Quirky
Kids

Quirky Kids

**Understanding and Helping
Your Child Who Doesn't Fit In—
When to Worry and
When *Not* to Worry**

Perri Klass, M.D., and
Eileen Costello, M.D.

January 2004

For Judy

With thanks for cheering me on!

Eileen Costello

BALLANTINE BOOKS
New York

To our families

A Ballantine Book
Published by The Random House Publishing Group

www.ballantinebooks.com

Library of Congress Cataloging-in-Publication Data is available from the publisher upon request.

ISBN 0-345-45142-2

Text design by Helene Berinsky

Manufactured in the United States of America

First Edition: November 2003

2 4 6 8 10 9 7 5 3 1

CONTENTS

ACKNOWLEDGMENTS

This book would not exist without the haven we were provided by the Ucross Foundation, in Ucross, Wyoming. In the time we spent there, we found the opportunity to write, to think, and to talk, far from our clinical practices, our chaotic homes, and of course, our six much-loved children. We thank Sharon Dynak and Elizabeth Guheen and the foundation, and we hope to go back someday!

In order to write this book, we interviewed a number of specialists and experts in fields ranging from special education to speech pathology. We are deeply grateful to Professor Elsa Abele of Boston University for her advice on pragmatic language therapy; Nancy Rappaport, M.D., consulting psychiatrist for the Cambridge Public Schools; and Jill Wittmer, Ph.D., of Beacon Services.

Many, many parents and grandparents generously agreed to be interviewed for this book and spent time and trouble detailing for us the complex and often very moving stories of the roads they had traveled with their children. Their accounts enriched our understanding of the subject, and we feel that their voices, as included in the text, enrich and illuminate everything we have written. They are the real experts, and the real champions. All of the names of the children have been changed, along with certain identifying details; we thank the children and their families. Some parents and grandparents preferred not to have their names mentioned, but we thank them for their help.

We also thank Niles Beland, Donna and Dan Bradley, Kate Collins-Wooley,

Jan Corash, Angela DeAngelis, Judy Fallows, Julie Black Gillman, Chelsey Goddard, Karen Halverson, Amy, Emily, Kevin, and Melissa Heaney, Mary Holland, Mimi Devine McLaughlin, Bob and Judy Natkin, Leda Nelis, Kate Nelson, Patrick Proctor, Connie, Dan, and Deanna Reiter, Jill Schiff, and Nancy Teich. Kate Collins-Wooley, Judy Fallows, Julie Black Gillman, Mimi Devine McLaughlin, Kate Nelson, and Connie and Dan Reiter also read sections of the manuscript and gave us the benefit of their personal and professional expertise.

This book has benefited as well from the expertise of Meg Johnson, a special education preschool teacher at the Early Learning Center West in Boston; Betty Kilgoar, the autism liaison for the Boston Public Schools; Jean Morelli, teacher at Boston Latin School; and Jana Feeley, admissions director at the League School of Greater Boston, who offered valuable comments on the manuscript.

Many professional colleagues took time from their busy schedules to talk with us about these issues and to read sections of the manuscript. This book draws on many different specialized fields, and we are not experts in any of them. As practicing general pediatricians, we send our patients to the experts we most trust for further evaluation and advice, and we were incredibly fortunate that many of these same experts—those who actually evaluate and treat our patients and also those whose writings and teaching have meant most to the parents we see and to us as well—were willing to help make this book more accurate, more representative, and more authoritative.

We were delighted when Carol Stock Kranowitz, whose book *The Out-of-Sync Child* has meant a great deal to many of the parents, therapists, and teachers we interviewed, was willing to read and comment on sections of our manuscript, and we are grateful for her insights.

Marilyn Augustyn, M.D., Director of the Developmental Assessment Clinic at Boston Medical Center, gave us the benefit of her considerable expertise and experience around the issues of school placement. Margaret Bauman, M.D., Associate Professor of Neurology and Director of the LADDERS Clinic at Massachusetts General Hospital (MGH), is a nationally recognized leader in the science of developmental differences and graciously took time to review our chapter on medical perspectives. Karen Bresnahan, M.D., developmental behavioral pediatrician and psychopharmacologist at the Center for Children with Special Needs at New England Medical Center, offered wisdom and perspective on the experiences that parents have in navigating the medical system and on the alphabet soup of official and unofficial diagnoses. Timothy Buie, M.D., pediatric gastroenterologist at MGH, who takes care of a large population of children with autistic spectrum disorders in the pediatric GI clinic, reviewed our medical section and offered a unique perspective on these children. Deborah Frank, M.D., Director of the Grow Clinic at Boston Medical Center, contributed her medical expertise. Steven Parker, M.D., Director of the Division of Developmental and Behavioral Pediatrics at Boston Medical Center—who has trained many developmental pediatricians and trained many pediatricians to be good developmentalists—kindly reviewed several chapters. Daniel Rosenn, M.D., child psychiatrist, founding member of the Asperger's Association of New England, and tireless advocate for quirky kids, has supported this book in numerous ways, and we are profoundly appreciative. Dana Rubin, M.D., pediatrician and child psychiatrist at Boston Medical Center, reviewed our chapter on medications in great detail and offered her experience on the newer treatments, as she offers it to our patients in daily practice. We both owe a very special debt to Barry Zuckerman, M.D., Professor and Chief of Pediatrics at Boston Medical Center and Boston University School of Medicine. Not only did he read and comment on sections of the manuscript, bringing to it his expertise both as a developmentalist and as a longtime advocate for children and parents, but he has been an important figure for both of us during our medical training and has always encouraged and supported our endeavors.

Once again, our gratitude to all of these wise and generous people; any errors or ambiguities in the book are ours alone.

We thank our colleagues at Dorchester House, Southern Jamaica Plain Health Center, and the Reach Out and Read National Center for putting up with the additional complexities that arose in our working lives as we wrote this book, and we are particularly grateful to Ellen Everson for all her patient help and great goodwill.

We offer personal thanks to Aurora Charron, Marion Cohen, Yolanda Cohen, Ellie Horowitz, Drew Curtis, Donna DeVaughn, Shari Feibel, Robie Harris, Alice Hoffman, Heidi Jay, Shana Lessing, Joyce Mallory, Lisa Masotta, Tricia and Scott Morrow, Christine Poff, Kay Shearer, Laura Sherman, and Jai Underhill.

We thank our agent, Elaine Markson, for shepherding our proposal along, as well as our editor, Nancy Miller, for her enthusiasm about this project, her understanding of the topic, and for helping us make it into a better book than we could otherwise have created, and our copyeditor, Susan J. Cohan, for her many hours of intelligent labor.

Our families, of course, have contributed to this book in a wide variety of ways. It's probably true, as we said above, that this book would not exist if we hadn't escaped them for a little while, but it is certainly true that it would not exist without their inspiration and support. They taught us much of what we know about the vagaries and realities of family life, and they put up with our often haphazard mothering styles. And then, on top of it all, we took extra time away from them to write this book—whether by going off to Wyoming, with barely concealed grins of delight, or by locking ourselves in the attic and refusing to arbitrate even urgent bathroom-related questions. We would like to thank all six of our children—Nolan, Geoffrey, Isaac, Orlando, Josephine, and Anatol—for the many lessons on the limits of parental and pediatric wisdom and, of course, for the recurring joys that make everything else worthwhile. Matt Gillman encouraged Eileen to write this book, sent her off to Wyoming to do it, and read and commented on the manuscript. Larry Wolff cheered Perri on through all the stages of putting the book together and has been especially adept at identifying interestingly quirky adult specimens in the halls of higher academe. Bob Gillman read sections of the manuscript with the erudition and perspective that come from a long and distinguished career in child psychiatry and with the emotional intelligence of a devoted father and grandfather; he is sorely missed since his recent death. Sheila Solomon Klass kept us company through the manic days of assembling the manuscript, read every line with close attention, and contributed the critical eye of a crackerjack proofreader and English teacher, the sensibility of a writer, and the wisdom of a mother and grandmother. Although Pauline Costello has never understood why mothers (like her daughter) work outside the home when they have so much to do *at* home, she undertook additional domestic burdens while this book was being written. She folded countless loads of laundry with the good cheer of a loving mother and grandmother. We thank all three generations of both our families.

Last, with profound humility and gratitude, we thank all the many children and families who have allowed us into their lives as pediatricians; we learn constantly from our patients and from their parents, and we hope that with this book we may offer some of what we have learned back to families in a way that will help them on their own journeys.

PART I

A World of Quirky Kids

Introduction

○ ○ ● ○

You're worried about a child you love. There's something different, something off, something eccentric, something quirky. You want to understand what's going on, and most of all, you want to help. Your job as a parent is to help your child grow and develop and learn and thrive, and to do that job properly, you have to understand your child as an individual, quirks and all. The world is full of quirky kids. They live with us in our houses—but they live in slightly different zones, seeing the world around them through idiosyncratic lenses, walking just a little out of step, marching and even dancing to the beat of different drummers.

Kids we are calling "quirky" are the ones who do things differently. Maybe you've noticed developmental variations—a child who doesn't talk on time or, alternatively, talks constantly but can't get a point across. Or maybe there's something in your child's temperament that makes daily life a challenge—a rigid need for absolute routine, a propensity for nuclear tantrums. Or perhaps you're uncomfortably aware of social difficulties—a toddler who always occupies herself alone while the rest of the playgroup lives up to its name. These are the differences—skewed development, temperamental extremes, social complications—that define the group of quirky kids. As pediatricians and mothers, we are in contact with kids every day, and we have become interested in the quirky kids among us.

As Aidan got older, I noticed more and more his inability to interact with other kids and his lack of interest in activities. I tried to do a Gymboree class with him. He had no interest whatsoever. He would not participate. He was more interested in the lights in the room, the stuff on the bulletin board, the numbers and letters. I felt so mad at him: "Why won't he do what the other kids do?"

The weekend I decided our son had autism—he was three, we were on Cape Cod, and it was too overwhelming for him, and he put his arms around this little tiny tree and shook back and forth the whole weekend long. He was wearing a sleeper with feet on it and sneakers, and he was wearing a watch, and he was hanging on to this tree. And I said to my husband, "I think he's autistic—this is so far off the curve."

Caitlin is good at math, but she can get completely stuck if there is a typo in the word problem. She's idiosyncratic. She cannot stand to estimate; she must have a precise answer. If the graph paper doesn't have enough lines, she gets stuck.

Trevor is an anxious child who now, at the age of nine, very much wants to be like other kids and wants the other kids to like him. He's an avid baseball fan and player, and that has helped him out in the social area, but he still has some residual "autistic"-type behaviors, like running in circles when he is excited. He writes or draws in the air when he is bored or feels uncomfortable.

Thirty or forty years ago, these kids would have been thought of as odd or eccentric, but they would not have had medical or psychiatric assessments, and they would not have been given diagnoses. Nowadays, you may find that helping your quirky child grow up will involve coping with a formal diagnosis—in fact, often with multiple diagnoses or with diagnoses that shift and change as she grows. This book is not about the children diagnosed with classic autism or with mental retardation or with major mental illness—schizophrenia, psychosis, bipolar illness. They are outside the scope of what we define as "quirky," and there is a great deal of very specific expertise out there to help their parents get them the help and support they need. We are talking about a group of children who inhabit a grayer zone, a zone of characteristics also found in normally developing children, a zone of shifting and overlapping diagnoses and rapidly evolving terminology. You may find, for example, that your child will be described as fitting within the autistic spectrum disorders, in particular as having Asperger's syndrome, or alternatively as having pervasive developmental disorder (also sometimes called pervasive developmental delay), nonverbal learning disability, or pragmatic language disorder. Depending on their strengths and weaknesses, as well as on who does the diagnosing, children may also be diagnosed with sensory integration dysfunction or social phobia or attention deficit disorder. It's important to note that these are all relatively recent diagnostic categories, which may be used to describe children who would once have just been called "eccentric"—or maybe harsher schoolyard names.

As a group, they're sometimes called quirky kids. We prefer this term for a reason. It's not pejorative. In fact, it's sometimes a compliment. But it does suggest the unusual features—challenging yet often charming—shared by an increasing number of children in our society.

Parents come to see us at our office with stories, with patterns, habits, and behaviors that they've noticed in their babies and their toddlers, their preschoolers and their elementary school children, and they ask our opinion: Is this normal? Is something wrong? We hear stories about toddlers whose tantrums seem off the scale by comparison to their siblings, about young children with intense obsessive interests, about children who don't talk on schedule or who do talk but in peculiar ways, about children who don't enjoy the games that delight the other members of the playgroup—or the rest of the third graders. We hear about strong preferences and prejudices—children's habits and routines that can come to dominate a whole family. All of these parents are looking to us, the professionals who see hundreds and hundreds of different children grow, for a little perspective and often a little help.

And as we watch parents struggle with a multitude of assessments, diagnoses, therapies, and medications, we have come to appreciate that life with a quirky child can be complex and difficult. We wrote this book to help you navigate and to help you do what you most want to do: know and recognize and appreciate your own child and help him grow and thrive. Everything you do—looking for the right diagnosis, investigating different possible therapies, looking for the best possible school, setting guidelines for life at home— is done toward that end. It is by that standard that you should judge any advice you get—including ours. Helping your quirky child become the person she was meant to be will involve getting to know and understand a remarkable individual.

Emma is ten now, and she's obsessively interested in cats. If she did a self-portrait or portraits of her family, they would be of cats and cat families. She hates loud noises. Restaurants are too loud. Fireworks are overwhelming. She cannot stand the loudness of the toilet flushing or the bath being drawn. Someone else has to do that for her. Then she is happy to take her bath.

George always had unusual obsessions—especially the vacuum cleaner. We have photos of him hugging the vacuum cleaner at six months of age. When he was older, he drew pictures of the vacuum and talked about it all the time. He had phobias as well. One was a phobia of pinecones—not especially functional given that we live in a neighborhood with lots of towering pine trees.

Quirky kids are outside the common patterns. They have a hard time fitting in. What comes easily to other children is hard for them. In particular, their ability to socialize with other children is impaired—sometimes mildly, sometimes severely. They may have unusual interests bordering on obsessions and insist on holding the conversation to these topics. They may have trouble fitting into the physical environment as well, finding themselves overwhelmed by sensations or sounds that the typical child wouldn't notice. They tend to be anxious, often "unchildlike." Other kids don't always know how to deal with them—hardly surprising, since sometimes their own families don't know either. In addition, their development is not by the book. Although eventually all of them walk and talk, they don't follow the expected time course, and they often have great difficulty with particular milestones. Developmentally and socially, these children are different.

We are not child development experts. We practice primary-care pediatrics in urban Boston neighborhoods and see hundreds of families each year. We are rearing, between us, six children of our own, ranging from six to nineteen years, in our respective households. As mothers, we have had our share of visits to the pediatrician, referrals to specialists, teacher conferences, and childhood social snarls to untangle. We have worked together for many years, starting as residents in training, and have swapped stories about our own kids and the kids with whom we work. Like all pediatricians in this fortunate modern era of pediatrics with so many new immunizations, we see fewer serious infections than our colleagues did a few decades ago, and we find ourselves talking about child development much more than did those previous generations of pediatricians, who were busier with measles and meningitis.

We plan to tell you what we have learned from our practice, as well as from our colleagues in child development and psychiatry, about the spectrum of developmental differences and disorders that encompasses the quirky child. We'll offer help at every stage: from the early worries of virtually all parents who suspect they have children somewhere on this quirky spectrum to the successes and surprises we have witnessed as these kids grow to adulthood.

We have talked with many parents who feel they *knew* something was wrong yet had their concerns dismissed by their pediatricians. We have also known many parents who worried desperately for a while, only to see their child outgrow the problem. As pediatricians, we understand the dilemma well: when you have seen the full range of "typically developing" children, as well as the range of quirky kids, you often feel that the proverbial "tincture of time" is well worth a try. So many kids do grow out of so many things. We'll help you make sense of when it's right to worry and when it's OK *not* to worry.

We'll follow children as they grow out of toddlerhood and into the preschool years, when it's often easier to see which children are really off the scale: which children may not be able to manage well in their preschools and schools because of their developmental issues or their social difficulties or their unusual learning styles.

We'll take you through the early school years and into elementary school, looking at the kinds of evaluation that may help pinpoint your child's needs and at the kinds of therapies and school settings that can help improve his skills—and that can offer him the most comfortable possible setting for growth and learning. We'll talk about finding the right teacher—and helping her do her job once you've found her. Although many quirky kids can function well in a regular education setting, others will need additional supports, such as an aide in the classroom or a more specialized school environment. We will discuss these decisions in detail.

We'll talk about how things go at home—about your quirky child, your other children, your extended family, and even about what you as parents may experience. We'll talk about bedtime and mealtime and homework and birthday parties—the daily details of life that get shifted around, a little or a lot, when living with a quirky child. We'll talk about friends as well and come back to those social issues we mentioned: how do you help your child connect with other children and maneuver in the childhood social world?

Almost all parents fear the complexities and turbulences of adolescence. Quirky kids can have an especially difficult time of it, given the often unforgiving culture of adolescence and the importance of fitting in. By this age, quirky kids are generally aware that they are "different," and their social struggles and self-image problems may place them at risk for depression and other mental health problems. Girls may be at even greater risk than boys, since the girl culture of adolescence allows little room for being different or "weird." The more equipped the child and his family are with knowledge and with strategies for success, the better this time will be. Still, it will not be easy. To be fair, no one, quirky or not, is guaranteed an easy time of it in adolescence.

Adults are infinitely more accepting than children and teenagers, and many quirky kids thrive in college or in vocational schools where they can pursue their interests. Look around you. Quirky adults are everywhere! Think about the bonsai grower at the flower show who knows everything there is to know about bonsai and talks bonsai all day long and goes home to read about bonsai. Look at your family: is that math professor uncle of yours a quirky kid grown up?

The truth is, of course—as every worried parent knows—that not every quirky child grows up to be a successful but quirky independent adult. However, the ability to succeed in life and to function independently depends on the whole package that is your developing child, not just the quirky aspects. The children about whom we are talking make up a spectrum—from the mildly affected to the severely disabled. As we have worked on this book, we have tried to be mindful of this spectrum. We know that to the parent of a child struggling desperately in school and at home and taking three different medications to modify his behavior, it will seem patronizing and even callous to talk about quirkiness in a tone that suggests that eccentricity is charming and that quirky is a synonym for genius. As one mother said to us:

I'm so cynical about all the people who say that kids with special needs are "special," that there is some profound joy in taking care of them. If there is a beautiful side to this, I am still waiting for someone to point it out to me.

On the other hand, we don't want to make things sound too bleak or too much as if early problems mean that your life's destiny is set in stone. Most of these kids manage just fine. And many parents, especially when the children are doing well, do manage to find much joy in their children and much pride in their achievements.

We see so many good things about Chrissie—her optimistic spirit, her warmth, her fun-loving personality, her offbeat sense of humor—that a lot of the time, we don't think about the stress that her problems have caused.

The more tools your child has for understanding his differences, coping with his difficulties, and playing to his strengths, the greater the likelihood of his having a functional and sometimes quite wonderful adulthood. There is a certain club—centered perhaps at MIT—of very happy "nerds"! We have talked with a number of adults who, in retrospect, clearly fell into this group of kids as they were growing up. Many of their childhood stories are heart-breaking, and yes, some are struggling with adult issues of intimacy or with occupational difficulties, but there is much to be learned from talking with them.

This book is not an exhaustive resource and is not intended to enable you to diagnose your child. We don't recommend that. We do recommend arming yourself with as much knowledge as possible. You will know more about the assessment process, about the professionals who might help you and your child along the way, about therapies and medications that might be recom-mended, and about what to expect as your child grows up. We'll try to be hon-est about our prejudices. We speak from a medical perspective, from within the pediatric profession. Still, we'll include plenty of quotes from parents who have felt ill served by our professional colleagues as well as from parents who have found help and support, and we'll help you get the best that medi-cine can offer.

We will also help you anticipate the inevitable issues raising your child will present: how to talk about these issues with relatives and friends; what and when and whether the child herself needs to know about what's going on; the impact on your other children, on your marriage and your other adult rela-tionships, and on you. We will remind you to take care of yourself *so* you can take care of your child. It's easy to get lost in the maze of appointments and therapies and expert recommendations, of Internet information and best-selling books. But in fact, as your child's parent and strongest advocate, as the one who knows and loves and appreciates this particular child best, you are fully capable of deciding what is and is not useful. Keep a healthy dose of skepticism about you and remember that this is *your* child. Don't listen to anyone—including us—who tells you something that doesn't jibe with what you know about your own child. But do keep an open mind. Listen and learn, and at the same time trust your instincts and trust yourself to do the best by your own particular quirky kid.

Last, and probably most important, we'll keep reminding you to treasure your child and your child's childhood. Quirky children can be incredibly endearing, often very creative. Many of them have unique views of the world to offer. This book is written in the spirit of embracing these kids and fostering their good health and growth, while recognizing and addressing the inevitable challenges that childhood, school, and family life hold for them. We don't minimize the real difficulties and heartaches of loving and living with a child who is different from other children, but we do urge you, as far as possible, not to let those differences define your entire family, your feelings about your child, your whole sense of yourself. The frustrations and irritations you may feel at times are real, but so are the joys and the pride you will take in your child's victories and accomplishments—and also the unexpected insights, the special quirky moments when you realize that your child's unusual perspective has enlarged and enriched the world.

1

○ ○ ● ○

"My Kid Is Different"

So what do you do when you're worried about your child? You wonder and agonize, you scope out other children, you read books on child development and parenting magazines, and you go looking for help on the Internet. You talk to your spouse or your best friend or your own parents or your day-care teacher. Maybe you lock up all the worry inside and say nothing to anyone, because you can't help feeling that by speaking the words, you will make them come true. Finally, usually, you ask your child's doctor. Maybe you make a special appointment and come in to discuss your concerns, or maybe you just wait for the next regular checkup and then you mention it, more or less in passing, needing to say it, hoping to be reassured. As pediatricians, part of our job is to look over babies and young children and decide whether their development is proceeding normally and on schedule.

We see our patients for short, busy interludes, often at moments when they are feeling more than a little bit stressed-out. Think of the one-year-old, cranky after a long stint in the waiting room, less than eager to be handled by a stranger, maybe remembering all too well that this too-chilly room is a place where they stick you with needles. So, as pediatricians, we examine kids and watch how they behave, but we rely most of all on parents to tell us what's going on. We know that many behavioral and developmental problems are subtle and hard to judge, and we worry that we may be missing something. On the other hand, part of our job is to reassure. If we sent every child who takes a little longer to walk for a full orthopedic, neurological, and developmental assessment, we would hardly be doing anyone any favors—not to mention what would happen if everyone who was a little slow to talk got a full oral-motor workup and a brain scan.

Is Something Really Wrong?

All children have bad hours and bad days and even bad weeks. Many children have difficult developmental stages or particular developmental tasks that they find frustrating and even miserable. Many parents who find themselves sufficiently and persistently worried enough to request diagnostic workups and medical and developmental evaluations end up looking back on something that turned out to be nothing more than a difficult episode in an otherwise straightforward childhood. A persistent worry doesn't tell you what the end result is going to be, but it does signal a need to pay attention and ask the right questions.

Medical students famously diagnose themselves with every syndrome they study. And as parents, reading about children and the various things that can go wrong in their health or development, we measure our own children against the most ominous medical syndromes.

But if you've picked up this book, your concern is more than the occasional reflex anxiety that falls under the heading of parental love. You may be worried that your child is somehow developmentally different in a significant way. You may already have started making your way through the maze of diagnosis and assessment, and you may in fact already have had a diagnosis—or a label or a formulation—assigned to your child. But wherever you and your child are in this journey, it probably all began with some worries that somehow he was different: worries that didn't go away with the morning sun or disappear when teething ended or move to the back burner when you found a better day-care center.

Early Signs

For many parents, this nagging worry that something is wrong comes early in the child's life. Maybe it's an unusually intense expression of a standard baby stage: the infant whose colic doesn't end at twelve weeks or the toddler whose tantrums reflect an underlying frustration out of proportion to the "average" toddler. Maybe it's an unusual pattern of behavior or interaction—the baby who won't make eye contact, the toddler who plays obsessively with only one or two toys. Or maybe you're looking at developmental delays or differences that are just too numerous or too intense to write off as a variant of normal.

We knew John was different from the beginning. He had a lot of trouble learning how to nurse. I remember this nurse at the hospital saying he's got a sucking disorder. I knew once I got him home, he would be fine. He was, but he nearly starved to death in the process. It was three or four days before he got the hang of it. Then, for the first four months, it went OK. I went back to work, started giving him some formula. But he couldn't make the transition to eating. His intake started dwindling. I remember thinking, "It's because I've gone back to work." With baby food, he couldn't figure out what to do with it when it was in his mouth, and from four to nine months, he had a totally flat growth curve—didn't gain any weight at all.

I first noticed differences between Abby and other kids as early as two months. We were in a playgroup, and I felt Abby wasn't with it to the extent the other babies were. Her fists remained clenched longer than the others, she slept more, her motor milestones were slower even at that early age. Throughout her first year of life, I referred to all the usual books about milestones, and I couldn't relate to any of them.

These parents, though, are looking back on the infancy of a child who turned out to be genuinely quirky. For most of us, those early anxieties are more nebulous, harder to understand and classify. You have this sense that your child just doesn't fit—doesn't fit the books, doesn't fit the group, doesn't fit your expectations. You listen to other parents talk, and you feel more and more certain that something in your own home is out of step.

There are comprehensive lists of developmental milestones available for parents who want to check out whether their children are keeping up with the normal trajectories. In this section, we want to take a somewhat more global look at the kinds of concerns that parents often have, which may be less about a particular age-related milestone than about a general sense that something is "off": usually in the child's general behavior, in his language and communication skills, or in his social development—and often in all three areas. So we'll give you a few very basic yardsticks for measuring general development and a Web site to go to for a more detailed tool. We would also encourage you to follow up on your worries even if there is no specific missed milestone on which to pin them. And if your child has actually "lost" milestones—has regressed in his development, so that his speech or his social skills are less advanced than they used to be—that should send you looking for help immediately.

TEMPERAMENT AND BEHAVIOR

Parents may become concerned because a child's temperament is extreme— unbelievably irritable, as if not quite comfortable in his own skin, desperately needy, chronically frustrated. These are babies who arch, who shriek as if in frequent pain, who never seem to settle down. They're the fitful, disorganized sleepers, or maybe toddlers who don't seem to need any sleep at all.

Andrew didn't sleep. We would walk him around. He was uneasy right from the beginning. He threw up all the time. He wouldn't eat. He had repetitive behaviors. The early intervention people would come with toys, and he would just open and close the doors but not play with the toys.

I had planned to go back to work when George was six or seven weeks and put him in family day care. I couldn't actually leave him there. He was just too delicate, and he actually had separation anxiety at six weeks. He always had a worried look on his face. He was an anxious, hyperaroused baby.

More rarely, there are babies who are remarkably, even disturbingly, placid—children who don't seem to demand anything from the world. They're easier to care for, but their parents may become troubled—and rightly so— that they are somehow out of touch.

With older children, parents may note unusual behaviors, repetitive movements like spinning, hand-flapping, or rocking. They may run in circles and flap their hands whenever they get agitated. A child may constantly touch or spin or roll some particular object, ignoring all others.

Think about whether you're looking at repetitive or obsessive behaviors, extraordinarily rigid routines, or any evidence, as children grow, of obsessional behaviors. One good question to ask yourself is whether your family's daily routines are dictated by these aspects of your child's temperament. Do you truly live in fear of the meltdowns that occur if regular rituals are varied? Does all family equilibrium depend on keeping this particular child calm?

As children grow out of toddlerhood, quirky kids may have terrible trouble with transitions from one activity to another. They may throw outrageous tantrums that last longer than routine toddler rages and that go on occurring well after the child should have outgrown them. They may show extreme sensitivity to sensory stimuli as well and be completely unable to tolerate things routine for other kids—the noise of a movie sound track, the sensation of water on the skin, the motion of a swing at the playground.

What comes easily to most children can be terribly difficult for quirky kids. If you are watching your child struggle with some of the routine activities of daily life, and if your family life is being reshaped to accommodate her needs and preferences because she herself cannot accommodate at all, it may be time to look into what's really going on.

SPEECH AND LANGUAGE

During the first three years of a child's life, many parents become concerned about speech and language, noticing either that the child is slow to develop speech or else that the child seems uninterested in the speech of others. Some children get tested for hearing loss because they pay attention so selectively—ignoring human voices, say, but responding to a certain tune played by a music box or a favorite TV show. Some are slow to speak, but others speak early and precociously and in fact use their speech and language to manifest early obsessions.

Aidan spoke early. He started talking at nine months and knew the alphabet at twelve months, could recognize some of the letters. By eighteen months, he insisted on learning phonics. He read early and became interested in numbers, directions, things like that.

Emma's language was slow to develop, and we used to say she spoke "Emmaese." She prattled on in her own language, which was incomprehensible to anyone else. By two and a half, she babbled but did not talk at all. She did respond to speech. She always loved music and Disney movies. I just sensed that she was off the beam early on.

Whereas some quirky kids are speech-delayed and need to use other forms of communication while they're young (screaming, pointing, making grunting sounds, pulling on a parent's clothes), others develop normal speech at a normal pace but find themselves with impaired *language*. A child may be able to talk endlessly about her obsession but be unable to carry on a basic conversation. She may develop functional language that allows her to ask for what she wants but have no interactive language. (In other words, maybe she can say "I want juice" but is incapable of a sentence like "This juice is good!") Some children can only use and understand concrete words for concrete objects.

Patterns of speaking may also raise the alarm. Children with *echolalia* repeat the last few words of whatever is said to them. Children who perseverate may ask the same question or make the same statement over and over. Finally, some quirky kids have "robotic speech," and whatever they say comes out in a strange monotonous tone.

Some milestones to watch for:

- A baby should babble by six months, and the babbling should increase in complexity and in how close it sounds to spoken language.
- By nine months, a baby should respond to his own name.
- By fifteen to eighteen months, a child should be able to say a couple of words and should understand simple spoken instructions.
- By two and a half to three, a child should be speaking in sentences, with a certain amount of fluency and inflection—that is, a question should sound like a question.
- By four, speech should be completely intelligible to those outside the child's family.

SOCIAL INTERACTIONS

Some quirky children are uninterested in toys, or they play with their toys in unusual ways—lining them up or fixating on certain textures and stroking them over and over. Some fixate on one particular object—appropriate or inappropriate—to the exclusion of everything else. Many parents become concerned when their babies or toddlers don't seem to look at them or engage in the early games of peekaboo. Then, of course, there's the social outlier—the child who can't or won't or doesn't want to join in the sandbox games or the circle time at day care or the birthday party mob.

Looking back, I think Abby's total disinterest in toys was a clue and also inter-fered with her language development, which remains her greatest challenge today. I went to a playgroup meeting with Abby and her "wiggle worm," which looked brand-new. Another mom asked, "How did you keep that so clean?" When the other child's was tattered and worn well, Abby's was so clean from never being used!

Caitlin was always very determined and knew what she liked. For example, she liked a certain color, a bluish-green color, and before she could walk or talk, she would crawl over to the laundry basket to let me know that she wanted to wear something that was that color. She has had severe temper tantrums from early on. And at her first playgroup, she had no interest in the other kids. She just clung to me.

With the increased publicity in recent years devoted to early child develop-ment and to autism, many more parents are making careful observations about their children's social skills. Some key behaviors that may raise concern in an infant include failing to make eye contact and failing to pay attention to nearby conversations. In a toddler, parents might notice that the child doesn't really seem to care whether the parent is present or not. In general, these chil-dren tend to be uninterested in "joint attention"—in joining with you, whether by pointing or by talking, in looking at something and thinking about something together. They also show a lack of reciprocal play: when they're babies, they may not respond to their names or play peekaboo; when they're toddlers, they may be unwilling to acknowledge another child's pres-ence, let alone join in a group game.

As children grow up, there are usually more opportunities to see them with their peers. You may be concerned about a child who bonds tightly to an inap-propriate object—carries a certain CD everywhere, perhaps, as one of our pa-tients does—or about a child who is completely uninterested in being around other children. Hardest to watch for most parents is the child who is deeply interested in other children and eager for social contacts but goes about it all wrong and always ends up crying, or making someone else cry, or just plain left out. Generally, these kids have trouble with imaginative play. They just don't get what the other kids are doing.

Some milestones to watch for:

- Babies younger than four months should already make eye contact and respond with a social smile when a parent smiles.
- By one year, a child should be gesturing—pointing, waving bye-bye.
- Children under two enjoy being around other children and seem aware of them but don't necessarily engage them in play activities.
- From the age of two on, children should have real interactions (not all of them positive!) and should be able to play games that involve some back-and-forth.

But Is This Something "Real"?

There are irritable babies and placid babies, children who talk early and children who talk late. Plenty of children, quirky or not, fixate on one particular toy or transitional object. But when parents of young children become concerned about some combination of communication patterns, unusual behaviors, social interactions, and developmental irregularities, those concerns may indicate a child who needs extra attention.

Other parents experience the early years of their child's life without noticing anything particularly concerning but then, later on, see problems emerge once the child leaves the cocoon of the family and starts school. Often these parents, looking back, can see patterns and behaviors in infancy and toddlerhood that they now understand differently, as part of a larger pattern.

In day care, he was a little odd about his clothes. The other kids would get naked, run around outside, pee on the pee wall. He wouldn't even take his shoes off. In the toddler room, I remember them saying about him, "Well, Brian seems to be fine just as long as he is allowed to use the certain trucks he wants, and the kids have learned that if they just leave a six-foot radius around Brian and his trucks, everything is fine." And I said "OK," and I just accepted it. I think they were trying to say something to me and I didn't want to hear.

The "Pivotal Moment"

For many parents, there is a pivotal moment when they acknowledge that something is really wrong. Maybe it's some public fiasco—a child who can't enjoy what other children can, a child who falls apart at what ought to be a treat. It's not that this one episode is so absolutely decisive, but taken against a backdrop of lots of concerning behavior, lots of parental worries, one particular episode may make the parent feel that it's time to take action.

Abby became "hypervigilant"—afraid of noises like the vacuum cleaner, afraid of being touched, afraid of unknown people or anything unpredictable, like someone laughing when she was in a group of people. She was too scared to go anywhere. There was an episode at the zoo. She got so scared of all the strangers that she screamed and clutched me until I decided to put her back in the car and go home. We realized we needed help right away.

It has to be said: virtually every parent has a story of a public meltdown, a disastrous tantrum in a public place. One disaster does not a quirky child make. But on the other hand, one extreme performance may be what it takes to crystallize in a parent's mind all the floating anxieties and worries of many months. Other pivotal moments involve extreme, impossible-to-explain-away behavior that resonates with the parent's long-considered and long-avoided fears.

When you first start looking at each other like my husband and I did when Brian was in second grade—the thing that really pushed us over the edge—he developed a phobia about going to the bathroom. He had to know where the bathroom was and how to get to it before he could be comfortable anywhere. It made it difficult to drive in the car, visit a zoo or anyplace. He got anxious. He was having trouble making sense of the world. In retrospect, it was clearly an anxiety disorder. The thing he would grip on to was that he needed to know where the bathroom was.

Talking It Over

For many parents, it's hard to put these worries into words. Sometimes parents feel that articulating this kind of observation about a child will make it real—will stamp their child with a disorder. Sometimes, as a parent lives with a growing suspicion that something is wrong, there is comfort in putting off the discussion, the confrontation, the moment when the anxiety is admitted to another adult, who may either confirm the observation or else reassure in a well-meaning way.

When Jacob was about eighteen months old, I started noticing some backsliding in terms of development, and the onset of some unusual behaviors. He liked to watch the washing machine spin around. He played soccer obsessively, and he was fascinated by numbers on elevators. Also, by twenty-one months, he had lost most of his language skills and his social skills, and he became much less affectionate and less "connected" to other people. He began making strange shrieking sounds; having severe, prolonged temper tantrums with lots of screaming; and started head-banging. He became fearful of new people.

So you read a little (or maybe a lot) about child development, and you find some scary symptoms that seem to match those of your own child—but lots more that don't. How do you decide whether your worries are real enough to pursue? And what does it mean to pursue them? And maybe most important of all, how can you keep doing the job you need to do with your child and your family, even while you're watching and worrying? Where are you going to go for help and advice?

YOUR PARTNER

It's not uncommon for a child to have one worried parent—usually, the one who spends the most time one-on-one with the child, maybe sees the child around other children and makes comparisons—and one serenely untroubled parent, who is absolutely sure that everything is going to be fine. These discrepancies can be major sources of tension, with one parent feeling that the other is in denial or with one parent furious that the other keeps looking for problems when nothing's really wrong. Some of these gaps in understanding or acceptance can persist for years, well beyond those early suspicions and into the process of diagnosis and treatment.

My husband took a lot longer to accept that there was something wrong, having come from a family where everyone was high-achieving. When we were around his family, nobody knew what to say about John.

- Think about your different personalities. Does one of you tend to be the worrier, whatever the subject? Do you naturally fall into roles, with one parent raising problems and the other dismissing them? Acknowledge these patterns—and try to get past them to talk about your child.
- Discussing your concerns with your partner may make them seem more "real" and may carry significant emotional weight for you both. If you aren't both convinced that there really is a problem, you might agree to watch and wait for a short, well-defined period of time, now that the issue has been brought out in the open.
- Even if one parent remains convinced that nothing is really wrong, when the watchful waiting is over, if the problem isn't clearly resolved (the child has in fact started talking, stopped throwing tantrums, or found good friends at day care), agree on some reasonable plan of action for getting your concerns addressed.
- Remember that you are in it together. Whatever worries you nurture, whatever judgments you make, you are both driven by love and concern. Even if you don't agree, treat each other well, take each other seriously, and take care of each other. Your child needs you both and needs you to be working as a team.

FRIENDS AND FAMILY

Taking your worries outside of your immediate family may seem like a big step. Some parents consult friends, sisters, brothers, cousins right from the beginning, but many hold back, probably from that same anxiety that speaking the words will make the problem real. We'll spend a lot of time, later on in this book, discussing the issues of disclosure that come up with quirky kids. But here at the beginning, when you aren't sure what you have to tell, it might be wise to confide in a few carefully chosen people, as you start looking for expert help and advice.

- By all means, talk to a few trusted friends, but be wary of telling all your worries to everyone you know or who knows your child. You run the risk that a year from now, when perhaps your child has outgrown some of the worrying behaviors, other people will still remember her as the one who . . .

- If it does in fact turn out that your child has a specific diagnosis and special issues, think carefully about whom you want to tell and what you want to say. At these early undefined stages, you might want to hold off. If everyone in your child's world knows all your worst fears, it may be hard to dial them down later on and have them see her as she is.
- If you cast this particular net too widely—that is, tell everyone you know about your worries—you may encounter certain parents whose own children have some particular problem and who therefore see the world from that very particular perspective. As one pediatrician told us:

The mother of one of my patients, who was recently diagnosed with mild learning and language problems, had a sister with a severely disabled child, who kept telling her, "This was just how my son started." And it was terribly upsetting for this mother, who felt that it meant her daughter was going to end up inevitably with all these same problems, on all these same medications.

YOUR PEDIATRICIAN

Most people start with their child's health care provider—usually a pediatrician, family practitioner, or nurse practitioner. We have parents come to us all the time with developmental worries—sometimes straightforward (how come my sister's child is a month younger and she already knows how to go up and down stairs?) and sometimes large and complex and difficult to define. We also find ourselves, quite often, in the situation of having to bring up developmental concerns with parents who have not been at all worried, because something about a child's development doesn't seem on course. Some pediatricians have additional training in behavior and development, and many others have at least a special interest in the area. But every pediatrician spends hours and hours looking at babies and young children and has some idea of the range of normal—and of the varieties that lie on the fringes of that range. That's not to say that your pediatrician knows everything about development. Nobody knows everything about development.

You and Your Pediatrician: Making It Work

In books about children with developmental issues, you may find bitter accounts of doctors who missed the boat. Parents were worried, parents knew something was going on, and the pediatrician dismissed the concerns, saying, "He'll grow out of it." Then, of course, it turned out that the child really did have a problem, and valuable time had been lost. We know these stories, we know they happen, and we want to make sure you don't end up feeling that way. On the other hand, we do have to say, we know the other stories, too—the ones that don't end up in the books because the children really did grow out of it and the problems were resolved. In all honesty, many parents bring up developmental concerns with us, and the majority of their children turn out to be just fine.

But of course, that isn't always true. Our job is to listen to your concerns and look carefully at your child and help make a reasonable judgment about whether it's time for further testing. We need to understand why you're worried, and just how worried you really are. You may come to the conclusion that you're dealing with the wrong doctor and it's time to move on, but we hope that most parents will find that their pediatrician is reasonably well informed and reasonably helpful in this complicated and sensitive process.

- *If you feel you have a pediatrician who listens carefully and has interacted with your child and examined your child and is not worried, that means something.* If you've expressed your worries and the doctor has looked carefully at your child but is not alarmed, consider letting yourself be reassured. It's not a guarantee, of course (we're loyal to our profession, but not blindly so), but it may well mean that what you are looking at is more in the going-through-a-phase category. It can be pretty hard to judge whether a two-year-old is off the charts in oppositional behavior and tantrums, especially with a first child (or a second child when the first was a totally easy kid). If you like and trust your doctor, you might consider letting it rest here, at least for a few months.

- *It's important to make these diagnoses early, but not on an emergency basis.* Obviously, we aren't talking about diagnosing a child who's deaf or a child with classic autism or a child with seizures. Children with major psychiatric or medical disorders need to be diagnosed and treated as rapidly as possible. The more obviously and severely delayed your child is, the more quickly things should move. Most of the kids we're talking about—the quirky kids—can be watched and sorted out a little more slowly or, most important, offered special help with the developmental tasks that give them trouble (speech therapy, occupational therapy) while you're figuring out the big picture. It's also important to remember that sorting out the issues that affect these kids can be a long, ongoing process. It may take years and involve multiple assessments and multiple diagnoses. There's no single vital test that needs to be done as soon as possible to get any one essential answer. In the words of one pediatrician:

In this neighborhood, there are lots of people with kids, and they know I work with kids, so they ask me if they think there might be a problem. I can't believe the extent to which people have asked me about things, told me they're really worried about their kids—and then I ask them later and it's just, "Oh, she got over it!" It's better to wait six months than be wrong. The labels are not always helpful, and they affect the way you perceive the child, and they don't change much about what you're going to do.

- *If you're really worried about something, communicate that to your pediatrician.* It's sometimes hard for us to tell whether parents are making a casual comment or whether they're expressing a deep worry, rooted in days and weeks of careful observation and concern. Go ahead, say it, in so many words: "There's something I've been noticing for weeks now, and I'm really worried. I read an article and it seemed to be describing my baby, so now I'm wondering if she has this syndrome. Could this be something really bad?" And if the doctor doesn't seem to register your concern, say it again. Parents may come away from a medical encounter believing they've told the doctor something, while the doctor leaves not understanding that it's a real worry. It's not at all uncommon for a parent to drop a casual question: "That birthmark—it's not going to turn into anything bad, is it?" "That funny sound he makes—does that mean he's going to have a stutter?" When the pediatrician is fully alert and fully sensitive, those questions get properly explored: "What do you mean by 'anything bad'?" or "Does stuttering run in your family?" But as we hustle through the day and try to remember all the necessary things on the long checklist of any child's annual physical, we may not be paying proper attention. Stop us, look us in the eye, tell us you're worried, and tell us exactly why.

- *Schedule a visit specifically about your child's development. Don't try to talk about it at the visit that's really about an ear infection.* Sometimes it seems as if parents deliberately avoid scheduling such a special visit. Again, maybe it makes the concerns seem too real. We all walk a fine line as parents between wanting to have our suspicions confirmed and wanting to have our worries set aside. However, you should come in, sit down, and tell us what is worrying you. The fact that you were worried enough to make the appointment will signal to us that we need to give this issue time and attention. If the visit is specifically scheduled to discuss your concerns, there should be time to get your most pressing questions answered and to make sure that together you and the pediatrician have agreed on a next step.

- *Your concerns should prompt your pediatrician to do some kind of systematic developmental assessment, not just "eyeball" your child.* These concerns, expressed at such a visit, should prompt the pediatrician to do a full and systematic developmental exam, looking at how your child rates according to age-appropriate norms in motor development, gross and fine; cognitive skills; language; and social interactions. These screening tools have been developed to be used by general pediatricians, not specialists, and can be done quite quickly. They may give you a handle on whether a referral is indicated. Many pediatricians will use a test called the Denver Developmental Screening Test, asking your child to perform certain tasks right there in the office (pick up a raisin, for example, or build a tower of blocks) and asking you to describe other behaviors you've witnessed at home (does your child imitate housework?). While looking over a child in the exam room, a pediatrician might also make note of the child's response to the usual sensory stimulation that goes on in a doctor's office, such as an otoscope in his ear or a tongue depressor in his mouth. Children with sensory issues may find this sort of stimulation unbearable. In addition, a simple assessment of a child's neurological skills can help determine how these skills compare with the child's progress in speech and language development.

I had a friend who kept a developmental screening test on her refrigerator and checked off each developmental milestone her child reached. When I saw it, I realized

I could never do it, because John didn't have any of the check marks he should have had, and he didn't have most of the ones he should have had six months ago. It reminded me of how, when John was born, I wanted to keep baby books on each of my kids. At a certain point—he was maybe a year and a half—I just stopped doing it. So much of our life was consumed with his delays—the fact that he couldn't talk—it was just too sad. I felt I would be fabricating his childhood, ignoring the major part of our life with him, which was early intervention and speech therapy and occupational therapy.

- *If you really don't feel as if you're being listened to, get a second opinion.* OK, we've already stuck up for our specialty. Pediatricians are not all alike. Some are more tuned in to these issues than others. Not all pediatricians are the same. Not all *good* pediatricians are the same. Even those of us who would classify ourselves as interested in developmental differences and sensitive to parental concerns have gotten it wrong in certain cases.

Throughout Abby's first year of life, each time I talked to my pediatrician about it, he reassured me that everything was fine. I remember the lines people used to reassure me: "She's developing at her own pace." "She's on her own trajectory." "Don't compare her to others." "You're a first-time mom. Just relax." I felt that the doctors and also our family and friends thought we were crazy. But I had a gnawing feeling something was up. In the pediatrician's office at age two, something set Abby off and she started tantruming. She was fearful and overwhelmed, and she couldn't stop. The pediatrician said, "I would just ignore all this. This is just attention-seeking behavior," and told me he thought I was decompensating and referred both of us (my husband and me) to counseling.

So why isn't your pediatrician worried? First and foremost, your child's behaviors may not be as worrisome as you think. Range-of-normal infant colic can be pretty awful. Standard two-year-old tantrums have driven many a parent over the edge. Second, your child may have some truly concerning quirks but come off overall as pleasant, appealing, well connected. People may not worry as much about developmental problems in a happy, attractive, engaging child. Third, you may be seeing certain extreme behaviors that are "saved" for you and just don't show up in the doctor's office. Last, of course, you may be presenting something that is just beyond the knowledge and expertise of your particular pediatrician. In any of these situations, you need a second opinion, either to confirm your own suspicions or to dial down your anxiety.

Aidan's pediatrician felt he was within the norm. He became oppositional as soon as he could talk, and he talked very early. His tantrums simply couldn't be ignored. He would scream and hang on to me, save his worst behavior for me. And again, the pediatrician felt this was the usual oppositional/control issues with a toddler—and his recommendations didn't help. It was impossible to do time-out with Aidan. You would have to hold him down the whole time, which defeats the purpose of the time-out.

- *Where do you go for a medical second opinion?* When faced with a pediatrician who keeps telling you there's nothing to worry about, you should probably request a referral to a specialist in child development and behavior, so your child can be more fully evaluated. Many people find themselves hesitant about challenging a doctor's authority even by requesting a second opinion. Depending on your financial situation and your health insurance, you may prefer to locate the developmental clinic on your own and make the appointment yourself. (There will be a clinic at any major academic medical center or children's hospital.) But if your health insurance requires a referral from your primary-care pediatrician, remember that you are completely within your rights to request this referral. Explain that you continue to find yourself troubled by these questions, and you'd like your child to be formally evaluated, even if only so you can be reassured.

The Big Picture

As you look at your child, be sure you don't take just one developmental milestone and focus on it. Every child reaches some milestones early and others late. Ask yourself whether there's a pattern here: Does my child have trouble with many motor skills? Does my child seem weaker or clumsier than other children? Does my child have trouble with words or with communication in general?

There was something wrong in so many systems—and what was wrong was so basic. Our son just wouldn't eat. It was just mind-boggling. People would say, "Oh, he's not going to starve to death. People don't starve to death," but he certainly did not have a normal drive to eat. We used to count those little rotini pastas—"Oh, he ate six of those for dinner!"—we would be so excited. Plus his head was small, plus his motor skills were so weak, plus he wouldn't talk. By a year, he wasn't doing most of what a normal one-year-old would do.

In our clinic a couple of months ago, we discussed a nine-month-old girl who wasn't crawling. Her mother had come in very concerned about this: she thought her daughter should crawl. We asked her, "What *is* your daughter doing?" It turned out she was doing a lot. We asked all the gross motor and fine motor questions: Does she pull to stand? Does she sit upright in her high chair? Does she pick up a raisin? And yes, this child wasn't crawling, but she was doing every other thing. She was babbling, she was communicating her wants, she was beginning to say "Mama," and sometimes it even seemed to mean "Mama." This girl was, we decided, on some basic level, completely on target developmentally. And sure enough, on physical exam, she was strong and vigorous, she had normal muscle tone. So under those circumstances, as doctors, we take a deep breath and tell the mother not to worry. When this little girl came back for her next visit, at one year of age, she was walking. She skipped crawling—went right to walking. We were, no question, relieved. Every time we make the decision to reassure parents like these, we think of the occasional child who *doesn't* go on to walk or crawl—the child who is truly signaling a developmental delay.

Children develop in many directions at once. Developmentally speaking, some kids are "motor machines" who roll, sit, crawl, and walk early, yet their language skills lag. Other babies happily sit in one place and babble away. It's as if some of them can't do both at the same time. When you look at your child, look not just at gross and fine motor skills but also at cognitive skills, at communication, at talking and understanding. Look at social skills and personality: does your child cry and act up around strangers but talk and laugh with people he knows? A child who is doing fine in most respects but has one particular area of difficulty is not as worrisome as a child who seems to struggle on several fronts. Even if you have a specific worry that you want to pursue, it's important for your sense of your child to keep all these developmental trajectories in mind and to recognize the many different kinds of progress, wherever they occur.

Even as you pursue your worries into the world of diagnosis and testing, don't let yourself reduce your child to a symptom, a problem, a set of missed milestones. Look at the whole child, with all his strengths and weaknesses, preferences and quirks, and find as many ways as you can to cherish the days of his childhood. We don't mean to minimize the seriousness of your concerns or the pain that comes with worrying about a child, but it's also true that everyone gets only one childhood, one family, one set of parents. Look for ways to enjoy and appreciate the child you have, even as you are looking for answers and help.

And so we move, as parents, from nebulous worry to special appointments to discuss a nagging fear to evaluations at specialty clinics, where we will find ourselves surrounded by children with the full spectrum of developmental difficulties. And so we move, as pediatricians, from looking a little more closely at a given infant—checking and rechecking the child's muscle tone, perhaps, or asking extra questions about speech development and social skills—to articulating our anxieties to the immediately worried parents and to involving our specialist colleagues and waiting for their multipage assessments. As you journey across these borders, consider how this fits into the lifelong story of you and your child.

Everything looks different in retrospect. If you end up with a diagnosis, with a child whose life is truly shaped and affected by a developmental syndrome, you will look back at your early anxieties as loud warning signals and at everyone who did not take them seriously as dangerous and incompetent. On the other hand, if there is no specific diagnosis and your child outgrows most or all of the worrying behaviors, you may forget all those moments when you thought something might be wrong. In judging the people to whom you went for help along the way—and most of all, in judging yourself—remember that these are all complex, individual stories. It can be very hard to predict the future. Don't be too hard on yourself if you feel you missed various warning signals. Don't kick yourself for not understanding right away that your child needed intense speech therapy, or that your child would never be one to enjoy crowds or loud noises or parties. You weren't blind or obtuse or cruel. You were just figuring things out as you went along. All kids are works in progress; developmental trajectories and family dynamics change and shift with time. Your job with your quirky kid is a harder, more complex version of any parent's job: to find what works, to help and protect and teach, to shape the world to fit your child even as you help your child learn how to handle the world.

Last and maybe most important, do not let your worries or your anxieties overshadow your relationship with your baby or child. You need memories of your child's early years that are more than anxieties, diagnosis, testing, problems, and therapy. While you pursue issues of diagnosis and workup, make sure you build in time for whatever comes most easily and gives most pleasure—to you, to your child, to your family.

Despite all these difficulties, we carried on our life. We traveled with him, we took him to visit relatives. These things that bothered us didn't bother him at all. He was a happy kid. He liked to do a lot of things. There was a lot of pleasure in him. We had to try very hard, being who we were, not to let these things color our whole lives, but he was a fun little baby. He liked being around people. He had a nice disposition. And now that we know that he's basically doing pretty well, it's easy to look back and remember the things we had fun with.

References and Resources

Brazelton, T. Berry. *Touchpoints: Your Child's Emotional and Behavioral Development.* Cambridge, MA: Da Capo Press, 1994. This book is written with a real understanding of children's temperamental and behavioral differences.

Eisenberg, Arlene, Heidi E. Murkoff, and Sandee E. Hathaway. *What to Expect the First Year.* New York: Workman, 1996. This book is part of a popular series. For parents of quirky kids, of course, this isn't what you were expecting, but this book does allow for developmental differences and can help parents identify red flags that should lead to seeking advice or help.

First Signs Web site. The First Signs Web site, at www.firstsigns.org, is an excellent and informative site "dedicated to the early identification and intervention of children with developmental delays and disorders." A terrific place to start if you have a young child you are concerned about, it has a tremendous amount of information for parents *and* professionals working with quirky kids, in a user-friendly format. Don't miss it. It contains links to other sites that may be helpful as well as contact information for organizations around the country

Kranowitz, Carol Stock. *The Out-of-Sync Child: Recognizing and Coping with Sensory Integration Dysfunction.* New York: Perigee, 1998. Carol Stock Kranowitz is an educator in the Washington, D.C., area who has written a terrific book describing the various forms of sensory integration dysfunction and interventions to help. This book is on the shelf of most occupational therapists and bookstores.

Leach, Penelope. *Your Baby and Child: From Birth to Age Five.* New York: Knopf, 1997. Books like this are full of practical advice for a typically developing child, but it's not always helpful, and can even be disturbing, for parents of babies whose development is not on schedule.

2

○ ○ ● ○

Specialists, Labels, and Alphabet Soup:
ARRIVING AT A DIAGNOSIS

Once upon a time, most quirky children did not get assigned to formal diagnostic categories. They were called eccentric or odd and were humored as oddballs or tortured as weirdos, coddled as infant geniuses or ostracized as misfits. We all remember such children from our own school days, and chances are, they attended no special therapies, took no special medications, and carried no medical or psychological terminology on their journeys through childhood.

Look around those same classrooms and schoolyards now, and you'll see a host of diagnoses. Any child who doesn't quite fit the mold is likely to receive intensive testing, leading to diagnosis and rediagnosis and, in turn, to an individualized program of therapies, home-based interventions, and possibly medications. This is, we have to believe, on the whole a good thing. We are no longer taking for granted that certain children, the ones who have a harder time, ought to be left to struggle on alone. They can benefit from careful attention to their strengths and weaknesses, from extra help at an early age, and from a more educated and understanding attitude on the part of the important adults in their lives.

As doctors, we sometimes tend to speak of "having a diagnosis" almost as if it were a special distinction. "Well, does he have a diagnosis?" "So after all that, did the kid get a diagnosis?" As medical students, we were rewarded for coming up with long lists of possible diagnoses—the "differential," as it is called in medicine—and then, even more, for coming up with the one true diagnosis.

But it's a different set of emotions and judgments when you set out, as a parent, to look for a possible diagnosis for your quirky child, to let a variety of specialists and experts quantify your child's strengths, weaknesses, and quirks and then perhaps offer you a name, a syndrome, a single formulation. There are a couple of very important matters to discuss specifically with reference to quirky children and diagnoses:

- *What does a diagnosis mean to the parent?* Some parents see their children's quirks as wrinkles in development—personality variations rather than problems. Others, although grateful for help with whatever their children find most difficult, don't want any specific label applied to the child to explain those difficulties. Many fear—and with good reason—that a label may become a self-fulfilling prophecy, marking a child in the eyes of teachers and classmates and even family members. On the other hand, many parents feel a strong desire to give their child's quirks a diagnostic name, so that they can educate themselves, help the child as much as possible, maybe find other parents facing the same situation, and perhaps anticipate the problems that may lie ahead.

I thought if it had a label, there was some body of knowledge out there and I could learn what I needed to know and see where he was on the spectrum. Also, I wanted to know about recurrence and the risk to other kids we might go on to have. I thought it would be useful to know the likelihood we would have to deal with it again. Whatever it was, I knew it was in the family. We have pretty weird people on both sides. I'm just one of those people who wants to give things labels. This way, I could know the worst-case scenario.

When we got Abby's first diagnosis—sensory integration dysfunction—we felt that the weight of the world was off our shoulders. As a little kid, Abby was one of those kids who was just bothered by everything. She was very tough to take care of. And when we got that first label, we felt as if everything made sense.

- *Many children will accumulate more than one diagnosis over time, as they get tested and retested and as they grow and change.* Many quirky kids don't fit any single diagnosis. Depending on the child's age and developmental stage and on the orientation and training of the person doing the assessment, these children can receive many different diagnoses as they grow. Some diagnoses will fit for a while and then be outgrown, whereas others will continue to be relevant even as your child grows and changes. You may find yourself holding on to a particular diagnosis, not because it fits so well but because it helps you with the school system!

Ben has a diagnosis of Asperger's, made when he was seven, although along the way, he has had a huge number of diagnoses or formulations of what his particular brand of quirkiness is. Included in the list: colic, attention deficit hyperactivity disorder, generalized anxiety disorder, pervasive developmental disorder, obsessional personality, bipolar disease, learning disorder. . . . He's also described as having sensory issues and as being impulsive and reactive. Sometimes I still wonder whether they've got it right, but he's getting what he needs, so the label isn't that important.

I took George for an independent evaluation at a hospital. A neuropsychologist told me he was retarded and had a very low IQ. This was a very tough guy, who thought I was deluding myself. He actually said to me, "I have a normal four-year-old, and this is not a normal four-year-old." I knew that he was language-disabled, and that therefore the validity of some of the testing was in question, but it still had a huge impact on me. Then, next, he saw an occupational therapist, who also said that on the basis of the testing, he was mentally retarded, but she felt the testing wasn't really getting at him completely. The speech therapist described him as functionally nonverbal. I paid for these evaluations on my own and did not share them with the school department: I did not want George to start school with a diagnosis of mental retardation when I was quite sure this wasn't his problem. At the age of seven, he had another neuropsych evaluation. At that point in time, the neuropsych person said she had seen a number of kids like George but didn't know exactly what was going on with them. It was not until fifth or sixth grade that another neuropsych person hired by the school made the diagnosis of Asperger's syndrome but told me that although George wasn't classic, it was a term that the school understood, so I should use it to get George what he needed in terms of services.

- *There is a great deal of what is called comorbidity with many of these conditions—meaning that many of them overlap or occur in tandem.* Depending on a child's age and what is expected of her at that age, different skills become more or less important, different problems seem major or minor. In kindergarten, for example, whether or not she plays easily with other children may determine how happy she is in school. By second grade, learning issues may have become paramount. As we get better at recognizing these complex syndromes, older children are being diagnosed as well. Often, after years of persistent, but not devastating, school problems or social issues, they find themselves given "official" diagnoses during adolescence.

In this chapter, we look at the array of specialists and diagnosticians to whom parents turn as they try to sort out their children's behavior and development and as they try to help their children over some of the hurdles encountered in the early years at home and out in the world. We will look at the ways that different specialists—with different training, different orientation, different assessment tools—can offer you different kinds of information, some more oriented toward practical everyday function, others more attuned to recognizing syndromes and making diagnoses. We want to clarify, before we start on the nitty-gritty of diagnosis, that we feel the point of all this—the point of the workup, the testing, the careful consideration of your child by multiple experts—is *not* to come up with the right label, the right name, the right answer on some cosmic medical-student exam. The reason to have your child tested is to help your child—and to help you help your child. Diagnoses are worth having only insofar as they point the way to reasonable and realistic expectations, useful therapies, and greater understanding.

Evaluating Your Child

You've decided your child needs testing by experts. You need answers, advice, and explanations. Where to turn?

In a perfect world, you would turn to an immensely erudite but also tremendously sensitive team of experts who would come to your child without preconceptions and take the time and trouble necessary to get to know him through and through. Their recommendations would be realistic and practical, and the evaluation, along with any necessary follow-up appointments, would be fully covered by your insurance. Our goal is to help you get all or most of what you need . . . even in this imperfect world.

EARLY INTERVENTION

Early intervention (EI) programs are available in every state, as federally funded services for children with developmental needs in the first three years of life. For children under age three, your insurance company may sometimes insist on an early intervention evaluation before it will pay for any other kind of testing. EI programs will bill your insurance company or, if you don't have insurance, will still carry out the evaluation. If there are delays or peculiar development in several areas, however, a more comprehensive diagnostic evaluation may well be in order.

SCHOOL-BASED EVALUATIONS

You may find yourself beginning with a school evaluation, either because you think it will help provide some answers or because your insurance company requires it or because the school usually covers the expense. These school evaluations are often reasonable places to start, but we offer several cautions:

- The waiting lists can be long.
- The quality of the evaluators varies immensely.
- There is no guarantee that any one of them will have experience with the needs of the quirky child.

We have heard parents complain about school evaluations that seemed rushed—or superficial—or too highly directed at putting every child into one of a few categories. On the other hand, we have worked with plenty of gifted school-based professionals who have helped many families enormously. Certainly, the school-based perspective can direct the evaluation specifically at many learning issues that are vitally important for children. Another tricky issue is that when a child gets a diagnosis that requires extra educational support, the school is required by law to supply that support. With shrinking budgets for special education services, many schools are in no hurry to offer a classification that will maximize help in the early elementary years, even though such help may make a huge difference over time. All of this is to say that, although you may need or want to start with a school evaluation, and it may provide you with very helpful information, you may well decide to go further in your diagnostic quest.

ACADEMIC MEDICAL CENTERS AND MULTISPECIALTY DEVELOPMENT CLINICS

As you move beyond EI—or alternatively, beyond the school—consider academic medical centers and multispecialty developmental clinics. From the insurance point of view, these are likely to require a referral from your pediatrician. This kind of evaluation should certainly be available in any major city and at any major academic medical facility, and your pediatrician should be able to refer you to the closest clinic. The evaluation should include speech and language; a neurological evaluation, which may or may not involve imaging studies (a computerized tomography, commonly known as a CAT scan, or a magnetic resonance imaging scan, commonly known as an MRI, of your child's brain); physical therapy and occupational therapy; and, if the child is old enough, neuropsychological or psychoeducational testing. Taken together, these assessments can provide a detailed and potentially helpful picture of your child's skills and deficits.

INDIVIDUAL SPECIALISTS

Parents who are not ready to have their children undergo a multispecialist evaluation, or do not live near any center that can do it, or who are interested more in functional help and less in diagnosis, may find themselves taking their children to several specialists individually. Thus, quirky kids may be assessed, in their time, by developmental pediatricians, speech and language pathologists, neurologists, physical therapists, occupational therapists, psychologists, psychiatrists, early childhood educators, early intervention specialists, social workers—and that's not even counting those who are taken to nutritionists, allergists, homeopaths, and toxicologists!

We know we're talking here as though the process of testing and diagnosis will inevitably involve many steps and perhaps many years—but quirky kids are the ones who don't quite fit diagnostic categories, so the tendency is to keep testing and keep looking for help. As your child grows and changes, the

knowledge and skills gathered as a parent will help you judge when further assessment might be useful and when it's OK to take a break.

Before we look at the different perspectives these specialists can offer, we
have one last word of advice on choosing your direction:

Trust your instincts. Go into this process with an open mind but also with a
healthy degree of skepticism. If someone tells you something that absolutely
does not fit with your sense of your own child, consider it objectively. Look at it
to see whether it's going to help you help your child. If it's nonsense, forget it.
Don't let someone who can't answer your questions adequately or who makes
you uncomfortable pursue a long-term therapeutic relationship with your
child, no matter how grand and glorious his degrees or his reception room.

*We have taken Abby to so many specialists over the years, I have antennae for
those who don't really "get it," and I don't have a lot of patience for them. My task
is to cut it short as soon as possible without being too rude, but there have been
times when a specialist has shown such a lack of understanding that I've had to
say, "I don't really care what you think." Life is too short to waste time with people
who do not understand my child.*

Thus, armed with notebook, questions, reasonable expectations, and a certain amount of skepticism, let us approach the list of specialists who may look
at your child. It's important to remember that different professions mean different kinds of training, different professional experiences. Different frame-
works will be brought to bear on your child, depending on who is doing the
evaluating. Each specialist will see your child against the backdrop of the other
children regularly seen in that specialty. Each specialist will be asking different
questions and using a different set of diagnostic tools to get at the answers.

Therapies and Specialists

EARLY INTERVENTION PROGRAM

Parents with infants and toddlers who seem to be having developmental problems may turn to early intervention (EI) programs, which exist in every state.
You can be referred by your pediatrician, or you can refer yourself for evaluation. This evaluation usually includes:

- A home visit to check out the child's social environment.
- An assessment by a developmental educator, focusing on play skills, such as the use of toys and the ability to engage in pretend or symbolic play, and social interactions with people both familiar and strange. A child's attachment to her caretakers is evaluated as well. Does she snuggle up with Dad out of fear of the strangers in her living room, or does she look away and rock back and forth?
- Assessments by occupational therapists, speech and language therapists, and physical therapists. These specialists form teams within many early intervention programs and are skilled at evaluating infants and toddlers. (The specifics of these evaluations are discussed later in this chapter.)

EI programs conduct evaluations of needs and provide services but do not diagnose children. Their job is to assess where the child is on the developmental spectrum and provide whatever help is appropriate in areas where catch-up is needed.

I remember wondering what they were thinking, yet they weren't diagnosticians. They didn't have a unifying hypothesis about any of the kids. Many of the kids in our therapeutic playgroup shared the same basic difficulties, though they were coming from many different places. There was one who'd had a stroke because his mother was beaten up when she was pregnant, there was one with Down's syndrome, one who had been born very prematurely. EI does a great service, but it doesn't give you a diagnosis. That's not what they are about. I wish I had known that at the beginning.

The combination of directed therapeutic help and no diagnosis may be exactly what some parents want and all that a child really needs, especially in the early years. More EI programs are now identifying very young children who have delays or behaviors that suggest a diagnosis on what some may call the autistic spectrum. Once identified, these children are sometimes referred for more intensive behavioral programs with outside agencies. Given the data that suggest that intensive early intervention can improve long-term outcomes—at least in the most severely affected children—early identification has become a higher priority.

As children get older, they show us what kinds of therapies help them most. For example, we've heard therapists describe "a real OT kind of kid"— that is, a kid who will derive the most benefit from the work that occupational therapists do. For those children, an early experience in EI may point the way to particular therapies that need to continue as the child grows. No matter what your child's issues, early intervention services only go up to age three. Clearly, many of these problems may last longer than that in a child's life.

OCCUPATIONAL THERAPIST

Occupational therapy and physical therapy overlap, but occupational therapists are generally more interested in the smaller muscle groups, like the hand muscles or the facial muscles used in eating. They also look at a child's ability to tolerate sensations, input, stimulations, from all of his senses. *Dysgraphia* (terrible handwriting), for example, is a problem for many of these kids and falls within the OT expertise. So do oral-motor assessments. There is a subgroup of occupational therapists who have special training and special certification in sensory integration. These therapists are specifically concerned with that elusive problem on which we touched earlier: how children exist in their environment. They are particularly useful for that quirky child who seems uneasy in his skin, not confident moving through space. As they assess your child, they will look for problems like "gravitational insecurity" and "rotational insecurity," referring to the child who cannot stand to have her feet off the ground (on a swing, for example) or to rotate or spin around. They will also look at your child's sensitivity to sensory stimulation. This would include, for example, the child who can't tolerate the tag on the neck of his shirt rubbing against his skin. With slightly older children, the OT will focus on whether the child can write; on whether she can be taught to type, can tie her shoes, eat with a fork, follow multistep directions; as well as on larger questions: Can she organize her body in space? How about her thoughts on a page?

SPEECH AND LANGUAGE PATHOLOGIST

Many people know that speech therapists help children talk or that they address specific problems like stuttering or speech impediments. They can also help assess a number of additional concerns in the realm of speech, language, and communication. Most quirky kids are not terribly speech-delayed. They can make words, they can talk; but they can't necessarily carry on a conversation in an age-appropriate way.

A speech and language assessment will include not only your child's ability to make words but also her *ability to communicate* using words as well as her *prosody*—the character of her voice as she speaks. The assessment will take into account the child's frustration tolerance and the nature and quality of her tantrums. And, like the occupational therapist, the speech pathologist will look at oral-motor function.

We got our first glimmer of this being more of a global thing when John was about two. I took him to see a speech therapist because he had lost a few of his language milestones. He also had failure to thrive. He wasn't growing because he wasn't eating much. We knew something was up, yet it was subtle enough that no one else who had seen him offered anything useful. She said, "Oh, he has motor-planning difficulties. He has oral-motor dyspraxia." I remember going back to my regular pediatrician and asking him what this meant, and he said, "He doesn't know what to do with his mouth!" The sensory stuff was so intense for him that he couldn't figure out how to get the words out of his mouth or the food in. It was the first time I saw the two as related, not as two unrelated things—that he couldn't eat and he couldn't talk.

PHYSICAL THERAPIST

Physical therapy evaluation focuses on muscle strength and weakness and co-ordination. The therapist will look at whether the child's muscles are weak, at whether she can throw and catch a ball, sit in a chair well enough to eat, walk up and down stairs. Many quirky kids are physically awkward, from either clumsiness or weakness. They may have instability of the trunk in which their muscles are not quite strong enough to control their upper bodies. This may mean that such a child would do better sitting in a chair with back support, whereas the "average" child could sit on a picnic bench quite comfortably. Evaluation by a physical therapist may include both playing games and carrying out the activities of daily living.

PSYCHOLOGIST

A psychologist has an advanced degree (master's degree or doctorate) in psychology but is not an M.D. Psychologists conduct evaluations of a child's intelligence and cognition. A school-based psychologist is often called upon to do a psychoeducation evaluation to determine the child's educational achievement and potential and to spell out which accommodations on the part of the school may be helpful.

NEUROPSYCHOLOGIST

A neuropsychologist has special training in the biological and neurological bases of learning and thought. This evaluation includes a battery of tests that most kids experience as "like being in school." The point of a "neuropsych eval" is to assess the level of cognitive and behavioral functioning and to serve as a basis for making recommendations about school placement and overall care of the child. This is the tool that is most likely to diagnose a learning disability, such as dyslexia. It may also diagnose attentional problems that interfere with learning. The tests will look at the child's ability to sit still, to focus, to process information visually and auditorily, to organize thoughts in his head and on paper. In addition, the particular learning difference most common in quirky kids—the nonverbal learning disability—is characterized by a specific pattern on intelligence tests administered during this exam. Most neuropsychological evaluations will include an interview with parents in which you'll go over the history of your child's birth and growth and development, focusing on areas of special concern. Of all the types of evaluations described here, neuropsychological testing is likely to be the most lengthy—and therefore perhaps the most stressful for your child and for you. To make it easier and more pleasant, many clinics split it up over a couple of days.

They said Brian should have neuropsych testing, so I went on a mission. What is a neuropsych eval? Who does it? Where do you get it done? It's a battery of tests. Brian's had it done twice, and it's six or eight hours of tests. First, he had the educational and the psych tests. He came out of that, and they sat us down after they did the tests, and clearly, he was puzzling and he was unusual. They said, "We're confused and we're concerned." (This was in the middle of the third grade.) "Clearly, he has X strengths and Y deficits, but there are these other things going on."

PEDIATRIC NEUROLOGIST

A neurologist is a physician with specialty training in the brain and nervous system. There are pediatric neurologists who have a special interest in children with atypical behavior or development. Attention deficit disorder, for example, is often diagnosed and treated by neurologists. (There are also child neurologists with less interest in this field who may focus on diseases such as epilepsy or brain tumors or cerebral palsy. Be sure you are referred to one who is versed in the quirky child.) A child whose overall picture includes a neurological disorder—such as seizures or a tic or a question of Tourette's syndrome—will certainly be seen by a neurologist, who may stay involved as the diagnostic questions expand past that particular disorder. A neurologist will examine your child in great detail, paying attention to the strength of each separate group of muscles and to the ability of his nerves to register sensation, as well as to reflexes, coordination, and mental skills—whether the child is nine months old or nine years old. Most important, a neurologist will be strongly oriented toward sorting out the possibility of medical problems that are not just developmental differences. For example, if the child's weakness or clumsiness has raised a question of cerebral palsy or of one of the muscular dystrophies, a neurologist's exam will be essential. A neurologist may want to get a look at the brain by doing a CT or an MRI scan—particularly if the child's behavior and development raise issues of syndromes that may actually show up as abnormal brain development. The likelihood of a significant finding on a scan of the brain is extremely low. More often, it serves to reassure parents that the overall appearance of the brain is normal.

DEVELOPMENTAL AND BEHAVIORAL PEDIATRICIAN
Often, the person directing the whole workup will be a pediatrician with specialty training in behavior and development. Even though these are often precisely the most overbooked doctors in town, you want, ideally, to look for a developmentalist who is particularly interested in kids on the quirky spectrum (as opposed to someone who specializes in kids with mental retardation and cerebral palsy, for example). This may be the person referring your child for neuropsychological testing, for a speech evaluation, or for any other kind of assessment. This may also be the person who gathers all the different pieces together and tries to form a coherent diagnosis, especially since, as we said at the beginning of this chapter, doctors are trained to think in terms of diagnostic categories. Expect to be asked a lot of (repetitive) questions about your child's development: how old he was when he first rolled over, sat, stood, walked, talked. Expect as well to be asked about problems that run in your

family, including autism, learning disabilities, or mental health problems like depression or bipolar disease. The developmental and behavioral pediatrician will do a careful examination of your child, looking to see whether there is anything unusual about his body. Like the neurologist, this doctor will also pay particular attention to the child's nervous system, noting physical strength and coordination as well as behavior, social responsiveness, and speech.

CHILD PSYCHIATRIST

At some point in the assessment, your child should probably see a child psychiatrist, a physician who has done subspecialty training in psychiatric disorders of children. The kind of information that a child psychiatrist will gather is both different from and in some ways more sophisticated than much of that described above. You will probably be glad to have this assessment and this diagnostic point of view. Sometimes, in fact, it's a child psychiatrist who directs the workup and receives and interprets the evaluations. A thorough neuropsych evaluation will be of great interest and help to a psychiatrist, but she is not equipped to do one herself.

Psychiatrists interested in quirky kids are likely to assess the "theory of mind." Theory of mind refers to a child's ability or inability to view experience through another person's eyes. The inability to see another's perspective, sometimes called "mindblindness," is often considered the underlying feature of the quirky child's social difficulties. The assessment involves something like this: The doctor will tell your child a story about two children who have candy. In the story, one child leaves the room, and the other puts the candy someplace new—for example, into a box. The psychiatrist will ask your child to explain where the child who was out of the room will look for the candy when she comes back in. Children with this trait of mindblindness will answer, "In the box," because *they* know that's where the candy is. Other children, by the age of four, can project themselves into the child in the story, who does not have that information—they know she'll look for the candy wherever *she* last saw it. Most children enjoy their visits to child psychiatrists (beware of the psychiatrist whom your child doesn't enjoy!) and look forward to an opportunity to play a variety of games and talk openly about the things they find challenging. Psychiatrists rarely do the one-on-one therapy for which they are famous in movies but rather periodically check in after the assessment period is over, to monitor symptoms and perhaps medications.

We have two kids on the spectrum and have really enjoyed and appreciated our relationship with the child psychiatrist over the years. They both look forward to seeing him, and we need his counsel and experience from time to time. He, more than the other professionals we have seen, seems to really enjoy the kids and sees them as interesting rather than as problems that need to be fixed. The kids sense this and appreciate it as well.

Evaluating the Evaluators

As you move with your child through this maze of experts, your job will be to track and evaluate the information offered and to make important decisions about when to look further and when to pause.

- *Make sure you understand your cast of characters. Ask the specialists you see about their qualifications and their particular fields of expertise.* It's important to know whether you're dealing with a neurologist or a neuropsychologist, or with a neophyte speech pathologist versus a master's-level expert with a special interest in the autistic spectrum disorders. Even if you aren't completely sure how to integrate the specialist's background with the assessment and the advice, your pediatrician and the other specialists you see may understand the opinions you've already collected better if you can help them understand who was doing the evaluating.

- *Talk to the evaluators! Ask questions! Write down what they say!* Some parents just don't—or can't—get their questions answered in any kind of detail by the people doing the evaluating. Sometimes this happens because there are still tests to be scored or conversations that need to take place among members of the team doing the evaluation. At the very least, you should go away knowing *when* you will hear and *how* you will hear what the assessment has yielded. For the most part, someone who has just spent a while with your child should be able to give you at least a few reactions or observations. It is completely reasonable to let evaluators know that you'd like a few minutes at the end of the session to get a sense of what they think. Take notes. You may be more tense than you realize, and it may be hard to remember exactly what you did or didn't hear. Ask to have unfamiliar terms spelled out and explained. Ask whether there's anything you can read for more information. If you've had a full multispecialty evaluation done, consider making an appointment to come back in, sit down, and discuss the results.

- *Keep a notebook. Write everything down.* As time goes by, you will think of questions you want to ask, observations about your child that seem significant, ideas for further assessment or therapy. Write it down. Keep a record of the specialists you see, the tests they do, the information they give. Jot down phone numbers of programs or specialists you learn about from other parents as well as contact data for someone who isn't that helpful now but may be in a few years. A notebook will help you track your child and your own understanding. It will also help you use your time with the specialists to ask the questions you've been wanting to bring up.

- *Don't expect a single "eureka" moment.* We'll say it again because it's so important. By and large, quirky kids don't fit neatly into diagnostic categories. Having your child assessed, considering different diagnoses, is an ongoing process that is very valuable if it points the way to helping your child. Still, it's probably not going to yield you a single all-explanatory moment when you finally find out what's "really" going on.

- *Remember that some specialists—or some clinics—will give almost anyone a diagnosis.* If you look hard enough and long enough, eventually you will come across someone who will pin on the label—maybe because it's the same label everybody gets at that particular clinic. Be especially wary of labels that carry immediate recommendations for expensive therapies. Don't let anyone prey on your desire to help your child along. It's probably worth getting a second opinion or discussing the recommendations with your own pediatrician.

We saw this psychologist in private practice who looked at my son and recommended all these other evaluations—like functional optometry so that an optometrist could see how he tracks when he reads, for example. She had particular names of people she wanted us to see—and I felt as if she was going to keep her friends in business and they were going to keep her in business!

Most of the people you will encounter with your child as you look into assessment and diagnosis will be honorable and professional. It must be said, however, that there is something of an industry out there in providing diagnoses and therapies to kids with developmental variations. This brings us back again to our preference for the academic medical center.

Diagnoses and Labels

So you've been to a specialist—or specialists. You've asked your questions and noted down the answers, kept copies of all the assessments, sat with your pediatrician to discuss the results. Bear in mind that each of these experts looks at your child through a different professional lens. Thus, a diagnosis of Asperger's syndrome, say, is more likely to come from a psychiatrist or a behavioral/developmental pediatrician, whereas an occupational therapist might describe the same child as having sensory integration dysfunction. A speech and language pathologist might call the problem a pragmatic language disorder. A neurologist could see a right hemispheric weakness, and a neuropsychologist could call it auditory-processing disorder or nonverbal learning disability. The tests you do and the training you have determine the diagnoses you are most likely to make. Many of the diagnoses on this list overlap and coexist. Some describe overarching syndromes, whereas others pinpoint a specific dysfunction. Your child is your child—not the sum of any number of these. The objective of the diagnosis is to point the way toward something you can do to help. Different ways of understanding what's wrong may actually point you toward different ways of helping.

Most of these diagnoses are relatively new. Although they may be relevant and useful, and may represent our current best guess at what's going on, we have to face the fact that many of them will probably evolve and change in the years to come. Some may even disappear as our understanding changes. It's OK to feel a little wary if you sense that your child is being bent and twisted in order to fit the hot diagnosis of the moment.

The terms that follow may be spoken to you about your child by any one of the specialists who sees him. Some are nothing more than descriptions. Some are more global terms that could describe difficulties in many different areas. For any of these problems, there will be whole books that address the details. We will try to point you toward some good ones. All these words can be scary. Depending on your experience, your reading, and your background, some can be downright terrifying in their implications. We won't promise that what we say will necessarily reassure you, but we would argue as strongly as we can that none of these diagnostic terms should be heard either as the end of the world or as a distinct and final pronouncement on your child's potential. They are clues and constructs, approximations, best guesses, and often works in progress. That said, what are some of the words you may hear or read or lie awake worrying about?

DESCRIPTIVE DIAGNOSES

Descriptive diagnoses generally pinpoint areas of weakness or difficulty, which almost intrinsically suggest particular therapies. You may be more likely to hear these terms from therapists or educators, people who evaluate your child with the idea of matching her up to the most helpful therapy.

RIGHT HEMISPHERIC DYSFUNCTION

A neurologist or neuropsychologist may use the term *right hemispheric dysfunction* in describing a particular child's strengths and weaknesses. The right hemisphere, or right half of the brain, is the region believed to be involved in all of the disorders subsumed under the quirky-kid diagnoses. The right half of the brain is responsible for, among other things, visual-spatial perception, integrating information, and intuition and getting the "gestalt" of what is going on around you: the big picture. The left side of the brain handles skills like categorizing, rote learning, following rules. Most quirky kids have trouble intuiting, or understanding nonverbal information—ways of understanding the world that come naturally to the typical child. Because of this right brain weakness or immaturity, the cognitive part of a neuropsychological evaluation will yield a lower score for the "performance" compared to the "verbal" intelligence quotient—as if the brain has all the information but can't quite use it. This can become important when considering the distinguishing features of one diagnosis compared to others. Possible therapies for this diagnosis include occupational therapy and special education services with extra academic support.

SPEECH AND LANGUAGE DELAY

The speech and language delay description reflects your child's progress in speech norms for his age. In fact, a full speech and language evaluation will provide detailed information about what your child can and cannot do with language. Older kids on this spectrum should definitely get an assessment of *pragmatic language skills* (the ability to understand the give-and-take of conversation, to pick up cues about when the other person is bored or no longer interested). Speech therapy can be helpful for both verbal and nonverbal aspects of communication. Not all quirky kids are speech-delayed. Some of the kids we are talking about actually develop language early. Some, quite dramatically, learn to read as they learn to talk—called *hyperlexia*. Thus, not all quirky children will be evaluated early in childhood for speech delay, but even some of the precocious talkers may need to be seen later in childhood when their communication difficulties emerge. For many children, initial concerns about speech delay lead to other questions about communication, social relations, and patterns of thought.

Trevor was developmentally delayed and had no speech at age two. Then, almost before he learned to talk, he started reading, and my husband saw an article about hyperlexia. So his first evaluation was with a hyperlexia specialist, who said, yes, he does have this syndrome. When he did start to develop language, it was slow and echolalic. He had other unusual mannerisms, like waving backward, his palm facing himself, and mixing up pronouns.

George talked a lot but used "scripted speech" from movies or books. He had an incredible memory and would remember a line appropriate to a situation, but it would be directly from a book or movie. When he was three and a half, we had a storm and lost our power. We took out the flashlights, and his grandfather told him not to play with the flashlight, because it wasn't a toy. George responded by saying, "I know, Grandpa. It's a big responsibility, but I'll take good care of it." His grandfather looked at me and said, "And you are worried about his language?" But it was a line directly out of a book we had read about taking care of puppies. At about this time, he had his first full evaluation, and the speech therapist said he had no "functional language."

PRAGMATIC LANGUAGE DISORDER

The term *pragmatic language disorder* is used largely by speech and language pathologists to describe the idiosyncratic social impairments of quirky kids, due to their difficulties in verbal communication. Although some kids may be able to wax eloquent about their area of special interest, they may *not* be able to figure out when it is time to stop. This is pragmatic language—using words and the nonverbal behaviors that go along with them to understand another person. Quirky kids often miss the boat in this regard. They keep on talking. They talk in monotonous voices. They change the subject midstream. Or they do not understand the facial expressions of the person with whom they are speaking. They interrupt with no regard for the interuptee; the concept of turn-taking in a conversation is foreign to them. This is a major handicap, even for a comparatively young child in the first few grades of school. Pragmatic language therapy, discussed in more detail later, is directed at teaching children these skills. Given the rules of the game, many quirky kids can learn what came naturally to most of us.

MOTOR DELAY

Children with motor delay have fallen behind with respect to the motor skills you would expect them to be developing for their given ages. Motor delay can refer to a specific skill or milestone that the child has not mastered, or it can refer to the quality of the child's movements, to clumsiness or unsteadiness or muscle weakness. A great number of quirky kids have difficulties with motor coordination and weakness. This can show up early as delayed motor milestones like sitting up or walking; or you may notice it later, if the child cannot hop or kick a ball or seems to lose her balance easily. Motor clumsiness may persist throughout life, but many children have made tremendous gains in this area with a combination of occupational and physical therapy.

MOTOR-PLANNING DIFFICULTIES

The term *motor-planning difficulties* refers to the ability to plan an action with your brain and carry it out with your body. Motor-planning difficulties, called *dyspraxias*, are frequent in quirky kids. In medical terms, this is similar to what you see in an adult who has had a stroke in a particular area of the brain. She may know exactly what she wants to do but cannot get her body to do it. One part of the brain is not working right, and therefore, despite all her intelligence and memory and understanding, buttoning her shirt is a difficult, if not impossible, assignment. In kids, motor-planning difficulties manifest as the inability to carry out tasks—maybe simple tasks like chewing and swallowing, or maybe complex tasks like getting dressed and tying shoes. We hear many stories from parents about their children's not being able to perform seemingly simple tasks like putting on their pants:

We noticed pretty early that John had trouble getting things done. He was never that motivated to get dressed on his own, and we coaxed him to try when we got busy with the younger children. We watched him lay his pants over his legs. He knew how they were supposed to look once they were on, but he couldn't figure out how to get his legs inside. There were, and continue to be, many things like this.

SENSORY INTEGRATION DYSFUNCTION

Most likely to be used by occupational therapists, the term *sensory integration dysfunction* describes the child who seems out of sync with her environment. We have worked with a number of kids who fit this description and have benefited from treatments directed at this problem. Sensory integration (SI) refers to the capacity to take in information from the senses—visual, tactile, auditory, taste, and smell—and process it. This capacity is hardwired in the central nervous system in the right hemisphere of the brain, as discussed above. The ability to integrate this sensory information enables us to get the big picture. When this system is faulty, it is nearly impossible to make it through the day smoothly.

Ben's sensory overload comes mostly in the form of visual overload. He doesn't like loud noises but has no trouble with movies or loud performances. He has sensory abilities most of us don't have or screen out without thinking about it. He suffers from recurrent ear infections, and at age six, he told his pediatrician, "I can feel fluid moving around inside my ear."

The child with SI dysfunction, eloquently described by Carol Stock Kranowitz in her book *The Out-of-Sync Child*, may be oversensitive or undersensitive to sensory input. The child may be extremely sensitive to touch or textures, loud noises, visual stimulation—and because of this sensitivity may try to minimize the stimulation. Alternatively, if the child is much less sensitive than usual to such input, he may seek more of it than most people can tolerate. When you think about the oversensitive child, think of the kid who cannot stand the wind or the sand at the beach, not to mention the water. Or the boy who covers his ears at movies. Or the girl who cannot stand the seams on her socks, the tags on her sweater. However, the child who *seeks* stimulation of her senses may need the volume up high, may put everything in her mouth, may enjoy spinning or twirling around as a way of sensing the world. In retrospect, parents often describe these oversensitive kids as fussy, prone to screaming or arching, difficult to console. The undersensitive child may be remembered as excessively placid or as so easy that the parents worried—but probably didn't get much sympathy from anyone! Sensory integration therapy is designed to help kids with these issues.

Here's a story from a mother of two kids with SI-like symptoms on opposite ends of the spectrum:

I was at the beach with both of them when they were about two and four. I knew it was going to be hard for John, but I love the beach myself so I decided to just give it one more try. One breezy afternoon, Sam was so happy he just couldn't get enough of it. He jumped in and out of the water, rolled around in the sand, squealed and shrieked with joy in the brisk breeze. At one point, we decided to take a walk along the beach. Sam was completely naked except for his sunglasses and thoroughly enjoying himself. John, on the other hand, was fully clothed with socks and shoes, a terry-cloth bathrobe, a bicycle helmet, and goggles, so as not to feel the wind or get any sand in his eyes. I knew other moms were noticing us. We must have been quite a sight.

NONVERBAL LEARNING DISABILITY

The term *nonverbal learning disability* describes the "learning profile" often seen in quirky kids, with certain specific findings on neuropsychological testing—for example, a stronger verbal score compared to the performance score. It's a *nonverbal* learning disability because the child's verbal scores are fine; she runs into trouble with her nonverbal skills of integration and abstract reasoning. Children with NLD tend to be bright, have a great vocabulary, are terrific at rote learning, and reliably notice certain details. Yet they cannot integrate them into a unifying concept. An example is the child who seems to be a great reader in terms of figuring out the words yet has no idea what he just read. Although these kids may be strong in math in the sense that they have excellent computation skills, a word problem can really throw them off. Anything that requires abstract reasoning is a real challenge to a child with NLD, and academic performance will falter as more of these skills are required to succeed in school. Problems with visual perception can manifest themselves as physical awkwardness or clumsiness. Many of these children suffer from sensory defensiveness, usually manifested as sensitivity to certain kinds of touch or textures, loud noises, and so on. NLD is a global disability that makes the processing of new information challenging. These kids are quite literal in their interpretation of language and cannot appreciate metaphors or "read between the lines." This can be of great concern to parents, as it puts the NLD child at risk for abuse or other dangerous situations. These kids will need help from special education services, pragmatic language therapy, and sometimes occupational therapy.

DISTURBANCES IN EXECUTIVE FUNCTION

The executive-function skills are the higher-order thinking skills required to organize a plan and carry it out. Many quirky kids, despite high intelligence, have great difficulty in day-to-day life due to executive-function difficulties. These problems can impede their progress academically, socially, and in the working world. These kids might answer any individual academic question perfectly well—maybe even brilliantly—but can't put it all together, can't actually outline the project and see it through, can't complete the whole assignment. Teachers with special education skills can be helpful here, and some occupational therapists can work on organizational skills.

Despite his high intelligence and encyclopedic knowledge of facts, Gabriel can't put it all together in a decent report for school. He's much better off with short-answer questions or multiple choice—anything that doesn't require organization.

MEDICAL DIAGNOSES

Terms and diagnostic categories discussed in this subsection are those that you're more likely to hear from a medically trained person, such as a pediatrician or a psychiatrist, a developmentalist, or a neurologist.

ANXIETY DISORDER

Familiar to all of us, anxiety is more familiar to quirky kids and their families. Children can manifest their anxiety in any number of ways, but it is almost always part of the quirky-kid package. That is not to say that all quirky kids "qualify" for the DSM-IV diagnosis of "anxiety disorder." ("DSM-IV" refers to the fourth edition of the *Diagnostic and Statistical Manual of Mental Disorders*, a psychiatric reference book. See the "References and Resources" list at the end of this chapter.) Some manage anxiety much better than others. Some are truly debilitated or devastated by their anxiety, whereas for others, it's a smaller piece of the puzzle. Still, most tend to be anxious. Perhaps your child needs someone in his bedroom until he is completely asleep. Perhaps he does not separate and explore the world at the expected time because he just can't let go of you, or then again, perhaps his fear of strangers is all-consuming and debilitating. As children get older, anxiety can show up in many different ways in particular situations—around animals, say, or about having to perform in class—or with anxiety-driven behaviors. Anxiety disorders are broken down into subtypes:

- *Generalized anxiety disorder* describes a person whose worry is pervasive and difficult to control and is out of proportion to any real threat. The worry is associated with physical symptoms—having trouble sleeping, perhaps, or palpitations—and causes enough distress to interfere with everyday life.

- *Social phobia* means the anxiety is focused on social situations or situations in which the child must "perform" in public. In young children, this may look like excessive shyness or fear of strangers.

Abby was so afraid in social situations, we stayed home most of the time. In her toddler years, she was terrified in groups, and anything unexpected could set her off—like a sudden laugh or someone coughing. We avoided family gatherings, or one of us would go and the other would stay home with her.

- *Separation anxiety disorder* describes a level of distress and worry about leaving home or separating from a parent that is way out of line for the child's age. Some of these kids are unwilling to go to school because it means separating from the parent, or they may even be unwilling to go to sleep, for fear of something happening to the parent.

- *Obsessive-compulsive disorder (OCD)* is a syndrome in which the compulsion to do something over and over is an attempt to ward off anxiety.

For some families, this is the first symptom that brought them in for evaluation.

Eventually, Brian developed an hour and a half of going-to-bed rituals. I used to read to the kids every night, and he would have to go to the bathroom after I finished—and he would do it again and again.

When John was about three, he learned to tell time, which was a great surprise to all of us. By four or five, he had a collection of watches and clocks—some analog, some digital, some on military time. He often wore three or four watches at the same time. By age five, he started lining up his clocks along the side of his bed and synchronizing them before he fell asleep. If they weren't synchronized when he woke up, he'd become very anxious. This prompted our first visit to a child psychiatrist.

OCD-like symptoms can be a major source of stress and disability for quirky kids. Although this is not a primary quirky-kid diagnosis, virtually all quirky kids need to deal with these issues along the way. However, we should point out that comparatively few of these children will actually have true obsessive-compulsive disorder. Many of them will have obsessions and compulsions, but not to the degree that constitutes this diagnosis. Therefore, these will be features of their lives and problems with which they'll have to deal. For most of them, OCD will not be the chronic, lifelong disability that it can be. If, however, these problems get to be really troubling for your child, they are among the most amenable to medical therapy (see Chapter 10).

ATTENTION DEFICIT DISORDER

Attention deficit disorder (also sometimes called ADHD, for attention deficit hyperactivity disorder) is a very common diagnosis frequently applied to quirky kids. Although often it fits the bill, this diagnosis is *so* common that parents need to be sure the evaluation is complete enough. It may point out an attentional problem, but does it answer the question of whether or not attentional issues are the whole story?

Problems with attention are the common denominator of so many neurologically based disorders of childhood that attention deficit may be only part of the story. More common in boys, ADD is found in as many as 3 to 5 percent of school-age children. Kids with ADD can't maintain their focus, and this manifests itself in three major ways: inattention, hyperactivity, and impulsivity. Children with inattention are easily distracted, disorganized, they have a lot of trouble following through, and of course, they have a hard time paying attention. Hyperactivity means constant motion—from squirming and fidgeting at rest to nonstop running and climbing. And impulsivity suggests a tendency to act without thinking. A child may have only inattention (often how ADD shows up in girls), hyperactivity together with impulsivity, or most commonly, all three symptoms.

Although these behaviors can start quite early, it is difficult to diagnose ADD in anyone under six years old. To "qualify" as having ADD, a child must manifest these behaviors in different settings (not just act up in school, for example, while behaving normally at home), over the course of at least six months, and they must interfere with the child's functioning. The ability to concentrate for long periods of time on television or on video games does not mean that a child does not have ADD, since those particular activities offer a kind of frequent repeated stimulation that actually works well for children with this problem. Therefore, a child who can't pay attention in school or to activities with friends and siblings at home may have ADD, even if he spends long periods of time staring at screens.

This diagnosis can be made by some general pediatricians, though others prefer to send kids to neurologists or behavior and development specialists or psychiatrists for full assessment. The diagnosis may involve asking parents to fill out questionnaires describing the child's behavior at home while his teacher is asked for a description of school behavior.

Children with these problems can be quite isolated from their peers because of their difficulties—which require a disproportionate amount of attention from adults. Teachers, coaches, camp counselors, and even parents will think of these kids as particularly troublesome and labor-intensive. Other kids may resent them for taking up so much attention or for disrupting activities and making trouble in school. The children themselves end up lonely, depressed, and sometimes act out even more wildly. Medication is standard therapy for children whose ADD is interfering with school function. There are also many teaching and learning strategies that can really help.

Kids with ADD have a higher-than-normal risk of many comorbid conditions, including other behavioral disorders, Tourette's syndrome and other tic disorders, anxiety, depression, and speech and language problems. Up to 15 to 20 percent of these kids will have some kind of learning disability that may manifest itself as an imperfect ability to perform tasks required for academic success.

OPPOSITIONAL DEFIANT DISORDER

Although all kids are oppositional at times, the term *oppositional defiant disorder* is reserved for the child who seems incapable of compliance with her parents' wishes. It is commonly seen along with ADD, and we hear quite a lot about otherworldly tantrums in quirky kids, who have difficulty modulating their reactions to fit the situation. Kids with this "official" characterization must meet certain criteria put forth in the DSM-IV. They lose their tempers easily, argue with adults, often defy or refuse to comply with adult requests, annoy people on purpose, blame others for their own misbehavior, are easily annoyed, and come off as angry, resentful, spiteful. These are challenging qualities in a child and sometimes constitute the reason parents seek help. Although the diagnostic criteria are descriptive, they do nothing to explain the cause of this behavior. Our experience suggests that many quirky kids are simply overwhelmed by the world around them, aren't flexible enough to go with the flow, miss all kinds of cues that might avert a meltdown in the average child, and pop a gasket when they can't manage any other way. Sometimes called "explosive," these kids are not well liked by their peers or their teachers. By and large, they are not happy—and neither are their parents. Many end up on medications, and they often find it useful to see counselors and learn to discuss their feelings and impulses.

TOURETTE'S SYNDROME AND OTHER TIC DISORDERS

Many people have now heard of Tourette's syndrome, though some expect this neurological disorder to involve outbursts of profanity as its most prominent feature. In fact, the hallmark of Tourette's syndrome is the presence of tics, sudden involuntary movements or sudden involuntary sounds. Tics can range from brief jerks or twitches to head-shaking or gyrating . . . and yes, they can include obscene gestures or bad language.

To be called Tourette's syndrome, a child's symptoms must meet a set of criteria—multiple motor tics as well as at least one phonic (sound-related) tic, tics that occur multiple times in the day or else continue to recur at least occasionally for more than a year, tics that change over time. Tics in general, and Tourette's, are much more common in people with ADD and OCD, and—as with many of these syndromes—this one does tend to run in families. Tourette's syndrome typically shows up between the ages of three and eight, and it's most severe around the age of ten. Tics are gone by the age of eighteen for more than half of the kids with Tourette's. Medication helps many children with tic disorders.

AUTISTIC SPECTRUM DISORDERS

The term *autistic spectrum disorder* is widely used to capture the overlap of symptoms among many quirky kids. Although it is *not* a category in the DSM-IV, it is indeed a category in the minds of many pediatricians, child neurologists, and psychiatrists who work with children. The unofficial *autistic spectrum disorder* term is used by these professionals to underscore the reality that a given child may have features of several of these conditions but not fit exactly into any one in particular. The closest category in the DSM-IV is the unfortunately named pervasive developmental disorders, which consists of autism, Asperger's disorder, pervasive developmental disorder–not otherwise specified, Rett's syndrome, and childhood disintegrative disorder. In this subsection, we will describe the various diagnoses—with the exception of Rett's syndrome and childhood disintegrative disorder, both of which are extremely rare.

Looking at these disorders, note the way that quirky children, in their rich variety, have made it necessary to create certain categories that are defined by *not* fitting into any categories. This is a broad spectrum, and individual children will require individualized combinations of therapies—often including medication, occupational therapy, physical therapy, pragmatic language therapy, and psychotherapy, as well as academic support. Later on in this book (Chapter 9), we'll help you design the particular mix your child needs.

There is controversy among the researchers working in this field, as well as among families of affected children, about the use of the term *autism*. Whereas classic autism is a severe condition familiar to most people, many quirky kids bear little resemblance to autistic children. The use of this term may serve to confuse and frighten rather than enlighten. We cannot defend this nomenclature, but we will do our best to explain it. Current thinking is that autism is not limited to the severe classic autism—with which most of us are somewhat familiar and which usually (85 percent of the time) includes mental retardation. Severe classic autism—outside the province of this book—has shadowed this terminology, so that many parents are terrified to hear that their child may have an "autistic spectrum disorder." In fact, this is a spectrum, with autism at its most disabling end but with many milder forms as well. What all of these disorders have in common are problems with communication and social interactions. We will briefly discuss three of the milder conditions currently placed on this autistic spectrum. Some of these disorders are described in the psychiatric manual DSM-IV, where specific criteria for each diagnosis are laid out. Because the characteristics are so clearly defined, parents are sometimes told that although a child does not meet the criteria for any of these syndromes, the child has autistic features. Scary words to hear. Frankly, they can mean everything or nothing.

Although parents often see some of the characteristic traits of these disorders in their infants and very young children, and though they can sometimes be diagnosed as early as the age of two, there is no way to tell how severely affected the child will be or the category into which he should fall. Children with the less severe forms are especially hard to detect early. With the increasing incidence of these diagnoses, it is important not to rush to these conclusions too early. If you diagnose Asperger's syndrome—the mildest form of ASD—before a child is four or five years old, writes Janice Ware, Ph.D., associate director of the Developmental Medicine Center at Children's Hospital Boston, there is "the risk of either underestimating the risk of symptoms not yet expressed or overestimating the severity of behavioral symptoms that may represent a variant of typical functioning or another form of learning or behavioral problems other than ASD."[1]

Asperger's syndrome is perhaps the most familiar and well characterized of the quirky-kid diagnoses, though that does not necessarily mean that the term is familiar to the average person or even the average pediatrician. As with all of these diagnoses, children can fall anywhere on the continuum—from mildly to severely affected—and no two children are exactly alike. Although there is even controversy about the features that distinguish Asperger's children from those with atypical autism, high-functioning autism, and other PDD diagnoses, there is some agreement as to what generally constitutes this diagnosis.

Reasonably normal language development (specifically, two words by age two and three-word phrases by age three) is a distinguishing feature of Asperger's (compared to children with true autism or even high-functioning autism). Kids with Asperger's often have impaired social interactions, repetitive or stereotyped behaviors, preoccupations or interests, motor delays or clumsiness. A characteristic finding on neuropsychiatric testing further distinguishes the Asperger's child from one with high-functioning autism: Asperger's children consistently score higher on verbal rather than performance IQ—a finding also described in children with nonverbal learning disability. Some people have suggested that NLD and Asperger's are the same, whereas others feel that it is possible to have one and not the other.

What does this mean in plain English? These are the classic quirky kids. They are often, though not always, able to function within regular school environments, albeit with some supports either in school or around the edges. They tend to have special interests—sometimes bordering on obsessions—that may be abiding over time or may evolve into others no less intense. The interests themselves can serve to further isolate the child or can be a springboard into social relationships (when the interest is sports, for example). The brighter kids, and those without major learning issues, have it much easier than the children who struggle academically. Those with stereotypes associated with autistic kids—like hand-flapping or rocking—struggle more than those without them. Virtually all these children have trouble making friends; their behavior is just strange enough to make other kids uncomfortable or scared. The inability to see another's point of view, the anxiety, the tendency to have rigid expectations of others, and the lack of flexibility combine to make this child more alone in the important social world of childhood. Many Asperger's children are infinitely more comfortable with adults than with other kids. Adults are more able to accommodate to the child's differences, are less likely to do unpredictable things, and are often charmed by these kids.

At two and a half, Caitlin started a playgroup three mornings a week with a child psychology graduate student. She made a video of the children and sent it home, and we were horrified. The other two girls played with the teacher, did "ring-around-the-rosy," etcetera, while Caitlin sat in a corner by herself. We were worried. We knew that she needed help. At the pediatrician's office, I brought it up, that I was worried about my daughter's development, and I was told she was fine, not to worry. Then the graduate student came over to talk with us and told us, in an excited grad-student type of way, with a big smile on her face, that she thought Caitlin was autistic. Thus began a series of evaluations and therapies that still continue. I called the pediatrician's office looking for the name of a child psychologist and was sent to someone who said that Caitlin's main problem is that she is just so smart! This was not helpful. After a couple of other visits to psychologists, including one who wanted my husband and me to call our mothers and find out the age at which we were toilet-trained, we went to this child psychiatrist who saw her once, when she was about five, and said, "This is Asperger's." What characteristics of Caitlin's behavior made it so easy for him to make this diagnosis? She was always very rigid and insisted that things had to be the same. As a toddler, she would only wear clothes that had ducks or numbers sewn on them. She had terrible eating habits and horrendous temper tantrums. She could not engage with other kids. She loved swings, but to an extreme degree.

High-functioning autism (HFA) is a term sometimes used interchangeably with *Asperger's syndrome,* but these individuals are in fact a distinct group. They are slower to acquire language and have weaker verbal scores and stronger integrative skills (visual-spatial skills), and they are less likely to overlap with nonverbal learning disability. Due to their weak verbal skills, they have a big discrepancy between verbal and performance IQs, but it is the opposite of the discrepancy found in people with Asperger's syndrome. One distinction is that children with HFA are not particularly interested in social relationships, whereas children with Asperger's are deeply interested though unable to understand the rules.

Atypical autism, also referred to as *pervasive developmental disorder–not otherwise specified (PDD-NOS),* describes kids who are perhaps closer to true autism yet are atypical either in the age at onset of symptoms or in the symptoms themselves. Like the child with Asperger's, these children have abnormal social interactions and restricted or repetitive behaviors, interests, or activities. Their play skills are impaired. However, this term is reserved for children in whom these abnormalities become evident after the age of three years and whose impairments cannot be explained by some other developmental disability. A child with these qualities who also has a clear-cut speech or language delay may fit here. This is a broad group of kids who, for whatever reason, do not fit into one of these other categories. This can be seen as something of a catchall category, and it's hard to argue that it really exists as a single specific diagnosis. (Look at the name: "not otherwise specified"!) The range in these children's level of function is also quite broad, and kids characterized as PDD-NOS can fall anywhere on the continuum of disability.

Rebecca was speech-delayed, and the pediatrician recommended an evaluation for her because her brother is autistic. She was evaluated by a group at a hospital and diagnosed with PDD-NOS. I feel that at this point she really fits the diagnostic criteria for Asperger's, but I want to keep the current label because, thanks to this diagnosis, Rebecca is getting all the services she needs right now.

This list of diagnoses helps sort kids out according to which symptoms and behaviors are most prominent and most problematic. Even if your child is not classic for any of these syndromes, careful testing and thoughtful diagnosis ought to give you a boost toward a relevant body of knowledge and experience—and most important, toward therapies and techniques that may make things better.

References and Resources

Although there are useful references regarding the screening and assessment process, no written resource can take the place of a developmental evaluation with an experienced professional. Do not try to make a diagnosis yourself! Use these references to educate yourself as you embark on this process.

American Psychiatric Association. *Diagnostic and Statistical Manual of Mental Disorders: DSM-IV.* Arlington, Va.: American Psychiatric Publishing, 1994. The fourth edition (1994) is the first edition of this manual to include the pervasive developmental disorders as diagnoses. A more recent revision, published in 2000, is called DSM-IV-TR (the "TR" is for "Text Revision"). Some parents find it helpful to look at the criteria for the various diagnoses straight from the horse's mouth.

Attwood, Tony. *Asperger's Syndrome: A Guide for Parents and Professionals.* London: Jessica Kingsley Publishers, 1998. A basic and readable book outlining the typical challenges faced by an Asperger's child.

Baron-Cohen, Simon. *Mindblindness: An Essay on Autism and Theory of Mind.* Cambridge, Mass.: MIT Press, 1997. This is the classic volume on the theory-of-mind concept.

Bashe, Patricia Romanowski, and Barbara L. Kirby. *The Oasis Guide to Asperger Syndrome: Advice, Support, Insight, and Inspiration.* New York: Crown, 2001. This terrific book on Asperger's syndrome includes a huge amount of information, advice, and anecdotes from families who have communicated with the Online Asperger Syndrome Information and Support (OASIS) Web site over the years. Don't miss it.

Hallowell, Edward M., and John J. Ratey. *Driven to Distraction: Recognizing and Coping with Attention Deficit Disorder from Childhood through Adulthood.* New York: Simon & Schuster, 1995. If you're thinking about attentional issues, and worry about the possibility of ADD as part of your child's picture, this is the book to read.

Kranowitz, Carol Stock. *The Out-of-Sync Child: Recognizing and Coping with Sensory Integration Dysfunction.* New York: Perigee, 1998. Once again, we recommend this book for anyone seeking a comprehensive guide regarding sensory integration dysfunction.

3

Dealing with the Diagnosis:
GRIEF AND LOSS AND MOVING FORWARD

Your child has a diagnosis. Someone has tested her and has assigned her to a category. You've been given a name—a label—and told that it belongs to your child. Maybe it's a familiar name, or maybe it's a term you've never heard before. Perhaps it feels strange, unexpected, unrelated to your perception of your child and what's really going on. Or maybe it seems so right that it has a kind of inevitability. Maybe it's even the diagnosis you've been expecting all along. Or perhaps—and this can feel worse yet—you've been told that she doesn't quite fit *any* particular category, and you're left wondering what to do next.

As pediatricians, we've seen parents in the days after they received these diagnoses. Sometimes we've even been the ones to deliver the news, explaining evaluation results or interpreting a too-technical letter. However well educated and well prepared parents may be, the experience of dealing with a diagnosis of this kind is intense, emotional, and highly charged.

There is nothing that hits as hard or hurts as much as finding out that your child has a serious problem. When you think something might be wrong, you lie awake and agonize. When those worries are confirmed, you're often devastated—no matter how well prepared you thought you were.

For one thing, many of the diagnoses that are offered to parents are terrifying in their implications. Are you hearing something that will determine the entire course of your child's life, circumscribing his possibilities and limiting his reach? You may also legitimately feel that you are being told something about what a hard job is in store for you: you are going to be the parent of a child with special needs. Many of us grew up hearing those words as code for mental retardation and severe disability. No matter how prepared you thought you were to hear a diagnosis, you may find that the actual "label" clangs in your mind like a kind of death knell.

This one doctor was the guy who I had decided was going to tell us either yes or no—and I guess I was hoping he would say, "Well, your child is definitely a little different and he's got this, this, and this, but he doesn't have Asperger's"—but really, I was expecting it. But I was still sad when he said, "Yes, he's pretty classic." Afterward, my husband said, "I don't see why you're so upset. You were expecting this"—I was weeping—and I think it was because some other person in a position of authority and expertise had said this. I wasn't just a neurotic parent. We were going to be dealing with this his whole life. It was really mammoth.

A Sense of Loss

A specific loss and sadness is evoked by your child's diagnosis. As parents, all of us start out with a mixture of hopes and expectations and fantasies. It's the great adventure of our adult lives, this remarkable experience of starting out with an infant and looking ahead to helping shape a whole new life. It's a complicated blend of falling madly in love and working harder than you've ever worked before, of redefining your family and your sense of self.

Every year at the school where I taught, there were one or two kids. People knew I knew about this because of my son, and the parents would end up coming to see me in the science room and closing the door and talking about their kids. And I could see that they didn't know what to do, and they were in between denial and grieving. "This is not the child I was expecting. This is not the way I expected my child's upbringing to go." There's a grieving process that goes along with getting this kind of diagnosis.

We come to the experience of parenthood with lots of expectations and complications—in fact, lots of "baggage." We're going to do it right even if our own parents didn't. We're going to protect our precious children from every danger; make their childhoods as happy as possible; control, as far as possible, the environments in which they live, the schools in which they learn. This isn't wrong or evil or arrogant—only impossible, as we come to learn. But in addition to our unrealistic fantasies of childrearing, we bring fantasies of how our children will perform, how they will do what we did—or surpass us—and how they will do us proud. These fantasies are part of the anticipation and enjoyment of parenthood.

Your quirky child has served you notice that all will not go as predicted. The diagnosis, when it comes, may seem to be the epitaph for all your fondest hopes and dreams. Many parents hear that first diagnosis as the end of fantasies. *No, my child will not* _____, and you can fill in the blank. *Won't be at the head of his class. Won't go even further than I did in tournament tennis. Won't have the successful, untroubled, socially confident adolescence I never had. Won't go to Princeton as I did—or as I didn't but hoped she would.* Or just, *won't grow up to be a happy, normal, well-adjusted adult.* How can he? He's got this terrible diagnosis. He's in a different category.

Understanding the ramifications of the diagnosis may mean coming to terms with some scary realities about what he—and you—will have to contend with as he grows. There may be real limitations on his immediate and distant future. In our pediatric and personal experience, we've learned that parenthood is never what you expected it to be. Still, we also acknowledge that right now, this might be cold comfort for the dimming of some of your brightest hopes.

No matter how much you thought you wanted it and needed it, you may experience your child's diagnosis as a blow and as a loss. That's perfectly fair. Your job is to adjust and find ways to use this new information, to become informed as a judge and an advocate. But before you do that, you may need a little time to mourn.

And after you acknowledge your grief at the loss of some of your hopes and some of your fantasies, you must then build and maintain new hopes for your child's future, even as you adjust your expectations. Your parental job of helping your child grow and thrive as an individual is going to mean believing in that individual.

- Remind yourself that the purpose of the diagnosis is to direct you toward information, resources, and therapies that can help your child function as well as possible, at home, in school, in life.

- Remember that many of these kids accumulate many diagnoses as they grow and that the first one that you are given may or may not have long-term relevance or predictive value.
- Consider joining a support group or other network of parents.

I am not the support-group type but have met many parents in various waiting rooms over the years, and that became a support group of sorts. We'd share anecdotes, laugh about how weird the kids were, and reassure one another that we were not alone. When my son was really young, it helped me to see the older kids who had made great progress and to hear their parents say, "You wouldn't believe it if you saw him a few years ago!" It gave me hope, a sense of perspective, and someone to call when the going got rough.

- Whatever diagnostic term you're dealing with, remember that it necessarily reflects a spectrum of children—from more impaired to highly functional—and don't let your expectations be colored by examples from the more severe end.
- Remember, most of these diagnoses are works in progress. The diagnoses themselves may evolve over time.
- Above all, don't let the diagnosis shadow too heavily your own picture of your child and your sense of her potential.

All of this is not said to encourage you to question the diagnosis. If it makes sense to you and if it's being offered by experts you trust, we urge you, at this difficult and emotional moment, to keep the diagnosis in perspective, to use it as a tool toward understanding and helping your child, and to keep an open mind about what the future may hold.

Parental Reaction

We've watched parents split up the intellectual and the emotional—one parent insisting on more, always more, information, while the other does the weeping or sits there looking stunned. Some parents, given a clue, turn into desperate detectives, spending hours on the Internet, accumulating shelves of books and scientific reprints, outexperting the experts. This can be highly admirable. But watch out if you've completely split the duties and one of you is in charge of information while the other confronts the emotional implications. Chances are, you really need each other right now. You both probably need to acknowledge both head and heart.

You also need to acknowledge the mourning process. That may mean naming some of the fears that this new diagnosis has elicited for each of you. Is there a person who came to mind, someone you are worried that your child may grow up to be like? A child in your school who was marginalized or mistreated, an adult family member who never got it together to lead a normal life? Are there specific images of parenthood to which you feel you are bidding good-bye forever? There are certain parental experiences that maybe only the other parent can truly understand, and we would urge you to give each other some help and comfort. Also, be ready to seek outside help and support if either or both of you need something more. There are moments in life with a quirky child when you may want to talk to someone—therapist, counselor, clergy, psychiatrist. Certainly, the emotional roller coaster of receiving a diagnosis has the potential to send you in that direction.

Yes, I am in therapy and on meds myself now—both things I thought would never happen. But my life as a mom is not at all what I expected and has been so deeply affected by having a child like David that I needed something to help me stay the course.

Many people respond to a child's diagnosis by demanding a cause, an etiology, a reason for what has gone wrong. We have had parents come to us asking whether the problem was caused by an illness in infancy or by a medication the mother took during pregnancy—or, of course, by environmental toxins or by childhood immunizations or any of the other theories that are currently seen as causes for developmental differences. As we'll discuss at more length later on (Chapter 5), there are many parents for whom the quest for a cause becomes a mission, even an obsession.

Even more commonly, though, what we hear in the office is a parent explaining cause and effect by assigning familial blame:

- "It's from my family, I know. My brother's oldest child is hyperactive."
- "My husband's really upset because he knows where this is coming from.

He has this brother who has seizures and tics and all kinds of stuff, and he's scared our son is going to be the same way."

- "My mother just told me about a cousin she had who was mentally retarded. Does that mean this is in my genes?"

Not so rarely, this takes on a tone of accusation, whether bitter self-accusation or even bitterer accusation of someone else: "I should never have had children." "You should have told me about your cousin before we got married." For some parents, this can be a valid issue. There probably is a genetic component to some of these syndromes, and many, many people can point to family members who seem to be affected by this range of diagnoses. Part of that is the high frequency of quirks and quirky kids in the general population, even back before most of these diagnoses existed, but part is that these diagnoses do indeed run in families. We'll discuss the genetic components more in Chapter 11.

Chrissie's dad has a history of ADD and learning disabilities, and he was held back in the fifth grade. He used to get locked in the closet because of his high activity level. And actually, I wonder whether I myself am on the spectrum. As a child, I listened to music obsessively, all day long. I wanted to be a disc jockey, and I read all the disc jockey magazines. In fact, I still want to be a disc jockey.

Where did this come from? I feel that I myself am the most likely culprit. I've always been excessively shy. In school, I was the quiet smart one in the class. And I'm still shy. I have several very close friends that I've had for years but not a lot of acquaintances.

Thinking in terms of blame and guilt when it comes to heritable conditions is a terribly slippery slope for parents already facing a situation that will require them to summon all their strengths and support each other through hard times and tough questions. So although you may want at some point to consider the genetics of whatever is going on with your child—seeing a genetic counselor and tracing out a family pedigree and looking at the odds that a future child will be affected—this is probably far down the line and most likely to come up for those whose children are most severely impaired.

Look beyond blame and try for understanding and sympathy. Any illness or problem or major life stress puts an enormous strain on a couple's relation-ship and probably increases the odds that they'll end up fighting, even split-ting. Take time now to confront this new challenge and try to make up your minds to pull together for the sake of your child, yourselves, and your family. You need to be able to discuss what's going on, and even what might have caused it, without assigning blame. No one deliberately passes on a problem to a child. Nobody did this on purpose; nobody wanted it to happen. You want to understand, to help, and you want to do it together. Build on what you have in common—your commitment to each other and to your child—and don't rip yourselves apart.

I guess I always felt that my husband and I were in it for the long haul, whether we drove each other crazy or not, but once we had this diagnosis, I felt it much more acutely. John really needs us both, and he's doing as well as he's doing because he has two loving parents, and if we made his daily life unstable, I don't know what would happen.

And for just one more responsibility at this difficult moment, make sure you look around and see how your other children are doing. We've seen par-ents become so preoccupied with the new diagnosis and its implications that a sibling feels abandoned or neglected.

The problem was, Brian started having these problems when his sister Jenni-fer was about twelve. So she was maybe fourteen when we were getting these diagnoses—and she just withdrew. The way she presents it now is that she felt she needed to become more self-sufficient because her parents had this problem that they needed to deal with. She describes how she orchestrated her applications to middle school all by herself. I was amused at the time. She drew up all these charts, and she checked with me that I had called people, and she put the pack-ages together for all of her teachers and she addressed the envelopes. I thought this was sweet and cute at the time, but now I understand that she felt she had to do it because if she didn't, I wouldn't, because of what was going on with her brother. I think she's wrong. I hope she's wrong.

Talking about It

You're handling the diagnosis: you've allowed yourselves to grieve a little, you've helped each other and refrained from casting any blame, and you're feeling ready to launch into the endeavor of using this new information to help your child. Before you begin, there are a couple of issues to settle.

WHOM ARE YOU GOING TO TELL?

Who needs to know, who ought to know, and who probably should know? There's no easy answer here, but there are a few guidelines to consider as you make your decisions.

If you have close friends or family members or people who care for your child—who have been involved every step of the way in your child's evaluation—obviously, you're going to tell them about the diagnosis. If you've been more reticent about your worries and your investigations, you might want to hold back a little with the diagnosis as well. This is not because there is any shame attached to any of these diagnoses or any need to keep them secret. But it is perfectly true that some people may have trouble seeing the child if the diagnosis gets in the way.

I told one friend who is a little too hovering. Every time she reads an article about Asperger's, she sends it to me. She means well, but she's more neurotic about this than I am.

Tell people whatever they need in order to help and understand your child. That doesn't mean that if he acts up in public, you have to stand there saying over and over, "I'm so sorry. He has PDD-NOS." All children act up in public. The correct thing to do as a parent is to set things as much to rights as possible, remove the child when that isn't possible, and apologize to anyone who has been bothered or inconvenienced. However, close relatives need to be offered some information to help them understand a child they love who may behave strangely at times. You can explain the behavior, you can offer your best strategies for dealing with it, and you can present and explain the diagnosis—but you might want to do all this by degrees.

Clearly, this is an area in which opinions differ. There is no single right answer. Our advice is to think it through carefully and maybe, when in doubt, hold back a little rather than rushing ahead, for the reasons discussed above.

My advice is to lie low for a while and not go blabbing it to the whole neighborhood or the schools—unless you have to. Also, don't talk to the child himself, unless he asks you directly, until he's old enough to understand or very disturbed by his differences—which, with boys, to be honest, doesn't usually happen till eleven or twelve when they realize how different they are!

We have been very careful about who we said what to. One of our relatives is a child psychiatrist, and he had a lot of opinions. He made us feel as if this was all our fault.

I have told my mother, but it doesn't mean anything to her. She loves her grandson; she knows he's different; she knows he needs a little extra help. The name doesn't mean anything to her. For his teachers, it's been very helpful. They've read about it; they've talked to his shrink and his therapists. They've taken him on as a project.

One reason to think about this carefully is the issue of your immediate family. If you have other children, and they are old enough to understand, the way you present your quirky child to grandparents and aunts and uncles will quickly transfer over to siblings. There are situations in which a child's behavior is so extreme that siblings need special explanations—but it cannot be denied that there are also plenty of situations in which the best thing for a quirky child is to be treated normally by his less quirky siblings.

We don't talk about Gabriel in our family as if he has a diagnosis. I think we can address the fact that he doesn't know his nose is running without saying, "Oh, it's your Asperger's again." If my other kids ask, I say generically, "He doesn't like loud noises, and we're his family and we have to make sure he doesn't have to hear too many of them." And then I point out ways we accommodate to their quirks, too. He just has about twenty times more!

In other words, the decision about what you are going to say within your immediate family will, of course, be affected by the ages and personalities of your other children and most of all, perhaps, by how extreme are the behaviors with which you need to deal. It's possible that siblings may need to understand that one child has a special problem and mustn't be teased about it, but you may be better off casting this—at least, at first—as standard household politeness: you are not allowed to tease your brother about his obsessions (trains, clocks . . .), and he is not allowed to tease you about yours (NSync, Britney Spears . . .).

For the school-age child, it usually makes good sense to inform the school. If he needs special services to succeed academically, or needs occupational therapy or speech therapy, the diagnosis will help you get those services. Also, a diagnosis that school personnel understand may help when a child's behavior gets difficult to manage.

Perhaps the most complex issue of all is what you are going to say to the quirky child himself. There are people—and organizations—who feel that disclosure is almost always right, and the sooner the better. Certainly, it is better for your child to learn about the diagnosis from you—with understanding and love and information—than to have it thrown at him in school or by an angry sibling. The question of who else you have decided to tell certainly affects this. On the other hand, children need to be given information as they are ready to understand it. Some quirky kids, in particular, can be very young for their ages. We're going to come back to this issue and spend a lot of time on it—discussing her "differences" with your child. We're going to have to approach it as an evolving understanding, in which the child may need new language, new information, new definitions, as time goes on.

Whatever you do, be wary of using the diagnosis as an excuse for behavior that you wouldn't condone in other children. Your own understanding of what may lie behind some of your child's unusual behaviors should not mean that all is permitted. It is perfectly legitimate to look for new strategies—and of course, to forgive what the child cannot help—but the quirks and the diagnoses don't excuse you from your job as a parent. You still have to help your child learn to behave and get along as best he can.

Your child has a diagnosis. Maybe you feel that nothing will ever be the same. Nothing is ever the same anyway when you're watching children grow and develop. Here, then, are the most important take-home messages of this chapter and, in fact, of this book:

- *Keep loving your child, and do not confuse your child with his diagnosis.* See him for who he is—strengths and weaknesses, quirks and quibbles—and love him for it. Don't let your vision of him be too strongly affected by new terminology. You already knew he was different in certain ways. He's the same child he was before he was diagnosed.

- *Take a deep breath: you have a long road ahead.* A diagnosis is not the end of anything—not the definitive end of your fantasies, not the end of your child's hopes and possibilities, and not even the end of your quest to understand and help your quirky child. We don't want to minimize the complexities that the diagnosis may imply or the special challenges your child may face as she grows.

- *Keep an open mind about what the future holds.* Remember that these diagnoses involve behaviors that fall on a spectrum. Remember that children grow and change, and any given child may grow from one diagnosis to another. You need to find a blend of realism, good sense, and hope. All parents do, in fact, but in your case, that blend has to take the diagnosis and its implications into account—without letting them define the whole future.

- *Don't fix on blame, and don't fix on a cure. Fix on your child and what she needs and how you can help.* It's completely normal to fantasize about a cure and to search for magic bullets, but none of these diagnoses is amenable to easy answers or overnight cures.

- *Don't forget to take care of your spouse, your other children, and yourself.* It can be a challenge to live with a quirky son or daughter or sister or brother, and there's a danger of forgetting that everyone else in the family has needs and emotions, too. Your quirky child will profit immeasurably from growing up in a caring family. Take care of everyone, and keep the family on course.

- *The diagnosis is a tool. Now it's time to learn how to use it to help your quirky child.*

If anyone had told me five years ago, when we first got his diagnosis, that George has perfect pitch and would be playing in the high school band and dancing with girls at dances, I would never have believed it. He's come a very long way!

References and Resources

Bashe, Patricia Romanowski, and Barbara L. Kirby. *The Oasis Guide to Asperger Syndrome: Advice, Support, Insight, and Inspiration.* New York: Crown, 2001.

Paradiž, Valerie. *Elijah's Cup: A Family's Journey into the Community and Culture of High-Functioning Autism and Asperger's Syndrome.* New York: Free Press, 2002. An excellent first-person description of the emotional, physical, and financial drain of parenting a quirky child, this book is ultimately uplifting and optimistic.

Quinn, Barbara, and Anthony Malone. *Pervasive Developmental Disorder: An Altered Perspective.* London: Jessica Kingsley Publishers, 2000. This practical primer on PDD and associated conditions includes the experiences of parents.

Silver, Larry B. *The Misunderstood Child: Understanding and Coping with Your Child's Learning Disabilities.* New York: Three Rivers Press, 1998. A book by a child psychiatrist with a special interest in learning disabilities and ADD that covers these issues throughout the life cycle.

PART II

○ ○ ● ○

Growing Up Quirky

Literary Glimpses

Bradford ... their genius five-year-old son ... was sitting on the living room floor, pulling books off the bottom shelf of the bookcase that took all of one of the few existing walls. Without looking up at us, he started to mumble some barely coherent comments about how we'd interrupted him in the middle of what he was doing. ...

"He's arranging all of the books in the house according to height."

"According to color!" Bradford cried, "I'm arranging them all by color. ..."

"Would you be willing to reveal your system for arranging the colors?" Arthur asked.

"Yes; it's a very simple alphabetical arrangement. If you'll look on that bookshelf behind you, you'll see that the black ones are first, then the blue, then the green, the orange, the red, and the yellow. Those are the basic categories."

"Hey, Brad," I said, "what about the browns?"

"I'm putting the browns together on a bookshelf in the other room, off by themselves." —Stephen McCauley, *The Easy Way Out*, 1992

Was it because people were a little afraid of him that they whispered about the Murrays' youngest child, who was rumored to be not quite bright? "I've heard that clever people often have subnormal children," Meg had once overheard. "The two boys seem to be nice, regular children, but that unattractive girl and the baby boy certainly aren't all there."

It was true that Charles Wallace seldom spoke when anybody was around, so that many people thought he'd never learned to talk. And it was true that he hadn't talked at all until he was almost four. Meg would turn white with fury when people looked at him and clucked, shaking their heads sadly.

"Don't worry about Charles Wallace," her father had once told her. Meg remembered it very clearly because it was shortly before he went away. "There's nothing the matter with his mind. He just does things in his own way and in his own time."

—Madeleine L'Engle, *A Wrinkle in Time*, 1962

"He's five, just turned five," Morris Sapersteen said. . . . He set down the suitcase with a sigh. "Gosh, you'd never believe how heavy those things can be."

"What have you got there?" Marjorie said.

"Airplanes."

"Airplanes?"

"Forty-seven airplanes. Neville won't go anywhere without them." . . .

. . . Neville left his chair and catapulted into the dining room, yelling, "Daddy, I want my airplanes! Give me my airplanes!"

Morris jumped up, forgetting that the suitcase was open on his lap; the suitcase slipped, he clutched at it and upset it, and the forty-seven airplanes went clanking and tinkling all over the floor under the table. . . .

"No, no," screeched Neville. "I don't want them picked up. I've got to make a parade!" He dived under the table and could be heard crawling, and sliding airplanes along the floor.

"What's he going to make?" Mrs. Morgenstern said nervously. . . . "Get him out from under the table, please."

"A parade," [his mother] said. "He won't harm anything. He just lines them up three abreast. In perfect formation."

—Herman Wouk, *Marjorie Morningstar*, 1955
(Note that this is happening at a large family Passover Seder.)

Introduction

In Part II, we're going to take a closer look at the three most important domains in which your child has to function on a daily basis: family, school, and peer group. It would probably be safe to predict that how a child feels about herself as she grows up will reflect her sense of how well she is doing in these arenas.

Whole books have been written about each of these topics, but parents tell us that the advice in most books does not really apply to quirky kids. Having a quirky child can shift the perspective, causing all the standard worries and concerns and considerations to become more complex or slightly turned around or maybe arranged in a different order. Not everything in Part II will be relevant to every quirky child. The knotty problem of school will be different for the eccentric math genius whose town supports a math-and-science honors school than for the child who struggles mightily with letters, numbers, and attentional issues. That math genius, by virtue of being at a school with others like herself, may find many aspects of her adolescent social life much more straightforward than she would have if she'd been in the big general high school.

There are many shades of quirky, and many children, over the course of their childhoods, move into and out of different phases. All children, quirky and not, wrestle with school issues, social life issues, and family issues. Parents need to be a little wary of attributing every problem that comes up in a child's life to that child's quirks. It's also true that all of these issues are harder, more complicated, and sometimes more painful when you're growing up on a different path.

We'll look at the educational choices—and issues—at the different levels of school, from preschool through high school. We'll take the same through-the-years approach to discussing a quirky child's social life and try to offer some philosophy and some helpful strategies for navigating each stage. And we'll talk about the quirky child in the context of home and family, from the small everyday challenges and logistics to the larger emotional ramifications of being part of a quirky child's family.

Before we take on these big issues of the external domains in which your child must live, we want to address the most basic domain of all: his sense of self. We want to talk about what is technically called disclosure.

DISCLOSURE

What is your child's understanding of why he needs to attend physical and occupational therapy once a week? How does he think about his inability to ride a bike or swim? How would he explain the reason he gets pulled out of class three times a week for extra help or why nobody else in the second grade is interested in train schedules or what those pills he takes every morning are all about? For the youngest children, the toddlers and preschoolers, what you do with your day is simply that—what you do. It usually doesn't occur to a young child that his experience is different from that of other kids his age. However, as the child grows up, you will need to give some thought to his self-consciousness, self-image, and self-knowledge. For a child with a specific diagnosis—Asperger's syndrome, sensory integration dysfunction, pervasive developmental disorder, nonverbal learning disability—many experts recommend formal disclosure. This means revealing to a child that he has what is called Asperger's syndrome, for example, and that this explains many of the ways in which he thinks and functions. You would tell him that there are many other people with Asperger's and that he will have things in common with those people that will make them in some ways different from everybody else. Many of the organizations and parent support groups that work with Asperger's feel that disclosure is essential. There are many published examples in which children—and adults—describe the relief that came with knowing that their differences had a name and that there were other people with similar differences.

Kenneth Hall, a ten-year-old boy in Northern Ireland who wrote an excellent short book about himself, *Asperger Syndrome, the Universe and Everything*, puts it this way:

> When I was eight I found out about my Asperger Syndrome or AS and since then my life has changed completely. Before that life was very hard for me. I was always depressed. Life was depressing. I always knew I was different and that I wasn't quite like other children. It's hard to say exactly how I knew. I detected some differences and I felt that things were not the same for me as

for other children. Other children seemed to behave differently, play differ-ently and talk differently, but I didn't know why. . . . When I heard that I had AS I was very pleased because I had been wondering why everyone else seemed to be acting strangely. So I felt a bit relieved. My life has completely changed now and I am much happier.[1]

One collection of accounts around the theme of *Disclosure and Asperger's Syndrome*, put out by the Asperger's Association of New England, contains an essay by Bob Stuart, an adult with Asperger's, in which he offers the following advice:

I believe the earlier in age the diagnosis the better. Children who know about Asperger's can better prepare themselves to deal with school and other chil-dren. They can get coping strategies to not feel different, strange, or alone. They would have a better chance of succeeding academically. Teachers could learn how to deal with the child while also gaining knowledge about AS. When telling other students, I imagine there would be a mixed reaction; some may be supportive, some may dismiss it or possibly tease the child. So the child could start by telling friends first then gradually tell more students if they need to.[2]

There seems to be a strong feeling on the part of many adults with As-perger's and some of the groups that advocate for people with this syndrome that early and full disclosure to the child is almost an obligation and usually a blessing for all concerned. In fact, many of these children find their ways to the diagnosis themselves:

In third grade, Caitlin found the article about Asperger's syndrome that I had saved from the newspaper to share with my husband. Caitlin read it, brought it to me, and said, "I think I have this!"

For those children who are not classic for any diagnostic category, the question of disclosure can be more complicated. What if the child has some Asperger-like features but in other ways does not fit the diagnosis? What if the child does not seem to sense herself as different from others? How do you know whether a child is ready or what she needs to hear? *The Oasis Guide* offers a balanced discussion of both how to decide when it is time to tell a child about Asperger's and how to do it. We will adopt some of its suggestions here, generalized to a larger and more varied group of children.

Let us confess a certain bias, which may not put us completely in line with the people who believe most strongly in the virtues of full and early disclosure. We have a general prejudice in favor of dealing with children mostly on a need-to-know basis. That is, we believe that most children ask, in one form or another, the questions that are bothering them. They deserve to have those questions answered fully and honestly. But we also believe that information for which a child has not asked and for which she is not developmentally ready can be at best irrelevant and at worst distressing.

Some general points on talking to children about their quirks:

- The single most important determinant of what you say and how you say it is where the child is developmentally. You may need to explain to a three-year-old why he is getting occupational therapy ("because your hands don't always do what you tell them to"), to a five-year-old why she is taking an antianxiety medicine ("because it helps make all those worried thoughts get softer and softer, until you can't hear them anymore and you can think about other things"), or to an eight-year-old why he has to be in a different class from the kid next door ("because you learn things in a different way, and this teacher has some special ways of teaching that we hope will fit better with the way your brain learns"). Whatever the case, you need to suit your language and your images not just to your child's chronological age but to your child's developmental stage.

We were fortunate that it came up while Brian was in elementary school because it was easier for him to accept. His self-image wasn't formed yet. I talked to a woman who had a kid whose problems were more clearly social, and he wouldn't accept the Asperger's diagnosis at all. He refused to have anything to do with it. It really felt as if it was saying there was something wrong with him. But he was thirteen or fourteen, while Brian was ten or eleven, and it was easier to get the concept across that we need to think about doing things with you a little bit differently because these things have been going on for you at school. . . . So we sort of think that you're wired a little bit differently than most kids, and we're going to do things a little bit differently. Of course, he didn't want to be different.

- This is not something you do once, then it's done. This is an ongoing conversation, involving you, your spouse, your child, friends and family, teachers and therapists. As your child grows, he will continue to refine his understanding of his quirks—as his understanding of himself deepens and changes. Your goal in the earliest discussions could well be just to open the door, to show that all questions are welcome and that you are happy to have these conversations whenever he wants.

- You want this to be a positive experience, and as far as possible, you want to present the information to your child in a positive light. With a young child, that might mean saying something like, "Your brain learns in its own way, and that's part of what makes you who you are." It definitely means reminding the child of her skills and talents anytime that you are discussing her deficits and limitations and usually emphasizing that people vary, that everyone finds some things easy and other things hard.

- One wise piece of advice offered in *The Oasis Guide* that applies equally to children with any diagnosis or syndrome, quirk, or wrinkle is that disclosure should never happen in the midst of a bad moment—a school failure, a disciplinary meltdown, a major social frustration.

- If a child brings up the why-am-I-different question in such a setting, deal with the immediate problem and make a promise to sit down together and have a talk about all the other issues soon. Keep the promise.

- Similarly, if a child brings the subject up on line at the supermarket or while you are driving madly across town to pick up his brother, answer whatever short question is closest to the surface and then acknowledge that this is an important subject and deserves a serious talk. Promise that the talk will happen soon. Keep the promise.

- Be wary of announcing a new diagnosis to your child. As an individual child grows, you might want to give yourself a little time to find out whether this particular term is really going to add anything to the discussion or to your child's understanding.

- Listen to the question that your child is asking and make sure that you answer it. There are lots of stories about three-year-olds who ask an innocent little question like "Where did baby Lulu come from?" and get the whole fallopian-tubes-and-seminal-vesicles shebang from an anxiously informative and thorough parent, when all the child really meant was, "Is it true babies come from their mommies' tummies?"

- If a young child asks why she has to get some kind of special help or therapy, the best answer is a concrete and practical one: to help you do this, to make it easier for you to do that.

- Having given that specific and functional answer, listen to whether she wants to take it a step further: Why is it so hard for me to do that when it isn't hard for most kids? How come I always need special help with stuff?

- If she's asking those bigger questions, they need to be answered. And yes, there are six- or seven-year-olds out there who want the formal diagnoses. There are also eleven-year-olds out there who don't want to take it any further than "My hands don't always do what I tell them to, and I worry more than other kids." Either way is fine. Tell your child what he wants to know.

- As your child grows, this discussion should continue. You want to avoid leaving a child with the sense that something important about himself is being kept from him. He should hear all the most relevant words from you in a positive and affectionate context.

- Older children need more complex and complete answers—sometimes more complex and more complete than you can give. If you know that it's time to sit down and talk with your ten- or eleven-year-old, you might actually want to read up on any of the questions you need to discuss—or have a book ready that the child can read herself.

- However, by the time a child is eleven or twelve, you probably have a pretty good idea of that child's makeup, his strengths and weaknesses, and the relevant diagnoses. You will be able to direct the discussion accordingly. Our experience as pediatricians in practice is that children of this age will ask what makes them different. (Our patients with chronic illnesses, for example, will start asking why they are always at the doctor, always having their blood drawn or chest X-rayed, why they are taking medications that their friends do not take.)

- Be prepared for how you want to handle these questions, with appropriate seriousness and in proper detail. If you have a good working relationship with your pediatrician or with some other doctor or therapist, consider doing it together. We have had many such conversations with families over the years and have found them useful and moving for all concerned. Kids feel cared for and attended to, and parent and pediatrician alike benefit from having this discussion in a supportive environment—where questions can be answered and the future discussed.

Children's sense of themselves—and of how different they are—varies tremendously, according to intelligence, self-awareness, social awareness, and perceptiveness. Some children, especially when they are younger, may hardly notice their quirks—or may comfortably assume that the rest of the world is like them. Some kids remain blissfully clueless and go about their business without suffering the fear of social isolation. Other children are painfully aware from the very beginning of even minor differences. Some of this awareness—or lack of awareness—will reflect the family, the school, and the social milieu.

Chrissie is ten now, and she's very relieved to know that her difference has a name and that there are other kids like her.

We wish we could offer you hard-and-fast guidelines for helping your child understand and appreciate his own unique perspective as he grows. You will need to be aware of his level of understanding at any given point, of his level of self-consciousness, and of his feelings about himself and how he is doing. The only way for you to be aware of all these things—especially as your child grows into a middle schooler and then an adolescent—is to keep the conversational door open. Ask questions and listen carefully to the answers. Be sure that you are answering the questions asked of you, whether asked directly or indirectly. Your goal is not to protect your child from the knowledge that she is different but to help her integrate that knowledge into a reasonably happy picture of who she is. Just as you have learned to cherish her for all the different things she is—including her quirks, her eccentricities, and her struggles—you have to help her learn to understand herself, appreciate herself, and cherish herself. There is no more important single thread to growing up quirky, no more important responsibility for the parents, no more important developmental task for the child.

The disclosure process with George (now fourteen) has gone on over a few years. His older sister, who is a junior in college, has been very helpful in the process. She has attention deficit disorder herself, so she used this to explain to him that he, too, had learning differences. Since he adores her, it didn't seem so bad that he had something she also had, because he thinks of her as so smart and competent. We got Mel Levine's book for kids about different kinds of minds and they read through it together, and I think that was much easier for George than it would have been if I had read it with him. Then I called the Asperger's Association, and they sent the Disclosure book, and we read through the stories together, and there was one about a seventh-grade boy that really resonated with George. I wanted to be able to talk about Asperger's the way we talk about his sister's ADD. We all know she forgets everything and gets lost, and we ask her if she has a map and a compass when she's leaving the house. It's a kind of gentle teasing. Now that George is eager to be accepted by the other kids, he wants to be told when his behavior or mannerisms are "Aspergery." For a couple of months, we all talked about it a lot. Finally, George's younger brother said, "Every time you say that Asperger thing, I think of cheeseburgers and it makes me hungry!" So now cheeseburger has become our code word for George when he is acting too weird.

References and Resources

Asperger's Association of New England (AANE). *Disclosure and Asperger's Syndrome: Our Own Stories.* Newton, Mass.: AANE, 2000. A collection of personal accounts. Write to AANE, 1301 Centre St., Newton MA 02459. Their Web site is www.aane.org.

Bashe, Patricia Romanowski, and Barbara L. Kirby. *The Oasis Guide to Asperger Syndrome: Advice, Support, Insight, and Inspiration.* New York: Crown, 2001. Contains an excellent discussion on the issue of disclosure.

Hall, Kenneth. *Asperger Syndrome, the Universe and Everything.* London: Jessica Kingsley Publishers, 2001. This is the book we mentioned by the ten-year-old boy.

Hoopmann, Kathy. *Blue Bottle Mystery: An Asperger's Adventure.* London: Jessica Kingsley Publishers, 2001. This is a fictional story, aimed at nine- to twelve-year-olds, about a boy with Asperger's and his friend.

Levine, Mel. *All Kinds of Minds: A Young Student's Book about Learning Abilities and Learning Disorders.* Cambridge, Mass.: Educators Publishing Service, 1992.

Shore, Stephen M. *Beyond the Wall: Personal Experiences with Autism and Asperger Syndrome.* 2d ed. Shawnee Mission, Kans.: Autism Asperger Publishing Company, 2003. A first-person account of growing up quirky. Offers insight into the mind of a successful quirky adult.

4

○ ○ ● ○

Family Life:
THE HOME AND THE WORLD

The single most famous line ever written about family life is probably Tolstoy's opening sentence in *Anna Karenina*: "Happy families are all alike; every unhappy family is unhappy in its own way." As pediatricians who have spent countless hours sitting with any number of families, we humbly suggest that all happy families are sometimes unhappy and that no two families are actually alike for more than a few minutes at a time. In this chapter, we are going to talk about family life with a quirky child. Before we even get there, we have a few things to say about family life in general.

First of all, it's hard work. Family life is intense, highly charged, and for most of us, extremely concentrated in terms of time and space. Second, family life is colored for all of us by our own childhood experiences, by our fantasies of what marriage and childrearing would be like, and by the images and messages sent to us by the culture in which we live. We measure ourselves and our homes against the fictional TV families we see and the images of real people who live more perfectly and more beautifully than we do. We also, of course, measure ourselves against the people whose family lives go awry, the movie stars on their umpteenth divorce, with the kids shuttled back and forth among the mansions, or the people in the paper who have just been arrested for horrific mistreatment of their children.

Finally, we measure ourselves constantly, and often rather harshly, against the other parents and children we know—the families in the day-care center, our siblings and cousins and their families, our friends, our colleagues . . . There are all kinds of subtle and not-so-subtle competitive games that parents play. There's the mother who casually drops into conversation that, of course, her six-year-old is rereading the Harry Potter books now, and she's just desperate to find him something else that will really *challenge* him (often said after some other parent has just bemoaned the fact that her own six-year-old refuses even to attempt *The Cat in the Hat*). Or how about the father who agrees that your daughter will have a wonderful time playing casual intramural soccer this year but happens to mention that his own daughter, the same age, has been recruited for the all-state team, and whew, what a schlepp that's going to be for everyone.

For parents of quirky children, these parenthood realities are particularly intense and charged. Life at home can sometimes feel like an hour-by-hour struggle. It doesn't help much to have well-meaning friends assure you that, of *course*, they understand, small children are *always* messy—or siblings are *always* fighting—it's just the way of the world. In fact, for many parents whose children are outside the usual developmental parameters or manifest consistently eccentric habits, it can be particularly frustrating to be assured that their off-the-scale family stresses are just what everyone goes through. We'll talk about some of the common family life experiences of families with quirky children and offer practical help for getting over the humps.

Family life with a quirky child is more fraught with tension, more difficult, and subject to all kinds of stresses, or to more intense versions of the usual stresses. The daily routines of family life can be complicated by your child's eccentricities. Your relations with your spouse, your other children, your own parents, and your entire extended family will all be colored by this brush. Although we don't mean in any way to make light of the stresses and strains that families encounter, we do encourage you to hold on as tightly as possible to your sense of humor. Every parent needs one, and the parent of a quirky child needs a sense of humor that is downright, well, quirky. It may be hard to believe, but you will probably get to the point at which all your worst family-disaster stories become familiar jokes. When you tell them, don't be surprised if you find at least a few other parents groaning in recognition!

Temperament and Goodness of Fit

Let's begin with two concepts dear to pediatricians, developmentalists, and psychologists: temperament and goodness of fit. The child's temperament and the "goodness of fit" between that temperament and your family environment, not to mention your own temperament, will shape and color the tenor of your life together. By temperament, we mean the behavioral and psychological characteristics of the child that many people believe are inborn or hardwired and that certainly appear to be established quite early in life. We describe temperament by looking at where a child lies along a spectrum for each of several qualities, including:

- *Distractibility:* How hard does the child concentrate? How easy is it to draw her attention away to something else?
- *Irritability:* Everyone knows that some babies are more irritable than others. Many parents, looking at two siblings, are astonished by the contrast between the easy one and the screamer who arches and cries at any stimulation.
- *Ability to manage transitions.*
- *Ability to self-soothe:* That is, whether he can calm himself when he gets upset. The infant or toddler who sucks his thumb or twirls his blanket when he's overwhelmed will be easier to live with than the one who howls, scratches himself, or withdraws.

A young child's temperament, her skills and problems, don't exist in a vacuum. The concept of goodness of fit tries to get at the way a child either is or is not in sync with her environment, with family expectations, with her physical setting, and with the temperaments of those with whom she lives. There are all kinds of classic examples of bad fits, children who might be just fine in a different family setting but pose all sorts of difficulties in the family to whom they are dealt. The high-energy child in the calm, serene home with the two older contemplative parents—she might have had an easier time as the third of four in a busier, crazier, noisier household where her demands would have to compete with those of the other children. Or the quirky precise little professor math genius in the highly active sports-oriented household—

wouldn't it be nice if we could give *him* to those two older contemplative parents who are going out of their minds chasing that little girl! Or the fussy, difficult-to-transition child with the parents who are anxiously determined to do everything right and interpret every cry as an accusation—let's give him to that happy-go-lucky, take-it-as-it-comes family over there, in exchange for their obsessive little girl, who will do much better with these equally anxious parents. She'll show them how to do everything right, and they'll do it.

It doesn't work that way. You love your child and your child loves you, and you are bound together for life. But there are easier fits and harder fits, and it's important to look at your quirky child and see clearly that the puzzle piece has more than one side. Don't let yourself think of him as a square peg without carefully looking at what makes the hole so round. Be aware of your own temperament, your own expectations, and your own habits. Although we don't mean to suggest that you are the one who has to do all the adjusting, you *are* the grown-up and therefore are the one who is supposed to figure out how to make this work.

I know my own personality has a lot to do with how I respond to my son's nervous habits, high energy level, and constant need for interaction. He has really never had much ability to entertain himself. I remember when he was a toddler: there was none of that exploring independence and then checking back with us to be sure we were still there. One of us was always right beside him, holding his hand, exploring the environment. Now I understand that this was his anxiety getting the best of him. And now, many years later, it takes a different form, yet still, one of us has to be right near him in order for him to do anything he needs to do—like reading for school, homework, etcetera. I find myself craving the child who will sit down and do something, anything, alone. And I know this isn't fair. I try to keep these feelings in check, and when I can't, I know it's time for a break.

Rages and Nuclear Tantrums

INFANTS AND TODDLERS

Life is harder when a child is miserable all or most of the time or supremely irritable or subject to tantrums and uncontrollable rages. Some parents remember that their quirky children "cried all the time" as infants or toddlers, and this may become even more intense in children who are deeply sensitive to sensory stimuli or who are language-delayed and crying in frustration at not being able to make themselves understood. If you have such a child, it may be worth looking beyond your regular pediatrician to see whether a behavioral specialist might be able to help. We know all too well that many pediatricians will write off the excessive crying of a baby who otherwise seems to be healthy and who is growing and developing well. We tend to offer strategies: set limits, try time-out, consider behavior modification, reward him when he's good, try a sticker chart. These strategies work for many kids. But a child who is off the scale, or a parent who is truly worried that something else is going on, deserves a second look.

My daughter had a tantrum right there in her pediatrician's office on the exam table. I hoped that he would finally see what I was talking about and offer some suggestions or advice, or at the very least a little compassion. But he just never got it. Instead, I felt that the doctors, like our family and friends, all thought we were crazy.

TANTRUMS AND RAGES

Many quirky children go through periods in their lives when they are subject to intense rages or tantrums. Again, many children, quirky and not, have tantrums, but the quirky kids tend to have the tantrums that are just plain *more so*—the ones that can't be touched by any of the wise strategies that are advised by the pediatrician or the magazine article or the well-meaning passersby. Quirky children have tantrums that don't go away if you ignore them, that don't lend themselves to limit-setting and time-outs. It's not our intention here to provide you with specific strategies to handle your child's tantrums, because quirky kids vary so widely. It is, however, very much worth the effort to figure out what your child's triggers are and to try to address them. Some kinds of behavioral therapy are directed at exactly this type of analysis. Maybe it's all about frustration at the things she can't do that other children can. Maybe there are certain variations in her routine that she just can't handle. Maybe it has to do with sensory issues: maybe it's noise, maybe it's crowds. Knowing some of the triggers doesn't necessarily mean you can head off every tantrum, but it helps you understand what's going on with your child and offers possible strategies to consider.

Chrissie had these paint-peeling tantrums from very early—at the littlest provocation. She still has several major meltdowns per year at school, and she will insist that I be called and that she must go home. And she misunderstands people's motives. If another kid says, "Can I help you with that?" she thinks the kid is making fun of her, and she cries.

Major rages at home, and the occasional terrible tantrum in public, can make you feel like a failure as a parent—especially during those moments in public when all sorts of helpful people seem to be coming from miles around to express unsolicited opinions about how to handle what's going on. Even in the privacy and safety of your own house, as you watch your child move deeper and deeper into a tantrum, you desperately feel that there must be *something* you could do to get him out of the cycle, to solve the problem, to make things better. Remember, parents don't create the rage in their quirky kids. Tantrums, in most quirky kids, are a combination of their developmental differences, their sensory problems, and their peculiar emotional wiring. You can help your child progress developmentally, filter and accommodate the sensory stimuli, and handle the emotional impulses, but you must do it without laying blame, either on him or on yourself.

That highly cranky, oppositional, nonverbal, rage-prone child is also a child who may provoke a lot of anger and even violence from even a loving and tolerant parent. These kids can drive their parents crazy, and these parents may feel pushed toward physical discipline and toward shows of uncontrolled anger themselves. *It's important to recognize the danger signs in yourself and to know when you're getting near the edge.* Know whom you can ask for help—whom you can trust to take care of the child and give you a respite, to listen nonjudgmentally to your lamentations and offer an honest opinion, or just to take you out for a little fun when you need it most.

The Vulnerable Child

The quirky child is often seen as the family problem, as the child who is somehow in jeopardy, about whom everyone, especially the parents, is always worried. In pediatrics and child psychiatry, we talk about the "vulnerable child syndrome," in which parents worry excessively about one particular child, usually because that child has been severely ill or badly hurt in the past. Each quirky child can play into this syndrome differently. Because her development may be less regular and less predictable, she may stay dependent on her parents longer than other children. Because they love her and worry about her, they may identify with her every disappointment or difficulty and exert themselves to protect her from all the hardships that they fear may lie in wait.

A parent's sense that one child in the family is especially vulnerable and in need of protection may translate to the other children as a lack of attention or a lack of caring. "You can ride the school bus, but your brother gets driven to school." "I'm sorry we had to come late to the school picnic, but your sister had to go to her language group." One persistent theme in this chapter is the importance of building in time that is *not* centered around the issues of quirkiness and their consequences.

If I followed everyone's expectations, I would be out every afternoon and every night doing something that might help her, and we would have no family life—never have dinner together, never be lounging on the bed reading aloud—the things that make up our family life. So there are times when I've decided that something had to give, and it's usually the special appointments. I resent the time they take away not just from the other kids but also from my daughter herself and the normal things in her life. She can't have a therapeutic appointment every afternoon!

A Note about Siblings—and Only Children

Plenty of quirky kids are only children, and this family configuration can be both a blessing and a curse for parents. It is easier to manage the day-to-day life of the family when you have only one child's behavioral issues to contend with. Without siblings competing for time and attention, it's easier to maximize the interventions and available help without guilt and remorse about other children. But that same sibling rough-and-tumble can teach a quirky child some important skills that may be harder for an only child to acquire. A family with more than one child will require more flexibility from everyone—including the quirky child, who may find herself learning a whole variety of adaptations and coping skills from the sound and fury of sibling relationships. When the temperaments of siblings as well as parents need to be considered, the quirky child has more opportunity to interact with others and to resolve conflicts. This is more like the real world, where little is tailored to any one person's temperament. Although exhausting for parents, the endless discussions and negotiations that occur in families with multiple children are beneficial for kids—quirky and nonquirky alike.

Everyday Life

Life at home is complicated, often chaotic, and a very particular blend of the routine and the wildly unexpected. To keep a home chugging along requires all kinds of logistical balancing and managerial organization. The volume of detail involved in keeping everyone clothed and fed and present at the appropriate activities with the appropriate equipment and then getting them all home and feeding them again is enough to make you feel like just pulling the covers up over your head and hoping they don't find you. Add a quirky child, and everything gets just that much more complicated.

MEALTIME

I do have the wish and the expectation that our family will sit down together for dinner—all three kids and at least one parent, and maybe half the time both of us—and the reality of what happens when we do has been kind of hard for me to take. I think this was a very important value of mine, in my fantasy of how my family life would go. My own family never did it when I was growing up—things were always too crazy—and I believe in it as a value for kids growing up. So I thought that with my kids—well, they would tell us stories of how things went at school, we would tell about what happened in our jobs, we would eat together.

So, instead, the reality: Just getting the dinner on the table with these kids who need my constant attention is a challenge. I tell Sam to get the milk and the butter and the grated cheese and put them on the table, and on the way to the refrigerator, he gets distracted and notices something on the bulletin board, and I either yell at him or I get it myself or I tell John to get it, and there's condensation on the milk bottle and he doesn't know to hold the handle and there's milk all over the floor because he's just not strong enough to hold the bottle. . . . Meanwhile, my littlest, Charlie, is just totally oppositional: "Get the plastic cups." "No!" "I'll give you three plastic cups; put them on the table." "No!" "You'll have to go in timeout." "I don't care!" And I guess that's maybe normal for his age, which is four, but still, on top of everything else. . . . I guess I have this fantasy that I won't be everyone's slave and I will have some help. So I have special little occupational therapy knives for John, but he's not strong enough to cut anything, and Sam is such a space shot, I'm afraid to let him do anything with knives. So maybe I ask him to help me peel shrimp—but he has no staying power, and he stops after the first few.

Next: the getting-ready process. Everybody has to wash their hands, and usually they balk. And I mean, John is eleven, you'd think he would care a little about washing his hands, but he doesn't. They come to the table, and then there's the question of who should have a lid on his cup. Four out of five dinners where there's not a lid on John's or Sam's cup, particularly John's, it'll fall over. We send him to school with juice boxes, even though his hands are so weak he can't manage the straw and puncturing it. He can't open a yogurt container.

And now, the moment you've all been waiting for: I bring the big bowl of pasta to the table! And basically, I want them to leave their butts in a chair for ten minutes, and it's really hard to get them to do that! Sometimes I turn the timer on and time them. John gets so distracted and he's not that much of an eater, though Sam loves to eat and eats large quantities of food. There's almost no conversation. There's a lot of Charlie screaming because Sam is teasing him! Basically, though, there are no reciprocal conversations, the kind we would like to be able to have with our kids. Sometimes we'll ask a direct question, one will start to answer, one will interrupt, the other one will start screaming.

And then, of course, something will get spilled. We're trying to give John a cup with no lid at the table, so it always gets spilled. And then everyone will get up and leave, and that's that.

Oh, and table manners I've completely forgotten about. They're just so far down on the list. It's just another way that dinner is very challenging at our house. By the time we eat, we're all pretty tired, especially John. His reserves are just low at the end of the day, and drinking from a cup or using a fork or sitting in a chair for ten minutes, it's all harder at the end of the day. But I think it's not so much the table manners, it's that we can't have conversations and that they fight and scream and tease each other at the dinner table are the two things that bother me most.

All kinds of behavioral and emotional issues come to the fore at the dinner table. For many families, it's the one certain moment of the day when everyone sees one another—although in other families, people eat in shifts according to their schedules and preferences. But feeding your quirky child definitely brings up a number of special concerns:

- *Reasonable expectations:* All parents learn—often the hard way—what can be expected of young children in this most primal social setting. A quirky child, who lags developmentally and socially, is going to tax your patience well past those early years. Adjust your expectations given what you know of your child's abilities and temperament. Those harmonious family dinners may come, but it's probably going to take a while.

- *Mealtime routines:* Some children will drink from only one particular cup. Some can sit comfortably only in a certain chair. Some eat their food in a ritualized order, and others, famously, get upset if any food is touching any other food on the plate. Quirky children may elevate these preferences to near obsessions. Pick your battles carefully. Go ahead and label the cups or the chairs, if that makes for a peaceful evening. TV dinner–style plates with raised divisions have saved many a dinnertime.

- *Picky eaters:* The children with sensory issues can have extremely strong preferences about textures. They'll eat only soft, or they'll eat only crunchy, or they can't take too hot or too cold. The obsessive quirky child may have all manner of very definite food preferences. We know one child who will eat only food that is white and lives on rice and white bread and plain yogurt and pancakes. Many parents complain that their children are picky eaters, and our response to parents is that as long as the child is growing normally, this is a place to choose your battles carefully. Food and feeding issues can become a major battlefield, and this is not a place where we want our children, especially our daughters, feeling that they need to exert more control. It's the rare toddler or even four- to seven-year-old who eats what her parents would consider a healthy diet, and the truth is that most children do just fine even if they severely restrict the range of what they are willing to eat for some period of time.

Megan continues to have funny food things. She stopped eating meat when she was three years old, because she made the connection between the cute little animals in her books and the food on the table. She has never eaten meat since. She has a lot of aversions and particular likes and dislikes. For example, she will eat green but not red grapes.

To preserve your own sanity, we recommend setting limits: "This is what I am making for the whole family, and if you don't want to eat it, you can have a peanut butter sandwich," or some other basic no-cook food that the child will accept. It's usually a bad idea to get pushed into catering individual meals, though certainly there are parents who just make macaroni and cheese every night for the kids and then save the real dinner for themselves. If your child's diet is clearly deficient (no fruits or vegetables, ever), add in a chewable children's multivitamin, and above all, keep offering. Many picky eaters, as they grow, abruptly expand their repertoires by suddenly accepting a taste of some unlikely food and discovering that it's OK. As much as you can, don't allow a picky eater's preferences to dictate the menu; if everyone else likes take-out Chinese food and one person just eats plain rice, so be it.

- *Slow eaters:* Because their motor control is poor, simply getting the food to their mouths can be a challenge for quirky kids. They can be distracted, or dreamy and far away, or develop obsessive rituals around food. These behaviors can drive everybody crazy at the dinner table, but it's the slow eater at breakfast who is often the most problematic. Some quirky children have to be reminded to take each new bite and then, it can sometimes seem, to chew it and swallow it. And there's many a quirky child (and, for that matter, many a nonquirky child) who finishes his breakfast strapped into his booster seat in the back of the car on the way to drop off an older sibling—which is why God made bagels.

When my son was a preschooler, every meal revolved around how many bites of food he actually ate. Once we were told that he had "oral-motor-planning difficulties" and declined the surgical solution of putting a tube though his skin into his stomach to feed him, we took on his meals with a vengeance! This involved sitting in front of him, offering him a bite, and then singing our "chew-and-swallow" song to the tune of a song we'd learned at his music therapy. Everyone else who might feed him—his grandparents or his baby-sitter, for example—had to know the song. We cheered when he actually swallowed something and then started the whole routine over again. Meals took forever, but we didn't know what else to do. We worked with occupational therapy and a "feeding team," but none of that really made all that much difference. Now he's ten and still doesn't eat that much, but he grows along his skinny curve, and we don't sing the "chew-and-swallow" song anymore.

If you're living with a truly slow eater, don't get too obsessed with it. The last thing you want is to find battle lines drawn or to make your child more self-conscious. Try feeding him when he is really hungry. If he comes home from school ravenous and consumes a big bowl of macaroni and cheese, you can relax while he dawdles over his dinner. Don't expect the rest of the family to stay at the table until the slowest eater has finished. Maybe one parent will keep him company, but it's also OK to go ahead and start doing the dishes. And, as with the picky eater, if you can find a couple of reasonably nutritious foods that your slow eater likes enough to gobble down, don't feel bad about serving those foods over and over—at least to him.

- *Table manners:* This issue looms much larger for some families than for others. But let's assume here that most of us do care about teaching our children to eat properly—and let us further argue that parents of quirky kids have a special obligation. Because quirky children, as they grow, are at high risk of being socially marginalized, teased, and ostracized, anything you can do to help them learn good manners is extremely important. Yes, the biggest, toughest jocks in the middle school may belch at the table or spill their food with total impunity, but that doesn't mean that your quirky child is going to get away with the same behavior without being teased or shunned. As we will discuss in the chapter on therapies, this is an area in which a relationship with an occupational therapist can be of real help. How can you as a parent teach manners? By nagging and more nagging; by praising excessively the child who remembers and correcting promptly the child who forgets; by narrating, over and over and over, the order of steps in cutting food properly with a knife; by serving easy-to-manage food sometimes, especially when company is there, but serving harder-to-handle items as well, on the assumption that a child might as well wrestle with his first solo steak in the privacy of his own home.

This means that family mealtimes for years will include that constant repetitious dialogue: *Watch your elbow—you're going to knock over your milk. Close your mouth when you chew. Say "Excuse me" when you burp.*

Use your knife as a pusher, not your finger. Use your napkin. Cut smaller pieces. Take smaller bites. Chew before you swallow! And along with that go all the other instructions: *Say "Thank you." Say "Please." Don't say "Yuck" when you don't like something. Ask politely to be excused.* It's not pleasant all the time—and the special problem with a quirky child is that because of fine motor issues and social dislocation, it can go on long beyond the point at which you might reasonably have expected a child to need such constant correction. As with food preferences and picky eating, you want to try to do the best you can here without letting it dominate family life. That may mean every now and then letting the whole subject go or serving something for dinner that is obviously finger food, with all the drinks in juice boxes and not a fork or a napkin in sight, and just letting everyone, including the parents, relax and enjoy. Oh, and don't forget to go out for a pleasant adults-only dinner every now and then. When you do, resist the reflex urge to criticize each other's deportment or cut each other's meat.

• *Dinner conversation:* Some parents of quirky kids, especially as the children grow older, feel that poor language skills are their child's most significant problem. And although many of us, looking back on our family dinner tables, don't actually remember a great deal of general and good-natured conversation, it's also true that as most children age, parents who emphasize the family dinner table are rewarded with the occasional episode of civilized discourse, which can certainly make it all seem worthwhile. Quirky kids, with their obsessive tendencies and poor social and fine motor skills, can make for fairly agonizing dinner table conversation.

What is dinner table conversation like? Well, it depends. Sometimes our son monopolizes the conversation with his news, with talk about sports, etcetera. His ex-therapist told us he's probably on the autism spectrum, too (sigh). Occasionally, Chrissie will come up with something sort of gross, but we just tell her it isn't appropriate. "Nice people don't talk about that stuff at the dinner table!" Which is pretty much the way my parents brought me up. It's sort of hard to keep her on topic, but she is getting better.

Standardize subjects, make family rules, and set guidelines: five minutes a night of conversation on each child's favorite subject and then on to something chosen by the presiding parent. Don't try to do this more than a couple of times a week; it's quite an effort for all concerned! And let us just say, once again, that you need to reward yourselves with some adult meals in a sane, pleasant atmosphere—at which you will inevitably end up discussing your children!

PLAYTIME

We hear over and over again from parents that they began to notice that their children were eccentric because of the ways that they played—or didn't play—when they were young. Maybe the child showed no interest in mobiles, toys, or games but preferred some particular random-seeming household object, to which he became profoundly attached; the child's toys sat on the shelves, perfect and untouched, while her anxious parents kept bringing home new ones.

We had a playroom at home that looked like a toy store. In my quest to find something that Abby would play with, I acquired a huge number of toys that were never touched. Then, by the age of one, she developed overwhelming fears and anxiety. So in addition to no symbolic play, no apparent interest in any toys, she became anxious and frightened. She threw things around rather than play. Her fine motor skills were bad, so she couldn't hold a crayon. She became overstimulated easily. We had an infant seat with colorful plastic toys on a bar at the front, and I had to remove all but one because it was too much!

Other quirky kids are willing to play with toys but only in ritualized and unusual ways. Lining them up. Arranging them in particular patterns. What most of these kids *don't* do is the standard symbolic play, in which you pretend the doll is a baby or the toy truck is a real one. The quirky child may be more likely to be lining up all the dolls, head to toe, or setting up the cars and trucks in an unalterable grid, or spinning the wheels on his trucks for long periods of time.

My son liked toy cars, but he just lined them up around the edge of our guest-room bed in a U shape. We would get on the floor and try to show him where's the driver, where are the children, but he just didn't care.

Parents of quirky children need to strike a balance between allowing the child the freedom to enjoy the things that give him pleasure and excite his interest, and attempting to lure him into trying, and perhaps liking, some of the typical pleasures that don't immediately attract him. Let him line up the trucks, if that's what gives him pleasure. But by all means, try to expand the game a little from time to time, relating the toy trucks to the real trucks you see outside or talking about the driver and showing the child how to make sound effects. We believe firmly that right from the beginning, a child is entitled to certain domains of his life in which what counts are his preferences, his talents, his interests, and his inclinations—even if they're eccentric. Don't make every moment of your child's life into a therapeutic opportunity and don't press too hard for a specific kind of play. Children can sense, often enough, when their parents are disappointed in them, and there are plenty of disappointments in life without making a child feel bad that she isn't interested in dolls or in the train set. However, toys truly are useful tools for all kinds of therapeutic interventions that work well with young children. You may find yourself down there on the floor, teaching your daughter to roll a ball back and forth as a way of getting her to practice social interactions and motor skills.

PLAYDATES

These unusual play habits make the issue of inviting another child over for a playdate seem complex and even fraught with tension. We would suggest that you think carefully about just why you are interested in setting up such play-dates and whether your child is in fact ready. Many quirky kids are not socially ready by preschool age to play one-on-one with another child without adult help and supervision. Many are not particularly interested in kids their own age. Some prefer adults or older children, whereas others gravitate toward babies.

When a kid would come over to play with John, we couldn't just leave the two of them alone. We'd have to have a plan, like "We're going to play checkers and then build a fort and then go out for ice cream." John was always interested in his one thing, whatever it was—telling time, the weather—and he just couldn't shift into anything else. And he was scared so easily, and one friend used to like to play pirates and he would create these scary scenarios and John would get scared. And then the other kid couldn't really shift either. You know, even typical kids at six to seven years old, they're not that flexible.

If your young child has siblings at home and attends some kind of pre-school or day care or early intervention group with other children, it may not be vitally important to arrange quantities of playdates. Some parents find themselves doing it because they are aware that all around them, there is a busy world of playdates and parties and sleepovers. But if your child shows no interest, you may want to wait a little while, keep an eye out for the best possible match in terms of playmates, and generally take it slow.

For more thoughts on playdates and children at different ages, right up to high school and dating, look at the chapter on the social lives of quirky kids.

TEASING

For many parents, the idea of teasing looms as one of the big terrors. *He's going to seem weird. The other kids will make fun of him. He's going to be tormented, bullied, excluded.* These legitimate worries will be addressed head-on in the chapter on the social lives of quirky children. Here, though, we want to talk about something a little different—namely, the kind of teasing that routinely goes on in families, among siblings. This kind of teasing is not happening just because a child is quirky. Brothers and sisters tease one another in pretty much every real-life family.

Teasing requires a certain social sophistication, an ability to put yourself in the other person's place and figure out what would really touch a sore spot. The little sister who intuits her older brother's sensitivity about the pimple on his forehead and teases him about it relentlessly is a good observer and a keen student of social dynamics. The little brother who responds to his older sister's teasing about how he spilled his milk again by throwing a screaming tantrum at the table and then stabbing himself with his fork is less well suited to the give-and-take of sibling life. A child's siblings are going to know his weak spots, and at hostile moments, that is where they're going to aim. The quirky child may not even understand that he is being teased; he may be bewildered by the mix of sarcasm, humor, and cruelty.

You might want to institutionalize a modicum of gentle family-style teasing, helping your quirky child get used to it as a kind of ritual. You don't want to create a situation in which every family member *except* the one quirky child gets teased now and then. In other words, if Mom can be teased about always forgetting where she left her car keys, and Dad gets laughed at for not understanding how to program the VCR, and Big Sister is being teased because she spends so much time on the phone, why shouldn't Little Brother take some ribbing for all the food spread out on the floor under his chair after dinner? Or alternatively, you can make general rules: *No teasing anyone about any aspect of physical appearance. No teasing anyone who feels bad. No teasing at the table.* Speaking both as pediatricians and as parents, we tend to believe that the kind of teasing that goes on in the home, unless it gets out of hand and too cruel or persistent, is valuable practice for many quirky kids. Parents should consider making a commitment to monitor it, explain the rules, and even help the quirky child respond in kind.

HOMEWORK

We have come to the uncomfortable conclusion that many schools assign a lot of homework, especially in the early grades, that is meant in large part as discipline for the *parents*. Oh, sure, the schools will claim that they are building good study habits and helping children get used to the whole idea of working in the evening, but quite frankly, we don't always buy it, especially when it comes to quirky kids. The kind of homework we are talking about tends to be profoundly repetitious—copying out letters, words, sentences, coloring in drawings, completing work sheets. However, homework, as a child grows up, can offer a real opportunity for a parent to help both with study habits and with academic strategies, and keeping an eye on your child as she does her homework can give you a real sense of what is easy for her academically and what is hard.

Homework was hell for Megan. It took so damn long to get anything done. She just couldn't focus. She would do a little, then she would rock back and forth like a human rocking chair; sometimes she'd flap her hands and that was always accompanied by running around in circles, usually around a piece of furniture. It really did upset me and I had no idea what it meant at that point in her life.

Lisa will decide it's difficult beforehand, and she will have her good days and bad days. If I ask her to do her homework, she'll actually start crying sometimes. Even though I'm really pressed for time in the mornings, I find she's better after a good night's sleep. After school, sometimes she's overloaded, everything seems overwhelming to her.

HOMEWORK ISSUES

- For many quirky children, especially in the early grades, a full day of school is pretty exhausting. Trying to wrestle with their attentional issues, with the social matrix of first or second grade, and with the specific learning-related challenges of reading and writing and numbers can leave a child pretty wiped out by 3:00—not to mention the sensory issues of noise and movement or the constant struggle to follow the rules and not get in trouble.

- Many quirky kids already attend extra therapy sessions of one kind or another after the school day is over. It seems to us that these kids deserve to come home and in some way relax. A seven-year-old who has spent a day in school trying valiantly to cope with his fine motor problems and then gone to his occupational therapy session after school should not then come home to face a work sheet, more struggle with his handwriting, and more frustration.

- Quirky kids—like all other kids and like most adults—will do the things they enjoy and find easy first. There's a real danger that at the end of the evening, when the child is most tenuously balanced, what will be left will be the hardest, most hated piece of work.

- Although the point of homework is supposed to be in part to teach independence, almost all parents of almost all children find themselves drawn in, at least in the early years, supervising, policing, correcting, helping . . . and so on until you cross the line and find the architect father sitting up all night making his fourth grader's ancient Rome diorama out of toothpicks!

- Homework is rough on parents, too, sometimes, and on whole families. The tired, frustrated child, up a little past his bedtime and crying because the assignment still doesn't look right (while his parent knows that what the child needs most is a good night's sleep), is no academic triumph for anyone.

- As children grow up, homework success becomes more and more about organization. If you switch classes for different subjects, can you keep track of what each teacher wants done tonight and handed in tomorrow? Can you track the due dates of longer-term assignments and upcoming tests? Can you bring the right books and papers home from school and write down the correct pages to read, the correct math problems that are due, the correct list of topics that are on the test? These can be real challenges for quirky kids.

• In the older elementary grades and in middle school, homework becomes much more serious. Some schools pride themselves on assigning large amounts of homework, as evidence of academic rigor. A child's learning issues and learning disabilities may really show up here; it may take much, much longer than it should to struggle through the history reading assignment or to write out answers to ten short-answer identifications.

• Sacrificing sleep to homework is a chronic problem in many high schools. Quirky children may be at special risk because of the learning issues that make the homework hard, because of organizational difficulties that make it problematic to structure their time, because their overall stamina is less, or because of an obsessive or perfectionist need to have everything absolutely right.

• Fatigue exacerbates attentional problems, learning difficulties, obsessions, anxiety, and social distress.

• On the other hand, homework can be of real benefit to the middle school or high school child who finds the social world confusing or intimidating or is bothered by the sensory overload of changing classes and worrying about class participation. Homework can be an opportunity to concentrate on academic issues without all these tensions and distractions.

HOMEWORK STRATEGIES

• *Consider homework groups.* Some families we interviewed told us they use this approach to help motivate their kids and make homework more fun. Invite one or two kids from your child's class to come over and do a little homework together. It can be an effective way to get a look at other children's studying strategies, and if there's a chance to play for a while when homework is done, that's a strong incentive to do the work more efficiently.

• *Use a flexible approach.* As you plan your child's elementary school program, look into whether there is any flexibility with regard to homework. You might be better off if homework involved reading together, in a situation in which you can do more of the reading as the child wears out and in which the reading time can also be pleasant one-on-one contact.

• *Consider your child's daily rhythms.* Most children, and most especially children with attention deficit problems, do much better if they do their homework relatively early in the day—maybe not immediately on coming home from school but certainly before supper. (Everybody deserves a break, and these kids, in particular, may need a chance for some physical activity before they have to sit down again.) Some quirky kids are notoriously early risers, and that can be a terrific time to get homework done. Kids who have rotten handwriting usually find that it deteriorates over the day and looks best first thing in the morning.

• *Have a plan of attack.* Sit down and strategize the day's homework with your child: How much has to be done? What looks easy? What looks hard?

• *Have a specific place to do the work.* How can you minimize distractions, if that's an issue? How available do you, or some other supervising adult, need to be? You can try to set up a dedicated homework place, which can be either in the child's room or, if his room is actually the place most full of possible distractions, in some boring adult setting: a little desk in the living room or some space on the kitchen table.

• *Reward accomplishments.* We are big believers in small, tangible rewards for small, tangible accomplishments. Finish your work sheet and you'll get a cookie. Finish all your homework and we'll go to the playground for fifteen minutes before dinner. With the assignments your child really hates, there's nothing wrong with offering an M&M or a grape or a gold star for every single successfully completed sentence on the work sheet or math problem on the list.

• *Don't overschedule.* If you fill up every afternoon with therapies and activities, then homework will have to wait until later, and that may be hard. How about moving some of these activities to the weekend? How about getting your child accustomed to bringing his homework along if you know there's usually a wait in the physical therapist's office? Some schools send home a packet of assignments for the week that is due on Friday or the following Monday. This allows for more flexibility in planning, and the final product is more likely to be relatively neat and well thought out.

- *Plan for supervision.* Think about homework supervision as you make your child-care arrangements. If you have a baby-sitter overseeing some of these after-school hours, can you give her clear instructions for helping with homework and make sure she understands that, if possible, it needs to be done before dinnertime? If your child spends time in an after-school program, is there some provision for homework? Many of these programs offer a supervised homework room, where kids can work in peace and get help if they need it.

- *Organize.* For many quirky kids, just keeping track of papers and assignments is a big task. Organizational issues are major developmental tasks for all kids, especially in the later elementary years. Quirky kids will be in good company. Still, as with other tasks, getting organized may take longer and require more help for the quirky child. Whoever is picking the child up from school may need to review with either the child or the teacher whether there is homework, and whoever is taking her in the morning may need to check and be extra sure that the completed assignments are packed and ready to go. When an assignment is given at school, the child should know exactly where to put the paper so she'll be sure to bring it home. After homework is done, the child should pack it up in whatever special folder or backpack is going to school the next day. No matter how carefully you plan, every parent has at some time or another driven over to someone else's house late one evening to borrow the assignment sheet that was left at school or driven madly back across town one morning with the forgotten, left-at-home important assignment. You just don't want to have to do it every day.

- *Check in with the teacher.* If the assignments are not always clearly indicated, or if your child has trouble figuring out exactly what is expected, you should either check in with the teacher on a regular basis or else establish a connection with another parent who seems relatively clued-in, so that you can, in a pinch, call for advice and instructions. Some teachers are available by E-mail, and some even post homework assignments on a Web page.

- *Evaluate the type of homework assigned.* If it seems to you that the assignments your child is bringing home are not particularly helpful or valuable to your child, you need to bring this up with the school. As we said above, our basic prejudice is that homework in kindergarten through third grade should be token at most—a fifteen- to thirty-minute assignment that reinforces what's going on in school while showing the child that such arcane activities as reading and writing and arithmetic can in fact go on at home, without benefit of a teacher, and while teaching the habit of, well, doing homework. We have seen children sent home with assignments that seemed, quite frankly, completely useless: coloring in coloring-book pictures of Disney characters, copying words over and over in different colors—first red, then blue, then green, then yellow . . . These jobs may be reasonably easy and entertaining for some children, but if they play right to your child's most distressing issues, then you need to be able to go in, meet with the teacher, and try to negotiate an exemption. No one ever suffered major consequences in later life from not coloring in a drawing of Minnie Mouse.

- *Bend the rules.* By far our favorite homework activity for young children is reading—reading together, letting the child read to the parent, and of course, letting the parent read to the child. We'd like to express the hope that homework reading programs will recognize the pleasures and comforts of reading aloud and will allow children to select the books that interest them. If you find yourself with a homework reading program that is taking all the fun out of it, you may need to make some discreet alterations at home—with or without notifying the school.

- *Stay informed.* If it seems to you at some point that too much homework is being assigned, talk to other parents. You may not be the only one who feels this way. When children have multiple teachers for different subjects, it's important that the teachers connect with one another and synchronize, so that everyone doesn't load it on the same night.

- *Use tools to plan.* Help older children plan their time—not just for any individual evening's work but for the bigger, longer-term assignments. Some quirky children are unable to understand how to break these down into manageable steps, and a chart or a checklist or a calendar with separate due dates for each task can be really helpful.

- *Find ways to compensate.* If you think you're seeing your child struggling unduly with a particular kind of homework, be ready to reopen the possibility of a learning evaluation. Remember that smart kids can compensate amazingly for all kinds of learning disabilities, and it may be only when all the other kids catch up and become fluent readers, for example, that your fifth grader's language-processing differences come to light, as it takes him a long time to read and digest printed text. Talking with your child's teacher can help you develop strategies to help. Maybe your daughter should listen to her books on tape while reading along. Maybe your son needs a laptop or the much cheaper AlphaSmart on which to type his assignments.

• *Encourage appropriate family participation.* Homework should not dominate the evening life of children in kindergarten, heaven knows, or in the first three grades of school. From then on, it should gradually assume more and more importance, since after all, by high school, we all hope it is dominating our children's evenings (because we have begun to imagine the alternatives!). Families need to treat homework matter-of-factly, as a child's responsibility to complete. It is also the whole family's responsibility to provide support—with proper supervision, with a comfortable place to work, with quiet when there needs to be quiet, and with special attention when there is a big test coming up or a major project due.

• *Remember the power of praise.* Try to make homework time a period that is associated with a certain amount of praise, with some physical comfort, and even with the occasional treat. It won't make your child love work sheets, but it may start to seem like a known, familiar, relatively pleasant interlude in the day—or at least, like a doable assignment.

PERSONAL HYGIENE AND GOOD GROOMING

Personal hygiene is a big deal for a lot of quirky kids. The tensions and strains around using the toilet, keeping clean, wiping runny noses, getting dressed, and all the rest can loom as highly fraught with tension and downright crazy-making for lots of parents. Not only that, but as a child ages and still doesn't seem to get it when it comes to basic self-care, a parent looks at him and imagines social disasters to come. For some of these children in later elementary school and middle school, the personal hygiene issues do become the focus of teasing or bullying or social ostracism. The eighth-grade girl who picks her nose all the time is going to get noticed and probably shunned. A second-grade boy who's been running around outside for hours will smell of dirt and dust and energy, but an eighth-grade boy better understand about taking a shower and changing his clothes. Even for their parents and other relatives who love them dearly, it's just plain easier to cherish a relatively clean, un-snotty, pleasant-smelling child!

These are issues that stress out almost all parents: the daily maintenance and supervision of small children's bodies, the necessity of civilizing them and teaching them self-care. It's a long journey from the cuteness of that first new-born poopy diaper to the two-year-old—or the three-year-old or the four-year-old—who can reliably pee and poop in the potty. Then you still have to know about it and hear about it, not to mention help wipe! And once again, parents of quirky kids get it all more intensely and for a longer time. These children need more supervision, and they need it further along in life, which contributes to that whole vulnerable child syndrome, in which parent and child feel more tightly tied together than is usual. There's nothing like han-dling someone's bathroom behavior and wiping her nose to give you certain special kinds of boundary issues.

Max would not become potty-trained, though the counselors told his father he knew exactly what to do. He just didn't care to do it. Finally, at about six or seven, his mother bribed him with a day-trip to the beach if he would urinate in the toi-let. He did but would not sit on the toilet to defecate, and only now, at nine, is he almost fully "trained."

He has never been able to stand water in his face, especially in his eyes. We re-member watching his very first bath through the window in the newborn nursery. He was screaming and arching and so clearly miserable. At the time, we thought that he must be cold or that all babies must hate their first bath. The fact is, it's never changed. He completely hates taking a shower if he needs to wash his hair. He seems to lose his sense of himself when his eyes are closed, and the sensation itself drives him nuts. We just started having him shower with goggles on, and that does help some. Of course, the goggles are always too tight so they hurt or too loose so the water gets in anyway. It's always a struggle of some kind, and frankly, it's gotten really old.

What can we tell you that you don't already know about quirky children and personal hygiene? You need patience, organizational abilities, resilience, a sense of humor—and of course, your love for your child. The following subsections offer some specific suggestions that may help.

USING THE BATHROOM

These kids are notoriously late to graduate out of diapers. Some are generally slow developmentally or at least verbally. Others are somehow out of touch with their bodies and physiological impulses. Your child will have to take these steps when he is ready. If that's later than you would like—and although you will, of course, encourage him and cheer him on—there are risks to making this into a struggle or a test of wills. It's common in our practice to see children, of many different ages, who develop constipation or who continue soiling their pants as toilet training goes awry. Even after a quirky child has managed the great transition, he is likely to need more teaching, not less, about the mechanics of using the toilet, of wiping, of flushing, of washing hands. You may find yourself repeating simple instructions over and over and over or posting signs to remind a child to wash his hands after using the toilet. Some children find damp wipes easier to use than toilet paper. You may find sticker charts very valuable: a star for every dry night (or for every poop in the toilet, depending on the issue) and a reward for a whole week of stars.

PERSONAL GROOMING

Personal hygiene rules, like many other social customs, may never come easily to the quirky child. They won't make sense to him or fit in with his view of the world. A child with fine motor delays or weaknesses may have trouble with the details of dressing or grooming herself and may need help or at least careful inspection long after all the other children her age can button their shirts, comb and arrange their hair, or get the spinach out of their teeth. What you probably *can't* do is depend on peer pressure to convince your quirky child that these issues matter. You'll hear parents saying from time to time, "Oh, when he starts to care about girls, then he won't want to have spinach on his teeth." This is much less true with quirky kids. They have trouble decoding the social rules and therefore can't quite make the connection, or they just don't care. Waiting for your child to learn the rules independently and make good personal resolutions is unlikely to work. It may in fact lead to intense teasing that hurts your child but doesn't succeed in reforming him.

Morning ablutions, in particular, need to be kept to the bare necessities in most families, just because of the realities of trying to get out of the house. Frankly, as pediatricians, we recommend to parents of young children that they teach detailed teeth-brushing skills in the evening.

I use a lot of bulletin boards and dry-erase boards to keep up with Trevor's lack of organization. Mornings can be really hard, especially if he senses that I am losing patience, and I am not a patient person. I am an impatient person with a very slow child. I take a train to work, and there is very little wiggle room. If the morning isn't going well, it can be a disaster.

Keep an eye out for modifications that make life easier: a toothpaste that your child likes—or at least dislikes less—is more likely to get used. Occupational therapists sometimes recommend shower chairs for children who find it hard to keep their balance. A telephone shower may be easier than an overhead shower for the child who hates water in his face. Goggles may keep the water out of his eyes and help make showertime tolerable. Search till you find the right extremely soft towel for a child who is sensitive to sensory stimuli. You may want to keep hair short, especially if washing or brushing feels unpleasant to your child.

CLOTHES

Many quirky kids are slow to dress themselves—slow in the sense that they can't do it till they're older than you might expect and also slow in the sense that it takes them many minutes to get ready. Choose clothing that is easy to manage—elastic-waist pants, shirts without buttons or snaps at the neck, jackets and shoes with Velcro fasteners. Tying shoes is a complex motor skill and comes late indeed to many quirky kids. Fortunately, we live in an era of slip-ons, all-terrain moccasins, and Velcro. It's usually easier to deal with clothes that are a little bigger rather than a little smaller. Many children have strong preferences about what textures they can tolerate next to the skin; when you find the perfect seamless socks or the ideal cozy, warm sweatshirt, buy large quantities. Try to budget time in the morning so that a child who dresses slowly is awake first and there isn't as much pressure. And no matter how much we want to foster independence, there are always going to be morning moments when you just grab the child and stuff her into her clothes and run. One mom we know put her son to bed in his clothes for years, so he would be dressed and ready to go in the morning. And you have to praise and praise and congratulate and congratulate and reward and reward—recognizing that even if you yourself feel these behaviors should be completely routine by this age, your child may be struggling. Finally, be aware that your child may not perceive the social implications of clothing—that is, he may happily dress in outfits that other kids will find odd or even ridiculous. You can help here by making sure that his dresser drawers are stocked with standard-issue kid clothes in the appropriate sizes. Keep an eye out for what other kids are wearing, and don't hesitate to shop the big chain stores; the more generic, the better.

Chrissie's clothes are often crooked, and sometimes she doesn't realize exactly what she is wearing—you know, striped tops with flowered pants. I just tell her she needs to change because the colors clash. And she usually does it, after I explain why she needs to do it. Her wardrobe is pretty limited because she hates wearing jeans and pants that snap or button. She prefers elastic waists. I've told her it's OK by me, but as her tastes change, she's going to have to adjust her preferences if she truly wants the latest clothes. I'm thinking I might want to take mother-and-daughter sewing classes with her at some point.

Ben is very particular about his feet, especially his socks. If his feet are sweaty, he will not touch them to put on his socks and needs me to do it for him, even though he's eight now. He has slip-on shoes, and I went out and bought the next three sizes now that I've found a shoe he will wear and put on by himself.

Of course, in the evening, you have to take all those clothes off and go back into the bathroom. Then, finally, thank goodness, to bed. If there is some part of your child's bedtime routine that he especially looks forward to, make it conditional on getting through the appropriate evening bathroom ritual. Yes, I went to the bathroom, I flushed the toilet, I washed my hands and my face, I brushed my teeth, I took off my clothes and put them in the hamper, I took my shower, I put on my pajamas, so now do I get a chapter of my airplane book? And yes, of course, a good chapter, rich with diagrams and technical terms!

BEDTIME

Some quirky kids are good sleepers, some less so. Some are the historically bad sleepers, especially as infants and toddlers—the ones who can never seem to settle, who certainly can't sleep in any unfamiliar place, who toss and turn and fret. Maybe it's an early manifestation of that sense that many quirky kids seem uncomfortable in their own skins. Maybe it's a neurological correlate of sensory integration imbalance. Maybe it's just bad luck.

Parents of quirky kids often find bedtime even more difficult with a child who may have more than the usual dose of fear and anxiety, or a more intense attachment and great trouble separating from the parent for the night. On the other hand, some parents we've talked to have told us about their experiences with quirky kids who just love to go to bed! The effort to make it through the day can sometimes leave a quirky kid exhausted and eager to sleep.

Occasionally, when he's in bed, my grandson Max will permit a back rub, but more often than not—more most recently now that he's nine—he does not want me in his room at bedtime.

Some special quirky-kid issues around bedtime—and some coping strategies:

- Think about what can make the separation of bedtime easier for an anxious child—whether it's a night-light, an open door, the promise that a parent will come in and check on her, or a favorite tape by which to fall asleep.
- Indulge bedtime rituals, but keep an eye on time. You don't want the whole evening to be taken up by the many elaborate steps of getting a child into bed. And don't allow the ritual to require only one particular adult. Mom *or* Dad *or* Grandma *or* a sitter must be included and allowed to participate.
- All the well-worn comforts of transitional objects and familiar bedtime stories or songs may be even more important to a quirky child—and may go on mattering even after other children have outgrown them. Never disdain any strategy that helps get your child happily into bed.
- Many children (and adults) with sensory integration issues like to sleep either in the cocoonlike environment of a sleeping bag or under a heavy comforter. This anchors them physically, comforting them by enclosing

or pressing down their bodies. Be open to the idea that she may want to sleep in a sleeping bag, zipped up tight, all year round.

John sleeps in a sleeping bag twelve months a year—he likes the feeling of closeness. And he likes the room to be absolutely dark. You'd think he'd want a light on because he gets frightened so easily, but no, it has to be totally dark.

There were a lot of things I used to fight with Lisa over that now I understand— like the heavy blankets she liked to sleep with even in the summer. It was a nightly battle, that and all the toys she wanted to sleep with, and how they had to be in certain positions. I thought she just didn't want to go to sleep, but with the sensory integration dysfunction, she needs those blankets to feel weighted down so she can relax. She needs those animals so she can find her place. It was so much easier once I understood it.

- If your child is taking medication, any abrupt change in sleep habits should be discussed with his doctor in light of the medication, the dose, and the timing. We often move children's dosing regimens around, giving them the same medications but at different points in the day, trying to help them be awake and alert during the day at school and then able to relax and go to sleep at night. You can read more about this in Chapter 10, on medications.
- Life with a quirky child can be wearing. As a parent, you are entitled to factor in your own need for a little break in the evening, for a little adult time to pause and regroup and think about what comes next—or maybe enjoy a glass of wine and a good trashy novel!

I was a maniac about bedtime. We followed the rules for how to make sure they know how to go to sleep by themselves—and they all learned. Sam was my most challenging. He would stay up later and set himself up in any number of places around the house. Sometimes we'd find him under the piano or the dining room table. He liked the feeling of the hardwood floors against his skin. He told me, "I just need to hear the sound of your voice." For the most part, he would manage by himself, so it was OK. I just needed that break. I needed to know that at the end of the day, there would be some time when they weren't in my face!

It's worth remembering that since this is, by definition, the moment in the day when children are most tired and sleep-deprived, it's probably a good time to indulge rituals and preferences.

BABY-SITTERS

Every parent of a quirky kid ends up with a baby-sitter horror story or two—although, to be fair, so do many parents of all kinds of kids. And, to be even fairer, most baby-sitters have a couple of good stories of their own. But here you are, thinking of leaving a more than usually challenging child with another caretaker, and you would really like it to work out, so that you can do your errands, hold down your job, see your friends, or just enjoy that candlelight dinner out together that we were recommending a few pages back!

Decide what kind of expectations you have of your baby-sitter. It's one thing to be hoping for an occasional evening out or a Saturday afternoon free to run errands, and it's another thing to have a baby-sitter who picks your child up from school five days a week and spends the afternoon with him. Let's think about that more serious, longer-term baby-sitter first. Are you expecting her to be your child's playmate, his tutor, his therapist—or will you be happy if she just keeps him safe and alive and relatively clean until you get home?

Toddlers and preschoolers who are involved in early intervention programs or behavioral programs will need a baby-sitter who understands the program. A baby-sitter might take turns with you accompanying your child to the early intervention playgroup or might participate in a behavioral program with a home-based therapist. For the more intensive behavioral approaches, usually reserved for the younger and more severely affected children, the therapist will insist that any regular baby-sitter be involved in the program so there is consistency.

A baby-sitter who is doing school pickup and afternoon hours is going to be faced with homework supervision and perhaps with getting the child to and from appointments. These responsibilities and expectations need to be clearly discussed. You should not by any means assume that just because someone is in college, she can do a second-grade book report or fifth-grade math! You need to make it clear to your baby-sitter exactly what you mean by helping with homework, both in terms of the help you expect her to give (show him how to look up the words in the dictionary, correct him when he reads aloud and makes a mistake) and the help you don't want her to give (do the math problems for him, color in the Minnie Mouse herself). You also need, here as elsewhere, a clear set of instructions for what she's supposed to do if she runs into a problem. No parent is happy to learn that the baby-sitter has invented a new punishment or restricted a privilege without asking.

The whole issue of punishment and expectations brings us to perhaps one of the most complicated questions that comes up with baby-sitters: how much does she need to know? If she's actually going to supervise the end of the child's school day and much of his homework, she probably needs to know everything she can about how your child functions and how he learns. However, if she's going to do the occasional evening and that's it, you might just give her an orientation about the child's evening habits and bedtime behaviors, and leave it at that.

You do need to warn a baby-sitter if there is any chance she's going to have to deal with any dramatic or potentially dangerous events, like seizures or major tantrums. Again, you need to leave clear instructions about how you want these situations handled and a way to reach you. Any baby-sitter who is asked to give medications needs to know what she is giving and whether there is any possibility of a reaction.

Remember that baby-sitters will vary enormously in their experience of the world—and of children. Just as you may have relatives who refuse to believe that there's anything different about your child (except, maybe, a lack of parental firmness!), you may encounter baby-sitters who doubt your interpretation. Experience and attitude are by no means tightly tied to age. We have heard stories of older baby-sitters who did not believe that any of these syndromes exist—or that anything was going on that couldn't be cured by a little discipline. We have also heard stories of older baby-sitters who brought a kind of wisdom and experience to handling quirky children that made everyone's life much easier. Similarly, we have heard about some younger baby-sitters who were completely overwhelmed by the oddities and pressures of quirky children but then about others who brought energy and sympathy—and sometimes recent training in child development or special education—to certain lucky families.

We had one baby-sitter who just thinks it's all total nonsense and there's nothing wrong with any of my kids except I'm too indulgent with them. Now we have a new sitter who sort of gets it and has strategies to help deal with it. At one point, she had two of my kids playing a card game and one building something, and I was in awe, because they weren't screaming at one another.

We hired a young woman to help with our kids after school. She came with solid references and a lot of experience. We went to great lengths to explain the issues of our kids and how we expected her to deal with them. When I came home the first afternoon, she met me at the door and said, "I cannot do this." I was stunned. When we spoke about it, I realized that she herself was too high-strung and inflexible to manage with our kids. I was actually grateful to her for figuring it out so quickly and moving on.

Look for a baby-sitter who seems genuinely to like and appreciate your child, however she may formulate her understanding of his quirks. Quirky kids, as we all know, can be endearing, eccentric, and exasperating, sometimes within the space of about five minutes. A sitter who can't indulge and appreciate your child's intense feelings—about baseball statistics or beetles or bus schedules—is going to miss all the fun of getting to know him. A sitter who thinks that allowing her to follow her set routines and rituals, or offering her the extra help she needs with dressing and personal hygiene, is just "spoiling her" is going to communicate that attitude and is unlikely to bond successfully with her charge.

When you think you've found that sitter who likes and appreciates your child, treat her well! Just as your job is harder than the average parent's job, her job is harder than the average sitter's. Acknowledge it when she goes the extra mile, pay her well, and thank her often.

Of course, many children behave differently with the baby-sitter than they do with their parents. In many families, baby-sitter nights are understood to be nights when the familiar routines are varied a little, the rules are relaxed, and a good time is had by all.

The Quirky Child Goes Out

Small children, by and large, do not really know how to behave in public places, and that is why Raffi concerts exist. One of the great joys—or one of the heavy burdens—of childrearing is the chance, or the obligation, to spend time in playgrounds, theme restaurants, creative puppet shows and theatrical presentations, water parks, cartoon matinees, and places where you pay good money to climb around in a great bin full of colored plastic balls. Most parents begin by taking their children out to these child-centered places, and then, when the child seems ready or when the parent absolutely cannot stand to listen to another repetitious, squeaky-voiced song, they try, somewhat tentatively, a real restaurant, a show that isn't just for kids, a concert, or tea at the Ritz.

With a quirky child, you have to take it a little bit more slowly and carefully. Even the usual child-friendly activities can prove highly unfriendly or highly challenging for quirky children, and their reactions can attract attention and censure even in places where routine childish misbehavior is going on all around you. Every parent has a story or two of a child who misbehaved so outrageously that they can never go back to the restaurant or the store or even, they feel, the state in question. Parents of quirky kids have more stories, and the stories are more extreme. The sense that other people are judging you and your child really hangs over many parents.

You're not the only one who's ever been publicly humiliated. To give you the courage to venture out again, we'll offer you some strategies for coping in public. But first, a few general pieces of advice:

- Think carefully about why you are doing whatever you are doing. Are you taking your child to *The Nutcracker* because she has expressed interest or loves music or watches enthralled whenever there are ballet dancers on TV—or are you taking her because it's always been part of *your* fantasy of having a daughter that you would dress her in a velvet dress and dream that Sugarplum Fairy dream together? Generally speaking, your chances of success in public endeavors are much, much higher if the child has expressed an interest.

- It can help a great deal to rehearse a scenario with your child. This allows you to think ahead about what may be tricky moments—loud noises, tight crowd scenes, scary sights—and it also helps the child understand step-by-step exactly what is going to happen and prepare for it. But just because you've given your child the restaurant scenario or the birthday party scenario one time through, you can't assume that now she knows it and will keep it stored somewhere for next time. You're probably going to have to do it each and every time and accept that going over the scenario itself is probably reassuring to her, a familiar prelude to what is becoming an increasingly familiar activity.

- Keep your sense of humor. Yes, we know we keep on saying that. But the truth is, there is nothing that ages as well for most parents as the memory of a public disaster. You'll find yourself telling the story to other parents to console them for the disasters that they've been through or offering it up at dinner many years later to the howls of your entire family. You need, as you go along, to identify a few good friends who can listen to your stories and are guaranteed not to respond with accounts of their own perfect children at the all-county deportment awards ceremony, and then you need to keep laughing, even if it's sometimes through tears.

RESTAURANTS, MOVIES, PUBLIC LIFE

Start slow with restaurants, and take it easy—basic commonsense advice for all parents of all small children. Go at hours when things aren't too busy; go to places that aren't aiming for a hushed and romantic atmosphere. This doesn't mean you have to sacrifice good food. There are fabulous ethnic restaurants everywhere you look, good "family restaurants" in many cities and towns, and any vacation destination is likely to have casual joints with great food.

As for the quirky child who eats only the same three things? Well, if you want to take him out to a restaurant, you'd better pack up thing one, thing two, and thing three and bring them along. Confide in a server, beg an extra plate, and then order plenty of food for those of you who *are* eating.

Being in a restaurant with your quirky child may make you acutely aware of how different he is developmentally from other children his age. Even if *he* isn't self-conscious about his table manners or about needing you to cut his meat, *you* may find yourself smiling nervously at other adults—or even other children—and wishing that your child could, for heaven's sake, grow up a little.

Last night we were at an Italian restaurant with friends. He was sitting next to this little girl, and they brought hot rolls, and my son hands one to the girl next to him and says, "Can you butter it?" And she looks at him. I mean, he's eleven and he can't butter his roll.

Restaurant trips are an excellent opportunity for the kind of scenarios we talked about above. Go over with your child the mechanics of a restaurant meal: we'll arrive, we'll park, we'll go in, we'll sit down at a table, someone will come and give us menus, we'll choose our food, you'll tell me what you want to eat, someone will come to take our order—and so on right through to paying the bill and saying thank you.

Similarly, a trip to the movies may be easier for a quirky kid who knows exactly what to expect, from the concession stand in the lobby to the coming attractions to the credits to the movie itself. For most quirky kids, you would be better off starting out with movies that are more or less known quantities rather than expecting them to be surprised or delighted by movies they don't know. You don't want to have to deal with the consequences of a too-scary or too-disturbing scene, and you don't want to have to answer loud, persistent questions in a public place. Movies can be very loud and very overwhelming for the kids who experience sensory integration problems. The right pair of earplugs can make the difference between pleasure and pain.

With any new outing, any new activity, take it slow. Don't let yourself be carried away by the experiences of the nonquirky kids who are the same age as your child. There's an awful lot of variation among children, and one child's favorite movie is another child's screaming trauma. Some kids think Ursula from *The Little Mermaid* is simply hilarious—so horrible she couldn't possibly be real. This is less likely for an anxious child or a child who can't make the imaginative leap into that Disney world. For him, Ursula is absolutely terrifying and the source of nightmares. Learn as much as you can about the movie before you go and tell it to your child, breaking the whole thing down into a scenario or script that lets her know exactly what's going to happen, step-by-step-by-step. And then you go, and try to have fun—but stay ready to bag the whole thing and get the hell out of there if it starts looking like a disaster in the making. And despite all your preparations, that can happen, and it can make you feel really bad.

We took Aidan to the Christmas-tree–lighting ceremony. Lights came on and music started playing all at the same time. It was just too much for Aidan. He was way overstimulated, and we needed to get out of there pronto! It made us very sad we couldn't do this special thing.

If you have other children, being ready to make a getaway often means having two adults present so that, in an emergency, one can take the unwilling child out in the lobby or out of the restaurant for a walk without ruining the treat for the rest of the kids.

And here, as elsewhere in public life, you may occasionally have to deal with officious strangers. Try not to be unduly rude to these people, but remember that you owe them no explanations and no information, only a polite apology if your child has in any way intruded on them. To the kindly lady (the technical term is *interfering buzzard*) who crosses the street to tell your child that if he would only take his hands off his ears, he would really enjoy the parade, you need only reply, "Thank you so much for your suggestion."

ACTIVITIES, SPORTS

Life, of course, is not all restaurant trips and movies and parades. There can also be team sports, music lessons, religious school, skating lessons, gymnastics, dance, and practically anything else you can think of. And for a given quirky child, any one of these may be a good activity—or even *the* activity, the be-all and end-all. Be careful, though, about overscheduling the quirky child or, again, about filling her schedule with activities important to you but not to her. The child who faces additional struggles in school and with homework, and maybe has a couple of extra therapy or special-help sessions every week, is unlikely to thrive on the addition of violin lessons (because every child should play an instrument), ballet (because it will help her grace and coordination), soccer (because team sports are so important for teaching kids to get along in life), and religious school (because we really want her to know her heritage). That regime is the kind of schedule that has recently provoked all kinds of books and articles about overscheduled children and the perils of pushing too hard. For a child who is already struggling just to meet academic and social expectations, it's out of the question. Choose activities that really matter. Ideally, they should be the activities that really matter to your child, not to you. In the words of one elementary school teacher:

I look at Annie—she has attention deficit disorder, she has some traits of Asperger's—and I think that her parents, who are very upscale, very success-oriented, were just expecting this perfect child: you know, she comes home and does a wonderful job on her homework, she practices the violin, she works on her community service project. And you know, it just isn't like that. And maybe there's someone else in the family—you know there's always someone else in the family where the sister's daughter or the cousin is like that—but it sure isn't Annie.

Giving up your fantasies can be painful for parents, but it shouldn't be painful for the child. It's important not to restrict your quirky child completely and to allow her to pursue her interests. It's also important to remember that if a child is truly determined to play baseball—or the piano—that determination may accomplish more than years of occupational therapy.

Children's team sports are a great big subject. There are towns where every girl plays soccer on Saturday or where spring is heralded by the appearance of Little League T-shirts. Your child may want to be part of the action. It's best to give team sports a try while your child is young. The youngest divisions in these leagues are rarely highly intense or highly competitive. This will give you a chance to assess your child's skills and see how much she enjoys the whole process.

LOGISTICS

It's important not to underestimate the importance of logistics, the details of getting from place to place. With all their extra appointments, quirky children can end up with complex schedules. Certainly, anyone who has more than one child is faced with a great deal of detail in the masterminding of daily life. Similarly, a single parent is going to be more stressed by logistics and perhaps face even more difficult financial and work-related decisions. And of course, there are some quirks that can make all the logistics that much more complicated.

For example, some quirky children simply cannot handle the school bus. It's too noisy or too crazy, or they get teased. Whatever the reason, you may be faced with the necessity of driving this child back and forth—which can greatly complicate your own life and excite the envy or the scorn of less quirky siblings who did, or do, just fine on the bus.

With all the therapies and appointments, it gets more complicated. Someone is always schlepping a kid here or there, always trying to remember what to bring along, always running a little late. This has financial implications for the family: Is someone going to cut back on hours at work? Does the baby-sitter need the car so Mom has to take the bus to work? It also has time and stress implications for all concerned. Inevitably, siblings find themselves getting dragged around to therapy appointments, as they do to one another's music lessons or sports events. This can bring on a great deal of groaning and complaining and also a certain amount of teasing, as your child's siblings look around at the other children in the physical therapy waiting room, for example, or the other kids attending the pragmatic language group. It would be easy to say that it's best not to bring siblings along to these appointments, but it's just a fact of life for many families. It means parents have a real obligation to teach the sibling how to behave. Some offices do have toys or puzzles, but these will rarely satisfy week after week. Bring activities—books, toys, homework—for the child who will be doing the waiting and thank her (and maybe reward her) for her patience.

If you sometimes feel as if you're slogging, it's probably because you are. Keep your eye on what really matters—your child, your family, your marriage. Cut your losses when you need to. And remember that you are doing a hard and important job. Logistics matter because they get the children to the activities they enjoy or to the special help they need. All this detail and schlepp and exhaustion will make sense as you watch them grow and learn and progress.

References and Resources

References and resources on family life will be found at the end of Chapter 5.

5

○ ○ ● ○

The Rest of the Family:

SIBLINGS, PARENTS, GRANDPARENTS, CELEBRATIONS, DISASTERS, AND "YOU'RE JUST LIKE YOUR UNCLE JOE!"

In this chapter, we're going to look more closely at the relationships that different family members—both immediate and extended—have with their quirky brothers and sisters, nieces and nephews, grandchildren, cousins, and all the rest. Our goal is to point out some problems that may arise, suggest some strategies and approaches—but also to celebrate the wonderful and positive impact that a supportive and accepting family can have on an eccentric child's life. We'll also look a little more directly at how parents can take care of themselves and of everyone else as well.

Siblings

The siblings of your quirky child are probably much on your mind as a parent. Are they getting their fair share of attention? Is the household so oriented around one child's needs that the less needy are sometimes left to fend for themselves? Do they feel ashamed of a weird brother or sister or cringe inside when someone at school laughs or teases—or are their own social situations compromised as they rush to defend or explain or intercede?

Jack and Rebecca have an older sister, Nina, who is very bright and capable in school and in all other areas. So Nina is the oldest child with two very impaired younger siblings and has adopted a caretaker role with both of them, especially her truly autistic brother. When other kids come over and see him doing his self-stimulating behavior, she just says, "That's my brother who is autistic. He doesn't talk, but he goes to a special school where they are going to teach him to talk." When she sees him after school, she runs up to greet him with joy and affection. This has been great for him to have such a sister as Nina. We worry about her as well as the other two, however, because she assumes this role both at home and at school. There is a child in her class with Asperger's, and she reaches out to him and takes care of him. When we go to functions for families of these kids, there she is, right in the middle with all the quirky kids, helping them out. We were worried she was growing up too soon, accepting too much responsibility for her age. So we brought her to the school counselor and asked her to work on this. We want Nina to have a childhood. She will probably end up in the caring professions.

My granddaughter Sophie is very strong and protective of her brother, Max. But one night, as I was sitting on her bed as she was falling asleep, a soft voice came up from the pillow and said, "Sometimes I think it would be so nice to have a brother who didn't have autism." I nearly cried.

There are children who grow up with a special kind of assurance, that special confidence which can come from knowing that you are the nonquirky, high-achieving, "perfect" child, and there are children who grow up feeling ignored and neglected. All we can do here is suggest that you think through the decisions you make about your quirky child from the point of view of how they affect her siblings and try to be sure, as we've said before, that the quirkiness and the accommodations to it do not become the all-defining features of your family life.

The nonquirky sibling needs:

- *To be sure of a certain amount of privacy, of protection from the more extreme moods and behaviors of your quirky kid.* It's not fair to expect a sibling to sleep through nighttime crying or to manage a tantrum. He needs to know that when things get extreme, it's not his problem or his responsibility—and that he has a place to go and get away, in his room or in some other reasonably safe and private spot, while you deal with what's going on.
- *To be able to keep her important possessions and her school stuff safe.* Young

children with autistic spectrum disorders can be highly destructive. Children with good intentions and poor fine motor skills can inadvertently spill or rip or knock things over. You want to avoid the scenario in which your child is always angry at her quirky sibling, always screaming, always upset. One way to do that is to make sure that her stuff is safe and that she knows that if anything does get spoiled, you're good for a replacement. Everyone will probably benefit from a general family rule: all children can keep important possessions in their rooms—or in their special drawers—where they are absolutely off-limits to other family members. Anything left out in the common space may be handled by all comers. After all, it might easily be the quirky child who is profoundly distressed by having a sibling touch or move or wreck her stuff. Maybe the trucks got moved out of formation because a younger brother actually wanted to drive one across the floor, yelling "Rrom-rrom, here I come!" Maybe a precious spatula (oh, yes, there are children who bond to spatulas) actually got used to flip the pancakes. And in this case, you again have to try to protect the quirky child's rights: "OK, this will be your *special* spatula, and your sister can't use it." "If you set up your trucks in your room, we can close the door so your brother won't touch them."

- *To be encouraged to help—and acknowledged for helping—when he is able.* You may find that a sibling has the ability to comfort or soothe or engage a quirky child who is generally harder to reach. At the risk of sounding trite, siblings can be great for quirky kids and vice versa. Sibling relationships provide models for friendships and present ways for kids to try to live harmoniously with others, life skills that they all need. Quirky kids usually need more practice, and brothers and sisters can help a lot.

When I go to their house to take care of my grandchildren, Sophie is quite helpful and occasionally quite "in charge" in terms of dealing with Max. "I'll do it, Nana," or "No, Nana, that is not the way to do it," or "This is what Max needs," and so on.

- *To find ways to deal with the embarrassment she feels about having a brother or sister who sometimes behaves strangely.* You can help your child with this by acknowledging the embarrassment or the distress without making a big issue out of it. Help the child find a reasonable formulation to explain what's going on: "My sister gets upset when she hears loud noises because her ears are so sensitive." "My brother really needs to do everything a certain way. Sometimes it's a pain, but we can just go do our own stuff and my mom will take care of it." Make sure the sibling has protected space to have a friend over. Don't expect your quirky child to be included or press for a game that everyone can play. Consider distracting the quirky sibling or even taking him out for a different activity or a treat, so that at least occasionally, the other child and her friend(s) can have full run of the house.

There is one rule that applies in any household to any set of siblings: however you may treat one another at home, you take care of one another, protect one another, stick up for one another, when it comes to the outside world. In the household with a quirky child, it goes a bit further: it is never OK to make fun of the quirky child to others or to initiate or join in any teasing or tormenting. This rule is inflexible.

The way that you and your family deal with your quirky kid, and the way that you feel about her and the way that you convey that feeling, will have a great impact on her siblings. Many children with more severely quirky siblings are acutely aware that as certain parental fantasies and ambitions are given up in the face of the other child's development, those same parental fantasies and ambitions may attach with even greater strength to the more typical, higher-achieving brother or sister. This may be a considerable burden to carry, and there are occasionally even children who, in one way or another, crack under the pressure.

I worry about Sophie forming attachments in the future, in terms of letting Max go and in terms of what her expectations of herself as well as of the other person would be. I worry about Sophie feeling free enough to make independent decisions for her own life. I worry about Sophie not developing resentments of all sorts, directed at Max, at her mother, and at her father. Yes, I worry about Sophie. Her childhood has been limited; I hope somehow she will be able to fly free when she grows up.

There are many children who look at a quirky sibling and worry that they, too, will develop the more troubling behaviors or symptoms, whether severe anxiety or seizures or tantrums. This can play into the preoccupations of a parent, who may be unable to stop himself from anxiously watching his other children for danger signs. We found this to be especially true for parents when the first child was the quirky one. Any mild variation in the second child's development or behavior will almost automatically be viewed as the onset of more serious and familiar issues. Many a younger sibling has been subjected to extra scrutiny because the parental antennae are up! In fact, parents do have good reason to be concerned and anxiously attentive: children who fall into any of the quirky-kid diagnostic categories *are* more likely to have siblings in these categories as well.

The only advice we can offer for families here is simple to give and difficult to follow: try as hard as you can to view each child separately, as the person he is, as her own unfolding individual. Comparisons are famously odious, and comparisons made among siblings have been paying therapy bills of one kind or another ever since God liked Abel's offering better than Cain's.

One common issue you face with siblings—one quirky and one not—is the situation in which a younger child surpasses an older. There's no easy way to deal with it when a younger sibling achieves a developmental milestone first, masters a skill that the older one still struggles with, passes him by academically, or even gets to some social landmark (a sleepover party, a first date) that has not yet—or may never—come to the older. It's awkward for everyone—unless your older, quirkier child is genuinely immune (uninterested in the sport or the skill or the social scene). It would be a noble younger child indeed who could refrain from remarking on having got ahead of the older. You have to remember that, to small children, birth order often seems like a mandated footrace. It's only natural to crow when you pass the person who started out ahead.

Fortunately, John has some splinter skills, so, for example, Sam knows that John is good at math. He's developed a persona at school as this kid who's big in math. But then again, Sam is constantly comparing himself to John: "Well, I took the deep-end test when I was seven. He's ten, and he hasn't even gotten in the pool yet!"

You have to be matter-of-fact and frank about this, and you can't let your concern for your quirky child's feelings stifle whatever celebration or congratulations are indicated. You certainly don't have to compel the quirky child to participate, but you can't downplay the achievement itself. So, no, you don't have to drag the ten-year-old boy who is physically awkward and uncoordinated to his eight-year-old sister's gymnastics championships. But you'd better be there yourselves, and you'd better bring her a bouquet, and you'd better put that picture of her with her team and everyone wearing rosettes up on the wall. Then look for something to celebrate with her brother.

Sibling relations are often awkward and touchy, even when everyone does everything in strict birth-order chronology and even when everyone is equally high-achieving and sunny-tempered and is aware of receiving an equal and fair share of parental notice and appreciation. Well, actually, this has never once happened in recorded history, but we suspect that even if it did happen, there would still be some touchy intersibling issues! When one child is on a genuinely different developmental trajectory, it gets more complicated and touchier. The less you measure your children against one another, the harder you come down on anyone who does, and the more you find ways to distinguish and celebrate each one, the better off you'll be when the crunches come.

By far the most basic and widespread issue for the siblings of quirky children, however, is the constant daily rub of being in a situation in which one child in a family is unusually needy and the parents have had to arrange life so that those needs can be met.

Although her father tries to give Sophie "special time" and enrolled her in gymnastics classes, Sophie is free to do "her own thing" only if Max is involved in a program that takes care of him.

Anything that parents can do to address this imbalance is helpful. Special time scheduled with each child, whether formally or informally, is important. Kids need to be with their parents sometimes and have their parents concentrating fully and solely on *them*, not on the family conundrum. Rotating choices (what to pick up for dinner Friday evening, what to do on Saturday afternoon) so that everyone gets to choose in turn (rather than catering only to the person with the most restrictions—even if that sometimes means that he can't participate) can help siblings feel that their own lives aren't being unduly truncated by preferences and dislikes they don't share.

By the time John was about five or six, I started planning these mom/son weekends away with each child alone. I felt they deserved some of my undivided attention, and I deserved the chance to truly revel in being with one of them at a time, without constantly feeling guilty that I couldn't meet anyone's demands because they were all so needy.

Megan's younger brother is a sophomore in high school. Now that she's gone away to college, it's really nice for us to have time with him, because so much of our energy has always been taken up trying to help Megan out. There always seemed to be some kind of crisis, and he honestly did not get the attention he would have gotten if she hadn't been his sister. Anyway, he's with us alone now, and it has been so nice—the meals, the conversations, everything.

Above all, remember that the complexities of family life, and of rubbing up against siblings, can be the best thing in the world for a quirky child. A child who needs help with social dynamics will find plenty in the direct speech of her siblings. The home environment should be a safe place to relax and have a little fun—free from some of the anxieties and strictures that apply during the school day. The love and understanding and tenderness of siblings at different points over the life span can mean a tremendous amount to your quirky child, and the returned affections of a quirky brother or sister can enrich siblings' lives.

Our son is a pretty understanding sort of kid, which isn't to say that his sister Chrissie doesn't drive him crazy from time to time. She does. But I've always had one rule: you don't have to love each other, you don't even have to like each other, but you must be polite to each other. That means, no name-calling, no excessive teasing, and especially no hitting, shoving, etcetera. Oddly, since I've given them the freedom to hate each other's guts, they seem to get along fine.

The Extended Family

For some parents of quirky kids, it is in their extended family that they find help and support and acceptance. For others, the most difficult, most tense, and most unpleasant day of any season is the family gathering.

Our relatives think, "She's just a wacky kid and will outgrow it." But I thought Chrissie needed more help, because I knew that day-to-day life with her was not just "wacky" but painful.

We're very concerned about where Aidan will go to school. We live in a tight community with my husband's extended family close by, which is a great support, but the city doesn't have the best services for a child like Aidan. It would be a really major decision to move, and there are no guarantees that it will work out.

Extended families, looking at your quirky child, will react according to their own histories, their expectations, their wisdom, and their experiences. In other words, everyone brings a lot of baggage.

My brother has a son with pervasive developmental disorder, and he and his wife basically locked themselves up. For years, they didn't come to any family celebrations because Paula couldn't tolerate the way people looked at their son. She thought she was seeing reproving looks—that everyone thought it was all her fault. They wouldn't go to the beach with the family in the summer anymore. That created a big rift in the extended family. Nobody could understand, she wouldn't tell them, and she just wouldn't come. The family interpreted it as Paula thinks she's too good for us, or she has something better to do. They didn't know it was painful for her. To some extent, Paula was right; people were blaming her. On one occasion, an old family friend said to me, "Look what they've done to that child." On the other hand, I've seen people with very impaired kids just taking them along, and if other people in the family ask questions or object, they say, "Well, this is my kid . . ." So some people can adapt to the potential social environment better than others.

Think carefully about exactly how you want to discuss your child's issues within the circle of your family. Of course, keep in mind that in most families, news travels. This is one place in which it is really worth deciding carefully what language you want to use and how up-to-date you want everyone to be. We aren't saying that you should keep the issues secret—though we admit to a certain bias toward keeping information limited, straightforward, and relatively practical—just that you should give some careful thought to what formulation makes you most comfortable and is likely to produce the kind of tolerance and acceptance that your child needs.

Some problems—like many learning issues, for example—really don't need to be discussed in great detail. Your child may be asked to explain why he's reading easier books than his cousin when she's younger, but chances are, that's a familiar kind of question for him, and he should have his answer ready. (A simple "Because she's a very good reader" is often effective.) Major social oddities are obviously going to be easier for people to take if they're prepared, as are any really noticeable speech or motor delays. If your extended family doesn't see you or your child regularly, the more you can do to prepare them for what he's going to be like, the easier you'll make it. It may be much less valuable to say, "They're thinking now that he looks like he has some features of obsessive-compulsive disorder, though they also see some Asperger-like behaviors, and of course, there are a lot of issues with fine motor weakness," than to say, "You'll notice he's totally obsessed with dinosaurs, and he'll absolutely talk your ear off. He simply doesn't know how to make conversation about any other subject, and he's got some obsessive little routines that the doctor wants us to go along with, so you may notice him dividing his food up into very tiny bites. And oh, yes, his table manners are still pretty lousy. I'd really appreciate it if you could sit him next to me so I can help him cut his turkey!"

FAMILY GATHERINGS AND CELEBRATIONS

Every child has at some point or another disgraced herself and her parents at a family wedding, Christmas, Thanksgiving, Bar Mitzvah, christening . . . You do get, thank heavens, some slack in the family circle. Parents tend to remember these disgraceful events that starred their own children more clearly than anyone else does! Family events are, after all, highly charged, often emotionally complex, and rarely full of people acting their most adult selves. However, you probably want to take part in the family traditions, in some form or other. You may also find that both you and your child receive special kinds of help and acceptance there. Most parents want their kids to be familiar with their cultural rituals. Most extended families think children are an important part of landmark events like weddings and even funerals.

There are also the bad ideas: no, your quirky, difficult, obsessional screamer of a three-year-old should not be the ring bearer at your sister's long-planned, everything-must-be-perfect formal evening wedding for five hundred of her closest friends. Got that?

Here are some general tips for strategizing your way through family gatherings:

- Anticipate the event and the expectations as much as possible. Think about things that might set your child off—loud music, camera flashes, crowds. Talk it through with the child, bring essential supplies (earplugs, a familiar and comforting book), and praise good behavior extravagantly.

- Talk in detail about the rules of behavior in an unfamiliar setting: the getting up and sitting down in a church or synagogue, the need to be quiet while a ceremony is going on. If you know a big event is coming up and your child is unaccustomed to religious services, it might help to take her once or twice just so the whole atmosphere is somewhat familiar.

We took John to this big Bar Mitzvah in Chicago. The music was so loud, he just started crying, so it was good we were staying in the same place, and we could take him up to the room. It turned out that there were lots of little boys who were not exactly interested in the big party and would rather play Pokémon cards than eat a wonderful dinner. Now when these events come up, we plan an escape route so we can all enjoy ourselves.

- As a general rule, at family-only celebrations, the custom is that you put up with everyone's quirks and peculiarities, but at big formal events to which many people are invited, different rules may apply. If it's a highly elegant dinner, and a child who can't manage a knife and fork is going to give offense, then you might want to think twice about whether it would be kinder to your child and to yourselves to arrange things differently. This will probably have something to do with whether your child actually wants to go and will feel bad about missing the event. Don't start a family feud over an invitation that means nothing to the child.

- Plan who is going to be with your quirky child the whole time you are at the event. These are, by and large, not the kids you blithely send off to the children's table and never think about again. One of the parents, or a genuinely dependable older sibling, has to be responsible for keeping an eye on how things are going at all times, interceding at danger signs, making sure that food and drink are manageable, and generally troubleshooting.

Right around now, I'm anticipating the holidays and the get-togethers. I feel we shouldn't expect to eat anything because we will need to help Aidan through the events. All those other kids running around and playing. We don't expect him to play with the other kids, but we always have to worry that he could become overstimulated and start one of his tantrums.

- Think about who might be able to help your child enjoy the event. Is there a special relationship with Grandpa or a cheerful aunt who seems to enjoy listening to your daughter talk endlessly about cats? Ask ahead of time if that person can pay her some extra attention. Sometimes there is a quirky adult in the crowd who is just as interested in iguanas as your child or who will play chess or otherwise engage a child to your utter delight and relief!

- Prepare your child for any questions he is likely to be asked. Children with social difficulties may find it intimidating to have lots of semi-strangers coming up to claim acquaintance and ask them questions. The fact is, adults tend to ask the same questions over and over of children: "How old are you?" "What grade are you in?" "What's your favorite subject?" Or they make even more personal remarks that aren't really questions: "Isn't that a pretty dress you're wearing?" If you can rehearse your child in giving a few simple answers and even make a little game of it ("Let's see how many people tell you you've gotten taller!"), you can take away a lot of the tension. Absolutely stereotyped repetitive conversations, after all, can play right into a quirky child's social style, and you should take advantage of this. Many children love being let in on the joke of adult predictability. For some, it can be a real social lifesaver to know they have pat answers ready for the most common questions.

Sam should be going into fourth grade, and he's going into third. He's very aware of this, so when people ask him what grade he's in, he says, "Well, my school doesn't have grades," and he kind of goes on from there about his school. I didn't teach him this—but it works, it distracts people. "If we had grades, I would be going into fourth, but we don't have grades."

- Have a getaway route planned. There is truly nothing worse than playing out a bad scene with your whole extended family looking on.

- Make a parental plan: who's going to be responsible for taking the child out if things don't work, and what's the first-line destination? Playing Game Boy in the lobby? Going out to the car for a game of cards? Some people swear by some quick physical stimulation. Try twenty jumping jacks in the lobby or run around the block. Try anything! Work it out and agree on it, so you don't end up with a big marital argument in the middle of somebody else's wedding.

- Think a little about what you're going to say if people make any comments. If you don't want to go into detail, especially at a large event where lots of the people are not in any way close to you, then don't. Even if your child acts up and has to be taken out, you still don't owe people anything more than a prompt and heartfelt apology—a specific apology for the behavior, not a general apology for your child's overall weirdness, let alone his very existence.

AUNTS, UNCLES, COUSINS

In many families, each new generation of cousins serves as a kind of field of comparison. Brothers and sisters who are themselves close, or who are being kept in close contact by their mutual parents, may find themselves feeling either pleasantly supported or miserably competitive—and sometimes both in syncopation. How are you supposed to cope with your sister's absolutely perfect gold-medal children? How about with your brother's youngest, who looks to you suspiciously like your own quirky child at that age? Or what about if there's already another quirky child—or quirky adult—in the family?

My sister started giving me all kinds of diagnoses of Lisa. Well, her son is a problem, he has seizures, he's probably on about fifteen to sixteen medications. When Lisa was diagnosed with sensory integration dysfunction, she kind of descended on me: "You gotta call this person and get this done and call that person and get that done." And when my son had a fever seizure, she descended on me:

"Oh, that isn't a febrile seizure, that was something else, and you're going to have to deal with all these seizures." She just terrified me.

- People need to be sensitive about the differences among children. Everyone is always aware of the comparisons, and the parents of an obviously way-ahead-of-her-age and brilliant and socially poised ten-year-old have a certain obligation to roll their eyes and complain about her bad moods at home—or her terrible taste in pop music. Complaining about how tired it makes them driving her to all these state championship swimming meets does not count. Of course, your sister or your brother may not adhere to this rule—in which case, you have little recourse other than to smile, praise the child in question to the skies, and absolutely and positively refuse to be drawn into any comparative conversations. "He's doing really well, and we're proud of him" is a perfectly adequate remark to make about your own child. It is by any reckoning better manners than making everyone listen to a long list of prizes and achievements.

People looking in from the outside—grandparents, aunts and uncles, classmates' parents—they think they have some advice for you. They think they have an answer you haven't found, because they were successful with their kids and you aren't. It's like people without kids giving advice about kids, only worse, because I know that their experience was nothing like mine in raising her. None of that advice applies, and it's infuriating to have to listen to it sometimes. I always feel that the subtext is that she would be more normal if only we did this or that.

- In a large family with a whole group of cousins of similar age, the quirky child may appear as a real and obvious outlier. Maybe all the rest, younger and older, are out on the lawn playing touch football, and your child is over there lining up his cars or reading that book about the Civil War that he already knows by heart. It's your job to stick up for him, stand by his preferences, and help him find an identity within the family. Maybe you can teach him a little about touch football so he'll feel comfortable playing or keeping score. If not, maybe you can include him in the adult conversation or link him up with one particular relative who is in no way interested in the football game. Maybe he can help Grandma put the marshmallows on the sweet potatoes.

My sister-in-law has three kids, all high-achieving in every sport. Each plays multiple instruments and practices each of them every day. She's got it all planned out for them to go to a good college. Sometimes she asks why my kids aren't playing an instrument. She just doesn't get it! She doesn't understand that it's all we can do to get through homework.

- Be careful about the temptation to compare your quirky child to other quirky relatives. It's sometimes reassuring and even delightful to look at a beloved, if eccentric, uncle and see links to your child, but it also poses certain dangers. Sure, if Aunt Molly also loved astronomy as a child and could name all the constellations, too, and now she's an aerospace engineer, that's a fine comparison to make. Whether or not your son actually has much in common with Aunt Molly, it may make for an easy way for the family to see and accept his peculiarities. But let's face it, if Uncle Harry is still living in that strange little room up over his parents' garage, and if no one likes sitting next to him because he spills so much when he eats, well, that's not a particularly nice destiny to wish on your daughter with the poor table manners at age ten. You don't want your family to make a comparison like this and thereby, in a sense, write your child off. And you don't want to be in any danger of doing it yourself, either.

- Once again, cousins and aunts and uncles can mean a lot to a quirky child. They are a built-in social network, a group of people he will see over and over in his life who will, with luck, accept him and embrace him and acknowledge him as one of the tribe. Quirky children, who sometimes seem to be outsiders in any group in which they find themselves, need that feeling of belonging and of family connection.

GRANDPARENTS

Most of us grow up with the certainty that whatever our parents may believe, our grandparents think we are perfect. The world is full of bumper stickers that say things like, "IF I HAD KNOWN HOW WONDERFUL GRANDCHILDREN WERE, I WOULD HAVE HAD THEM FIRST!" It can be particularly valuable for a quirky child to know that kind of unconditional adoration, that sense that just by coming into the world, she has accomplished a miracle. Unfortunately, it can also happen that grandparents can find a quirky child's eccentricities or developmental slownesses hard to tolerate and, maybe in part because of a childrearing mind-set that evolved before many of these diagnoses were commonly known, may be somewhat inclined to blame everything on parental laxity or on other aspects of the way you are treating your child.

My parents are very clear that the problem is day care. They never put their children in day care and can't understand how anyone could do it. This is their way of understanding her developmental delays—that she doesn't get enough of our attention, that it's because we put her in one of "those places." In other words, we brought this on ourselves.

Grandparents can mean a tremendous amount in the life of a quirky kid. They can be his biggest and most sincere cheerleaders or your absolutely life-saving baby-sitters or the people who provide a little family context and perspective. After all, they knew *you* when you were young, and they may see some connections! Obviously, this is all highly dependent on geography; on whether they see you every other day, every month or so, or once a year; and also on their situation in life and state of health. But for many families, even the grandparents you see only every so often are eager to help any way they can. However, depending on your relationship with them and their beliefs, they may be the very last people you want to let in on the details of how you are managing with your child.

My mother-in-law doesn't know John is on meds. I feel it's none of her business, and I guess I'm not entirely immune to other people's opinions. I just don't want to hear what she might say about it. When John was little, her take on him was, "He's fine, and why are you taking him to all these appointments?" But now she'll say, "Oh, that was so awful when he wouldn't eat and he wouldn't talk!"

My husband's parents are very supportive of everything with Jack and Rebecca; in fact, they're in a grandparent support group. For a while, they were bringing home articles about crazy diets and nutritional supplements, but I don't go in for that stuff, so I asked them to stop it. Now they bring different kinds of information. My mom, on the other hand, has the "He'll outgrow it any day" attitude toward Jack and thinks there is nothing wrong with Rebecca at all.

Many parents with quirky kids speak about a grandparent who refuses to believe that anything is wrong or of concern or even different. If the children are academically smart, and especially if they have prominent splinter skills, many grandparents will define them as geniuses and accept them—and boast about them—in those terms.

Aidan's paternal grandparents are very interested in learning—Grandmom is a teacher, Grandpa is a librarian—and they are so pleased with how bright he is and how early he knew the alphabet. He can do no wrong.

Our general advice would be to allow grandparents the pleasure of believing—and boasting—that their grandchild is a genius, while presenting her problems and your concerns as the eccentricity that everyone accepts often goes along with that genius state. The grandparent who believes that she is nursing a budding Einstein is a grandparent who will be able to provide that happy unconditional love and pride that can mean so much to a child— especially a child regarded by others as the family problem!

With children who are more delayed and less easily seen as eccentric geniuses, grandparents, just like parents, have to confront the loss of their own fantasies. Many grandparents are heavily invested in their grandchildren's following certain paths or mastering certain skills. You will need to remember the evolutionary process by which you modified some of your own expectations in order to be tolerant and helpful as your parents modify theirs. Try hard not to get too angry at a grandparent who perhaps does not see your child every day and who seems to be persistently puzzled by his lack of developmental progress. It's a hard personal journey, and a little sympathy and support will go a long way.

The other interesting issue that often arises with grandparents is the familial reverberations. Many a parent has been astonished to learn that he himself (or maybe his brother) was highly quirky in his youth, in ways that perhaps did not have a name back then but that resemble or shadow or interestingly contrast the ways in which his child is now developing. Other grandparents, having staked their claim in some way on their own children's normalcy, having refused to acknowledge problems and eccentricities the first time around, are not about to open that retrospective can of worms now.

My husband's older sister was very developmentally delayed, both speech and motor, as a child in the 1950s. I remember their mother telling me things about her, but she never herself related it to my kids' being the way they were. She never wanted to go that far. Her daughter had had both speech and motor delays and some significant learning difficulties that must have been simply impossible to deal with then. So that's a forty-five-year-old story—and you would think there would be all these bells and whistles when they saw our son and all his delays, but no. It was like there was something in their family code that kept them from talking about it.

My husband is one of three kids. His brother was very hyper as a child but became very depressed as an adult and committed suicide in his thirties. My mother-in-law recognizes her deceased son in her grandson, Ben, and is very supportive of me and of my husband for all we do to help him. She says she wishes she had been stronger to have gotten her son the help he needed when he was young.

There can be all kinds of complexities involved in negotiating the emotional balance among the three generations, but grandparents and grandchildren are generally held together by strong bonds. Grandparents, like parents, are in this for the long haul, and for many families struggling with complicated quirky children, grandparents provide some welcome help and hope and respite. Grandparents are often the baby-sitters who aren't really baby-sitters—because it's a treat to visit them or to be visited by them, or simply because they're the ones doing this for love, not money.

Some general points about grandparents as baby-sitters:

- Teach routines all you want, but it is a time-honored truth that at Grandma's house—or when Grandma is baby-sitting—all bets are off, and all kinds of treats happen. As long as your child is happy, relax and enjoy it!

- A grandparent who is going to do any significant amount of baby-sitting needs to know how to handle peculiar or alarming behaviors—though don't be surprised if you come home to the serene report, "He's always just as good as gold with me!"

- If your child is engaged in an intensive behavioral program, anyone who spends a significant amount of time with her will need to be educated in the system you are using. This includes grandparents, who can often find it even more difficult to respond as the program has prescribed.

- Make reasonable allowances for age and health. Some difficult quirky kids really take a lot of running, a lot of lifting and carrying, a high level of energy. If you have a grandparent who is eager to help out but maybe limited by health or energy level, keep those baby-sitting visits short and sweet—or ask for some late-night hours, after the child is asleep, and go out to a late show or a candlelight dinner. A couple of families we talked with have used a younger teenager and a grandparent together as a "baby-sitting team." This can take the pressure off grandparents for tasks requiring a lot of physical stamina and provide some good on-the-job training for the teenager at the same time.

- Grandparents can help you make sure all siblings get some special adult attention. Don't let the "problem child" monopolize all the baby-sitting time that grandparents offer. Make sure the other siblings get some time alone at Grandma's house or a special outing once in a while.

We hear again and again in our pediatric practice about grandparents who refuse to acknowledge that anything is wrong or different. It's every parent's own decision whether you need to pursue the question. A grandparent who blames your childrearing practices for any problems your child encounters can really wear you down. You may find yourself wanting to do some educating— or some screaming. But a grandparent who is letting you know that as far as she is concerned, these things don't need diagnoses, that her grandchild is his own special self and just needs to be loved and appreciated—well, that grandparent is correctly representing the thinking of her own parenting days and is to be cherished and appreciated.

Parents

It's time now to say some specific things about how life with your child can affect your own life and your spirits and your relationships with the significant adults in your own life (your spouse, your partner, your good friends) and about how you might want to think about protecting and cherishing them all, so that you can do as good a job as possible at everything that matters most— including taking care of your quirky kid!

SINGLE PARENTS

Single parents have it a lot harder, no question about it. All the additional pressures and sorrows and tensions of life with a quirky child devolve on that one parent. There may not be another adult easily available with whom you can discuss the child at length, strategize, and look for help and comfort. Try to develop a community of friends or relatives who know your child (or children) and can offer support and respite when you need it. You'll need a regular break from doing it on your own. Don't wait until you've completely lost your cool before setting up some time just for you. Do it regularly. There are support groups in most communities for single parents and even some for single parents of quirky kids! This is a long haul. The more support you garner for yourself, the better off you and your children will be.

YOU AND YOUR PARTNER

A quirky child can stress a relationship mightily. We have certainly seen couples polarize and even split up over the disagreements and logistical pressures of regular childrearing plus. Other couples are simply so stressed by the rigors of life at home that one parent starts spending less and less time there, the other resents it more and more, and the couple's own relationship ends up in trouble.

What created marital tension was this: his dad believed Jacob was normal and didn't agree with me about an evaluation. Meanwhile, I was very concerned. Now my husband and I have separated, and the stress around Jacob and his issues was one of the main factors.

What can you do to prevent these problems or to deal with these disagreements and with the extra stresses of daily life?

- Acknowledge the stresses and their dangers. Help each other through the process of acknowledgment and/or diagnosis. Talk about your hopes and your disappointments and your fears.
- Fights and even divorces can happen over the anger that is generated when one parent is more concerned than the other. One thinks something is really wrong, the other that it's nothing and the child will outgrow it. You

probably cannot rear a child together, as any kind of partners, unless you find a way to formulate and understand that child that makes sense to both of you. That may take work and expert help. As in all partnerships, nothing is ever completely equal; one of you is likely to do the lion's share of the work involved in parenting a quirky child. There are certain advantages to this: one of you will get to know the professionals, the therapies, and a community of similar families. Two of you do not need to be at every appointment. Be careful, however: too strict a division of labor regarding your child can leave the more involved parent feeling isolated and overwhelmed and the less involved parent excluded and marginalized.

- Give careful and respectful attention to each other's opinions, both about what's going on with your child and about the best way to address her needs.

- At the beginning of any new therapy or treatment, it's important that both parents meet the doctor or the therapist or the teacher and agree that they feel comfortable with the person and the plan.

- Give true and serious attention to the logistics, the who-is-going-to-pick-her-up-after-physical-therapy-when-it's-also-Peter's-Boy-Scout-night questions. It's rarely possible for one parent to handle these completely unaided, whether that means getting help from the other parent, from a baby-sitter, or from a friend.

- Talk frankly about your financial situation and the implications of your child's issues. If you are thinking that one parent may need to stop working or cut back on hours, discuss the impact on the family finances. Many extra expenses come along with quirkiness—therapies, special after-school programs, medications, private schools, tutors, baby-sitters to help take the edge off the after-school hours. How can you budget for these additions? If you are actually considering relocating, do you both agree on a town that you think has good public school programs that might be right for your child?

- Take care of each other. You love each other, you both love your child, and your child's best bet in life is probably for the two of you to stay together, to keep loving each other and taking care of him together. This is a hard road to go alone. Try very deliberately for some conversation every day that is not purely logistic in nature and that does not focus on the issues of your quirky child. Don't let your sex life become completely swallowed up by the busyness, fatigue, frustration, and sometimes depression that can accompany life with a quirky child.

I can't say that Chrissie's disorder has taken a toll on our marriage. We have our moments—we had about a month of them recently—but in general, we put our marriage first.

- Pay attention to the adjustments and efforts that your spouse is making: to the endless patience with which your husband practices question-and-answer with your daughter or the clever way your wife has reorganized the bathroom so your son can reach everything he needs.
- If your own relationship is under severe stress—if you're fighting all the time or not talking at all or never having sex—see a therapist. Get help as soon as you realize there is a problem. Be on the lookout for signs of emotional overload in yourself and in each other. Depression in parents of quirky kids can go unrecognized because it seems so reasonable to be sad. Depression can wreak even more havoc on your family, so if you are worried about yourself or your partner, check it out.

ENVYING OTHER CHILDREN

Many parents find that in the course of watching their children at school or at sports or at other activities, or in spending time with friends, they become at least intermittently possessed by envy of other parents with "normal" kids. You can watch your best friend's son hit a home run or play his violin, and you can think, "Surely this is the child I was meant to have." Or you can listen to another parent complaining at length about her obviously typical daughter's obviously typical whininess, and you can think, "Honey, you have no idea!"

Family vacations with Caitlin and our extended families are very difficult: there are multiple families with about fifteen people, lots of kids. I usually become very sad and realize all over again how much easier it is to raise "regular" kids.

Almost all parents go through various disappointments and challenges to their most precious heartfelt fantasies when they watch their kids grow up.

However, when you find daily life shadowed by ugly moments of resenting all the other parents in the world, whose kids seem to be just fine, and resenting all their typical, normal, perfect, high-achieving kids, remember:

- First of all, this isn't true. You know it isn't true. Every family has issues. Every child has issues.

- Second of all, you don't want to turn into one of those awful people who goes around hoping to hear bad news: *Yes, sure, he hit a home run, but he's on five different kinds of psychotropic medications! Sure she plays the violin like an angel, but did you hear how she went after her sister with a knife?* If those stories become your secret comforts, something is wrong inside.

- Even if you hold on to your sense of perspective and your basic good nature, there are going to be moments when you feel yourself ready to burst with the emotion that comes with seeing what seems to come easily to every other child or with hearing the fond complaints of parents who have no idea what life is like over on the quirky side of the playground.

- Come up with a couple of basic strategies, statements that explain what you're feeling but don't upset anyone else. You are entitled to a rueful smile and a wistful comment: "I look at those kids and I really, really wish my daughter could enjoy the beach, but that's who she is and there's no changing it."

- Do not, ever and under any circumstances, rain on another parent's parade. When someone else is glowing with one of those proud parental moments, dizzy with the joy of a child who has just hit a ball or spoken to the company in Chinese or buttoned himself into his first tux and gone off to the prom or gotten into Columbia—well, that is not the moment for you to say, "My child has problems. My child may never do that particular thing," and by implication, "How dare you be so insensitive as to let me see your exultation!"

- Perhaps the hardest moments for many parents are not actually the achievements of someone else's child. What can actually be much harder are the public moments (at the pool, at the circus, at the playground) when it can just seem that every other child in the world knows how to be a child and have fun—except yours.

- Practice reality. Make a joke of it when you can. Relish your child's quirks and eccentricities. As long as you can find pleasure and joy in the child you have and the life you lead, by all means give yourself permission to feel sad sometimes for the child you don't have and the life you didn't get.

YOU AND YOUR JOB

What about your career, your job, your professional future? Some parents' work lives continue on much the same trajectory, quirky kid or no. Some parents make modifications. Some give up their jobs. Some change jobs and end up devoting their lives to some particular aspect of the quirky-child universe.

For me, I find my job is very grounding, and I like the job I have despite petty annoyances. I know that if I didn't get to get out of this house and go to my office, where I feel like a grown-up and have a certain amount of authority and control, I wouldn't be able to come home and take care of my kids.

I am an artist, but my work schedule just had to change because of having a child with so many needs. I have spent so much of my life in doctors' offices and waiting rooms, and so much of our money has gone to getting help that our insurance doesn't cover. But the fact is that we believe that we have helped her, that she is doing as well as she could be doing, and she could be doing much worse.

There are plenty of parents, most often but not always mothers, who end up scaling back their jobs or quitting altogether because of the exigencies and stresses of caring for a quirky child. This can happen because one parent has a job to which he—or she—is not particularly attached or just because the logistics of family life get too complicated to accommodate more than one parent with a serious job. Clearly, this has financial implications for the family. In addition, it may mean that that parent becomes more and more tightly tied to that child.

It is, of course, perfectly true that tending to a quirky child can take any amount of time—as can tending to any child. There are plenty of mothers who quit their jobs and devote themselves full-time to tending nonquirky children, too. There may be some quirky children so complicated, or some situations so difficult to manage, that a full-time parental pilot is the only—or the best—solution.

I quit my job for a while to spend more time with Jacob and to get him the help he needed. I am now trying to restart my career. It was the right thing to do at the time, and I do not regret it.

Other parents, with high-powered or demanding jobs, sometimes use those jobs to escape their less-than-relaxing homes, their demanding and puzzling children. When one parent does this, the quirky child—and indeed, the whole family—loses a necessary balance. When both parents do it, the quirky child is given over to therapists, baby-sitters, doctors, and teachers—all of whom may be supremely dedicated and loving, but none of whom can take your place as parents.

Let us confess our own frank prejudice, as pediatricians and mothers. If you can manage it, it's generally better for both parents to keep their jobs, however modified, and to avoid that strict division of labor which so often seems to follow when one person earns the money and the other cares for the kids. In other words, mothers (or rarely, fathers) who work and who like their jobs should not be pushed or shamed or harassed into quitting their jobs to become full-time advocates, therapists, chauffeurs, and tutors to their quirky children.

By keeping your job, you bring in more money, and you keep the marriage a little more balanced. It isn't all the financial clout on one side and all the parental clout on the other. You also protect yourself from becoming completely identified as the mom of a quirky kid. You will have someplace in your life where you can go and be someone else.

I love to go to work. Sometimes I get so entrenched in the appointments and evaluations, I forget that I have another life. It's such a relief to go to work and talk with other adults about anything. I find there is more of me to give when I get home, because my universe is greater than the "mom of a child with differences."

There are lots of different ways to balance your children and your professional ambitions and opportunities and your finances and your marital and family logistics. Speaking as mothers who have found it worthwhile and psychically necessary to pursue reasonably demanding careers while rearing our own children, we appreciate firsthand the rewards of taking your work seriously, even while you take your children seriously.

MAKING IT YOUR MISSION

And then there are the parents—again, usually but not always the mothers—who take on their children's issues and needs with such energy and thoroughness that they end up making some aspect of having, or being, a quirky child into a lifework. Sometimes an unexpected twist in the road of your life really does show you the way to a larger destiny. There are parents who have taken on Asperger's syndrome or school issues or sensory integration dysfunction and found ways to use their own knowledge and experience to help other parents and other children and even to change the world a little bit. We salute them and we honor them, and we cite many of their books and Web sites and organizations in this book, hoping to hook you up with people who will understand all the different aspects of the parental journey on which you are embarked, because they have been this way themselves.

We do offer a brief caveat: making your own single quirky child into your life's mission can be dangerous. If your whole life becomes taken up with and taken over by the needs of your child, by fighting her battles and ferrying her to her appointments, if you're there in school almost as much as she is, and you spend your spare time surfing the Net for more information on her disorder, this may be unhealthy—unhealthy for you, for your primary relationship, for your other children, and even, perhaps, for your quirky child.

This may sound harsh or unsympathetic. But we have observed that when a parent becomes almost obsessed with a quirky child, the family ends up out of whack, and the child himself has to bear the significant burden of that parent's full-time adult concentration. It's not always an easy thing to be another person's cause or the object of another person's every thought or another person's reason for living.

ONE FINAL NOTE TO PARENTS

Family life is hard at times for everyone. Making a couple work is hard. Figuring out how to blend careers and adult ambitions and children's lives is hard. And taking care of a quirky child is hard in itself and can make all of these other jobs that much harder.

I ended up myself on Paxil at the end of his fourth-grade year when he had come down with obsessive-compulsive disorder. It's another diagnosis. We were talking about putting him in residential treatment. I remember driving him in the car, thinking maybe it would be better if we just went off the road, let's end it, and I said to myself, "Time to go to the psychiatrist and get antidepressants." You kind of have to realize that it can take a long time, and you don't even know what's the place you're going to get to.

This past year, I realized that I was doing too much of this alone. My husband's work schedule required that he travel a lot, and I was home trying to keep everything going—school and homework, piano practicing for my other kids, various appointments and medication evaluations, the works. I gradually became totally overwhelmed and had real trouble getting pleasure out of anything. I got some help, but more important, I realized that I need to set limits for myself. I can only do so much for my son, and sometimes that means I just can't do everything.

If you find yourself in trouble, get help. Marriage counseling, pastoral help, psychiatric help—whatever you need to make it through. Do not think of the responsibility of caring for a quirky child as something that you are going to tough out. Don't feel guilty that you have needs of your own. Talk to your friends, your spouse, your doctor. Call a hot line if you have to or a parent support group. Borrow money from your parents if you have to or sell off a few pieces of the family silver or take a credit-union loan at work, but get help. Everyone feels overwhelmed and depressed at times, but if you're chronically overwhelmed, chronically sad, unable to take pleasure in the things that usually make you happy—or if you even *fleetingly* contemplate hurting or killing yourself—please, get help. You will be glad you did, and you will be able, once again, to be what you need to be, to help the people depending on you, and to face another day.

The people to whom you are most closely connected, and who, after you, feel the strongest sense of family attachment and communion with your child, can greatly help you along the way. If you can find a way to glean support and perspective and a helping hand at critical moments from aunts and uncles and grandparents, you will have made the world a more connected, more welcoming place for yourself and also for your child.

Content

References and Resources

Greene, Ross W. *The Explosive Child: A New Approach for Understanding and Parenting Easily Frustrated, Chronically Inflexible Children.* 2nd ed. New York: HarperCollins, 2001. When tantrums are a prominent feature of your child's package, Dr. Greene's book is a great resource full of strategies to make life easier for everyone.

The Morning News. This periodical, published by the Jenison Public Schools, in Jenison, Michigan, and the Gray Center for Social Learning and Understanding, is a publication "dedicated to people with autistic spectrum disorders and those who work alongside them to improve mutual understanding." If you find Carol Gray's techniques helpful, these four quarterly issues are usually small workbooks for parents or professionals to work on together with kids to help address the predictable difficulties that will arise in the social arena. To subscribe, phone (616) 457-8955, fax (616) 457-4070, or write to *The Morning News,* Jenison High School, 2140 Bauer Rd., Jenison MI 49428.

Tanguay, Pamela. *Nonverbal Learning Disabilities at Home: A Parent's Guide.* London: Jessica Kingsley Publishers, 2001. This is a basic book about living with an NLD child, with advice about everything from buttons and zippers to understanding the theory of mind and how it manifests in day-to-day life.

Turecki, Stanley, and Leslie Tonner. *The Difficult Child.* 2nd ed. New York: Bantam, 2000. Written by a child psychiatrist, this book is the resource for a full discussion of temperament.

Whitney, Rondalyn Varney. *Bridging the Gap: Raising a Child with Nonverbal Learning Disorder.* New York: Perigee, 2002. This book, written by an occupational therapist, is another excellent resource for parents of an NLD child, with clear explanations and examples of terms and advice about helping the child along in life at home, in the world, and at school.

6

○ ○ ● ○

Choosing a School

As pediatricians, we look at life at school and school performance as essential measures of whether our patients are able to manage in their worlds. A child who is physically healthy but seriously unhappy, academically troubled, or failing in school is a child we worry about, and we talk to the teachers and the principal and the special ed teacher and the speech therapist, trying to figure out what is getting in the way of success and learning.

Making decisions about educating your child may present you with some of the most difficult hurdles you'll face as a parent. Making those decisions well will mean tailoring your child's every-day, all-day setting in a way that helps him function, adjust, and learn. We start from the assumption that a quirky child's experience in school has enormous potential to help the child learn to use all his skills but also from the realization that both the academic and the social aspects of school can be terribly hard on these kids.

The decisions about what kind of setting is most appropriate can change over time, like everything else with regard to your child. Here are some general thoughts on the process:

- *Take it slow and be open to change.* Don't let yourself be convinced that you have to make a permanent decision right at the beginning or that a "wrong" decision in kindergarten will have lifelong implications. All children grow and change, and quirky kids change in very unpredictable ways. Educational planning works best when you are looking realistically at where your child is and what she needs—right now. You can think about the longer-term future, of course, but don't set your heart too strongly on any one school or program. Plan for the next year or two, stay alert to how things are going, and be ready to reconsider.

• *Know your child and how to advocate for your child.* The more you know about how your child's mind works, and about how the school year is going, the more likely you are to see a problem early—and be able to address it. The clearer you are on the different roles of the people at the school, on all the available resources, and on the school's chain of command, the more effective you will be at making changes when they need to be made.

• *A rough few months in school—or even a rough year—is not the end of the world.* Almost *all* kids, quirky or not, have a rough year or two somewhere along the way—a less-than-ideal teacher, a difficult social situation, or just a period when the child's individual learning style and interests are a bad fit with what the school requires. It's not by any means necessarily the right response to change schools immediately or even to assume that all problems are the school's fault. A rough year can be a growth experience for a quirky child—or at least a valuable lesson in how to take certain setbacks in stride and keep on going.

There is no tried-and-true educational program that works for all quirky children, but you will come across parents and teachers with very strong feelings about what is right and what is wrong. Your job as a parent means taking into account individual learning styles; developmental, social, and interpersonal differences; and in some cases, mental health issues. Then you need to stay in close touch to make sure things keep working as your child grows and changes.

Some parents looking at schools will need to focus most intensely on academic programming, on the style and structure of the classroom, the backgrounds and orientation of the teachers, the academic philosophy of the school, or the availability of special education resources. Others might feel that their children will do fine with any good standard academic program but will have special concerns about social or athletic expectations or about the size or the general atmosphere of the school. The group of children we're discussing here, after all, includes children with learning disabilities, children with academic areas in which they shine, and children with a wide variety of behavioral and social issues—and all these may describe a single child! The parent's task, then, may include balancing all these considerations while looking realistically at what is available, affordable, and practical in the family's real-life situation.

Some of you will be looking at only one possible school—maybe because it's the only one around—and trying to tailor an educational program for your child within that school. Others will consider a few different schools, and some parents, especially in urban areas, may feel there are too many choices. Whatever your range of school choices, we want to help you think about a program that works for your child. We've collected stories of educational settings that work well for a wide range of quirky children. Finding the right school is a hard job, but it's a job that has been done successfully by parents working under all kinds of constraints.

Brian went to a private progressive elementary school. He went to a school for special learning for seventh and eighth grade—very small class size, a lot of social support, lots of tutoring, the capacity to individualize curriculum beyond what a resource room would be able to do. Then he moved back into a regular private high school, and he's doing fine. When I was in elementary school, I was considered not quite average. I was always in the lower reading group. I didn't come across as smart until science and math started to be important, in fifth grade, and I got a chance to shine there. I've said to Brian, "Clearly, this is the stuff you're good at, and when you get to high school or college, you're going to shine." And now people are calling him for advice on their homework.

Getting Started

- Know the territory: what kinds of classrooms and curriculum choices are available in your local public school system, which schools have what services for children with special needs. Go to whatever your community offers in the way of a "school fair," collect information from the school district, and visit the schools that interest you most.

- Contact your school district's special education office, where you will find specific information about schools in your neighborhood that offer evaluation and support services for a child who needs extra help.
- If you are considering private schools, you need to collect information on the possibilities. You may have to collect this school by school, or there may be an "independent-school fair," or you may find yourself looking to a consultant.
- If your child is already in day care or preschool or early intervention, talk to his teacher about your concerns and about her recommendations.
- Talk to other parents. You'll get useful information and may well discover options you haven't heard about anywhere else. If you can find some parents who have quirky kids a few years older than your own, they will be a valuable resource.

Gathering Information

Consider your options. Examine your own assumptions about how you want your child educated. You may be a staunch believer in public education—with fervent political and social convictions—only to find that there is no public school nearby that will fit your child. Parents who believe devoutly in the advantages of private schools may come to the conclusion that this particular child would be better served in a public school, where certain services are legally mandated and where the teachers might have lots of experience with special-needs kids. Or speaking of devout belief, you may have cherished the hope that your fantasy child would thrive in parochial school and come to the conclusion that, for your real child, it would be a disaster.

You definitely want to collect everything you can on what's available to you through the public schools. Don't assume that your local school will be able to provide information on the full range of options available within the public school system. Talk with other parents, talk with teachers, talk with the therapists or doctors or other professionals who know your child best. Ask for advice, follow up on leads, and collect as many recommendations as you can.

Some families have used educational advocates who act as consultants and are knowledgeable about school options in the area. If you choose to go this route, interview a couple of potential advocates first to be sure you can work together and ascertain that they have worked with other children with similar needs.

We found a school for Abby after long consultations with an advocate and the school itself. The school identifies itself as a school for mild-to-moderate learning disabilities. The consultant said other families she had worked with had been very pleased. We spent three years there struggling because it turned out that the learning disability the school is most comfortable with is dyslexia, and Abby is not dyslexic. Her nonverbal learning issues affect every aspect of her being, and trying to learn in an environment that is devoted to something else has been too hard. We are moving on for middle school to a school that, at least for right now, seems to understand her issues and embrace her anyway.

WHAT ARE THE OPTIONS?

Whether you are looking at public schools or private schools, you need to approach the school with a consumer attitude: are you offering what my child needs? Here are some questions to address as you look the school over:

- Does it provide specialists to help kids with learning differences or with physical, speech and language, or occupational therapy needs? Although all public schools will, in some form or other, many nonspecialized private schools may not. Is there a resource room? A reading center? A counseling service? An on-site school nurse?
- If these resources and specialists are available, just how available are they? Full-time? Once a week?
- What is the school's track record with those special education specialists and occupational and physical therapists? Have key staff members been there for a while, or is there a lot of turnover?
- What do parents think about the skills and flexibility of the specialists? About their accessibility and availability to discuss children's progress?
- How successfully does the school cope with children who don't fit into neat categories—who need special help in some areas but may have strong skills in others?
- Can the school foster a special interest or talent? Is the curriculum for math or music (or whatever your child's skill) adequate and engaging enough to keep your child on track?

Your Child's Social and Sensory Needs

In addition to your child's learning style and academic needs, you have to pay attention to what's going to happen outside the classroom. Because many quirky kids are of at least average intelligence, academic demands are often the least of their worries, especially in the early years of preschool and elementary school. So it can be the playground, the gym, or the cafeteria that makes a given school a good possibility or an impossibility.

The following considerations are of general concern to most quirky children:

- Size of the school—and therefore of the crowds at recess or at lunch. How many children in the school? How many children in a classroom? Think about how your child copes in a gymnasium or cafeteria with hundreds of kids and deafening noise levels.

John's experience in first grade was colored by the size of the school and the noise level. He found the cafeteria especially difficult because there were hundreds of kids. The noise level was very high, and he had trouble supporting himself on a cafeteria bench.

- How about the playground at recess time? How closely are the children supervised? How much organized activity versus how much running around? Will that fit with your child's activity level, social skills, and attention span? Do the teachers seem to be aware of the social dynamics, and will someone reach out to a child if he is unhappy?
- What's the general noise level? Is there a public-address system that injects frequent, loud, and sudden interruptions?
- How big are the classrooms? How crowded? Is there enough classroom staff to manage the needs of the kids or to help negotiate conflict? Does it feel organized, as if there is a system and the kids know what it is?

David's school, which is a small private school for children with special needs, does not have kids with behavior problems, which is good for David, who gets very distressed and anxious when kids are causing trouble. They have very clear and direct expectations about what they do and how they do it, and David likes that. There's very little wiggle room. He attends a sensory motor group where he is learning about himself, his likes and dislikes. For example, he will now comment, "I don't like this kind of shirt. I don't like loud noises." And he will come up with strategies to help himself when he feels uncomfortable.

- How are the classrooms set up? Desks in rows? Small groups of tables pulled together? Is there a range of styles?
- Are there kids in socks or slippers in a cozy "reading corner" with pillows?
- Is there a policy regarding teasing and bullying? What exactly is it, and how seriously is it adhered to?

Armed with your notebook or your clipboard, it's time to venture out into as many schools as you can visit.

It is helpful to get to know the cast of characters involved with the kids who need some extra help in your local school system. You may be referred to a particular person from a previous program your child has been in, or you may need to refer yourself. All public school systems have *someone* who will understand the mechanics of getting your child started in school. The sooner you get to know that person, and have an evaluation done to determine what services your child may need, the better.

The Individualized Educational Plan (IEP)

If you think your child has special needs—academic, social, attentional, or related to learning style—you have the legal right to request a full evaluation done by the school and its team of experts.

- You can do this before your child starts school or at any point in his educational career.
- If your child hasn't yet started school and is over age three, call the special education coordinator of your local school district and ask to begin the process.
- If your child is already in school, speak to the classroom teacher, the special education coordinator, and the principal about your concerns. You will probably need to make a formal request in writing. Be sure to date this request; the school is legally obligated to get the evaluation done within a specified time frame.

An educational evaluation done through the public school system consists of a number of specialists evaluating a child's achievement, potential, and areas of difficulty in meeting with academic success. The evaluation identifies problems, sets goals, and makes recommendations for services (for example, occupational, physical, or speech and language therapy, or time in the resource room for extra academic support in a given area). In some cases, a more restrictive educational setting may be recommended, especially for children with severe behavioral problems or serious weaknesses in several areas. The individualized educational plan is a legal document. Parents are asked to review the plan and sign it to show agreement. Review the IEP carefully before you sign it, and ask for clarification. The language itself can be hard to understand and sometimes seems downright silly:

Student will be able to write a cohesive story 80 percent of the time.
Student will be able to catch a ball 50 percent of the time.

For most families, the only IEP they ever see is their own child's, and so at the beginning, at least, they are reading it without a lot of experience and expertise. Before signing it, we recommend reviewing it several times, asking questions of the team, perhaps going over it with your pediatrician (only if she has experience and interest in these issues!) or with some other knowledgeable professional. If you do not agree with the assessment or the recommendations, discuss this with the evaluators at your child's "team meeting." These meetings are educational for most parents and should not be adversarial, even when there is disagreement. Remember that although you have rights under the special education laws of your state, it is in the best interest of your child to keep a positive working relationship with this team.

Though the IEP is a legal document, many parents find that putting its recommendations into effect can be challenging. In areas where school districts are suffering budget cuts, special education services are often the first things to go after art and music.

The team agreed that Sam needed intense speech and language intervention as well as help from the resource room teacher, but neither of them had any time in their schedules to take on another child. So where does that leave us? He has done more or less OK without it, so I know he is not a high priority for them, but

I also know that he is slipping in his schoolwork and it's not going to get any better until he gets the help he needs and deserves.

This mother's frustration has echoed time and again throughout our interviews. Our experience in practice has been that it is increasingly difficult to obtain the services a quirky child may need in school, especially if an evaluation determines that his achievement is adequate, which usually mean on grade level.

There is nothing easy about accessing or implementing special education services, and it is a rare school year in which a quirky child will be on "autopilot." Keeping track of your child's progress requires a lot of energy and effort and can involve a lot of stress. Parents of middle schoolers and high schoolers have commented that once a child has multiple teachers—different teachers for different subjects—it is the parent's job to be sure all of them have read the evaluations and are aware of the necessary accommodations.

It is worth mentioning the Individuals with Disabilities Education Act, usually referred to as IDEA. This is a congressional act mandating that all states provide services for children with disabilities. All states must adhere to this law, though we have found tremendous variation in its interpretation.

An IEP generally is in effect for three years, at which time the child has a complete reevaluation, in which each specialist on the team reassesses your child in detail. The purpose of these re-evals is to determine the amount of progress the child has made toward reaching her goals and to determine whether or not she will continue to need the services described in the original plan. Less formal ongoing assessments and evaluations ought to be happening as well. Some kids truly outgrow the need for a certain kind of help.

The summer John got interested in baseball, he played baseball every day with the zeal he had previously reserved for schedules and clocks and calendars. He had had some significant motor issues and we'd been told that his visual perception was off, so we didn't have great hopes that his interest would go very far. In fact, I was kind of heartbroken for him. What could be harder for him than swinging a bat and trying to hit a ball, or catching a ball that could be coming from any direction at any speed? I was also just plain exhausted from all the baseball playing he demanded of me! When we headed back to school and physical therapy in the fall, his PT asked how he did it. He had improved dramatically in virtually all the areas she had been working on, and she couldn't believe it. She told him he had designed his own PT program and was doing a lot better with it than he would do with her. He beamed. That was a few years ago, but I'll never forget it, and not just because it was two appointments a week I could cross off my calendar.

CREATING A PROGRAM

Once an IEP has been developed and accepted, the team will offer a program aimed at helping your child meet the goals that are spelled out. There are a lot of different ways to do this in the school setting:

- A standard classroom with no additional supports (which can hardly be called an individual program, but this is exactly what happens to some of the more functional quirky kids because their academic work is on grade level and the school doesn't see any need for extra help)
- Inclusion in an integrated classroom mixing typically developing kids and kids with a variety of special needs or learning disabilities
- A substantially separate classroom designed for kids with more challenging learning and/or behavioral concerns

Within any one of these types of classrooms, a child who needs special education services might get that help in one of several different ways:

- Services and therapy delivered in the classroom to small groups of children. This has the advantage, when it works well, of integrating this extra help into the other activity going on in the room.
- A "pullout," in which the child leaves the classroom to receive the services. This can allow a resource room teacher, for example, the opportunity to work intensively with one student or a small group in a setting designed to encourage concentration—important for many quirky kids!
- An increasingly popular option, albeit expensive from the school's point of view, is an aide in the classroom devoted to the child or children with additional learning needs. An aide can make or break a child's ability to function in a public school setting. This is a wonderful option for many quirky kids.

Some Thoughts on Public Schools

The vast majority of quirky kids are served quite well by the public school systems in their neighborhoods. Some communities have special education services at all of their schools, some have them only at a select few, and some have none at all. In that case, children who need those services are usually educated in a neighboring community at the home school system's expense or in a collaborative school shared by several communities. Virtually *all* quirky kids spend at least part of their school years in a public school setting, and it's probably a good place to start.

Chrissie started kindergarten in a public school program that worked well for her. She had a great teacher, and she made friends. In fact, I wanted her to repeat the year, but she couldn't because she was the age to move on. I think this is a downside of a public school system: they insisted on moving Chrissie through the grades because she is smart, but she's also very immature. Now she's in the fifth grade, and she has an aide in the classroom whom she shares with a couple of other kids.

Because public schools must cope with a wide variety of kids, they often have the necessary resources and a more inclusive attitude. Almost all public schools will have *some* staff trained in special education. There will be reading specialists, speech and language therapists, counselors, and psychologists. Many schools will have access to a psychologist specifically versed in the issues of the quirky-kid population. Virtually all public schools have a nurse on staff at least part of the day—a distinct advantage for children with medical concerns like seizures or complicated medication regimens. Keeping this in mind, look for someone within the school system—teacher, counselor, nurse, special education coordinator—who seems to understand your child and with whom you can connect. Many families do better if they find that one crucial ally who can help keep an eye on things within the school.

Many families also find that the public school experience is valuable for their quirky children for other reasons. They get to know the other kids in the neighborhood, and they go to school with what may be a more economically and ethnically diverse group of children than they would find in private school. In general, the public school experience may be closer to the real world; a quirky kid who can thrive, or survive reasonably intact, is well prepared to take on the challenges of adulthood.

We are aware of a number of families who have moved to communities with public school systems better equipped at handling quirky kids with their many potential educational and social concerns. Although this is a major undertaking and a big life decision with implications for the whole family, the fact is, many families *without* quirky kids do exactly the same thing for the same reasons: they are looking for the schools that will be best for their children. As long as you keep in mind that what's the best now may not always be the best, and as long as your other children are faring well, this is sometimes the best possible decision a family can make.

We looked around a lot, investigated various communities, talked with parents we knew through EI and speech therapy groups, and decided we really needed to move. We moved to a community known for its great schools (for typical kids, of course) that had wonderful special education services. We are lucky to have been able to do it. Our daughter is thriving, we are more relaxed and more available to each other and to our kids, and our other two children seem to have weathered the move reasonably well.

ALTERNATIVE PUBLIC SCHOOLS

Charter schools, pilot schools, alternative education programs—more and more, communities are offering publicly funded but more "progressive" or nontraditional schools and programs. Because they tend to be founded and directed by idealists and visionaries who aspire to education "outside the box," they may look appealing as possible places for the child who is himself clearly outside all the usual boxes. We would offer a caution about assuming that a quirky child and a quirky school will be an automatic good match. The occasional good match is possible—the music-oriented charter school and the intensely musical quirky child, the small alternative progressive program and the child who couldn't face the bustle of the regular big elementary school.

For younger children, especially those who need extra services during the school day, these programs may not work out. We have not seen many quirky kids who could thrive optimally in programs that were themselves in the process of growing, developing, changing, evolving, and sometimes struggling. In addition, many of these programs are somewhat delicately balanced, especially during their early years, and although they will strive to provide extra help and extra services for the quirky children they serve, the expense may be prohibitive and may even threaten the viability of the school itself.

By all means, check out the nontraditional public school offerings in your area, but keep in mind that most quirky kids need a certain amount of stability and do well with more experienced teachers and specialists.

Private or Independent Schools

Sending a child to private school will loom as a major financial commitment for some families, as an expected and planned-for expense for others, and as a complete impossibility for many.

In addition, you face certain important considerations as you look at private schools. Private schools are under no legal obligation to provide any special education services, and the vast majority of them do not. They are not required to do pullouts or provide an aide in the classroom—and they have no funding from the state to do so. Therefore, by definition, for the more needy or impaired children on the spectrum, a typical independent school is not likely to be a good match.

Many private schools do not want to admit kids with special needs. And for the most part, if the school doesn't want a child with your child's issues, then you and your child probably don't want that school. You can apply without specifying the issues, but if you get away with it, the school may offer you a place but be unable to meet the needs of the child. Before applying to private school, you must carefully consider how you feel about disclosing your child's particular issues to the school.

Certainly, there are parents who apply to private school without mentioning, for example, that a child has been receiving speech therapy or that a child is prone to extreme tantrums. You dress the child in his casual best, you take him to the interview, and you hope that he enunciates clearly and refrains from attacking any of the other children.

We're not saying you have to tell the school everything. Small problems that seem to have resolved, behavioral eccentricities that don't prevent your child from functioning in a preschool class—these may not be relevant. However, it makes no sense to go into this situation knowing that your child is going to need a lot of speech and language help but then keep it from the school—and then perhaps get upset when it turns out the school doesn't have the relevant specialists on tap. If your child's behavior is so explosive that he's already on his third medication and his second anger-management group, it's really not fair to the school to give the staff no hint at all of what they're taking on. Getting your child into private school can come to feel like a high-pressure and often somewhat unpleasant game. Certain parents are determined to win at all costs. Of course, the real object of the game is to find your child a place that's right for her.

We applied to a number of private schools for our son in the first grade. By then, we were pretty sure he could no longer survive in our public schools. We decided to be completely honest about his "stuff," hoping that one of the schools we liked would work out for him and knowing that we were signing up to do all his extra stuff on our time. One school did work out, and he has done wonderfully there. Of the ones that didn't, however, I most remember a wise woman who was an admissions director. She said, "This is not a good place for your son. He will not do well here." She was so clear, so honest, so direct—in very sharp contrast to the others who kept beating around the bush—and we were so grateful to her. It was painful to hear but so much easier to deal with and has become much less painful as time has passed. I actually remember her with a lot of respect and admiration.

There's considerable variety in the world of private schools. There are schools with certain educational philosophies (Montessori, Waldorf), with specific curricula based on theories of learning and child development. There are schools where kids wear uniforms (which can be very appealing to quirky kids—as long as they don't involve snaps, buckles, or neckties!) and schools where creativity is unfettered by the rules of standard spelling. There are schools run like military camps and schools with open classrooms and alternative educational principles. There are single-sex schools—and some advocates swear by this form of education. There are boarding schools where kids stay in dormitories or houses with adult supervision. There are small, homey, quiet schools designed to seem like family settings (easier, maybe, for children with sensory integration difficulties). There are academically intense schools for high achievers and arts-oriented schools for creatively gifted and talented kids. There are also larger, more traditional private schools much like public schools in scale and in terms of social demands on kids.

Private schools can offer a new range of pressures and problems, but they do also offer freedom from certain constraints that hem in the public schools. For example, many states now require major testing at regular grade intervals. The child for whom tests and anxiety are a problem may be better off in private school—exempt from the tests and the pressure. One distinct advantage of private schools in general is that they tend to be less rigid about kids' moving on to the next grade level simply because a birthday falls on a certain date. Because the social maturity of many quirky kids lags behind their ages and often their academic abilities, many will benefit from being among the oldest in their classes. Schools with classes that span more than one grade level, where one teacher stays with the same group of kids for two years, are terrific for these kids. Public schools are under pressure to move kids along if their academic work is on or above grade level, even if their social skills are not. In general, private schools create a somewhat more protected and protective environment for their students than many public schools. The same need to take all comers that equips the public schools with specialists and experience also may mean that the classrooms have to handle kids who might well be asked to leave in a private school. However, we know families who have found themselves in private schools in which every child seemed to be polished, perfect, attractive, athletic, well groomed, and well behaved—a situation that can really make the parent of a quirky kid yearn for a few rougher edges!

In private schools, class size is usually smaller, with more adult attention and supervision possible. Parents often get more feedback from teachers, with lengthy written comments and regularly scheduled conferences. Many private schools have extra facilities—art studios, music rooms, woodshops, large school libraries—and on into the stratosphere of rolling manicured campuses, ceramics workshops, and riding stables! There is no question that for some quirky kids, this can translate into a kinder, gentler school experience—but only if they get the services and the educational support they need.

Some families we know have developed programs for their kids that include a private school education with extra supports outside of school and school hours. Some have even put in place an aide for the classroom in a private school setting (at the parents' expense). One mom commented that this worked well for her son and minimized the attention to his differences.

Once we got an aide in the classroom for George, he seemed to settle down, he was less anxious, and he was able to learn better. In his case, he really needs her pretty close by most of the time, but she floats about the room and helps other kids occasionally as well. This has been a great help to him, and to his teacher, and has enabled him to stay put in a school where he feels comfortable and where his brother goes. The only downside is the expense.

It can be an advantage to separate school and supplementary therapies. Sensitive about how other kids see them, many children prefer to keep their therapies outside of the school experience. Of course, such a program is highly dependent on parental resources, knowledge, initiative, time, and money. Someone has to assess the child's needs, find the specialists, put together the program, pay the bills. And *someone* needs to be available to bring the child to his appointments!

Parochial Schools

Parochial schools offer some specific benefits that may make them absolutely terrific for some quirky kids—and out of the question for others. Most are fairly traditional in their approaches to teaching and learning, demanding that students wear uniforms in many cases, expecting even young children to sit still in class and pay attention, and requiring good behavior and a high degree of respect for the teacher—who in some cases may be a figure of some religious significance. Disturbing behavior in class is not tolerated, and punishments tend to be fairly traditional. These schools pride themselves on being academically rigorous and may give a good deal of homework from the early grades on. Most require some course of religious studies in addition to the regular curriculum, which may involve something as extensive as learning another language from a very young age (Hebrew at a yeshiva, Arabic at an Islamic academy). This may add hours onto both the school day and the homework evening.

The quirky children who do best in these schools are those who thrive on routine, who need a structured environment with clear rules and an emphasis on discipline and order. There are quirky kids who find the whole business of clothes and social conformity difficult and for whom uniforms are a real blessing (no pun intended). Some anxious children are troubled by any alteration in the daily routine. Parochial schools have for years offered parents, including parents in some difficult inner-city settings, a high degree of tradition, discipline, and order, combined with firm academic standards and, of course, a certain amount of ritual. These schools may be a real haven for the quirky child who responds well to clearly stated expectations and whose anxieties are allayed by the clear hierarchy of parochial school and even by the religious and social certainties on which the school and its curriculum are based.

Again, most parochial schools have few resources for getting students extra help. Parochial school is definitely not the place for the quirky kid who cannot sit still or who needs individualized teaching. Classes tend to be large, and the expectation is that children will sit still and behave or face the consequences. Choosing to educate your child in a parochial school should be based on the belief that it can meet his needs. If it does, the added comfort for you and your child of being in a familiar social group with familiar rituals will be a bonus! Some quirky kids take on their religious beliefs and history as a special interest! Can you imagine the positive attention she would get from the rabbi or the nun or the imam for that!

Schools for Children with Special Needs

An increasing number of schools—usually private but sometimes publicly funded—are specifically intended for children who are not succeeding in more standard settings. Some such schools are especially devoted to kids in the PDD/ASD categories. If these diagnoses have been suggested for your child, it is definitely worth knowing about these schools—and keeping them in mind as possibilities for your child at one point or another.

Our experience suggests that these "separate" schools are often where parents turn with their older children, after a solid try in other schools, sometimes several. Although some quirky kids have more profound delays or more worrisome behaviors as very young children and *start* these programs early, the vast majority do not.

For the older child, however, the issues may change, and sometimes these specialized schools can really be lifesavers. Perhaps the diagnosis and the learning issues have become clearer as the child grows up, or perhaps the later elementary/middle school years can be so terribly hard on quirky children. Most such schools have academic curricula geared toward the learning profiles of quirky kids, with extra therapeutic services such as sensory integration, occupational therapy, social skills or pragmatic language therapy, social workers or other mental health professionals, and in some cases, behavioral programs geared toward addressing undesirable behaviors (aggression, self-mutilating). A specialized school should do more than address your child's immediate learning needs; it should help you tease out important questions about the future and your child's potential for further education, work, and independent adulthood. Vocational training and off-site job placements for those who are not college-bound are important for older children struggling with the special learning problems, social issues, and emotional complexities of the adolescent years from the quirky side of the aisle.

We talked with staff at a number of such schools, including the admissions director of one school geared toward quirky kids who were not succeeding in their previous school placements and who in some cases had exhausted a number of less tailored programs:

When a family first contacts us about admission, we do a very detailed review of the child's educational and developmental history to be sure that our school would be an appropriate place and that they truly cannot find a less restrictive or less expensive alternative. Our goal is to work with a child and his family over a relatively short period of a couple or a few years so that he can return to a more typical educational environment. Most kids who come to us come at the middle school level, and many are able to leave for high school. The ones who do not are the ones who are unlikely to live an independent life, and we work with them to find job placements in the community, to teach them daily living skills they will need to live in a group home, and prepare them for young adulthood. The admissions process is not usually a happy one for the families, because they have had to convince their local school department that it cannot meet the needs of their child. The cost here is so expensive ($114,000 per year) that few school departments will easily accept that assessment without a fight. Families use mediators, advocates, lawyers to help them, and it can leave a lot of bad feelings all around.

Some specialized schools offer boarding as an option at the middle or high school level. This is a personal decision for most families, probably easier if others in the family have attended boarding school. In some cases, parents and siblings may need respite from the ongoing demands and emotional drain of caring for a complicated child. A boarding school with appropriate staffing and supervision may meet the needs of the whole family while offering the quirky child a chance for independence and a new environment.

Therapeutic Schools

A child's depression or anxiety, obsessiveness or psychotic tendencies, antisocial tendencies or outbursts can make education—not to mention a social life—nearly impossible. A therapeutic school will offer an environment of acceptance and a therapeutic milieu in which a highly trained staff works closely with the kids to address their psychiatric needs. This usually includes individual and group psychotherapy and a highly structured environment with clear expectations. The majority of these schools are boarding schools, and there are not many. They are tremendously expensive, and—unless you can convince your local school district to foot the bill, on the grounds that the district itself cannot meet the needs of your child—most families simply cannot afford these schools.

Homeschooling

Homeschooling quirky children is clearly not for everyone. However, some kids in these groups thrive when social demands are kept to a minimum and they are free to concentrate on their academic progress—usually in anticipation of attending school at a later date.

Some parents choose to homeschool their children *because* of the quirks. They feel that none of the school options available to them meet their children's needs. Other parents believe in homeschooling for its own sake for any of a number of reasons (academic, religious, philosophical) and find themselves faced with the particular challenge of tailoring curriculum and teaching methods to a child's needs. Homeschooling can offer solutions to—or at least ways around—some common quirky-kid problems. For example, a child who is especially distractible and struggles hard with attentional issues may do much better in an educational setting that is not a classroom full of other children. It's easier to control the noise and chaos in the home environment (well, as mothers, we tell ourselves it *ought* to be easier . . .), easier to carve the day into periods tailored to a child's attention span, easier to take a break for rest or physical exercise when one is needed. And of course, for a child who finds social relations complex, difficult, or even punishing, homeschooling offers a way out—though this way out does not provide that child with any social skills practice. A homeschooled child is blessedly free from being teased—but of course, parents have to make sure that she is not also free from playing with or talking to other children.

There are certain regulations regarding homeschooling, and you need to be sure you meet your state requirements. This ideal of homeschooling or any approximation thereof requires a parent with the time, the talent, and the inclination. Even then, it may only be the right answer for a specific segment of your child's educational life. As pediatricians and as mothers who doubt seriously that we would have the talent or the dedication to homeschool our own children, we do want to emphasize that this is an option worth considering for certain parents.

Making Your Choices

So what are you doing as you look around for a first educational placement for your quirky child?

- You're visiting as many schools as possible and asking lots of questions.
- You're looking into what's available to you in the public school system and requesting an evaluation and an individualized educational plan if that's appropriate.
- If it's an option for you, you're checking out some private schools and planning realistic strategies for what you're going to say about your child as you apply.
- You're thinking about whether you're interested in parochial schools or in homeschooling.
- Most important, you're talking with the people you feel have the best sense of your child and his learning style—his preschool teachers, for example, and his speech and language therapist. By all means, ask your pediatrician. We hear a great deal, good and bad, about families' experiences in the various schools available in the communities in which we work.

As more children are assessed at younger ages, these educational choices will come upon families sooner. We have been assuming here that you have a sense of your child's issues already during the preschool years and are in a good position to look at different elementary school options right from the beginning.

Sometimes a child's quirkiness doesn't become an issue until school problems arise. This scenario is more likely with children on the milder end of the spectrum, who make it through the early years at home but stumble when the academic and social demands of the elementary years hit. We've been pediatricians for a number of families whose children weren't evaluated and/or diagnosed until fifth or sixth grade. As their pediatricians, we saw them year after year without suspecting that anything was up. When we talk this over with the parents, those parents almost always say that they had worried, at least off and on, that something was amiss, but usually, it was some worry so vague, so uncertain, so hard to explain that they never actually brought it up with us at those annual checkups. After all, who brings up social awkwardness when a doctor asks if you have any worries about your child?

How can a child reach the later elementary years without an evaluation of some kind? Easily! For some, there may be only particular behavior that seems, as one mother put it, "off the beam." Because some quirky kids are so bright or have a "splinter skill" that actually puts them ahead of the pack, their eccentricities may be viewed as charming or delightful, and their parents may realize that other nagging worries about school function were lulled by the pleasure of enjoying certain specific triumphs.

John could tell time when he was three years old. We knew this was remarkable and were happy that he had an outstanding skill. One of his teachers, however, made such a fuss about how great it was that we felt she was missing all these other major red flags. It's one thing to be able to tell time, but it's quite another to have that ability take up so much of your time and attention. He always wore multiple watches, which had to be synchronized, and he spent a lot of time checking that all the clocks in the room were the same. It got in the way of his doing other things he should have been doing at that age, and he was using that skill to comfort himself and keep himself organized and in control. He continues, many years later, to be interested in timetables and schedules, but it doesn't take up so much of his energy.

In the elementary years, most teachers are quite adept at noticing which kids in the class aren't keeping up academically and which ones may need a different teaching style. A good and experienced teacher will also easily pick up which of her students are socially isolated and anxious and which have peculiar habits or behaviors that make the others uncomfortable. The seasoned teacher is likely to be able to predict which issues will plague a child throughout the school years and which ones can easily be incorporated into a regular classroom and school. Trust your child's teacher if she suggests taking a closer look at your child's differences, especially if those same concerns make sense to you. A good and perceptive teacher, of course, can make a tremendous difference in a child's life—or even in a whole family's life.

Brian was in the school where I was teaching, and third grade was a disaster from the first day. He was hiding in the corner, hiding in the bathroom. Within a week and a half, his teacher and some of the other teachers sat me down—after all, they were friends of mine, colleagues—and said, "He needs to be evaluated. Something is not going right for him. You need to do something about this." And right then, I went on a mission.

On the other hand, a teacher who misinterprets a quirky child's behavior can mean a hard school year for all concerned.

We started Caitlin at a small private school in kindergarten, thinking she would get more individual attention. She certainly did, but not the kind of attention we were looking for. She was just too different, too eccentric, too rigid to survive in that setting. The teacher called almost every week with complaints about Caitlin's "insubordination." When I asked for an example, she told me that when they were learning the letter K, Caitlin turned her paper over and wrote the entire alphabet multiple times, omitting the letter K. I think this was her way of saying, "I can already do this. I'm bored. I'll show you!" She did not fit the profile of the compliant kindergarten girl, and her teacher wasn't equipped to recognize her behavior as anything but defiance, or "insubordination." The director of the school called us and said she was not welcome back unless she had an aide in the classroom, for whom we would need to pay. We left the school at the end of the year.

When the teacher thinks something is wrong, you need to ask yourself honestly whether the teacher's observations resonate with your own. If they make sense to you in light of your life at home with your child, think about what you need to do next. Does your child need a full evaluation? Would it make sense to try a different school environment and see how that goes first? Are the problems strictly academic, social, behavioral, attentional, or a mix? If the teacher is concerned but you honestly don't recognize the concerns she is describing, talk with your child and find out whether this sounds like a bad match. It might help to sit with it for a while, offer your child some specific strategies for getting along with this teacher in this classroom, and watch to see whether that helps. Follow up with the teacher and follow up with your child. It also might be helpful to get some other opinions within the school.

The school-based evaluation is a good place to start for most families. Sometimes it's all the expertise that is needed, both to determine your child's needs and then to meet them. It's the same process we discussed above, in which a team evaluation yields an IEP, which the school is then obligated to fulfill. In the best school systems around the country, kids never need to move to another school because their schools are fully equipped, either with special classrooms or with adequate services around the edges of a regular educational setting. Unfortunately, this is not the case everywhere.

Children enrolled in alternative schools such as charter schools or pilot schools or in private elementary schools will face a different set of circumstances—usually more difficult logistically and emotionally. Because these schools are not eager to spend their education dollars on a few kids who require special education services, children who need extra help may face frustration and even experience discrimination. A school without the necessary resources is more likely to view a quirky child as a behavior problem. It's worth looking into it if you have had some concerns over the years and suddenly the school staff is labeling your child as a problem. It's not usually an emergency, but you do need to consider whether it's worth the energy to put up a fight for services in a school that doesn't already have them in place.

Although this law is under some protest in certain states, your child is eligible to receive special education services through your local system *even if he is not enrolled in the system.* You may have found a terrific school for your child that doesn't provide the occupational therapy you know he needs for his fine motor skills or sensory integration dysfunction. At this point, *you are completely entitled to request an evaluation from your local public school, and the school is required to do the evaluation, and to provide services if they are indicated.* You may get some dirty looks, but you are within your legal rights. Most school professionals understand that families choose a variety of ways to educate their kids and that parents usually know best.

Our son needed occupational therapy for many reasons, but his fine motor skills were probably his greatest area of difficulty. For several years, we have gone to our neighborhood elementary school in the early morning or the late afternoon for his OT sessions. This has worked well for him. He likes the fact that he does it outside of his own school, and they have a very nice relationship. His OT understands that his overall needs are better served in this way.

As you explore different options for your child and work to reconcile the impressions of the classroom teacher with the testing done by specialists, don't lose sight of the big picture. The point of all this is to respond to concerns about your child and how she is doing in school. Your goal is to provide her with a world that supports her growth and learning and welcomes her every day into a place where she fits in.

References and Resources

For references and resources on schools and education, see the end of Chapter 7.

7

○ ○ ● ○

The Quirky Child and
the Educational System

My visit to a school this morning was oddly emotional. Although I know that John has lots of difficulties, I have been pleased that he has done "fine" at a regular school. As he has gotten older, however, I am more aware of what a struggle it is for him, how exhausted he is, and how exhausted we are helping him to keep track of everything and get his homework done without a major episode. At the school I looked at this morning, a small private school for kids with learning disabilities, the admissions director talked a language we have unfortunately had to learn over the years—"attentional issues, nonverbal learning disorder, Asperger's syndrome, executive-function problems"—as if this was normal, or at least manageable. What a relief to know that such a place is out there for kids like John. The kids all seemed so happy to be there and talked to me with such enthusiasm and relief that they had found themselves at a place that embraces them.

The Preschool Years

The younger the child, the less likely parents are to have certain information about quirky habits or diagnostic categories to inform choices about child care or preschool. The younger the child, the more likely parents are to be reassured by well-meaning adults, including their pediatricians, that their concerns regarding their child's development are probably overblown. Since the average age of diagnosis for many quirky kids is six, parents of these kids are at a disadvantage in our label-driven society when it comes to figuring out an appropriate placement. For those who have not been in early intervention (EI) programs, a regular preschool or playgroup in the neighborhood is likely to be the first school experience. As parents see their child in this context, new concerns may arise, and differences in development may be more apparent. However, in infant and toddler programs and home-based day-care settings, teachers or caregivers may have plenty on their hands just meeting the demands of typical kids. They may lack the training to recognize or deal with those whose development is atypical. It is often only in retrospect that we understand the problems that quirky kids—and their teachers—encounter in these early years of education.

We didn't know at the time what our son's problem was, but we knew that he was developing slowly and didn't eat enough to gain weight. He started a small family day-care program with a total of six kids when he was a year old. It only lasted a year because, by the time he reached age two, we had a better handle on his delays. The day-care provider, who had been revered by several of our friends for the care she gave to their children, clearly had no clue what to do with our son. She probably had never encountered a child like him. She insisted he was just fine, she didn't notice anything at all different, yet he never spoke a word and did not interact with the other kids. We believe she was just uncomfortable talking with us about his development and thought it would all come out in the wash. It made us slightly crazy.

Whereas some teachers and child-care providers are unable—or unwilling—to talk with parents when a child seems somehow problematic, others can be too ready to jump to a conclusive diagnosis on the basis of a few pieces of evidence. Both approaches can leave parents bewildered and sometimes resentful. Considering and comparing the impressions that these teachers form of your child is often the beginning of a long process of obtaining the kind of support that *will* be helpful.

EARLY INTERVENTION

For the children under three, early intervention programs, federally funded programs available in all states, provide evaluation and therapy in a school-like atmosphere for preschoolers, in which their developmental delays are addressed in a setting of preschool games, songs, toys, and activities. As we learn more about atypical development, children are being noticed earlier and enrolled in EI programs at younger ages. What used to be largely groups of former premature babies with neurological impairments are now more eclectic groups of toddlers and preschoolers with a wide range of developmental differences and medical histories. As pediatricians become more educated, referrals can be made earlier. There is ample evidence, scientific and anecdotal, that early intervention makes a difference.

AFTER EARLY INTERVENTION

When the time comes to move out of an EI program (on or around the child's third birthday) and on into preschool, choosing the most appropriate place for your child will depend largely on what her needs are and what your options are. Generally speaking, areas around big cities are the best prepared to address the needs of these children, because there are larger concentrations of educators of all kinds and interests—and large numbers of kids of all kinds needing services.

This move to a preschool will be easier for parents and kids who have already worked with a team of specialists. Many EI programs have liaisons whose job it is to help with the move into a preschool. Such a liaison is probably the best person to advise whether your child should start off in a program geared toward children with atypical development. Even children who have not been enrolled in an EI program, however, are entitled to an early childhood evaluation through their public school systems at this age. It's worth getting the machinery in motion well before your child's third birthday because there are often long waits for evaluations. This period from ages three to five years can be one of great frustration for the families of the more academically and socially skilled quirky kids because the availability of preschool programs for this age is quite variable, and the less needy kids may not qualify for them. This can cause a gap in precisely the services that have the most potential to help.

Charlie attended a pleasant private preschool in the neighborhood that did not offer any services, but the director was very open to welcoming his occupational therapist, who came in for occasional visits to observe and offer some advice to the staff. He received his therapy at the local elementary school, which did not have a program for him because he wasn't "impaired enough"! This system has worked OK for us, but it wasn't ideal, and I hope we haven't lost precious time. Only time will tell.

Finding the best preschool match will require visits to the potential classrooms, interviews with teachers and principals and therapists, and talking with other parents. If you know your child will benefit from speech and language therapy or occupational therapy, look for a program that will offer these services. If, on the other hand, your child functions pretty well in all areas except the social, a friendship group or pragmatic language group outside of the school setting may be all he needs. Your goal during these years is not to overload your child with all possible therapies but to help him strengthen his skills in any way that may help him as he grows. Maximizing services early in a child's life, when you are in greater control of his schedule, will pay off later on.

CHOOSING A PRESCHOOL

What needs to be considered in determining a proper preschool setting? There are some specific issues to keep in mind that are especially relevant to this age group:

- *Structure:* There are preschool programs that are tightly scheduled and emphasize a group curriculum and others that are much less programmed. There are children who thrive on one or the other. Even for a child who is more or less on track developmentally but eccentric in her behavior, you need to think about what kind of structure—or lack of structure—would make her most comfortable. Most quirky kids will find free play quite challenging.

- *Curriculum:* This is related to structure. Some preschools are proud of teaching prereading skills, premath skills, and many other specific academic subjects, whereas others are more play-oriented. Your sense of whether your child is ready to start learning—or able to sit still and concentrate—is important here. For some four-year-olds, this can be a real struggle.

- *Class size:* The ideal, of course—and not just for quirky kids—is a smaller class with plenty of adult attention. A child who has real problems with social interactions is going to have more trouble learning to deal with a large group all at once.

- *Noise level:* There are noisier, crazier classrooms where a somewhat rambunctious child will not be a problem, and there are gentler, more serene settings where the child who is alarmed by noise and chaos may flourish. And in that context, it's worth noting that the questions we detailed in the previous chapter about cafeterias and playgrounds and public-address systems are just as relevant for this age group as for older kids, if not more so.

- *Teacher experience:* A challenging child is much more likely to thrive in a preschool setting with a teacher who has coped with a wide variety of children in the past.

- *Teacher/student ratio:* Be sure that you are putting your child in a setting where he can get the attention he needs, even if he sometimes absorbs the full attention of one of the available adults.

- *Discipline:* Think about what happens when your child gets upset or angry or frustrated and whether the preschool will be able to cope. What happens when there is too much stimulation? Does she shut down, or is there a danger of a major meltdown? What is required to handle the meltdown?

- *Length of the school day and availability of a summer program:* You have a good idea of your child's physical stamina. A quirky kid may need more downtime than others his age. Also, consider a summer program that may help him hang on to those hard-won gains over the summer.

DEVELOPMENTAL SKILLS

For children whose development is not precisely on schedule, there are all kinds of questions to think about with regard to the skills needed to participate in a typical preschool day. Developmental delays often mean three- and four-year-olds who speak much less than other children their age—or sometimes not at all. Nonverbal children usually need a preschool setting with small groups and a high teacher/child ratio. They can often do well in a program that uses a Picture Exchange Communication System (PECS). This system uses small cards with simple diagrams of things like a pencil, a glass of milk, a bathroom. A nonverbal child can use a diagram to communicate her wishes. We have seen remarkable amounts of communication with these cards—often a starting point for eliciting speech.

Think about the skills needed for your child to get through a preschool day:

- Does he understand spoken language?
- Can she actually carry on a conversation? (This is not the same as being able to talk.)
- How about her gross and fine motor skills? Can she climb stairs independently?
- Can he sit in a chair without any special equipment? Can she hold a pencil, or a crayon or marker, and write?
- Is she able to handle toileting or still in diapers?
- Is he able to interact and play with other preschoolers?
- Can she follow directions?
- Does he have any splinter skills, like a notably early ability to read (hyperlexia) or remarkable abilities in math or music?

LANGUAGE-BASED PROGRAMS

Some preschool programs are described as *language-based*—a term worth knowing about if your child has difficulty understanding spoken language or following directions and if she needs to hear things more than once or in several different ways. Many such children benefit from this approach in preschool and beyond. Although not all teachers or schools use this term to describe a teaching style, look for cues when you visit a class—posted schedules, so kids know what to expect as the day goes on; explaining directions for a project in several ways; using pictures or written words as well as spoken words to get a point across. This style of teaching and explaining comes naturally to many early childhood teachers but certainly not all. This kind of flexibility is helpful for many young children, especially the quirky. Rigid rules and expectations can spell disaster.

THE RIGHT CLASSROOM, THE RIGHT TEACHER

Although it is virtually impossible to find the perfect teacher, the ideal speech and language pathologist, and the optimal occupational and physical therapist all in one place, it's worth looking at all your options and trying for the best balance. The classroom teacher is the most critical. Throughout *any* child's life, a classroom teacher who understands him is the greatest gift of all. Put your energy into finding a teacher for the early years who will understand your whole child, not just her deficits. Early childhood teachers with special education training are often best equipped to do this, but some seasoned preschool teachers are just as likely to "get" the quirky child. What you want is a preschool teacher who appreciates and understands your child, in all her complexity. A teacher with a sense of humor, who delights in the child's quirkiness, who makes accommodations for his differences without drawing too much attention to them, is a valuable guide on your child's road through school.

For us, the decision about where Gabriel should go to preschool was actually pretty straightforward. We knew he needed every kind of special ed service he could get, and there were only a couple of possibilities. The early intervention liaison was a great help, and we trusted her recommendation. He spent three really good years in an "integrated preschool" in a public school in the neighborhood. Half of the fourteen kids in the class had some kind of special need. He got all his therapy in one place and had amazing teachers who were "on" to him. We learned a lot from them and still remember them with love and admiration for the work they do. It made a huge difference for Gabriel that he got off to such a great start in school.

CHECKING OUT A CLASS

When checking out a preschool class, look around at the classroom and think about your child. Think about behaviors your child has that may challenge the staff and how they might deal with them—yes, *those* teachers whom you are watching in *this* classroom. Does your child flap her hands or twirl around? Does he make distracting funny sounds? Does she have trouble staying on task or sitting still for a few minutes? Can he keep himself safe? Check to see how carefully the children are being monitored. Is this an environment in which she could learn? Will she find it too distracting? What about when he gets wild—will these teachers know how to handle him? Watch how they handle children who don't follow instructions the first time around or who get a little bit out of control. Are there other children like her? Are there more typical children from whom he could learn? Are the children *too* impaired to be playmates for your child? Are there enough adults in the room to help her out when the going gets rough? How many kids are in the class, and how would your child fit?

With the proper support in the preschool years, both kids and their parents can develop strategies for school success, focus therapies on important skills at a time when there are no overwhelming academic or social pressures, and anticipate the coming years with their eyes open. Many quirky kids need less intervention as time passes. This is the period to put as many supports as possible in place, helping your child make the transition to school as smoothly as you can, with all the help she needs. If, later on, it turns out that some of that help is no longer needed, more power to you, and more power to her teachers, and more power to your child herself. It will mean that all the time you put into finding the right program made a difference, that all the supplementary therapies you pursued did what they were supposed to do: they helped shape her development and her school function in the right direction so that life and school and learning could get easier, not harder, as she grew.

When Trevor started kindergarten, he spent half his time in a special education kindergarten and half in the regular education room. Gradually, over the course of the year, he spent more and more time with the typical kindergartners and eventually "graduated" into the regular class completely. He is currently in the third grade in a regular education class, with virtually no special education services. He is extremely bright in math and in an honors algebra class with kids from another school. He would be in an honors geometry class if his fine motor skills were not so poor.

The Elementary Years

Many experts believe the elementary years are the quirky kid's most important years. Elementary school is your golden opportunity to lay good groundwork for those future years. After all, as children grow up, parents have less control than they may want—over the school, over the peer group, and even over the child. It's usually easier to teach social skills to a seven-year-old, and help her practice, than it is a seventh grader. Seize your moment when you can. All too soon, we all find ourselves standing around with the peculiar helplessness of parents of adolescents, wondering whether anything we say will ever again have any effect!

When Lisa went into kindergarten, I was terribly worried about her, about how she would do socially with the other children, about what was going on at school. And she wouldn't tell me. She would just burst into tears. The school helped me a lot with staff members' observations that she reacted in strange ways to different situations, that she couldn't seem to sit in a chair. She said the kids were yelling in her ears. She's easily distracted, and it's hard to sit her down and keep her on task. But on her last report card, the teacher said that she was making good progress, even though she still needed help with being organized.

As quirky children age into the complexities of middle school and high school, the more coping tools or strategies they have acquired, the better off they are. By sixth grade or so, it is often clear which kids can succeed in regular schools and which ones may need a temporary or permanent educational setting outside the mainstream. The experiences of the elementary years will provide the data needed for such a decision. Approach the elementary school years not as a free-play zone before the serious work starts but rather as an opportunity to help your quirky kid learn how to learn, how to play to his strengths, how to get along with other kids and with teachers and principals as well.

WHAT KIDS LEARN IN ELEMENTARY SCHOOL

We expect kids to learn to read, to carry on a conversation, to tell a story that makes sense, to use language—both written and spoken—to expand their world, and to work and play with their peers. We expect them to learn the basics of mathematics. We expect them to learn to write and draw using a variety of implements. We want them to be able to follow directions, take turns, and understand the rules of community behavior: raising hands, taking turns, not interrupting. For older elementary school children in fifth or sixth grade, we expect them to be able to comprehend a variety of literary genres (not just science fiction or baseball stories) and be able to write about them. We want them to be able to sit and eat lunch with a group of peers—without grossing them out! Perhaps most of all, we want our children to make friends, to have a social life, to enjoy themselves on the playground, to know how to play, and to feel like part of the gang. These are tall orders. Any one of these standard, natural developmental or cognitive tasks can present a challenge for your child. Knowing which ones are most likely to be stumbling blocks can help determine the elementary program most likely to work for your child.

George did OK in the early grades because he was an early and good reader. So much of the first couple of years is just getting kids to read that he coasted through. Once he hit fourth grade and needed to read literature, it was a disaster.

Typically, it is during the elementary years that a child's difficulties declare themselves as real or not, or as mild, more intense, or downright severe. Many families have needed to move their child from one setting to another as things became clearer.

John was assigned to a first-grade class in an integrated program, and we were thrilled. He would get all his therapies during the school day, and the teacher was certified in special education. It turned out to be a disaster. Despite her training, his teacher was very rigid, and she was a real screamer. This terrified him, not to mention the sheer volume, which he found overwhelming because of his sensory defensiveness. One day I went to pick him up, and he was out in the hall crying. He told me he was in "time-out" because he couldn't keep his chair still and it kept rocking back and forth. When I spoke to the after-school teacher, she said she just knew he was doing it to bug her. In fact, the chair had one short leg, and he couldn't keep it steady. He was receiving PT right there at school for his truncal instability, but she just didn't get it. His anxiety grew as the year progressed, and we finally brought him to a psychiatrist, who blessedly diagnosed him with Asperger's and said, "He's in the wrong school." That was just the catalyst we needed to get going. He ended up in a small, cozy private school with loving teachers who make allowances for his quirks yet foster his education. The irony is that, on paper, that first program would clearly have been the right one, yet in reality, it wasn't. We learned a big lesson that year.

LEARNING STYLES

Kids understand early on that they are in school to learn and that all around them, other kids are learning. Children generally know where they stand with regard to their classmates and whether they are struggling with things that come more easily to everyone else.

If a child cannot learn, school becomes a repetitive exercise in failure. This, in turn, can get in the way of making friends or lead to all kinds of tactics to avoid school or to serious anxiety or depression. And of course, learning disabilities and learning differences are in no way the same as intelligence. Many kids with major learning disabilities are extraordinarily bright. Ironically, their intelligence may make things harder for them, or at least more obscure, because these bright kids can compensate much longer in school, using their brains and the skills that come more easily for them to cover for the problems they can't solve.

We had always had some concerns about Debbie, but she did well in school, so we didn't go looking for trouble. By high school, her grades starting slipping, and she was completely exhausted all the time. We thought she was depressed, and she was, but that wasn't the primary problem. The psychiatrist we took her to referred her for a neuropsychology evaluation, and it turns out she has a major learning disability. We were stunned at first but then realized that so many of her behaviors over the years made sense in this light. She is very bright and compensated with great effort for a long time, until the volume and complexity of the work meant the strategies she had developed weren't working anymore.

NONVERBAL LEARNING DISABILITY

Many quirky kids have learning issues that fall under the general rubric of nonverbal learning disability (NLD). For a description, refer to Chapter 2. Because an NLD child is impaired in many aspects of daily functioning, be sure the school you are considering understands what this means. Since it is a relatively new term, even some special education departments are unfamiliar with it.

PUTTING IT TOGETHER

Some experts in the field of quirky kids argue that there ought to be entire schools designed with these kids in mind, and there are a few around the country that are of great interest. If you are a member of a parent support group, this is a good resource for finding such schools in your area. You can also try looking up a specific diagnosis on the Internet—NLD, Asperger's syndrome, autistic spectrum disorder—and may find school-related information on some of the Web sites maintained by the support groups or parent associations. However, this is not an option for the vast majority of families of elementary-age kids. The most recent wave of special education laws has moved kids with atypical development into the mainstream. This is a concept well known to most parents—that typical kids and not-so-typical kids are best served together whenever possible. There is plenty of controversy surrounding this concept, but at this moment in educational history, this is where most quirky kids start.

MAINSTREAMING

Some school systems have developed programs to meet the needs of quirky kids whose problems are less severe within the public schools. With resources and extra help, they enable the mildly quirky to function in a regular classroom. This, of course, is in the best interest of the school systems, because it reduces the number of kids for whom the district needs to foot the bill for an outside placement in a more specialized school.

Children can be mainstreamed in private or parochial schools, too, of course—if they can manage with the regular school program or if the staff is willing and able to make some adjustments.

For some quirky kids in this age group, the ability to stay in a mainstream classroom depends on the availability of a classroom aide devoted to them. It's well worth considering before moving a child to a different kind of classroom or an outside placement. Teachers can be grateful for the extra help, and kids can make great progress!

Chrissie has an aide in her class whom she shares with two other kids, and this works well. She helps the kids reinterpret instructions they don't understand and helps to keep them on task. Chrissie has learned a lot more since the aide started and generally feels more successful at school.

PROGRAMS FOR CHILDREN WITH DELAYS OR BEHAVIOR PROBLEMS

For children with more significant delays in development or language or for those whose behaviors are more disturbing, specialized elementary school programs exist in most communities within the public school system. These children may need help aimed at addressing their behaviors or at helping them with their motor development or their language, along with an appropriate academic curriculum. Without that help directed at their other issues, they won't be able to do any learning. To find these programs, talk with your developmental pediatrician, your occupational therapist, your psychologist. Talk to other parents or support groups for parents of similar children. Most kids who find their way to a successful program do so through contacts in the world of quirky kids. We hear from parents that the best advice they've got has been either from other parents or from specialists who work with lots of children with the same kinds of needs. One mother in New York City found a terrific program for her child through his occupational therapist:

We found a "class within a class" for children with special needs right in our neighborhood. It was Jacob's OT who suggested it for him, and he has made a lot of progress. I don't know if I would have found it without her, and it is definitely the right place. I am doing a lot less traveling around to get him what he needs.

PROGRAMS FOR GIFTED AND TALENTED CHILDREN

The quirky kids with splinter skills, such as tremendous mathematical or musical ability, and those with high intelligence, may be well served in schools for gifted and talented kids—where there is a real premium on intellectual ability and less emphasis on social skills or sports. It can be a real joy to a quirky child who's good at math to find herself in a place where math is the only thing that really counts (pun intended). There is less need to worry about your child's quirks in this kind of environment because these places are full of quirky people. Sometimes they pride themselves on just how weird they can be! Your child is more likely to find another with the same or similar special interests—be it military history or Pokémon—in a school for the gifted and talented.

The Middle School Years

For many of us, the journey from sixth to ninth grade doesn't take us through the happiest or easiest years of our lives. The point of middle school is often to make it to high school and get through puberty relatively unscathed. Anything else is gravy. Most kids have at least some difficulties with the educational, emotional, and physical transitions necessary at this time, as their bodies leap forward into the changes of puberty or lag behind their classmates' and as they contend with the personal, family, and peer-group implications of turning into teenagers.

KIDS ON THE AUTISTIC SPECTRUM

This is by far the hardest developmental stage for most kids on the PDD/ASD spectrum. Even as young children, feeling comfortable in their own skin is challenging. As five- and six- and seven-year-olds, these kids were more awkward, more uncomfortable, more wary, more likely to be upset or injured or frightened by the imperatives of their bodies. Throw in the physical changes of puberty and adolescence, the dazzling and confusing world of flirting and dating, and many quirky kids are overwhelmed. The social demands at this time tax exactly the areas these kids find difficult, if not impossible. Most quirky kids lag behind their age group in terms of development and social maturity, making this time even more confusing. At the same time, increasing academic demands require an ability to integrate information that simply confounds many of them. Gone are the days of straightforward math problems with a single answer!

The change in nomenclature that broadened the diagnostic criteria for the PDD family of disorders occurred in the early 1990s. The kids now approaching adolescence are the first batch of kids entering middle and high school with such a description. These diagnoses and their educational implications may be almost new to some of the people in charge of your child's education. You cannot assume that school personnel at this level will have a comprehensive knowledge of the quirky-kid spectrum, and you may well find yourself in the role of an educator in order to advocate for your child.

MIDDLE SCHOOL PROGRAMS: FINDING A FIT

If kids will ever need a specialized or separate school environment, even for a year or two, this is the most likely time. The middle school programs specifically designed with quirky kids in mind are generally set up with an explicit plan to reintroduce them to more standard school settings by high school, when their quirkiness may be more likely to be accepted or even seen as a strength. Some sensible school districts devote most of their special education funds to the middle schoolers, because the payoff is the greatest when these kids can stay within their own communities and rejoin their classmates for high school. It is worth anticipating the middle school years in advance, knowing what your options are, and visiting a few places with your child's specific needs in mind.

David started in an integrated preschool with good teachers and got all his therapies at school. At this point, he still had no diagnosis; he was called "minimal brain dysfunction" or "language-impaired" and was receiving OT, PT, and speech therapy. In his integrated first-grade class, his teacher just didn't get it. There were so many different types of kids, it was nearly impossible to know all of their learning styles. In second grade, he moved into a substantially separate class, and again, his teacher just didn't get it. At that point, we started looking around for private placements and hired a lawyer to help us. We approached the school and, of course, met with resistance. The lawyers thought he "didn't look bad enough on paper" to require an out-of-district placement, but we kept pushing, and he ended up at a small, intimate private school, very well staffed with specialists. It's a much better place for him, and the school district is paying.

ACADEMIC ISSUES AND MIDDLE SCHOOL

For kids who have had an individualized educational plan (IEP) in place during elementary school, this transition will be smoother, since the educational machinery should be automatically updating the plan and assessing your child's progress and considering new options. For those kids who so far have been without an IEP but who seem to have some learning issues coming more and more to the fore, the move on to a new school is a time to reconsider whether additional services might help. Many quirky children have uneven abilities—strong in some areas and very weak in others. While the stereotype of the little professor is not entirely accurate and certainly doesn't describe all of these kids, it does indeed describe some of them and will help to expand the available options.

Smart kids can get away with a lot more in terms of their eccentricities. However, this is usually not an age at which kids in a classroom will make allowances for bizarre behavior.

One child got sent to me at the school where I was teaching science because he was kind of peculiar. He was continuously picking and rubbing his nose, he was chapped around the lips, he was very unattractive-looking. And he didn't want to do anything but read the dictionary or read about chemistry. He had the periodic table memorized in second grade. Anyway, his teacher wanted to know whether what he was doing, what he was reading and writing about, was correct. Did it make sense? What we ended up doing, he and I, was we spent an hour a week together for about six weeks, and we did a little chemistry together. They needed to get him out of the classroom, he was awkward, a social pariah, and they were sending him to me partly to support his individual interest and validate it and partly to gauge whether it was gobbledygook—and of course, it wasn't. We did a nitrogen unit and we cleaned the fish tank, and I got him to join my fish-study group, and he did a chart and talked about the nitrifying bacteria and the nitrogen-fixing bacteria, and he was in heaven.

On the other hand, kids who struggle academically need to be in a place where their disabilities can be addressed and where kids with similar profiles are succeeding. As with the elementary-age child, a good educational evaluation will be an important tool for determining the right place.

SOCIAL SKILLS AND MIDDLE SCHOOL

Almost no one remembers the social environment of middle school with tremendous affection, but there is no question that to get by, you need certain basic social skills. You need to be able to understand what's OK and what's not, what's weird and what's normal. You need to perceive and work within the various social hierarchies of early adolescence and find your place in the school's social networks. Finding that place will mean being able to participate in the activities that go with it, whether sports or friendly gossip or shopping or playing video games. How a child succeeds in that middle school social world can have an enormous impact on his sense of himself and on his mental health. A kid who doesn't get the give-and-take of conversation, who has habits or behaviors that make the others uncomfortable (picking his nose or skin, twirling around, or other self-stimulating behaviors), is more likely to be teased, ostracized, or banished from the social group.

Michael has always been different but because of his high intelligence made it through elementary school without too much trouble. He hasn't ever really cared about having friends. He's physically awkward and shuns sports, and he engages in some pretty weird behaviors. I am worried that the other kids will tease him if they figure out he soils his pants. He himself doesn't even seem to realize it, and when I talk to him about it, I draw a blank. He will not keep extra underwear in his locker at school.

Major struggles with depression and anxiety often begin or become more acute at this age, which is why a preexisting relationship with a mental health professional may really pay off now. But a child who is in distress may need more than someone with whom to talk. You may need to rethink the whole school question and find a better fit. By this age, school and the peer group become something close to a child's entire world, and the right school at the right time can be akin to a lifesaver.

Our daughter became very depressed because she was so isolated socially. It didn't help that her older sister was so popular, could play every sport, and had loads of friends. The combination of her depression and her learning difficulties prompted us to look for a school that could address these issues. We found a private school for special education where she is thriving. She's learning and she has friends, and though she sometimes feels embarrassed about going to a "sped" school, most of the time she is pretty happy. She even went to an overnight camp for two weeks and survived!

BUDDIES

Many adults expect their children to help classmates who are in distress, but parents of most quirky kids will tell you it usually doesn't happen on its own. A relatively mature child in the classroom with good social skills can be asked to buddy up with the quirky child for lunch or social activities. This can help to bullyproof the quirky child, especially if the buddy is a popular and well-liked member of the group. Although kids (especially girls) of this age can be brutal to one another, they can also be remarkably receptive to a little responsibility. Consider whether you want to discuss this possibility with your child's teacher at this stage. Be sure that he thinks it's a good idea and that there is a likely candidate in the class who could handle it.

Some quirky kids can learn how to manage in middle school, and some just can't. Some quirky kids whose lack of self-awareness or whose more limited intelligence prevents them from altering their behavior or learning socially acceptable means of interacting with others really need the protection of caring and understanding adults at this time, when conformity and self-consciousness are at such a premium. However, we have met a number of families who feel that the most important thing at this stage of development is really a couple of good friends, inside or outside the classroom.

Ken has never liked sports, and once all the boys in the neighborhood stopped coming over for LEGOs and wanted to play sports, he just couldn't get himself to do it. This year, he got interested in Magic Cards, and there is another boy in his class who loves them, too. This has helped a lot. He looks forward to seeing his friend, and they can sit in a corner and play with their cards and enjoy themselves! They insulate each other from the eyes of the other kids.

For some quirky kids, being good at something or intensely interested in something that happens to be of interest to the other kids can be life-changing:

Once John got into sports, he developed a kind of persona at school as the sports/math guy, and everyone knew him as that kid. Because sports are so much a part of the life of boys (and men, for that matter), it created a social world for him that he hadn't had before. Everyone talks to him about the latest scores, and he engages in imaginary sports (like making a three-point basket or catching a pop fly and turning it into a double play). Kids who know him seem to think, "Oh, that's just John. He loves sports." Kids invite him to play pickup games at recess. Before the sports thing kicked in, he would motor around the edge of the playground, observe the others, and wring or flap his hands. We can hardly believe this has happened. I think he might have needed a special school if it hadn't.

PUTTING IT TOGETHER

Some school districts have developed programs specifically targeting the quirky-kid group, with the aim of keeping the kids within the public schools, though this is the exception rather than the rule. Other systems seem to think that these kids are bright enough to function independently in a typical school environment, perhaps with a little support around the edges. Certainly, this can be true, but you know your child best. Your gut feeling about whether he can thrive (or survive) in a given environment is worth a lot. Know your options, even if you don't need to use them.

We visited a school geared toward kids on the PDD spectrum just to get a sense of whether our daughter would need such a place. It was great to know that such a school existed. It was clear that a lot of care had gone into the design of the building, the classrooms, and the other common areas. The corridors were wide to minimize the bumping and jostling that these kids find unnerving; the walls were extra thick to contain outside noise and prevent distraction. Even the desks were designed with the physically awkward child in mind. The rooms for sensory integration therapy and speech groups were cheerful and inviting rather than a closet—literally—where she receives her OT now. The staff is all certified in special education and understands the learning issues of these kids. For the moment, we think she can survive where she is, but there is comfort in knowing other options exist.

Again, at the middle school level, many kids who can't quite manage on their own may do better with an aide in the classroom, to translate or reiterate directions or keep a child on task. Of course, as a middle schooler, a child may be more self-conscious about having an aide than she was back in elementary school, but good teachers and a supportive school should help make it work. It is worth remembering that your public school owes your child an *appropriate* education under the special education laws, and a classroom aide can be just the thing to turn an inappropriate environment into that legislatively mandated appropriate setting. Few schools will come forward to offer such an expensive addition to a child's education plan, but it has worked extremely well for some of these kids. It keeps them close to home, and it's a lot less expensive than a placement in a school outside the district.

Both typical and quirky kids who pass through this stage of development relatively intact have gained many of the skills they will use throughout young adulthood. You could argue that after middle school, it gets easier and easier to be a somewhat odd duck as you proceed through life. High school can be a more accepting phase of development, when kids, and the adults around them, relax their expectations a bit and sometimes actually embrace the qualities that marked quirky kids as social outcasts a few years earlier. College is notoriously a time when kids who felt out of place in high school finally find their peers, and out in the adult world, quirky colleagues, neighbors, and relatives abound on every hand. So if middle school is a hard row to hoe for your child, try to keep in mind that it's probably going to get easier as she goes and that her struggles may begin to ease a little as she makes the next transition.

The High School Years

High school was much better than middle school for Megan. She was fortunate to get a spot in a small program within the big public high school. It was generally good, and she made some friends, but nothing that ever involved getting together outside of school. Things other teenagers would do made her feel uncomfortable. There was a special education teacher in the program, and I gave her articles on classroom strategies for kids with Asperger's, and that did help. After the pilot program ended, she was in regular education classes at the high school and got involved in things like the science team. She worked as an apprentice at the aquarium, went to biology camp one summer. I know there will be a place for her in the science world.

Older adolescence is a time when *all* young people are forging their individual identities and getting a better idea of their place in the world. If you look at almost any high school class, you can see the extent to which many kids are actively trying to be different. In fact, developmentally, it's a characteristic of this age group to declare independence—from your parents, from particular sections of your peer group, even from your friends. Think back on your own adolescence. Were there groups of kids to which you knew you didn't belong and from which you felt you had to mark yourself off? Even typical kids of this age are often interested in a special topic or area to the exclusion of all else.

It's also true that high school generally offers you a little more scope to pursue your interests and play to your strengths than middle school. High school offers most children the first serious chance to choose their own identities: the audiovisual squad or the basketball team, the chess club or the jazz ensemble.

In many places nowadays, geekiness is somewhat cool—thanks probably to Bill Gates and to the general awareness that in a highly technological world, geekiness can be strength. A bumper sticker we recently saw for sale in a Western-wear store in a small town in Wyoming proclaimed BE NICE TO NERDS; YOU'LL END UP WORKING FOR ONE. There are kids who are known by their peers and teachers as budding poets or writers and those who are brilliant in chemistry or applied math. Memorizing the periodic table can be seen as pretty cool at this age—at least, by a certain select group. Spending eight hours a day doing gymnastics or figure skating is not all that unusual in high school, and other kids can find this fascinating and appealing.

The fact is, if a quirky kid has made it to high school, he will probably find it more accepting and less stressful than middle school and may not feel quite so different anymore. His learning issues ought to be well understood by now and strategies for coping—books on tape or an AlphaSmart for assignments, for example—well developed.

ACADEMIC ISSUES AND HIGH SCHOOL

By the time quirky kids reach ninth or tenth grade, most of their families are knowledgeable about the kids' learning profiles and about what additional services are necessary to make things work in school. Parents usually also have some sense of whether their children are socially isolated, though that becomes harder and harder to tell as children grow into adolescence and in many cases become much more private.

As in the middle school years, schools devoted to kids with an interest or a particular strength in, for example, math and science or art and music can be wonderful places for quirky kids. Music and math are areas of strength for a subset of quirky kids and quirky adults as well. On the other hand, vocational schools can be terrific places for quirky kids. For highly educated parents (in the college sense of the word), sending your child to a vocational school can feel like moving backward. But remember, this isn't you; it's your child, and you want to give him his best shot at an independent livelihood.

By now, it should come pretty easily, when investigating schools, to decide whether or not your quirky kid could negotiate the corridors, the need to move from class to class throughout the day, the gym, or the cafeteria. The degree of structure is a major consideration at this time. Does your child thrive on structure, as many quirky kids do? Does she need to know exactly what's next and where? Can he tolerate moving to a new classroom every forty-five minutes? Is too much choice overwhelming? Look around at the other kids and their behavior with one another. Will your child's social behaviors be acceptable here? If many of the other kids are wearing only black or have ten piercings on their nose and eyebrows, will your daughter's need to wear the same jeans and T-shirt every day seem so outlandish? How about the noise level? Will it be overwhelming? Are there options about where to eat lunch or do a study period? Are team sports required, or are other options available for the after-school hours? Meeting with the special education coordinator and school psychologist will be helpful for most families, and talking with other parents you've met over the years will help determine whether a particular high school has a good chance of working for your child.

Separate schools for kids with special needs or with special skills will again be a consideration. It is rare that a high school–age student who has not required a separate environment in the past will need one now. On the other hand, kids for whom a separate environment has been successful at the middle school level may find the transition to a more standard school relatively easy at this time. The anonymity of the larger high schools is a bonus for a child coming out of a more restrictive setting. All kids are somewhat self-conscious. They come out of a pretty wide variety of backgrounds and school experiences, and the fact that some of them attended a special school is a lot less meaningful and may not even be noticed.

ADOLESCENT ISSUES AND THE QUIRKY TEENAGER

The developmental tasks of adolescence are challenging for all kids. As doctors, we are aware of the issues of the teenage years and on the lookout for problems that may arise—mental health issues for which the child is genetically predisposed, substance-abuse problems, eating disorders, high-risk sexual behaviors, questions about sexual identity or preference, reactions to longstanding family stresses. All of these problems are out there in all the high schools to which our kids go every day. In some ways, the quirky kids have it no better or worse than any other teenagers. Those with splinter skills or intense special interests may have an anchor that many of their peers lack. In the average public high school, most kids will be able to find at least a couple of kids like themselves, and quirky kids may find themselves appealing to other kids for the first time. As kids approach adulthood, their refusal to participate in certain activities has a lot less meaning. No one expects all teenagers—or adults, for that matter—to be the same, and accommodations start to come more easily to peers and teachers alike.

HE NEVER TELLS ME ANYTHING:
FIGURING OUT WHAT GOES ON IN HIGH SCHOOL

Your adolescent may communicate with you mostly in grunts, frequently look sullen, confine comments at meals to occasional sarcastic sallies, and shrug when you ask which teacher you should check with to see how she's doing. And this has nothing to do with quirkiness.

Indeed, with older children, it may prove more difficult to gauge their success. You may not have one particularly involved or knowledgeable teacher to fill you in on your child's progress. Academic performance, of course, is one good indicator: a student who is failing in all subject areas is not in a good environment for learning, or something major is getting in the way. Probably a more sensitive indicator of success at this age, however, is your child's mental health and independence. Because mental health issues such as depression, suicidality, anxiety, or obsessive-compulsive disorder tend to present around this age, and because of the complex comorbidities of many quirky-kid syndromes, it is worth keeping a close but not too intrusive eye out for any distress signals. Watch for increasing obsessional behavior or for disturbed sleeping habits. Be alert for the adolescent who unilaterally decides to stop taking her medicine. She may be stopping because she's having a problem, or she may have a problem because she's stopped. Watch for evidence of increasing social isolation. Depression can manifest as loss of appetite, as unexplained crying jags, or as anhedonia, the loss of the ability to take pleasure in the activities a child normally enjoys. If you think your child may be in trouble along these lines, don't depend on the high school faculty or staff to detect, diagnose, or treat the problem. You will probably need the help of a psychiatrist or psychologist (preferably one who has known your child for a while) to tease it out.

HIGH SCHOOL ISN'T EASY

Adolescents can be excruciatingly self-conscious, and dissatisfaction with yourself or your performance or your place in the high school world can be a powerful and destructive emotion.

For making the best of your child's experience, a good recommendation from one of the mothers we interviewed is to "think outside the all-or-none box." Many schools are willing to make accommodations to keep a child in his local school, but you may need to suggest them. For example, a child who simply cannot learn a foreign language or becomes anxious or obsessive in health education or is too uncoordinated for gym class can still thrive with relatively minor changes in expectations. Think creatively. How about an extra year of high school, with fewer classes per year, or an independent study or studio for a child with special interests or abilities? Don't focus too much on graduation requirements or college admissions, especially during their first couple of high school years. Save that for later, when you have a better sense of what the future may hold.

References and Resources

Bashe, Patricia Romanowski, and Barbara L. Kirby. *The Oasis Guide to Asperger Syndrome: Advice, Support, Insight, and Inspiration.* New York: Crown, 2001. This book has a terrific chapter called "Special Education Basics," at the end of which is a list of further references and Web sites.

Leicester City Council and Leicestershire County Council. *Asperger Syndrome—Practical Strategies for the Classroom: A Teacher's Guide.* Shawnee Mission, Kans.: Autism Asperger Publishing Co., 2002. This is a guide to pass on to your child's classroom teacher.

Levine, Mel. *A Mind at a Time: America's Top Learning Expert Shows How Every Child Can Succeed.* New York: Touchstone Books, 2003. Dr. Levine is a developmental and behavioral pediatrician who has devoted his career to understanding the ways in which children learn. This compassionate and informative book may help you understand how your child's "wiring" affects his school performance.

Silver, Larry B. *The Misunderstood Child: Understanding and Coping with Your Child's Learning Disabilities.* New York: Three Rivers Press, 1998. Currently in its third edition, this volume is a great resource for parents of any child with learning differences.

Stewart, Kathryn. *Helping a Child with Nonverbal Learning Disorder or Asperger's Syndrome: A Parent's Guide.* Oakland, Calif.: New Harbinger Publications, 2002. This is a guide for parents written by a psychologist who founded a California high school specifically for these children.

Tanguay, Pamela B. *Nonverbal Learning Disabilities at School: Educating Students with NLD, Asperger Syndrome, and Related Conditions.* London: Jessica Kingsley Publishers, 2002. Useful for both parents and teachers.

Twachtman-Cullen, Diane, and Jennifer Twachtman-Reilly. *How Well Does Your IEP Measure Up?: Quality Indicators for Effective Service Delivery.* Higganum, Conn.: Starfish Specialty Press, 2002. A practical, step-by-step guide to making the IEP process work for your child.

8

○ ○ ● ○

Social Life:
FINDING FRIENDS AND GETTING BY

School may be more important for his future, family life more fraught with friction on a day-to-day basis, but for all that, it's probably the social life of their quirky child that most gnaws at parents, keeps them up nights, provokes their fears and even their tears.

Over the short term, when parents worry about a quirky child's social abilities, they are worrying about whether he will be able to participate in and enjoy all the various games, jokes, and friendships that are a big part of life for school-age children. But over the long term, parents may worry about something bigger, more global: Will my child ever fit into the world? Ever have friends? Ever get along normally with colleagues? Ever find love? The social peculiarities can serve to isolate a child early on, perhaps even before the child has been evaluated, and can leave the adults around him bewildered.

I'm Jewish, and Andrew's father is Christian. Andrew has decided he prefers Christmas. When a mother came into his preschool class to talk about the Hannukah celebration, he yelled out, "I hate Hannukah!" The mother thought he was an anti-Semite. Fortunately, I was there, and I explained that he was half Jewish himself. Recently, he said, "I hate Hannukah; I hate Jesus. I only like the big bang."

Many quirky children suffer socially, to one extent or another, and their parents suffer with them. You have a child you adore, whose struggles and triumphs you recognize and celebrate. You see all his lovable, endearing qualities. It can hurt a lot if his classmates seem to see only a weirdo, a freak, an outcast. And it can hurt even more if now and then you see him through their eyes—his off-putting personal habits, his obsessive conversations.

Preschool and Before

During your child's toddler and preschool years, you have a certain amount of control, at least over the forms of her social life, if not the content. Parents arrange playdates for young children, make the call, schlepp back and forth, supervise as needed. Many day-care and preschool-age children are pretty willing to go on any playdate with any classmate; if there are toys and videos and snacks, or some combination of them, it seems like a treat.

On the other hand, many younger quirky kids just aren't ready for a lot of socializing. Early intervention will offer some social contact, and that may be enough for them. Socializing can be fairly stressful for many of these children, and they may need to decompress and relax without the additional pressure of a playdate. Maybe your child would be better off if you took him to the playground and let him play alone with his favorite truck while he has a chance to observe the other children. "Parallel play"—playing next to one another without actually interacting—is normal in toddlers and often lasts longer in quirky kids. Many like being around other children but without getting too close or without the pressure of having to talk, share toys, or take turns. Don't let your own wish to see your child as "normal" or your hopes that playing with other children will somehow be good for her push you into setting up a social life that she's not yet ready to handle.

PLAYDATES

When your child is in the preschool years, ages three to five, you will probably find yourself arranging at least the occasional playdate. Quirky children may require more supervision than other kids to make sure that the playdate is peaceful, that the guest's wishes are respected, and that both children come away feeling they've had a good time. In fact, for some quirky children, playdates are essentially supervised parental project times.

What are some of the special issues to consider as you think about whether your preschool child is ready for playdates and, if so, how to make them work?

- Play may be harder for a quirky child for any or all of several reasons:

    - Many have difficulty with symbolic play. Their imaginations work differently, and they just don't get the dress-up or the let's-be-pirates.
    - Language delays or language problems make it harder to play, to understand, and to be understood.
    - Sensory integration issues may make it hard to handle loud noises or the touch and texture of something that's part of the game.
    - Fine motor problems can make a child less skillful at all kinds of games—or just frustrated by his own inability to do something that the other child can do easily, whether it's dressing a Barbie or putting LEGOs together.
    - Tantrums may be so severe that they scare the other children.

- Negotiating the sharing and the turn-taking can be more complicated.

    - Because of different developmental trajectories, a quirky four-year-old may have as much trouble sharing toys as a more typical two-year-old.
    - And the more typical four-year-old with whom your child is playing is not going to have a whole lot of patience if she doesn't get her turn. Preschoolers, when they do master the sharing concept, turn into real sticklers about rules and fairness.
    - A particular toy or game or object may have extra meaning to the quirky child—a truck that has to stay in the lineup or a stuffed animal that always sits in a particular position on her pillow. Put away any objects that you think your child may not want to see another child handling or playing with.
    - Children with rituals may have trouble changing their rules and routines when another child is around. Talk it through in advance: "We're going to have a snack together, and *you* can eat all your raisins before we open the box of Goldfish crackers, but Susie might want to mix them up."
    - Keep these early playdates as short as possible. This is more reasonable if they don't involve long drives. In fact, this is one situation in which

a multifamily house or a congenial city neighborhood offers real advantages.

A lot of John's early social experience was with the boy downstairs. They would have short, sweet interactions, and when things started to escalate, it would end. That's the great thing about a multiple-family house: you don't have to go to any trouble to set this up or cart them for miles. I think it's much harder in a suburban or rural area where everything has to be arranged in advance.

- Tailor the playdate to your child.

  - Ask him with whom he most enjoys spending time at school.
  - Ask the teacher with whom he plays, talks, eats.
  - Think about an activity he enjoys that you think would work well with another child—a trip to the playground (outside time is often much easier than inside time), a game that you know he understands and can play competently.
  - Make a plan and walk your child through it. Quirky kids often do better if they know what to expect: "Susie will arrive with her mother, and you'll play hide-and-seek. And then when you get tired of that, we'll have a snack, and then we'll let Susie choose which video to watch. Then her mother will come, and we'll say good-bye."

- When your child is invited over to another child's house, be realistic.

  - Keep it short, especially at the beginning.
  - Consider the question of whether you want to stick around for at least the first part of the visit. This probably depends on how well you know the other child's parents and how concerned you are about how your child will do. Many parents, inviting another child over for a playdate, have in mind a couple of hours of relative freedom for themselves, the child happily occupied with a friend—that is to say, they aren't necessarily expecting to have to entertain another adult during that time.
  - Be easily reachable—by phone, by cell phone—and don't be too far away.

- It is perfectly acceptable to call in halfway through the visit and ask how things are going. Be prepared to come pick up early if necessary.
- Tell the other child's parent anything she absolutely has to know—that there may be a tantrum or a seizure or an episode of tics, that your child is phobic about water or dogs or vacuum cleaners.

- Whether the playdate is at your house or at someone else's, if something goes awry, do your best to figure out what it was and how it happened. You may be able to avoid that particular trigger the next time around or talk it through with your child.
- Don't assume that anything that goes wrong was necessarily on account of your child's quirks. It takes two to tango. Part of the give-and-take of playdates is figuring out what to do when your guest acts like a creep and won't play any of your games and mixes up all the different colors of Play-Doh and says she wants to go home after five minutes. This is your cue, as a parent, to be gracious and understanding toward the other parent and make her feel that you understand that all children have their good days and their bad days.

We don't mean to make this sound as if it's all hard work and always poised on the edge of disaster. In fact, plenty of quirky kids start having playdates during the preschool years, enjoy their friends, enjoy themselves, and go back to school with special bonds to the children with whom they've played. So as you sense your own child's interest and readiness, it can definitely be worthwhile to enter the game.

You should also have some scenarios in mind that take into account the less successful turns that a playdate can take—not to mention the disasters. You know your quirky child, and you know what to plan for—an episode of stereotyped repetitive behavior that will bewilder the other child, a tantrum—and you should have some options in mind, from a reliable favorite board game to a second parent available if the kids need to be separated. And just in case you do encounter a disastrous playdate (your child bites her guest; the guest bites your child; a favorite and irreplaceable toy is destroyed; both children end up in screaming fits, and the neighbors call the police), comfort yourself with the certainty that all children have a few calamitous playdates along the way. Then stop to think about what you might arrange differently next time.

Elementary School

THE SCHOOL DAY

Caitlin developed a phobia about flowers. For no reason we could ever completely figure out, she developed a strong aversion to flowers on fabric, clothes, curtains, etcetera. Ever try to buy clothes for a little girl with the caveat that nothing can have any flowers on it? If we went to a restaurant that had flowers on the china or even the furniture, we would have to leave because she couldn't tolerate it. And because her social skills were so poor, if anyone at school wore clothes with flowers printed on them, she would tell them they were ugly and she hated them.

The only way I ever know how my son is doing socially in school is either another mother tells me or I invite a couple of little girls in his class over for a playdate. This one little girl knows absolutely everything. I have learned all kinds of things that he never tells me. He's a boy, and all boys are to some extent clueless. So I'll say, "How was school, honey?" He'll say, "Fine." He seems OK. Then this little girl comes over, and she'll start telling me the teacher screamed at him and made him cry.

Social life in elementary school is highly dependent on the school schedule and the general school attitude. Some elementary school children have large amounts of essentially unsupervised, unstructured time—on the bus, on the playground, even at times in the classroom—whereas others are much more tightly regulated. Unstructured time is notoriously tough for the quirky child. A seasoned elementary school teacher will have a pretty close sense of what is going on socially among the children in the room, though this may be more true in first grade than in fifth or sixth.

David likes rules and doesn't understand the gray areas. At school, he couldn't understand why the other kids didn't behave properly and would tell them to behave themselves or he would tell the teachers what they were doing. This became annoying to the kids and teachers, but his motivation was more that he just didn't get it rather than wanting anyone to get into trouble.

It is greatly to your advantage to befriend your child's teacher, especially in the early grades. Don't overwhelm her with your expertise without paying deference to hers. There are parents who come in on day one with an enormous pile of information about their child's issues, about the most approved techniques for dealing with his eccentricities, about his social needs and emotional requirements—all without giving the teacher any chance to observe the child in the context of the classroom and draw some conclusions of her own. You want the teacher as a partner, an expert observer and interpreter of the school-day academic and social scenes. You should remember that she will have a different perspective on your child and his functioning, perhaps more attuned than yours to how your child reacts to the social exigencies of a boy—or a girl—of a certain age.

BOYS AND GIRLS

Boys and girls move through elementary school on substantially different social trajectories. These are generalizations, of course, but for the most part, girls are much earlier to develop complex social webs, cliques, interlocking nets of friendship and best-friendship, and intricate systems of in-groups and out-groups. Boys—at least, in the earlier grades—tend to be less socially aware, more physical in many of their activities, and more willing to consider other boys their age in the general category of friend. This can make the early years of school somewhat easier for a quirky boy than for a quirky girl. Chances are that in the second grade, say, a boy who pays no attention to his clothes and sometimes says some pretty weird things will be able to be included in a general pack of second-grade boys, whereas a girl the same age might already be clearly marked as an outlier. It may also mean that the gap between a quirky girl's social perceptions and social skills and those of her peers will be much bigger than the comparable gap for a boy would be.

Rebecca misses social cues. She wants to have friends, she's six years old, but she gets into struggles. She doesn't understand the rules other kids want to play by; she's extremely literal; she pulls phrases right out of cartoons, to which she is addicted, and uses them pretty appropriately, but they are not her words. One day, she screamed, "You don't love me anymore!!" I thought, what is this? Then I realized she had heard it on SpongeBob SquarePants, *the exact same line. She is impulsive and recently got into trouble for stealing in her class. She was sent to the principal's office, where she said, "I'm so bad. Please give me another chance. I won't do it ever again." Once again, totally scripted from something. The principal interpreted this as very "high-functioning," when in fact it was scripted.*

All this can make it pretty hard on the girls. As a parent, you may be able to help at this age by keeping a careful eye on what the other children wear to school, what they use to carry their books or their lunch or protect themselves from the rain, and helping your child get it right. You can support any friendship that seems to be developing and maybe try to cement it a little by becoming friends yourself with the child's parent.

PECULIAR HABITS

As children grow, both boys and girls become more and more aware of any behavior that marks a child as different. By third or fourth grade, the child with some repetitive personal behavior or some obsessive school routine or some personal hygiene black spot is going to be noticed and possibly teased or even shunned. And a teacher who draws attention to this habit as well, even if her intentions are good, may increase the degree to which the other children pay attention.

My daughter has trichotillomania. She picks at her scalp, pulls her hair out. We were trying to help her with this, and I mentioned it to her teacher—thinking, of course, she must have noticed this, so I was going to tell her some strategies that the behavioral psychologist had suggested. They didn't work, but still . . . So I mentioned it to her teacher, which was really stupid on my part. And she said, "I hadn't noticed." But then, apparently, she went crazy with my daughter and her head and was constantly telling her to stop twirling her hair, and all the kids in the room knew about it. So then I had to tell her, "Could you lighten up on the head thing?"

All you can do is try to see those possible troublesome habits as problems well in advance and target your behavioral modification at home, your work in therapy, or even your trials with medication partly at those behaviors. But even so, there will be visible quirks, and there will be other kids to point them out.

Is it ever worth visiting the school, explaining the whole situation to the other children, and asking for their tolerance and good manners? Absolutely. Children have been known to rise to the occasion, and we have patients whose parents have repeatedly visited the school, explaining, say, a young child's severe skin condition or the sometimes frightening aspects of a tic disorder or the absolute rituals of a child with obsessive-compulsive disorder (OCD).

When Brian was in fifth grade, they did a skit about differences—with a friend saying he didn't like the way Brian had to take a snack first and Brian explaining to the class that it was just his OCD, he couldn't eat something if someone else had touched it. OCD is easier to explain than Asperger's because you can see it, it's so concrete.

TEASING

A certain amount of teasing is a fact of life, but teasing in school can get out of hand, and it can be a parent's difficult and thankless task to assess the degree and intensity of teasing going on and respond appropriately. Elementary school is probably the time when your child is most likely to talk openly with you about being teased and least likely to forbid you to interfere.

Other kids teased me when I was growing up. I cared, but I didn't care. Nothing could stop me. I always thought I was the greatest painter in the world, even when I wasn't. I stopped caring whether other kids liked me. I would put it out of my head.

When teasing passes a certain point, especially if the object is a less-than-popular child, when teasing becomes ganging up or happens so regularly that the child becomes unhappy in school or reflects racial differences or the child's physical traits or behaviors she cannot control, it's time for the parent to talk to the teacher and time for the teacher—and the school—to do something.

Schools *can* do something about this problem. Don't ever let anyone tell you they can't. At the elementary school level, at least, the tone set by the teachers and the administration, and their response to teasing that gets out of hand, can make an enormous difference. It is not impossible to create an atmosphere of censure, in which the child who (inevitably) starts teasing anyway is himself shunned by other children who don't want to get into trouble (or don't want to have to meet and process it all over again). As with everything else, it gets harder in middle school, but that doesn't mean it's a futile effort or shouldn't be attempted.

Where your child goes to school does make a difference. With Sam, at his first school, he was getting teased because Cinderella *was his favorite movie. That's a girl movie, not a boy movie, and he was getting teased pretty badly. I brought it to the attention of the school staff, and they basically said, "We have enough on our plates. We can't take this on." You know, "Kids will be kids." But at this school, they take it on. They process it; they meet; they discuss how it makes the child feel; they say, "It's not OK"—and that makes a big difference.*

What danger signs should you look for if you think your child might be being teased?

- Tears, fears, anxiety about going to school.
- Asking to stay home or pretending to be sick—any "school-avoidance behaviors."
- Worries that seem to be directly connected to the less-supervised parts of the day—the bus ride, the playground, the lunchroom.
- General signs that your child is upset—increased anxiety, sleep disturbances, unexplained crying.
- If you think something is going on, ask your child about school in general, ask whether anyone said anything to him that he didn't like, and then ask specifically about those same less-supervised moments: With whom did you sit on the bus? Play at recess? Eat lunch? Anything unusual happen?
- Bring up the subject of teasing and discuss it, before it gets to be any kind of problem. You can discuss what teasing is—saying mean things to make other kids feel bad—maybe with reference to what goes on between siblings, and you can tell your child:
  - Never tease anybody else, because teasing is mean.
  - If anybody ever teases him, that person is doing something wrong.

- He should get help from a teacher. Teachers and principals don't like teasing.
- He should tell you if there's too much teasing in school.

What should you do if you think your child is being teased?

- Talk to the teacher or the bus attendant or the lunchroom monitor.
- Do a little reality testing. Does it seem as if this is really happening on a regular basis, or was it an exceptional moment?
- Think about whether the problem could be addressed logistically. Could the child sit at the front of the bus, near the monitor? Would adding an extra lunchroom aide help, even if it was only for a week or two?
- If you think that something bad is happening, ask the teacher to do something about it. If the teacher isn't sure how to handle it or hasn't handled anything of the kind before, suggest a consultation with the school counselor or a more experienced teacher—and suggest that they might want to talk to the class together.
- Set a follow-up with the teacher (a return appointment or a phone-call date), so that it's clear you will be coming back to hear how things went with the intervention—the class discussion; the separate session with the ringleaders, if it's clear who they are—and how they're going now for your child.
- If you don't get the response you want from the teacher, go to the principal.
- Make it clear that you see this as a serious issue and that you intend to stay involved.
- If your child is being teased partly on account of a disability, make it clear that you regard this as especially serious and possibly illegal.
- Should you, ever and under any circumstances, consider calling up another parent to say, "Can't you make your daughter stop teasing my son?" Certainly, if you're ever going to do such a thing, it would be in the elementary years. Once your child gets to middle school, it's probably pretty much out of the question.

  - If you do decide to do this, tread carefully. You may make an enemy.
  - The more you know about the other parent, the better, and the more contact you've had in the past, the better.

- Ideally, you want to present this as just one little up-and-down in the long careers of your children as they go to school together.
- Remember that you are placing another parent in the always uncomfortable position of hearing something pretty negative about his child.
- Try, as much as possible (this will be pretty hard), not to make it sound as if you think the other child is a horror, a monster, and a lower form of life.
- Offer a specific solution: "Rachel probably doesn't realize it, but Lisa feels really bad about not being able to read yet. If Rachel could understand her feelings better, I'm sure she wouldn't tease her about it."
- If you're making a threat, make it politely: "I'm afraid that if Rachel pulls Lisa's hair on the school bus even once more, they're going to ask Rachel to stop taking the bus, and I would really like it if we could put our heads together and talk to the girls and find a way to stop that from happening."
- Still and all, we have heard only a few positive stories of the parents-calling-parents variety, and a lot of nasty ones.

- You shouldn't have to resort to this, and we hope you never do, but there have been a number of successful (and highly public) lawsuits in recent years in which children who were bullied or teased unmercifully or sexually harassed in public schools have sued those schools for failing to protect them and have won large judgments. The teacher—or certainly, the principal—will be aware of this nightmare scenario, and it should make it much more likely that your highly reasonable and civil request will be taken seriously. If it isn't, and if things are really bad, you might then, in the end, have to talk to a lawyer.

In the upcoming section on middle school, we'll talk a little bit about bullying, which can also be an issue during the elementary school years, especially in the fourth and fifth grades.

THE COOL AND THE UNCOOL

Gabriel is pretty isolated a lot of the time, and as he's gotten older, it has become harder for me to do the behind-the-scenes planning to keep a social life going. Other kids are busier, and he's often excluded.

By first grade among the girls, and by fourth or fifth grade among the boys, the question of who is cool starts to become an issue. Quirky kids, by and large, are not cool. What we mean is, just because they aren't teasing your daughter doesn't mean that the cool girls are including her in the cool lunch table, where everyone wears the same matching barrettes. And although you can to some extent help fight your child's battles when it comes to teasing, at least in elementary school, there is no parent on earth who has ever succeeded in making the cool girls open up another place at the lunch table, no matter how many of the right barrettes she bought and faithfully pinned into her daughter's hair. And the problem is, as it gets more important to be cool, more children begin to worry that uncoolness may be catching, like cooties.

In Megan's grade-five/six class, it became more clear that her development was well behind the others in her class. The sixth-grade girls especially, who were trying to be more independent, made her life miserable, and she became an out-cast in the class. At that time, she started acting out. She actually kicked a boy in her class when he accidentally knocked a shell off her desk and it broke. She con-tinued her spaced-out episodes of looking out the window and missing what was going on in class. We knew that our family needed help.

Gabriel is definitely not cool. By fifth grade, the boys are getting to a point where there are cool kids. Cool guys are smart and funny and socially savvy, and they sit together at lunch—and Gabriel doesn't notice any of this yet. But his friend Ken is also not cool, and he's more aware, he's more with it. So Ken is cool enough to know that Gabriel is the weirdest kid in the class, so he's not going to hang around with Gabriel in school, even though they're friends outside.

All this, of course, is for some children heartbreak enough—not being teased but not being included. There is just not much that a parent can do about it directly, except maybe listen when your child wants to talk about it, offer comfort and reinforcement, and promise her that this, too, shall pass.

On the other hand, there are some less direct things you can do about it, strategies aimed at helping your child find a peer group, social contacts, and friends and thereby freeing him, to some extent, from the strictly limited so-cial dynamics of his classroom. We'll take those up under the general rubric of friendships.

FRIENDSHIPS

For both boys and girls, a single good friendship can change the world. Going through elementary school is much easier if you have a best friend. If the right one comes along for your child, that can be a blessing. Cherish that best friend, who may well also be a little quirky. Help them find time to be together so that the feeling that they really are friends, with a mutual library of experiences and in-jokes, grows and expands. If there isn't a best friend available at school (and there isn't always, for quirky or nonquirky kids), and if there doesn't seem to be a wider circle of generally friendly peers, it is probably worthwhile helping your child look elsewhere for friends and companions.

The single most important step that many quirky children take toward friendship is to find an interest—or even an obsession—that is socially acceptable among children of that age. A nine-year-old boy obsessed with baseball and baseball statistics, a seven-year-old girl who cares about Pokémon more than anything else—these are children whose obsessions may work for them socially and may help them appear not so different from many of their peers. Whatever the cards and collectibles are for your child's age group, whatever the collective fads, think about encouraging your child to participate.

Pokémon is what she fell into from going to school. Before that, it was dinosaurs, and I was happy with the dinosaur obsession. I became an expert on dinosaurs because she knew so much. We would go to the library and get books and I would read them to her, and she really seemed to absorb it all, retain it all. Right now, Pokémon is Lisa's obsession. Her father and I had bought her Pokémon cards and she had several good cards, and she went out with the neighbors and traded every one of her good cards for really crappy cards. And I said to her dad, "If it helps her get along with other kids, I'm happy." Pokémon seems to work for both boys and girls, whereas when she was obsessed with dinosaurs, it was hard to talk to other girls. Now she has a couple of good girlfriends at school.

- Think seriously about community activities—Boy Scouts, Girl Scouts, church groups, bowling leagues—especially for the older elementary school child. A somewhat more structured setting may make it easier for a quirky kid to interact with his peers. It will give him a wider circle of kids at school with whom he has something in common. We recently read about a mother who organized a Cub Scout pack specifically for boys with Asperger's, ADD, and other developmental issues, tailoring meetings and activities to their needs and interests.

- Look at school-based after-school activities. For younger children, this will probably mean the school-based after-school program, if one exists and if your child seems to enjoy going. Going to after-school, even a couple of days a week, can again give her the chance to interact with a slightly different mix of kids, some older and some younger. It will broaden her social horizons within the school and may help her learn to play more comfortably.

- As your child gets older, look at after-school extracurricular activities— band, orchestra, chorus—if the school offers them. A child with musical skills can easily make this into his most important peer group, and once again, it will mean children in other classes and other grades who say hi in the hallway or stop to ask if he knows what they're supposed to practice tonight.

- A child with a splinter skill may find his peers—and his friends—in a special program or an after-school enrichment class. There are math groups, computer classes, art schools to look at.

- When your child finds an out-of-school friend, make it work. Get to know that child's parents, figure out the logistics of getting them together every now and then, think about carpooling to and from their activity.

- Keep in mind, though, as you're looking for extra activities, that as we said earlier, the elementary years can often be the years most crowded by therapy appointments and other special supports, some of which, after all, are aimed at helping the child develop social skills. Ask yourself, which is more important right now, occupational therapy or math group? Keep in mind that these children grow and change. The mix that's right for now may not be right a year from now.

- Some children will find their friends—or even their soul mates—at those very therapy appointments. It may be that in a pragmatic language group, your child will encounter another child who is somehow just like him and that they will recognize each other with joy.

Caitlin has not had many friends but now has a friend through her social-skills group who also has Asperger's. They E-mail each other, and I have to say, E-mail is a wonderful thing for a child who misses nonverbal cues. She only has to deal with the words, and the two of them share interests, so it has worked very well. Otherwise, she is never invited over to anyone's house, doesn't get invited to birthday parties.

- Your extended family, if they are in the area, may be a source of companionship. Many kids accept cousins, a little older or a little younger or a little quirky, with a sort of tribal inclusion that doesn't necessarily apply outside the family. If your child has been in contact with cousins—or aunts and uncles not so far from his age—all his life, they may continue to serve as playmates and a special peer group as he grows.

- If a child needs social contact beyond what her school seems to be offering her, consider the possibility of a pen pal, nowadays usually an E-mail buddy. Many quirky kids learn to type and use computers fairly early. Some find it easier to E-mail, without the pressure of having to decipher the social cues of body language and tone of voice. There are E-mail lists for children with certain specific diagnoses (autistic spectrum disorders, learning disabilities), and it can be both a pleasure and a comfort for a child to E-mail back and forth with someone whose experience matches her own.

  Very important: If you do decide to go this route, remember that quirky children, like all children, need very set guidelines on Internet safety and, because they tend to be more socially naive, may be at special risk. A parent should check that the E-mail buddy is actually who he seems to be—is, in fact, a child—and probably should make contact (also by E-mail is fine) with that child's parents. If last names and addresses are to be exchanged, it should be by the parents, since a child's basic rules are: *Never give out your address or your last name on the Internet. Never arrange to meet someone over the Internet. Never post your picture on the Internet.*

- Finally, remember that many quirky children find that they enjoy spending time with children younger than themselves.

Before John found baseball, he liked playing with younger kids. They didn't challenge him socially, and they would help him catch up with things he hadn't done earlier, like playing with the train set or building with blocks, which he never did when he was supposed to!

Abby had a little girl in our old neighborhood who was three years younger, and they would ride bikes together and play dolls together, and the littler kid was flattered that here was this big girl who wanted to spend time with her.

BIRTHDAY PARTIES

Everybody has them—birthdays, at least—and most children have parties. As your child ages, depending on her social skills and her social milieu, she may have to face the heartbreak of not being invited. But while she's small, you are in fact more likely to have to face the heartbreak—or at least the severe stress—of her *being* invited and having to go and behave. There are certainly some children who don't like birthday parties at all—we know one boy whose mother always just says no—but many of them will want to go, even if the party poses a social challenge.

As my son gets older, he's better able to say, "Wait, that's not something I want to do," but you don't always know. He was invited to one birthday party, and he really wanted to go because he liked the kid, and it turned out it was a laser-tag birthday party. It was really loud, really dark, really scary—and he'll never do that again. And if it's a pool party at the Y, he's not gonna go because he hates water, or he'll just come at the end for the cake. We have to allow him the choice and help explain when he doesn't want to go.

Certain aspects of children's birthday parties are pretty ritualized. You can help your child prepare for those, from the blowing-out-the-candles-and-singing moment to the good-bye and thank-you-I-had-a-very-nice-time—which, in any case, has to be nudged along by parental prompting for a good nine out of any ten children. But it can be hard to predict the games, the activities, even the entertainment. That is why many parents of quirky children end up being the ones hanging around at the party, offering to help and planning to stick it out just in case the bowling or Murray the Magician or the treasure hunt somehow goes awry.

Keep your own child's birthday parties small when he is small. Invite grandparents, siblings, a favorite baby-sitter, a couple of playmates. The experience of being the center of attention is overwhelming for many quirky kids, and the social responsibilities that devolve on the host—saying the occasional thank-you, not winning all the prizes, not biting anyone—can just be too demanding. As your child moves along in school, however, you may find yourself in a setting where it is obligatory to invite the whole class—or at least all the boys or all the girls. You should at least consider some kind of short and highly ritualized party outside the home, if there is a venue that your child finds comfortable and pleasant—a pizza party, a party at the science museum, a party in a theme or fast-food restaurant, a party at one of those "activity zones." Most children nowadays seem to be so conditioned to these parties that they arrive knowing exactly what to do, eager to see the IMAX movie or the dancing rat, depending on the place. They depart feeling they have gotten exactly what they came for, and you don't have to deal with the question of whether you somehow gave a weird party because your kid is, well, weird. You also maintain a certain amount of family privacy by keeping the party out of the home and eliminating the possibility that a child might, for example, discover the personal hygiene sticker charts on your upstairs bathroom wall or the Barbie doll collection in a house where all the children are boys. And this may be much easier for many quirky children than having to entertain in their homes and watch other children handle their possessions.

Middle School

For many kids of all descriptions, the middle school years are the most troubled, the years when your body's changes can race ahead of your social readiness—or else lag behind everyone else's development. They're years of self-consciousness and self-doubt when many kids take refuge in conformity, in blending in with the pack and being one with the crowd.

Junior high school was hell. Megan's one friend moved away, and that was a tragedy for Megan. Also, the other girls in her sphere at school were into pop music and culture and talking about boys and clothes, and they would say mean things to her. At this point, we tried a girls' social-skills group.

THE SCHOOL DAY

Where your child is in school for these years really matters. Middle school grades are grouped differently in different systems. We know, of course, that many people don't have much choice: the town has one junior high, and that's that. Still, we will discuss the way these different arrangements shape up for quirky kids and hope that even if your choices are limited, you will be better able to prepare for your child's experience.

Generally speaking, quirky kids are much better off either in a separate middle school or in a kindergarten-through-eight setting. They are unlikely to profit socially from being with true high school students (although there may be some quirky kids for whom the availability of advanced math or advanced music or advanced art classes is an advantage). Since they may already be a little behind their middle school peers, they could appear hopelessly slow and hopelessly young in a world full of sixteen- and seventeen- and eighteen-year-olds. If your school system puts seventh and eighth graders in the high school, you need to find out what special arrangements are made to guide and protect the younger children. Eating lunch in a high school cafeteria or just hanging out in high school hallways is probably going to be a challenge. Could she eat her lunch quickly and then go to the library? Is there a counselor's office if she needs to talk? Can she go to the nurse if she's getting anxious?

When middle school is still part of elementary school, some quirky children find a certain relief from the social pressures of puberty exactly because they are in a place full of younger children who just aren't there yet. The unfortunate truth is that in many kindergarten-through-eight school setups, the last two grades feel a little vestigial. The building is not really built for their needs, and most of the teachers are oriented toward the early grades. However, this arrangement offers the comforts of familiarity and a known setting during some pretty confusing years.

A separate middle school, for grades seven and eight only (or for grades six and seven and eight or occasionally for grades seven and eight and nine), can work well socially for some quirky kids. These schools offer all children an opportunity to go through these awkward years without constant side-by-side comparisons either to true adolescents (comfortably on the other side of puberty) or to small children (innocent, un-self-conscious, and generally cute). Middle schools also, by definition, attract teachers who find this an interesting age, delight in what middle school minds can produce, and feel sympathy with the emotional and social currents these kids navigate. Since quirky kids are often more comfortable with adults than with people their own age, these particular adults offer both intellectual growth and emotional support.

There are certain educators who believe strongly that during these years, the differences between boys and girls are so extreme that they are almost two different species, from an educational point of view as well as from a social perspective. These educators argue that the needs of boys and girls are so different during this period that you cannot serve the girls properly without shortchanging the boys and vice versa. Although we don't want to make any claim as global as that, we would say, more hesitantly, that for any given quirky child who does not seem to be flourishing in a regular middle school or for whom middle school looms as an enormous social challenge, you might consider the question of whether an all-boys or all-girls school might provide a better answer. They do remove some of the social pressures that middle school kids experience. At some all-female schools, there is much less pressure about how girls dress and how they look in general. At an all-male school, the embarrassment of a voice that suddenly shifts registers may be much easier to live down.

There are quirky kids who need to be with other quirky children in a more therapeutic environment. They are the kids, usually, for whom major learning issues or major mental health issues are getting in the way. They may need some kind of special placement—often with the goal of returning to the regular high school. And although this placement decision is rarely made for social reasons, a separate school can be a real social refuge for a very quirky child, offering him a context in which he is in fact not an outlier and offering him as well, with luck, a social matrix of friends and acquaintances.

Whatever your middle school arrangement, you are probably going to have access to limited information about your child's social life during the middle school years. You will probably perceive certain truths about how your child's social life is going from his emotional state. And then, of course, there will be the obvious clues of how often the phone rings, whether there are friends you meet, weekend invitations, and a general sense of activity.

If your child seems isolated, or depressed, or angry and confused, these are years when a relationship with a therapist or counselor can make an enormous difference.

BULLYING

In middle school, the kids get meaner and sharper, and pressure to be like everyone else gets stronger and stronger. Any eccentricity can make a child vulnerable to teasing and bullying. Wearing an assisted-hearing device. Going to the school nurse several times a day to take medications. Walking like a geek. Of course, no one should make the mistake of thinking that bullying happens because the target is quirky. Bullies bully whomever they can. There are plenty of cases of children being picked on for no obvious reason or because they happened to be physically small or because they happened to be assigned an unlucky locker next to the bully.

Bullying is increasingly being recognized as more than a minor social problem in schools. As we said above, there have now been several successful lawsuits on behalf of children whose schools failed to protect them when they were bullied. Schools are taking notice of these results.

There have also been a number of protocols and curricula developed by psychologists and educators aimed at equipping children to deal more effectively with bullies and to protect themselves. These include at least one curriculum aimed specifically at children with autistic spectrum disorders and several programs that are designed for working with whole schools to counteract bullying. As yet, there is not a lot of evidence about whether these programs work for most children, but there are some important points to emphasize:

- Some programs teach children to reply with a smart comeback when they are teased. This is by and large not a great idea for most quirky kids, who are less likely to be able to gauge the effect of what they say.
- Carol Gray, author of "Gray's Guide to Bullying," offers this advice for kids with autistic spectrum disorders—memorize one sentence and say it well: "I need you to stop. I don't like that; stop it." Anyone with a child who has one of these diagnoses might want to examine Gray's full program, but the notion of one simple sentence as a response to bullying might work for many quirky kids of all different types.
- Basically, all antibullying programs rely on the child's getting some backup. The child, whatever she says to the bully on the spot, has to be able to go to an adult for help and get help promptly. The school cannot

have a "kids will be kids" or even a "boys will be boys" attitude toward
bullying.

• Retribution, swift and terrible, must fall on the bully.

Schools need to protect their students. Children should be taught strategies to defend themselves, bullies should be punished promptly, and the whole
school should cultivate an attitude of mutual respect and safety. We have had
to refer children for counseling because of bad experiences they had at school
with bullies, attempted to get school-bus arrangements changed because our
patients were afraid to ride the buses with bullies, and talked to teachers and
principals in attempts to protect children who were afraid to go to school.
Sometimes it simply has not worked, despite a willing school administration—
and sometimes, in all honesty, the school administration has not been all that
willing. And so we are left offering these less-than-comforting thoughts for
that worst-case scenario, the middle school child who is being repeatedly and
severely bullied:

• Being the target of bullying can be genuinely crippling for a quirky child,
  and the middle school years may be the most vulnerable.
• In addition to making him unhappy, bullying can interfere with your
  child's nascent social development during these complicated years, leaving him hurt and stunted in his ability to connect with other people.
  Many adults—for example, those with Asperger's syndrome—writing
  about their childhoods, identify teasing and bullying during these years
  as devastating.
• You need to pressure the school, and by all means call in your pediatrician or your child's therapist to help you. And if that doesn't work, you
  should consider legal action.
• Think about whether, in your child's best interests, you might in fact
  want to change schools. Yes, in a certain sense, it's running away, and yes,
  in a certain sense, the bad guys win, but it can also be an incredible escape and liberation for your child.
• And finally, we would once more bring up the subject of homeschooling, just because some quirky-kid families do in fact cite bullying as
  one of the factors that pushed them out of the schools they were in.

Homeschooling does not have to involve a multiyear commitment. You aren't necessarily promising to teach the child at home right through high school. But for the child who needs urgently to escape a middle school situation in which he is being tortured, and for the family with no satisfactory school options available, homeschooling can be at least a respite, a chance to relax and take stock and recover.

THE COOL AND THE UNCOOL

He takes everything to heart. When a boy in George's class was sick and out of school for an extended period, the class sent him cards. Most of them were eighth-grade-boy humor about dying and stuff. George wrote this really heartfelt card about how sorry he was that the boy was sick and how if he needed any help when he got back to school, George would help him, etcetera. I had to explain to him that a grown-up might like this card, but another eighth-grade boy would think it's weird.

In middle school, quirky kids are seldom numbered among the desperately cool. The lucky ones are over on the more oblivious side during these years. Boys, especially, can often avoid the whole issue and choose to remain a little more childlike a little longer. If you are lucky, your child will be in a middle school where there is an entire group of children who are simply outside the cool-uncool axis. That is, they are clearly not in the running, but they are also clearly not even competing. These kids, the ones not in any hurry to take on the prerogatives of adolescence, the ones not obviously dying to be asked to the parties to which they are not invited, can be the right and proper companions of your quirky child.

As we said in our chapter on schools, there is, nowadays, a certain nascent nerd-pride movement, at least in some schools. There seem to be many kids who are happy to identify themselves as nerds and to look out at the world from that perspective with a certain sense of superiority. Those who self-identify as nerds are unlikely to be torturing themselves over not being cool: they may actually be proud of it. As a thirteen-year-old boy once said to one of us in horror, "Are you kidding? I'm a nerd! Nerds don't go to school dances!"

The saddest quirky child is deeply aware of cool and uncool and longs, constantly and passionately, to join exactly that club which will never accept her as a member. This is certainly not unique to quirky children, but it can be heartbreaking to watch when a child combines the exquisite awareness of what she wants with certain traits and attributes that indelibly mark her as someone who will never get it. And so we are left with a certain paradox: the more oblivious the child, in many cases, the easier the social aspects of the middle school years may be. The more acutely socially aware the child, the more miserable she may make herself, appreciating not only her exact place in the hierarchy but also the place she wants and cannot have.

FRIENDSHIPS

Middle school friendships can be powerful. If your child finds the right friend— or friends—during these years, the difficult transition to adolescence and to high school can be much easier. Friends during these years reinforce a child's identity and preferences and offer advice—much more valuable, and much more readily heeded, than a parent's—about every aspect of life, from popular culture to school activities.

Chrissie did make a couple of friends last year. She's especially close to one girl, who slept over for her birthday in June. They visit back and forth pretty often. They've been eating lunch together in the school cafeteria. We'll see how long this lasts. Chrissie often takes the initiative to call her, which I think is great. She's overcoming her fear of the answering machine, she's able to leave messages that make sense now, and she's pretty happy when her calls are returned. So all in all, she's growing up into a nice, if slightly awkward, girl.

Girls tend to be more socially aware and more likely to appreciate the fine nuances and multiple webs of relationships through which middle-school girl culture operates. Also, girls are just plain meaner to one another than boys, with cruelties so complex and subtle that many grown men cannot understand them. Girls, even more than boys, may define themselves by their social place in the world. Boys this age often travel in a pack, with room in the pack for those who lag behind a little bit developmentally. On the other hand, a boy who does find himself excluded may become the target of physical violence, whether pushing and shoving or real fighting.

How can you support your quirky child through the minefield of middle school friendships?

- Accept that it's pretty much out of your hands. You can't just call the parent of a twelve-year-old, the way you did the parent of a six-year-old, and say, "Can Susie please come over and play with Mary?"
- More and more, a splinter skill, a special interest, or a talent may provide your child with a way to find peers, companions, and friends. If your child has something she likes to do and does well, she should spend as much time on it as possible in as social a setting as possible.

Megan joined the all-city chorus, which anyone can join, regardless of ability. It's a sixth-, seventh-, and eighth-grade chorus, and she did it for three years and enjoyed it. She also tried the debate team, which is a good thing for a kid who sees everything as black or white. It's not a negotiating team, it's a debate team, where you try to win people over with your arguments.

- This is when you are hoping that some of the groundwork you have laid with your child during the elementary school years—all those months and months of pragmatic language therapy, say—will yield a more socially skilled child.
- Support your child's friendships, as they emerge. Get to know the parents of his friends. Offer the occasional evening or weekend activity—a movie, bowling, pizza—as a treat for the kids.
- Don't go overboard. You don't throw all the house rules out the window just to please a potential friend. It's normal for kids this age to push a little bit for adult privileges, but that doesn't mean you have to say yes to a request that you take them all to a midnight R-rated movie.
- Keep those community activities in mind: scouting, church groups, sports teams, charitable organizations. Anywhere that your child plays and works with other children within a fairly set structure can be a great help.
- Encourage extracurricular activities, which are more important in middle school. Learning how to put out the school newspaper or serving on the student council can lead directly to high school activities and can give your child a circle of acquaintances beyond her class or her grade.
- E-mail pen pals are a wonderful social adjunct for many kids. They don't take the place of real friends, but they do help children establish a sense of connection and practice many of the communication and empathy skills they will need for friendships.

- Remember that sometimes you will strategize and plan, and other times your child will take over and show you the way.

One day, Megan came home from school and announced, "Every kid in my class is going to sleep-away camp this summer. I want to go, too." We were stunned. She was so dependent on us for everything and hadn't ever spent the night anywhere else. The morning she was supposed to leave, she asked us to call the camp and tell them she would come next year. She was terrified. We had to peel her off the house and force her into the car. We took her literally kicking and screaming. She cried and tantrumed for a very long time. The following morning, she had calmed a bit and actually went and had a wonderful time. She went for four summers for a month each time. The camp was a Quaker camp, a good match for her because of the Quaker values of kindness and inclusion. She loved animals, and there were lots of those, and lots of hiking and not too many sports. She really didn't have any friends there, but she was included in everything because that's the way of the camp.

THE APPROACH OF ADOLESCENCE

Go and sit outside a separate middle school, a building that houses only seventh and eighth graders. Watch the kids going in in the morning or coming out in the afternoon. You'll see boys who are six feet tall and boys who are four feet tall. Girls who look twenty-five, both in their physical development and in their hair and makeup and clothing, and girls who are almost indistinguishable from those four-foot-tall boys. Many girls will be taller than most of the boys. A few boys will have crashed right through puberty, while many others will be in the embarrassing in-between of breaking voices and strange new body odors.

Their social lives will vary just as wildly. Some of those eighth-grade girls are dating high school juniors and live from dance to dance. They know more than you think about drinking and drugs, not to mention sex. Some of their classmates are still, literally, playing with dolls.

George came home horrified that there were kids in his class smoking pot. He told me he was afraid they were going to die. I couldn't believe I was saying this, but I told him, "It's really not that bad. No one ever died from smoking marijuana. Don't act all horrified around the kids who are doing it. Just get yourself out of the situation as delicately as you can." This is in contrast to all the antidrug stuff the school does, because George takes that all too seriously. He's so literal.

The positive aspect of all this variation is that in most middle school environments, there is room at both ends of the spectrum. Everybody is going through a transition, some in fits and starts, some smoothly, some with terrifying speed, and some with agonizing slowness. Eventually, most of them will at least catch up physically, but it can be a strange, even scary, time.

PUBERTY

Puberty hits many quirky children like the proverbial ton of bricks. Their bodies erupt in all kinds of directions. Their emotions, maybe never under good control in the first place, take off on the hormonal roller coaster of adolescence.

Explain puberty to your child in terms that make sense for him—or for her. Tailor your explanation to where your child is developmentally—both in understanding and in physical change. When we ask our middle school–age patients whether they have learned about puberty in school, they always say they have but then frequently turn out to have absorbed only scattered pieces of information, much of it somewhat dubious. You need to go over the basics, and you probably need some clear pictures to look at. We often give out or recommend *It's Perfectly Normal*, by Robie Harris, to adolescents. That book has excellent chapters on puberty. For the child whose understanding is less advanced, she has also written *It's So Amazing!* You definitely want to have one of these—or some other book you like—around in the house so that your child can do some quiet private reading up *after* you have had "the talk."

TIPS FOR "THE TALK"

- Traditionally, this is done by the parent of the same gender. Some parents— and kids—are comfortable discussing these subjects across gender lines, but many find it easier the other way.
- You need to be able to use all the terms—that means the slang and the vulgarities—that your child may hear in school to refer to pubertal changes and other physical manifestations. Your goal is a child who understands what is happening to her own body and also is not bewildered by the conversation around her in school.

- This is not really the birds-and-bees conversation. You can provide as much information about human reproduction as you want, but the main goal is to equip your child to understand and survive the onset of puberty.

If You Have a Boy

- If there is no father in the home and the mother feels it would be better for him to talk to a man, enlist an older relative or a male pediatrician.
- Tell him frankly and clearly about wet dreams. Quirky children, sometimes not very in touch with their bodies, can be terrified by nocturnal emissions. He needs to know that they happen to all boys as they grow and that they aren't wrong or dirty or disgusting.
- Tell him about masturbation. Tell him it's OK, that everyone does it sometimes, that you did it, too. It's only to be done in private, a private thing that people do to make themselves feel good, and that this particular good feeling is a sexual feeling.
- Tell him about personal hygiene as he reaches puberty:

  ✓ His sweat will start to smell, so he needs to be scrupulous about showering after exercise and wearing clean clothes.
  ✓ Deodorant. Toothbrushing. Shampoo.
  ✓ If he is uncircumcised, he needs to start routinely retracting his foreskin and washing under it every time he showers.
  ✓ If he's starting to be troubled by acne, get it seen by a doctor sooner rather than later. Acne is much more treatable than it used to be. If untreated, it can make a kid feel really bad.

- Tell him about bad touching—about other kids or adults touching his body without his permission or in ways he doesn't like. Emphasize that he needs to come to you right away if anything like this ever happens.
- Tell him when you notice his body starting to change or by the time he is thirteen, whichever comes first, or if he asks you about any of this ever.
- Tell him again, at regular intervals.

If You Have a Girl

- Tell her about menstruation. Show her pictures so she'll understand what's happening. Tell her about the first time you got your period. We calculate loosely that daughters nowadays are beginning to menstruate about a year earlier than their mothers did, which may give you some sense of when to expect it for your daughter.
- Tell her, as clearly as possible, what she needs to do when she gets her period—at home or at school.
- Talk with her about how women handle their periods. Show her a sanitary napkin. Practice with her how to use one, how to know when it's time to change it, and how to dispose of it. Emphasize that this will be her personal hygiene responsibility.

When my daughter was of menstrual age, I had to take her into the bathroom with me and model for her how I changed a pad. She didn't want to talk about it at all. She definitely did not want to celebrate.

- For some quirky girls, the ones with sensory integration issues and awkward relationships with their own bodies, menstruation is no simple proposition. You need to start thinking about the routines and prompts that will make it easier.
- Talk about breast development and bras and special sports bras for exercise.
- Tell her about masturbation. Tell her it's OK, that everyone does it sometimes, that you did it, too. It's only to be done in private, a private thing that people do to make themselves feel good, and that this particular good feeling is a sexual feeling.
- Tell her about personal hygiene as she reaches puberty:

  ✓ Her sweat will start to smell, so she needs to be scrupulous about showering after exercise and wearing clean clothes.
  ✓ Deodorant. Toothbrushing. Shampoo.
  ✓ Emphasize regular baths or showers, especially during her period.
  ✓ Depending on hair growth and hair color, she may want to start

shaving. Once again, this will pose particular challenges for a girl with fine motor delays or with sensory integration problems. Show her how to do it. Buy her the best possible razor and creams.

✓ If she's starting to be troubled by acne, get it seen by a doctor sooner rather than later. Acne is much more treatable than it used to be. If untreated, it can make a kid feel really bad.

In terms of personal hygiene, Chrissie still needs a little push. Her skin is starting to break out, which grosses her out, so that has actually worked in our favor in terms of keeping her clean.

- Tell her about bad touching. Tell her that if anyone touches her without her permission or tries to get her to do something she doesn't want to do, she has to tell you immediately. Tell her that you will never be angry with her for telling you something like this and that you will always try to protect her.
- Talk to her when you see her body starting to change or by the time she is twelve, whichever comes first.
- Talk to her again. And again. It's an ongoing process.

DANCES AND DATING

What about dating? What about dances? We can't say we like it, either as mothers or as pediatricians, but there is dating in most middle school settings. The girls, at least, tend to be very aware of it. By eighth grade, there are often dances. In some schools, these are occasions for everyone to go in a pack, whereas in others, they are attended mostly by those kids who are already dating, already coupling off. Whatever the custom is in your school, you and your child are more or less stuck with it.

Encourage your child to attend school dances if she wants to and if she has friends to go with. Remind her to check with other kids about what will be worn, especially if she has trouble understanding subtle social cues. The dress code for some eighth-grade dances is jeans and sweaters, and others involve what look to the maternal eye very much like cocktail dresses. Warn your child that middle school dances often don't feature a great deal of dancing. A few of the already-dating kids get out there and dance. A big group of boys stands on one side of the room, shoving one another, and a big group of girls stands on the other side of the room, talking about the boys—or about one another's cocktail dresses. Or maybe the girls dance with the girls and the boys watch them.

Trevor is naive about social situations. He is immature. His friends tend to be a year or more younger than he is. He frequently misjudges his abilities and is confused by other kids' reactions sometimes. For example, he came home from a "dance club" meeting at which the other kids laughed at him because of the way he dances. He demonstrated for me, and indeed, he dances in a peculiar way that other kids would think is weird. He still didn't get it when I explained it to him.

George is very interested in girls, and girls seem to like him. He doesn't have a girlfriend, but seven girls asked him to dance at the first dance he went to. I think this is because he stands by himself, and it's not so scary for the girls to ask a boy who is by himself. A boy in a group might make fun of her. I asked his older sister if it was some kind of pity on the part of the girls, but she felt it wasn't. She felt that George is sweet and not scary or threatening.

It's generally a big favor to a quirky child to practice a little dancing first. Our parental generation is fortunately not stuck in our own parents' lament— "I just can't do that rock-and-roll stuff you kids call dancing." Most of us can do it just fine, and it's an easy kind of dancing for a quirky kid to learn, since it has no rigid rules and does not require body contact. Put on some music, loosen up, and try to leave your child with the sense that it's OK to go to a dance and then *not* dance but that if she tries to dance, she'll be just fine.

But what about dating? Let's assume that your quirky child is not himself leading the way, at this point, but may be functioning in an environment in which other kids are coupling off. Keep your eyes and ears open. If there are obviously couples forming in the school, ask your child if he has any feelings about that. Talk with your child about the fact that some kids are dating and others are not, about what dating actually means, and about her understanding of what is going on. Don't just write things off with a "Seventh grade is too young for that!" if it's clearly happening all around and it's on your child's mind. Make it clear that seventh grade is seventh grade, and most people live their important dating lives in high school, college, and beyond. In other words, from an adult perspective, what goes on in seventh grade is unlikely to be life-determining.

Your child may start asking questions about what your own social life was like in middle school—or about how her parents met. For some quirky kids, watching social patterns form among their peers, even if they aren't participating, opens up their curiosity for the first time about love and sex and relationships. She may also absolutely refuse to discuss the issue with you. Make sure she has access to some good books and knows that the conversational door is always open.

There is always more going on in the way of sex, drugs, and alcohol than parents would like to believe in middle school. That doesn't mean that all the kids are involved or even that your child has any idea about this. But somewhere in that middle school are a couple of kids whose sexual experimentations have gone well beyond a little kissing, and they may or may not be conveying their discoveries to the group at large. Similarly, somewhere in that middle school are kids who know more than anyone thinks they do about drugs and drinking, and they may well be passing it on. You will not find an absolutely protected school and social environment for your child, no matter how much you would like one. You need to be ready to help him interpret, understand, and judge—and above all, keep himself safe.

SAFETY

Quirky children's poor sense of social skills, their youngness for their age, and their eagerness to somehow be part of the group can make them vulnerable to being pushed sexually, even abused. That's one reason that that talk mentioned above should always include the subject of being touched when you don't want to be. Any middle school–age child going out to dances needs to know that sometimes kids try to push other kids into doing things they don't want to do—whether it's drinking beer behind the gym or playing strip poker. Your child needs to hear, over and over, that she is entitled to say no, entitled to ask an adult for help, and that you will never be angry with her for any of these things.

And for that matter, since middle school is often a time of increasing independence, it's worth repeating all the be-careful-of-strangers warnings, with a special emphasis on sexual predators. An eighth-grade girl needs to know that the guy who sits down next to her on the subway and asks if she goes to college around here is bad news, however momentarily flattered she may be. She needs to know that she is supposed to get up and change her seat, finding a place next to an older woman if possible, if he persists. To know this, she is going to have to have some idea of what he might be after.

Almost all parents keep their kids under closer supervision now than when we were children. Quirky children's parents are often even more protective. Parents of quirky kids tend to know where they are at any given point, to defer independent travel and escort them back and forth, to hover more closely. This can mean that these children reach middle school age without having a lot of practice and drill about not getting into cars with strangers, not talking to people who come up to them on the street, not responding to the questions of the guy on the subway. You're going to have to teach your child all this, over and over, putting it as clearly as you can, probably taking him on a few experimental journeys, where he takes the bus or the subway "alone" with you a few yards away or walks home "alone" with you trailing a block behind. This will not be easy, most likely, and you will worry about whether your child is really ready. However, you do not want to send your child into high school with no sense of the world's dangers and no practice in taking care of herself.

High School

High school is often a little easier, socially, than middle school. In most places—note that we said, in most places—the rigid conformity of middle school relaxes. There are more possible social strata, more groups with which to identify, a wider range of normal. To put it another way, maybe nobody is really normal in high school. Almost all adolescents struggle with issues of identity, risk taking, achievement, substance abuse, sexuality, family relations, and self-esteem. The developmental task of every adolescent is to separate, to become an individual adult. It is never easy to be the parent from whom that separation takes place.

Against this somewhat tumultuous background of change and rebellion and self-definition, the quirks that loomed so large in middle school or toward the end of the elementary years can be much less noticeable. Many high schools are more forgiving, more varied—or simply bigger.

However, high school is where some kids—and not just quirky kids, by any means—seem to go seriously wrong. Every parent of a not-at-the-center-of-the-crowd child has probably thought on one occasion or another about the boys at Columbine, for example, or about other marginalized kids who shoot up a school or shoot themselves or crack under the strain. As students get closer to adulthood, the ways in which they can hurt themselves—or others—get more dangerous, with cars and alcohol and drugs and sex coming into the picture in various combinations. We aren't trying to say here that the kids who committed the murders at Columbine—or at any other school—were necessarily quirky kids, by our definition, but rather that these relatively new and scary images have now come for most of us to be associated with high school loners and outcasts, with high school kids who become sullen and withdrawn, and even with the targets of bullying.

Nancy Rappaport, M.D., is a child and adolescent psychiatrist who does what is now called "threat assessment" for several large Massachusetts school districts. If teachers or administrators are concerned about a student's potential for violence, it is her job to assess that student and make a recommendation. She is keenly aware that eccentric high school students may nowadays occasion worries about school violence. "It may be that an odd kid says some oddball off-color things that really gets people going. They may say something that's inappropriate. They may think it's clever—may be inordinately focused on drawing weapons or drawing cartoons which have violence in them. Or maybe with an Asperger kid, their selective fascination may be guns. A school will have a very difficult time accommodating that interest." By having the child evaluated and asking an expert whether the disturbing behavior is linked to a psychiatric or medical diagnosis, the school may find a way to modify its disciplinary response, especially important in these nervous times when many schools have "zero tolerance" policies.

Parents of high school students now live with terrible fears of high school violence and certainly have a lower threshold of suspicion when it comes to a child—your own or any of his friends—making any kind of remarks about hurting anyone at school, blowing up the building, or taking revenge on enemies. If you sense that anything like that may be going on, you need to get help immediately. That child needs to be seeing a counselor, and you need to be in close touch with his school to find out what is going on in his classes and in his social life.

It's more likely, however, that your day-to-day sense of your child's high school social life will be affected by mundane factors, that your child will find a somewhat precarious footing on the rapidly shifting ground of adolescence and will eventually get safely across. But it can be a pretty winding, indirect, painful trip. Any quirky kid dealing with a couple of other issues along with common everyday adolescence surely ought to at least consider the advantages of having someone to talk to. Plenty of people who work with adolescents believe that basically every adolescent could use such a relationship.

FRIENDSHIPS

Almost every high school is divided into multiple little worlds, and some go on existing side by side for four years straight, never touching. The real secret to high school success is to find the right zone. For example, when we were in high school, the audiovisual squad was the right and proper place for a group of boys who would today be called nerds. These guys hung out in the AV squad office, to which only they were trusted with keys. They passed their spare time attempting to get the broken projectors running again. It was an identity, a clubhouse, a social network. There are other legendary watering holes for the nonathletic and the chronically uncool: the math club, the chess club, the computer club. There's also the orchestra, the debate team, or any other venue that reflects a child's true interests.

If the high school itself does not offer the right niche, think again about community activities and church activities. Some children simply do better with adults, and they just might be happier in charge of ticket sales for a local theater group or working at the garage every weekend. But if your child is doing something like that, keep suggesting that she look around for some high school equivalent—someplace where tickets need to be sold or motors need to be fixed—some way to connect back at least a little to her schoolmates.

You don't have to be defined by an extracurricular activity in high school, though it can be a major help in finding like-minded peers. You can find an academic identity if you have a subject you love. Teachers have pretty good noses for this, and the girl who gets totally carried away by geometry will probably be noticed and appreciated by her teacher. You can find your niche in art or shop or any vocational courses your school happens to offer, from auto mechanics to cooking.

George is exceptionally musical and plays the trombone in the school band. He has perfect pitch, which only one in ten thousand people in the general population has but one out of twenty with autistic spectrum disorders. His music teachers are thrilled. They've never had a kid with perfect pitch before. And George likes to play in the band. He'll practice when he is told to, but he doesn't spontaneously play on his own. He also sings beautifully but doesn't seem to realize it or care about it.

Every once in a while, a high school kid asks us for an excuse from gym. Sometimes he's getting teased or bullied in gym, but sometimes he just feels self-conscious about his body or inept at the games he's expected to play. Under those kinds of circumstances, we try to refer for counseling, we discuss body-image issues, but you know what else we do? We give the kid a note to get him out of sports. It's true that exercise is important for health. It's further true that some of the most self-conscious kids—the obese, the boys who are embarrassed by the breast development that is happening in part because they're overweight—would profit most from taking gym. However, it's hard to see that being forced, kicking and screaming, into a setting where people make fun of your body—or where you think they're making fun of your body or where you constantly disgrace yourself or get blamed for all your team's misfortunes—is going to leave anybody a lifelong convert to good habits of regular exercise. Sometimes a teenager needs a respite. More and more schools are installing exercise equipment, and some offer kids a fitness option for physical education in which they can work out and measure their progress only against themselves. For the quirky child who does have some athletic ability, a team sport can give an automatic high school identity, a circle of friends, and perhaps an area in which to shine even if academics are difficult.

With a little bit of luck, all the social skills your child has acquired through the years, combined with the wider variety of social options open, will allow her to find a peer or peers, a friend, or a circle. As a parent, you stand back and watch, try to express a certain amount of counteropinion about prevailing fads and fashions, and offer what advice you can. Certainly, you support the friendships that seem to you to be good ones, offering to chauffeur, to pick up at the movies, and opening your home for the occasional party or homework group effort or poker night. You are entitled to set certain limits, and with a quirky child, you should try especially hard to make those limits as clear and explicit as possible. Go ahead and set curfews; go ahead and demand the name, address, and phone number for any party to which he's going. Go ahead and say no to really dumb ideas (ten kids in the minivan that one of them just got licensed to drive, heading for the shore two hundred miles away on a holiday weekend). Wall yourself off with all the traditional parental lines ("If everybody else jumped off the Brooklyn Bridge . . ."). Quirky adolescents who have not always found it easy to be included can be so overjoyed to find an opportunity, a potential social slot, that they can be desperate to go along for any crazy ride. You just have to grit your teeth and go on saying no.

Through it all, you continue to exercise the prerogatives (and exorcise the anxieties) of every high school parent—trying to keep your child safe, setting curfews, making rules about drinking and drugs, and just plain hanging in there.

LOVE AND DATING, SEX AND SEXUALITY

Some quirky kids are going to make it all the way through high school and still not get what all the fuss is about. Really. These kids, girls and boys, will, of course, have undergone the physical changes of puberty, which they may regard with amusement or with disgust—or may again seem hardly to have noticed. However, they have somehow escaped a little longer than most the emotional upheavals, the susceptibility to crushes and to falling in love, the yearning and the fantasizing, that are the lot of most high school students. As a parent, you will, of course, worry a little about this, but you will probably also feel somewhat blessed and somewhat spared.

Megan was invited to her friend's birthday party. By this time, her friend had a boyfriend. She had started dating in tenth grade, and Megan, of course, had no interest at all in boys. So her friend spent most of the party with her boyfriend, and Megan didn't really know any of the other kids. She called her friend afterward and said, "I didn't like the way you acted at your birthday party." Her friend has never called her since, and the friendship is basically over. I know that her friend's mom is just as happy, because she never liked Megan. I think she would have preferred that her daughter not be friends with such an oddball kid.

Other quirky kids are swept away and turned upside down by their first rushes of sexual attraction, sexual fantasy, and romantic emotion. These, after all, are kids who have always been inclined to obsessional thinking. They may find themselves completely consumed by a crush, obsessed with a romantic object to the point of constantly thinking of and fantasizing about that person. They may even end up doing something that looks rather like stalking that person. In high school, the notion that somebody really likes a particular student and is always following her around, or has chosen her classes purposely to be with him, does not actually attract a great deal of attention. But quirky kids may overstep the line and make fools of themselves or may even occasion complaints or concerns about safety on the part of their adored.

Other adolescents—quirky and not—are tortured by doubts about sexual identity. Sometimes they are merely responding to the rather diffuse sexuality of these early postpubertal years, in which people often develop crushes on teachers, on close friends, on singers and movie stars, of both genders. Others are realizing that they are not heterosexual—or not exclusively heterosexual— which can be a complex and difficult realization for a high school kid. Any adolescent struggling with issues of sexual identity in a culture that for the most part is still pretty homophobic (and we're talking high school locker rooms here, after all) is at risk for depression and even suicide. Such a kid needs to feel there is unprejudiced support and unconditional love at home. A quirky adolescent, adding this on to already complex feelings about being different from other people and being outside the group, may be particularly bewildered, troubled, or depressed.

Dating scenes vary enormously from high school to high school. There will always be a certain group of kids coupling off and going steady, but in many circles, there is a good deal of group hanging out, even including couples, and this may be less pressured. There are formal school events, dances, and proms. There are, of course, parties outside school.

We'll say it again: wherever you are, whatever you think the school enforces, there is more going on with regard to sex (and drugs and drinking) than parents know or would hope to see. We live in an era in which many high school students are sexually active and with multiple partners. Whether your child is in that category or not, he is certainly exposed to the conversation, the information, and the behavior of those who are. Give him the values he needs to evaluate what he sees and the support he needs to function in that environment.

If your child does start dating, you can offer support and suggestions, but you are probably not going to be listened to. However, a willingness to do some of the driving, or an offer to treat to a special dinner or theatrical event, can help the relationship along and also give you some sense of where it's going. Just as quirky kids may be at higher risk of developing those obsessive crushes, they may also be more likely to be destroyed when a high school relationship comes to its natural end, which, of course, often involves someone dumping someone and moving on. For some quirky kids, not easily social, this ending may bring disillusionment, despair, and clinical depression.

As in middle school, that same desire to be included can make high school students vulnerable to sexual exploitation. It's an awful thing to say, but you should probably be suspicious of a daughter's sudden popularity, especially if accompanied by other danger signs: mixing only with older kids, all boys and no girls calling the house, vagueness about where she is going and what she is doing.

After all these negatives and fears, we should add that the increased spectrum of high school identity can mean that in their romantic relationships, as well as in their friendships, quirky kids can find new opportunities to make connections, to form affectionate bonds, and to care for one another. Adolescent affection, attachment, and even love can be both beautiful and moving and, of course, profoundly educational.

The romantic lives of many high school students are carefully protected from parental examination. If there's going to be a conversation, you probably have to initiate it:

- Talk to your child, about sex and also about love. Talk about the power of the emotion, the difficulty of fixing your affections on someone who doesn't return them. Open up the subjects.
- Use movies or TV shows or books or news stories as ways to discuss these subjects. Quirky kids often have unusual takes on human relationships. Find out how your child views the decisions made by Romeo and Juliet or any other characters who happen to wander onto the scene. (*Romeo and Juliet* is read in many eighth and ninth grades, and it is, after all, a story of crazy, obsessive love that ultimately destroys both characters!)
- Make absolutely sure that your child understands the physiology and mechanics of sex and the meanings of all the most commonly used terms, however vulgar.

- Do not assume that your child's sexual feelings will be heterosexual. You want a child who is struggling with issues of sexual identity to feel that she can come to you for help and support. Many people in early adolescence find themselves attracted both to their own gender and to the other.
- You owe it to your child to make sure that he—or she—has a good understanding of how to prevent pregnancy and of the dangers of sexually transmitted diseases and how to prevent them. Although you can make it as clear as you like that abstinence would be your preferred choice for your adolescent, the truth is, you need to talk about condoms and how important they are and how to use them.
- Once again, it is likely that your child has received all this information in school, up to and including watching someone put a condom on a cucumber amid general hilarity. But many quirky kids weren't emotionally old enough to be interested the first time around or were so hobbled by self-consciousness that they didn't really absorb the information.
- If you have a son, you absolutely *must* discuss with him the issue of date rape. A quirky boy who doesn't quite get other people's social signals and who pushes a girl too far is going to find himself in terrible trouble—thrown-out-of-school or locked-up kind of trouble. He has to understand that he must absolutely clarify whether each additional intimacy is welcomed and must desist immediately if it is not.
- Talk about it. Talk about sex. Talk about love. Talk about taking care of people you love and about accepting it when someone doesn't love you back. Talk about relationships and what happens when they go wrong and about all the joys and satisfactions when they go right.

DRINK AND DRUGS

Most of what there is to say about drink and drugs and the quirky adolescent could apply just as well to all adolescents everywhere. Let us make some specific points about quirky kids and substance abuse:

- Once again, the desperate desire to be accepted may make some not easily accepted kids do dumb things.
- Many high schools now have zero-tolerance policies, in which any breach in the drug or alcohol rules can land a student in serious trouble. Make sure your child understands the rules—and the danger.

- For adolescents taking psychotropic medications, it is a basic issue of health and safety to discuss with your doctor whether there are any interactions with alcohol or common street drugs. Your doctor should be willing to talk this through with your child and make it clear that the risks can be severe.
- Sometimes when teenagers find that alcohol and various drugs are available, they begin treating themselves for long-standing symptoms, without realizing what they are doing. Thus, for example, marijuana may calm the insufficiently medicated ADD sufferer.
- Be aware that there is a danger that adolescents may either share their prescription medications with their friends (or even sell them) or start taking their own medications in the wrong doses or on the wrong schedule in order to achieve a desired sensation. The stimulants—Ritalin, Dexedrine—are popular recreational drugs in some circles. Clonidine—which is often used along with the stimulants—is increasingly popular as a drug of abuse.
- Anyone who is near the edge of mental illness is at much greater risk when it comes to drug use, especially to hallucinogens. A single LSD or PCP experience can precipitate a psychotic break, especially in a person who was already tenuous.
- Your child may need very specific scenarios for how *not* to get into trouble with drugs or alcohol, the kind of step-by-step instructions that you once invented for birthday parties:

  - Never go to a party if the parents are out of town or not at home.
  - If you find yourself at such a party, call us and we will come get you, and we will not be mad at you.
  - If someone offers you drugs, say no thank you; go somewhere else.
  - If people are drunk or acting strange, call us and we will come get you, and we will not be mad at you.

- For many parents, the single greatest anxiety is about the mixing of drinking and driving. You need another set of explicit instructions here:

  - Never ever get into a car where the driver might be drunk.
  - If you are in a situation like that—however far away you are, however late at night it is, however against the rules it is for you to be there in

the first place—call us and we will come and get you, and we will not be mad at you.

- If, on the other hand, we ever find out about your driving with some-one drunk—or drinking and driving yourself, once you have a license—terrible consequences will follow, and you will have lost our trust.

Your job, as parents, is to help your quirky adolescent make the most of his high school years, reminding him at intervals of your love and acceptance, cheering him on in his achievements, and supporting him socially as best you can to help him enjoy the pleasures of his peer group without falling prey to the dangers. It isn't easy and it isn't always pretty—but together you can make it through.

References and Resources

Cohen, Cathi. *Raise Your Child's Social IQ: Stepping Stones to People Skills for Kids.* Silver Springs, Md.: Advantage, 2000. This is a workbook for families in which the author, a social worker, outlines her "Stepping Stones" program to help children who have social difficulties. It is intended for *any* child with difficulties in social situations and is an organized, step-by-step approach to try at home.

Gray, Carol. "Gray's Guide to Bullying." This publication can be ordered from the Gray Center for Social Learning and Understanding. Write to The Gray Center, 2020 Raybrook SE, Suite 101, Grand Rapids, MI 49546; phone (616) 954-9747; fax (616) 954-9749; or visit the organization's Web site, at www.thegraycenter.org.

Gray, Carol. *The New Social Story Book.* Arlington, Tex.: Future Horizons, 2000. The situations covered in this book include many everyday social dilemmas.

Harris, Robie H. *It's Perfectly Normal: Changing Bodies, Growing Up, Sex, and Sexual Health.* Illustrated by Michael Emberley. Cambridge, Mass.: Candlewick, 1996. This book is written for adolescents; *It's So Amazing!* (below) is for younger children. Look at both to see which is right for your child at a given moment. Both are humorous, frank, and extremely informative.

Harris, Robie H. *It's So Amazing!: A Book about Eggs, Sperm, Birth, Babies and Families.* Illustrated by Michael Emberley. Cambridge, Mass.: Candlewick, 2002.

Moyes, Rebecca A. *Incorporating Social Goals in the Classroom: A Guide for Teachers and Parents of Children with High-Functioning Autism and Asperger Syndrome.* London: Jessica Kingsley Publishers, 2001. An excellent tool, with lots of practical strategies.

Nowicki, Stephen, Jr., and Marshall P. Duke. *Helping the Child Who Doesn't Fit In.* Atlanta: Peachtree, 1992. Helps the socially clueless child learn the "rules" that govern interactions between kids; contains lots of practical exercises and advice.

PART III

The Science, the Medical Science, and the Pseudoscience of Quirky Kids

Literary Glimpses

○   ○   ●   ○

Hanno's gratitude to his teacher was boundless, and he abandoned himself to his guidance. The same boy who brooded over arithmetic without any hope of ever understanding it, despite all his special tutoring at school, understood everything that Herr Pfuhl said to him at the piano, understood it and made it his own—if you can be said to make your own what has always belonged to you. Edmund Pfuhl, however, seemed to him like a tall angel dressed in a brown swallowtail coat, who took him in his arms each Monday afternoon to lead him from his everyday misery into the realm of sound, where everything was gentle, sweet, consoling, and serious.

In his heart, Thomas Buddenbrook was not pleased with little Johann and how he was developing. . . . He would fix on these very points: the dreamy softness, the weeping, the total lack of vigor and energy. . . . He was not doing well in his subjects. He was absent too often because of illness and was totally inattentive because his thoughts would linger over some harmonic relationship or some unraveled marvel in a piece of music. . . . Senator Buddenbrook knew nothing about such details; but he saw that his son's development, whether as a result of nature or external influences, was not, as yet, headed in the direction he would have wished. . . . If he could have suppressed and banned the music at least—it was certainly not good for his health, absorbed all his mental energies, and made him ill-suited for the practical side of life. And that dreamy way he had about him— did it not sometimes border on simple-mindedness?

—Thomas Mann, *Buddenbrooks*, 1901

○   ○   ●   ○

Speak sharply to Jeremy and you will bowl him over; he can't stand up to things. You'll get further being gentle with him, but I always remember that too late. He puts me in a fury. I don't see how he could let himself go the way he has. No, letting yourself go means you had to be something to start with, and Jeremy was never anything. He was born like this. He is, and always has been, pale and doughy and overweight, pear-shaped, wide-hipped. He toes out when he walks.

His hair is curly and silvery-gold, thin on top. His eyes are nearly colorless. (People have asked me if he is an albino.) There's no telling where he manages to find his clothes: baggy slacks that start just below his armpits; mole-colored cardigan strained across his stomach and buttoning only in the middle, exposing a yellowed fishnet undershirt, top and bottom, and tiny round-toed saddle oxfords. Saddle oxfords? For a man? . . . [Our mother] thought the sun rose and set in him. She thought he was a genius. (I myself have sometimes wondered if he isn't a little bit retarded. Some sort of selective, unclassified retardation that no medical book has yet put its finger on.) He failed math, he failed public speaking (of course), he went through eighth grade twice *but he happened to be artistic so Mother thought he was a genius. "Some people just don't have mathematical minds," she said, and she showed us his report card—A+ in art, A in English, A+ in deportment. (What else? He had no friends, there was no one he could have whispered with in class.)*

—Anne Tyler, *Celestial Navigation*, 1974

○ ○ ● ○

He was still leaning against the wall. He had been leaning against the wall when I came into the room, his arms folded across his chest. As I pointed he brought his arms down and pressed the palms of his hands against the wall. They were white hands, sickly white hands that had never seen the sun, so white they stood out garishly against the dull cream wall in the dim light of Jem's room.

I looked from his hands to his sand-stained pants; my eyes traveled up his thin frame to his torn denim shirt. His face was as white as his hands, but for a shadow on his jutting chin. His cheeks were thin to hollowness; his mouth was wide; there were shallow, almost delicate indentations at his temples, and his gray eyes were so colorless I thought he was blind. His hair was dead and thin, almost feathery on top of his head.

When I pointed to him his palms slipped slightly, leaving greasy sweat streaks on the wall, and he hooked his thumbs in his belt. A strange small spasm shook him, as if he heard fingernails scrape slate, but as I gazed at him in wonder the tension slowly drained from his face. His lips parted into a timid smile, and our neighbor's image blurred with my sudden tears.

"Hey, Boo," I said.

—Harper Lee, *To Kill a Mockingbird*, 1960

Introduction

Many quirky kids manage OK at home and in school and even in the social realm, thanks to a vigilant and understanding family, a tolerant environment, a terrific school, a good friend at the right moment. But the truth is, those children are also the children who don't carry the heaviest baggage. Their quirks are not devastating or debilitating or even depressing. And there are many other children who—even with wonderful families, homes, schools, and friends—are still going to need extra help along the way. And then there are the many, many children whose life situations are more stressful, who may have to deal with a less-than-ideal school setting or a less-than-sympathetic peer group and may hit a bad emotional or developmental patch as a consequence.

In Part III, we'll look at the wide range of special supports and interventions that parents may find themselves trying: therapies, special home programs, and medications. We'll examine what is understood—and not understood—about these children from the standpoint of medical science. The more we can understand about the specific roots of these problems, the better our chances of finding real treatments that can be scientifically validated.

There are a lot of less-than-scientific theories circulating out there about quirky children and a lot of not so scientifically based therapies available, some of them extremely rigorous and extremely expensive, and some of them downright dangerous.

If you are just starting to delve into the world of therapies and medications, Part III may bring up some terms and outcomes that make you confront your biggest fears and worst-case possibilities. No one, looking at a quirky three-year-old, wants to think in terms of years of psychotropic medications and five different therapies. Not all quirky kids will need this many kinds of help. What we are saying is that many quirky kids go through a hard time at some point, and then you will at least want to consider whether a therapeutic intervention or a medicine might help. You need to know what's out there.

It is certainly not your job, as a parent, to accept every recommendation, to try out every therapy, nutritional program, behavior-modification exercise, and new religion that may be suggested to you. It is, however, your job to look at your child and try to see whether something is hurting or whether something that should be happening isn't or whether something is happening that shouldn't be. This is why we have organized the chapters on both therapies and medications according to problem or symptom. Whatever your child's underlying diagnosis, if his major daily problem is anxiety, you need to deal with the anxiety. For that reason, you may not want to try reading right through these chapters. You may find it most helpful to use them as resources and look up the specific problems that affect your child.

We watch parents wrestling with the obligation they feel to do as much as possible for their struggling child. There are always more possibilities, another doctor in another city, another therapist who supposedly has developed her own special intensive program, another blood test to look for some new trace element that someone thinks may be linked to the problem, another nutritional theory about how to modify the family diet. We don't suggest that you should stop looking for alternatives that may be right for your child, but we do want to say that you cannot go down every single path at once.

We try to take you through some of the science—and many of the controversies—that underlie our current understanding of this interesting and complicated group of children. We look at the issue of whether there are more of them around than there used to be and, if so, why. We talk about new theories, from immunization reactions to the mating habits of computer nerds. We tell you what's known about the genetics, the neurology, the biochemistry of quirkiness, and we discuss some of the more scientifically marginal but widely circulated theories that you've probably already come across. We try to give you an honest sense of how much there is still to be learned and understood about these children and what makes them tick.

In picking and choosing the right kind of help for your child, there are a few basic realities to consider:

- What kind of help your child needs will depend on who he is and what his "package" is: his strengths and weaknesses and skills and problem areas. This is not easily quantified at any particular age.
- The help she needs will certainly vary as she grows, in quantity and in kind. Your goal in certain respects is to try to get her help early on, so that she can acquire the skills she needs to function more smoothly when

she's older. There are other issues that come to the fore only as children age and need to be dealt with later on.

- The kind of help you get may differ depending on whom you ask. Psychiatrists tend to think in terms of psychopharmacology and starting kids on medications. Other therapists might want to try something else first. This is not to say that one way is right and one is wrong, just to point out that, as folk wisdom would put it, "If the tool you have is a hammer, everything looks like a nail."

- You should not make blanket decisions ("No behavior-altering drugs, ever!") without learning what the possibilities are. The goal is to help your child, and you will help him best by finding out as much as you can.

- You will have to get over your embarrassment at having a child who goes to special therapy sessions or takes a psychopharmaceutical medication. That doesn't necessarily mean that these things have to be everybody's business, but if your child senses that you are actually ashamed, she will be, too.

Children respond differently to any given kind of help. By reviewing what is and is not known about the medical science underlying quirkiness, you will understand that in fact we are far from being able to make clear scientific judgments and recommendations for many of these children. You will find out what's right for your child by knowing him well and testing everything you are told against that knowledge, against your experience, and against your common sense. You may only know what really helps by trying it. Sometimes you may try things that are no help at all and have to give them up. It's important to remember that even within one relatively narrow category of therapist or specialist, people vary enormously in their skills, in their personalities, in their general approach, and above all, in their knowledge of quirky kids. You aren't just choosing the therapy, you're choosing the therapist. How much good your child gets out of it may depend as much on the fit with the person as on the need for the intervention.

We saw an apparently good, highly recommended occupational therapist for two years for John. We were told she knows her stuff, and she was trained in sensory integration, which is a big part of what he has, but she spent a tremendous amount of John's time on his fine motor skills. They did mazes; he had to hold the pencil and try not to bump into the edge of the line. It seemed tedious and boring, and now he types on an AlphaSmart, and did we really need to spend two years getting him to write with a pencil? Now he works with a different OT who is much livelier and helps him work on stuff that really impacts his daily life— keyboarding, cello playing. In retrospect, I think the earlier OT experience was a complete and total waste of time. He didn't complain about it; I just don't think it made that much difference.

Your best bet in almost any field is probably going to be someone who has worked with quirky children and sees where his own particular brand of help fits in. Within any given field, training and experience can vary widely. You don't want your child to spend session after session with a speech therapist who focuses only on articulation issues if what he really needs is a speech and language therapist who will leave his diction alone and concentrate on helping him use language in realistic, practical ways.

Some parents speak of a eureka moment when they feel they finally met the person—the doctor, the therapist, the special ed teacher—who really understood their child, and their child's issues, all the way through.

When we met Dr. R, we could really see that he got our kids. We've met neurologists and OTs and PTs and our pediatrician, of course, but this was just a eureka moment, when we felt, we've finally met someone who gets the whole picture. And we feel like he's going to see us through. We'll probably see him for years, now and again, and if things get rough, we know he's in our corner.

Keep an eye out for that one person whose understanding of your child seems to be larger, fuller, more complex, and more informed by useful experience. You want to stay in contact with that person. You want her in your corner, helping you figure out how to respond to new challenges, adjusting whatever regimen you and your child have developed together.

All of this can add up to a rather major complication in the lives of parents and quirky child—and siblings, too, for that matter. Take it on piece by piece. We know there's a lot of information in Part III and much, much more available on each individual topic. Look at crisis situations first, if they arise, and deal with them as best you can. Then you need to regard the rest of it—the "getting help and evaluating the help you get" project—as a lifelong learning job, perhaps never to be definitively completed. The goal is to help, and help means different things at different times.

Give yourself a break. How your child does in life is going to be a highly complex mix of the package he started with—the genes, the biochemistry, the neurology and physiology—and then the environment in which he grew, the help he got, the times in which he lived, sheer chance and coincidence, and that thing called luck. You're going to do your best, keeping an open mind and trying to stay in close touch with how he's doing, ready to change the mix if things are slipping. There is no one right way, and there is no sense beating yourself up about how much better everything would be if you'd just done something differently. You do your best, and life only goes forward. The goal of therapy or medication or any other support is not to bring your child to some guaranteed absolute mark but to help her along her own trajectory, help her function as well as possible in her own life, as the person she is.

9

○ ○ ● ○

Therapies:

GETTING HELP AND
EVALUATING THE HELP YOU GET

Most quirky children will encounter some difficulties in mastering expected skills at the expected time. No two children are alike—and no two children with the same label are exactly the same. One physically awkward or clumsy child may need a specialized physical education program, while the next might be reasonably well coordinated but have problems with fine motor skills like buttoning or snapping. A third may have profound sensory integration issues that affect many aspects of daily living. Almost all of these children struggle with interpersonal difficulties, managing the social aspects of living with others and playing with others and going to school with others. Call it what you will—pragmatic language disorder, deficient theory-of-mind abilities, nonverbal learning disability, auditory-processing disorder—this aspect of development is skewed for most quirky kids, whether they are aware of it or not. Whether or not an individual child is aware, certainly his parents and teachers and coaches and camp counselors and therapists—and most of all, his peers—will be aware of the ways in which the child may need some help. In fact, as they grow and the social tasks expected of them become more complex (and the peer-group setting less forgiving of eccentricity), many children who did not get—or need—a diagnostic workup early in life will become objects of increasing concern and attention.

Deciding when or whether to pursue any of the enormous (and increasing!) number of therapies that are recommended for quirky kids is quite a task. Sometimes, the developmental concerns are so prominent or the delays so severe that children begin early intervention in their first year or two of life. Increasingly, the youngest kids are participating in therapeutic programs. These may either follow one specific approach (applied behavioral analysis) or integrate aspects of several different approaches (many therapeutic preschool programs). Some families embark on intense behavioral programs to deal with disturbing or disruptive behaviors or with noticeable delays. If families do start down this path in the early years, it usually makes sense to them that intervention, therapy, and special support will continue—though they may change in nature—as the child grows. Often this leads to a special education evaluation as the child approaches school age—and this evaluation will, in turn, recommend more therapy. As children progress through elementary school, their teachers may continue to suggest new evaluations and new therapeutic possibilities. This may be profoundly helpful. But you can't follow every suggestion. It definitely helps to pause periodically and take stock, asking yourself whether new recommendations—or in fact, the familiar therapies you are already pursuing—really make sense for your child, here and now.

Every time we went for a new evaluation, the doctor would recommend that we see someone else for yet another evaluation. It never seems to end. Finally, we decided that Gabriel was basically doing reasonably well, and we all needed a break from this constant running around to evaluations and therapies. I don't think many of the therapists ever tell you that your child doesn't need to see them anymore. I am getting suspicious that these kids are keeping a lot of people in business and that, as parents, we need to take some control over our time and money.

There's no question that many children derive real benefits from the range of therapeutic interventions—many of them relatively new interventions, developed or reconceived and elaborated over the past ten or fifteen years. Unfortunately, from a pediatrician's point of view, we have to face the fact that few of them can point to any serious research-based *evidence* that they really work. The few published studies that exist tend to be based on small numbers of kids. When we suggest some form of therapy for a quirky child, we see that help is needed, we take our best guess at where to start—but we have no business reassuring anyone that it will definitely have the desired effect. This is a process of trial and error, of finding the right therapy and the right therapists to address your singular child's particular needs and struggles and problems. In other words, it's an educated guess—not quite the same for a pediatrician as getting a positive throat culture back from the lab, diagnosing strep, and telling a parent that the optimal treatment for the child is a certain dose of penicillin for a certain number of days.

The Schlepp Factor

I'm exhausted. I had been working part-time as a librarian, and I quit my job because I couldn't keep up with all of Caitlin's appointments.

Keep the ever-present "schlepp factor" in mind: How much of your time and energy is the program you are designing for your child going to require? What are the ramifications for other areas of *your* life—your job, the rest of your family, your own spare time. (Yes, yes, we know. We are, after all, mothers. But if you think you have no spare time *now*, just wait and see what kind of schedule you may face as you start putting therapy appointments together!) If you're thinking of signing your child up for a therapy that is offered on the day you often find yourself staying late at work or the day you usually take her brother to karate or the only day you can take a yoga class or go for a swim, you should think really hard about (1) whether it's worth it and (2) whether someone else can get her there.

Guilt is potent for many parents, arising out of the pain they feel at watching a dearly beloved child struggle. It's easy to decide that a "the more, the better" approach is best for therapies, and it's a short step from there to the idea that you're doing something selfish by deciding to forgo any particular option. But more is not necessarily better. You and your child—and your other children, if you have them—are all entitled to lives. Therapies and appointments should enhance your quirky child's life, not run him ragged. The schlepp factor really adds up over time, and many parents reach a point at which they are just schlepped out!

The Right Program

What do we mean by a program? We mean a combination of therapies (or maybe a single therapy) tailored to your child and your child's development and needs—and the needs of your family and its schedules. If your child is already enrolled in a special school—for example, a school designed for autistic spectrum disorder (ASD) and pervasive developmental disorder (PDD) kids—or, in some cases, in a special ed program within a regular school, you may have comparatively little planning and scheduling (and schlepping!) to do. Most of these schools employ all the most likely types of therapists in addition to providing academic support. For anyone not in that situation, there's a lot of evaluating, planning, and thinking to do.

I've always felt that if he could survive in a regular education setting, that is best because it's more like the real world. What I didn't realize was that all the extra help he needs is on my time around the edges of the day. It takes a toll—on him, on me, and on our family as a whole.

Make sure you leave your child some time to kick back and be a kid. Hanging out with you in the kitchen or running around the playground may help him as much as any therapeutic regimen. Home is, after all, where most of a child's growth takes place. Be alert for opportunities to help your child at home.

While I limited television drastically for my other children, I felt that Arthur *and* Doug *were George's best social pragmatics intervention. Similarly, I let him have the forbidden fruit of gun toys because it stimulated some pretend play.*

The list of most commonly recommended interventions for quirky kids is growing—just as is the list of medications and even the list of diagnoses. In working with our patients, the two of us have watched different children experiment with the various therapies, and we have certainly developed some biases. We aren't real experts (that is to say, therapists) ourselves in any particular regimen, but neither are we ideologically committed to any one approach. Still, although we hope you finish this chapter with a better understanding of the kinds of help available, as well as the jargon that may be used to describe it, we also know that nothing really takes the place of checking out any interesting possibility for yourself, to see if it's a good match for your child. Many of the therapies we describe are very therapist-dependent—find the right person and you're golden—and that is going to depend on your judgment, your willingness to trust your impressions, and the help you can get from other parents in the vicinity, who know your local players.

Once we found the right person to help us, we felt so much better. The therapist who has helped Abby the most is a woman who is both an occupational therapist and a psychologist. She just got it from the start and seemed to know exactly what we needed to do to help her. It was a giant relief. In many ways, it was just the beginning, but it took a long time to find her, so in that way, it felt like the end. It has made an enormous difference.

WHAT BEHAVIORS OR CONCERNS CAN BE ADDRESSED BY WHAT THERAPIES?

Matching behaviors/concerns with potentially helpful therapies is a challenge. In this subsection, we consider some of the specific concerns parents of quirky kids have and what therapies may address them. (The accompanying table provides an overview.) Be aware that there is plenty of overlap—one child's occupational therapy may be remarkably similar to another child's physical therapy.

BEHAVIORS OR CONCERNS	THERAPIES
Her speech isn't developing normally. He's always repeating lines out of movies and books.	Speech and language therapy
My child just isn't with it. He doesn't make eye contact. He always seems off in his own world. She doesn't play with toys in a normal way. She just hangs on to that DustBuster. He doesn't connect with the other kids his age. He's always off by himself.	Play therapy for the younger child, pragmatic language therapy for the older child

BEHAVIORS OR CONCERNS	THERAPIES
My son isn't walking yet. My daughter falls off of benches. She just can't seem to hold herself up.	Physical therapy
She can't manage a knife and fork and spills whenever she pours something. He can't get himself dressed. He can't figure out how to get his legs into his pants. He can't figure out how to do things that come naturally to other kids: mount a tricycle, ride a bike, pump on a swing. She's klutzy and always breaking things, like toys, lamp switches, barrettes.	Occupational therapy
His feet never leave the ground. He's scared of stairs, curbs, swings, slides. She has a meltdown when something unexpected happens: a sneeze or sudden laugh, a touch. He misjudges the quality of objects—how heavy the pitcher is, how much pressure to use on the pencil. He can't erase without putting a hole in the paper.	Sensory integration intervention
She is pulling out her hair and eyelashes. He gives us these blank looks. He's washing his hands ninety-nine times a day.	Medications, psychotherapy
She is so completely spaced-out. She doesn't seem to hear half of what we say to her.	Play therapy, speech and language therapy, auditory-integration therapy

BEHAVIORS OR CONCERNS	THERAPIES
His behavior is driving us crazy! We can't take her anywhere, and life at home is a nightmare! All the baby-sitters have quit!	Behavioral program
She is completely disorganized. He can't see the forest for the trees. Homework is a nightmare. School projects are hell.	Occupational therapy, pragmatic language therapy, individual academic support
He is becoming depressed and more anxious as he gets older. She's much more aware of how different she is, and she feels really bad about it.	Child psychiatry or psychology, friendship groups

Many experiences in day-to-day life can be highly therapeutic. The right piano teacher, the right karate class, the right new school may help your child with some of the issues mentioned in the table. As children grow up, they are more likely to put time and effort and energy into activities they love. Your best strategy may be to help them find those activities and support their participation.

WHAT CHOICES DO WE HAVE?

Those children whose problems show up early in childhood will take part in some amount of speech and language therapy and occupational therapy, most likely through an early intervention program. Increasing numbers of the youngest children are participating in intensive approaches like applied behavioral analysis—also called discrete trials training. Many young children are receiving some aspects of this and other techniques in therapeutic preschool settings. Older children are more likely to be involved in pragmatic language or social-skills training, adaptive physical education, or a sensory integration intervention. Whether or not other forms of therapy are suggested will depend on your child's unique combination of abilities, issues, and, well, quirks. There are references available to help you learn more about each of these branches of therapy. We have no experience with some of the more esoteric ones, like swimming with dolphins. We practice in Massachusetts—far from the dolphin swim centers.

Many of these therapy programs expect the child's parents to be active partners and to keep the therapy going at home (well, maybe not the dolphin riding). You should expect to be invited to participate in most of the exercises and activities. When you do, you can form your own opinion of whether or not it's useful and learn strategies for home to make it more effective. Some of these therapies, such as applied behavioral analysis, absolutely insist on shaping not only the parents' behavior but the behavior of everyone who comes in contact with the child—so you have to think carefully about what kind of commitment you are willing or able to make.

Applied Behavioral Analysis

For toddlers and preschoolers whose behavior and development are clearly not on schedule, behavioral approaches are gaining popularity. These combine many of the elements of the other recommended therapies for quirky kids, with the same emphasis on language, social skills, and reduction in undesirable behaviors. The most widely disseminated technique for the youngest children is applied behavioral analysis, in which a child is bombarded with intense, often one-on-one and face-to-face interventions.

Among the many approaches to improving the behaviors of these kids, this one elicits strong reactions from parents and professionals alike. Based on B. F. Skinner's theories about behavior and behavior change, ABA was first introduced by Ivor Lovaas in 1968 in California. Dr. Lovaas's 1987 study, in which nineteen "autistic" children received forty full hours weekly of intensive ABA as preschoolers, claimed that nearly half of these children were vastly improved in terms of their overall IQ and were functioning well in typical classrooms seven years later.

This invited controversy because Lovaas used negative reinforcement for unwanted behavior—such as physical restraint, time-outs, and water squirts to the face. In addition, many experts feel that not enough is known about how those nineteen children were assessed or diagnosed and whether their improvement was as remarkable as it seemed. Finally, the study has never been replicated by another researcher. Nevertheless, this study provoked quite a response, and the ABA movement took off in the United States and abroad.

Through discrete trials, a child's behaviors are observed and analyzed by a certified therapist. Voluminous amounts of data are collected, aimed at determining what function an unwanted behavior serves. For example, does a child flap his hands or twirl around because he derives pleasure from this, to avoid doing something else, or to gain attention from others in the environment? Once the undesirable behavior is understood, the therapist gets to work with the child to extinguish the behavior through a series of trials, using positive reinforcers (like Goldfish crackers) to promote the desired behaviors. Negative reinforcers are fortunately no longer in vogue. Data are continually collected to document progress, immensely satisfying for parents.

Early in the movement, ABA was touted as the only effective approach for more severely affected younger children, those without any language or with regression in their developmental milestones. Indeed, there are still serious proponents of this method for such children. ABA is intensive and requires a substantial commitment on the part of the child, the family, and the therapist. Few if any children ever actually receive forty hours per week of ABA. It is prohibitively expensive and a huge drain of energy. More recently, less intense forms of ABA have been used successfully to treat problematic behaviors in much more functional quirky kids. A more typical program today may involve twenty-five hours per week and can take some creativity on the part of the family to put together.

When Trevor was two years old, he had no language at all. When he did start to talk, he had echolalic speech, he reversed his pronouns, and he had odd behaviors like waving backward. At about age three, we had him evaluated by a behavioral intervention group in California, and we started an ABA-type program with an emphasis on his social skills and fine motor skills. We did things like pretend birthday parties to help him learn the "script" he would need to use at a real party. We had to fly therapists to our home in the Midwest, because no one near us was doing this kind of work. We also hired students to help us work with him.

Although many major cities will have certified ABA therapists or organizations with a staff of certified therapists, they may be harder to find in small towns or rural areas. You want the best possible person working with your child.

Floor Time

The floor time approach, developed by child psychiatrist Stanley Greenspan, is a good example of a different approach to enhancing development without dividing tasks into areas such as speech or motor or sensory. Some of the families we interviewed have incorporated this program at home. Greenspan's theory is that a close emotional connection with a parent or another important person in the child's sphere will promote optimal development. Rather than addressing the child's deficiencies, this approach is more likely to build on areas of strength. It requires parents and close associates in the child's daily life to spend twenty- or thirty-minute periods of time on the floor, engaged with the child, *playing*. Many quirky toddlers and preschoolers have limited imagination and play skills. The kind of playfulness we expect from children just isn't there. Although this may sound obvious, letting go of your expectations and following your child's lead isn't as easy as it sounds. Because of their children's odd behaviors and atypical play skills, many parents find it difficult simply to play along without inserting their own ideas about how a child "ought" to play. As the attachment deepens (the theory goes), the child's skills develop.

Programs like ABA and floor time have helped many a quirky child, though, as usual, there is little hard data. If you decide to pursue an intensive program like ABA, you need to find an individual therapist you trust and with whom you can work closely, someone you feel is the right match for your child and your family.

Therapeutic School-Based Programs

Many communities now offer therapeutic nursery or school programs that incorporate many of the philosophies promoted as beneficial for quirky kids—again, with an emphasis on language, social skills, and functional abilities. We have become aware of a wide variety of programs across the United States, from the psychoanalytically based Cornerstone Preschool Treatment Program in San Francisco to the LEAP (*Learning Experiences: An Alternative Program for Preschoolers and Parents*) Program in Pittsburgh to the all-inclusive TEACCH (*Treatment and Education of Autistic and Related Communication-Handicapped Children*) curriculum in Chapel Hill. Although each of these programs is different, there are many similarities. Your child's options will be based largely on where you live and on which programs have gained popularity in your area.

Therapeutic Approaches to Specific Concerns

SPEECH AND LANGUAGE THERAPY

Speech and language pathologists are the friends and supporters of quirky kids, most of whom will have a speech evaluation for delayed onset of speech or for unusual development of speech and language. Speech and language therapists can be credentialed in a variety of ways—from a bachelor's degree to a master's degree and on to a Ph.D. Many of us remember a "speech teacher" who helped kids with "speech defects," but these therapists are trained to work with many different populations—including kids or adults with head injuries or strokes that have affected their speech; kids with oral-motor problems like feeding or swallowing difficulties and cleft lips or palates; as well as kids who are slow to acquire language and kids whose language is not intelligible.

For the very young child with absent or unusual speech development, a hearing test and a speech and language evaluation are critical. Sometimes the child is just a late bloomer, but when something more is going on, a good speech and language therapist will notice behaviors that you may not notice yourself and make suggestions for further evaluation. The earlier the delay is perceived and understood, the better. If your child cannot cooperate for an evaluation, that is useful information, too. Speech therapy intervention for the preverbal child can start at fifteen to eighteen months of age, if not earlier. Lots of quirky kids receive years of speech therapy for slow onset of speech, articulation difficulties, and general communication problems. Fortunately, most kids find it fun.

We started speech therapy for Charlie when he was about eighteen months. The speech therapist from early intervention came to our home twice a week, and Charlie attended a playgroup at the early intervention center that included a few different kinds of therapists. I would sit and listen as much as I could. Charlie loved it. He loved the extra attention, and he seemed to know that this was going to help him talk, and he was already frustrated. The therapist got right down on the floor with him, right in his face (after he knew her well enough to tolerate that), and worked really hard at getting him to produce sounds. He learned where the different sounds are made in his mouth and throat. I remember him saying frog and holding his throat as he made the hard "g" sound. She brought toys that he loved and used them to help get the words out. Now that I have learned so much about the things that help these kids, I see that she was using lots of strategies at the same time. How will I ever know if this is why he started to talk? I guess I won't ever really know, but he enjoyed it, I learned from it, and we got hooked into the world of therapies that have clearly made a difference for him.

PRAGMATIC SPEECH THERAPY

Speech therapists with additional training in the pragmatics of language are most likely to be of help to the older quirky child who has trouble communicating. Part of what we are calling quirkiness often involves difficulties with the "pragmatics" of language—that is, with understanding the dynamics of conversation beyond the ability to say words and form sentences. Problems with language pragmatics may mean that kids have trouble:

- Starting or stopping a conversation
- Knowing when the information they are trying to convey is getting across and when it's not
- Understanding that conversational style or tone of voice should change according to their audience, that people don't talk to a cop the same way they talk to their best buddy
- Reading the body language or cues of the person across from them

For typical kids, the ability to take another's point of view develops at around age four. This is the theory-of-mind concept: you can appreciate that another person has a different experience from you, that she sees things differently, may know things you don't know, and may not know things that you do. Many quirky kids can't do this or can't do it as well as other kids their age, and it wreaks havoc with their conversational skills. In addition, many have unusual behaviors that other kids find distracting or disturbing.

This is where *pragmatic language groups*, sometimes called "friendship groups" or "social-skills groups," come in. The point is to get a small group of kids together with a speech therapist and actually teach them the mechanics of conversation—such as making eye contact, assessing the level of interest of the listener, communicating your own attention to another speaker. A typical group has four kids, usually school-age or adolescents. Each session has a topic or a place to start that is chosen by the therapist, who then helps the kids navigate conversationally. This can involve frequent redirecting, gentle reminders about paying attention or reducing interruptions, videos of role-playing that the kids watch and then comment upon. For the younger elementary school children, there may be cooperative games or activities in which the kids have to talk to one another in order to get the game or project done.

Sam started a friendship group at a local university with supervision from a professor of speech and language therapy and some graduate students. He was in about second grade when we started, and he did it for two years. The group was all boys, and they all were a little off and needed some help with their social and conversational skills. They did exercises and games geared toward understanding facial expressions and nonverbal body language. They did role-plays, which they later watched on video—and of course, they loved that! Then they would dissect their own and one another's behavior, with a lot of assistance from the group leaders. Some days they played cooperative games—again, with a lot of help— where it was required to talk to one another to reach a common goal. He found it challenging at times, but I think it helped him to see the perspective of another person. We used the strategies at home a lot, over dinner especially, to help him get the social rules of conversation that seem to come more easily to other kids.

DOES IT WORK?

There are some promising unpublished data regarding both initial assessment and response to treatment, but the numbers are small. We don't really know whether gains that are made in treatment generalize to the outside world, to the child's day-to-day existence. Can a weekly treatment group really have a great impact? The jury is still out. We have talked with a number of parents whose children have participated in these groups, and although they were generally positive, the reviews about long-term benefits are mixed. We would suggest speaking about the potential benefits to the consultant who really knows your child, observing a group session, and trusting your own knowledge of your child and sense of her needs in deciding whether it's worth a try. Checking in with your child's classroom teacher can also help you assess whether a pragmatics group is helping. Teachers see kids interacting with one another more than most parents do and are in a good position to let you know if they see any improvements in social skills.

PHYSICAL THERAPY AND ADAPTIVE PHYSICAL EDUCATION

Muscle weakness or low muscle tone, motor clumsiness, and poor coordination are quite frequent among quirky kids, who can be pretty klutzy. Physical therapy (and occupational therapy) is often recommended to address these troubles. Parents are likely to notice delayed walking, poor balance or stability, low muscle tone or weakness, poor fine motor skills for eating or writing or dressing, and poor ball-playing skills. Physical therapy for the youngest kids is geared toward improving function through improved strength and balance, and improving coordination through ball skills, mazes, and the like. Most young children love it and love the equipment in the rooms. There are strong data to support the efficacy of physical therapy.

Physical therapists can be found in all early intervention programs, most hospitals, and most public schools. Also, independent groups of physical therapists working together with other kinds of therapists are sprouting up in many communities. Most school-based physical therapists these days will have some experience with the quirky-child population and what approaches are most likely to be successful. It is worth talking to an individual therapist about your child and what issues you most want addressed. Observing one or two sessions will help you determine whether your child and the physical therapist are well matched.

The physical therapist was David's first therapist, and we were referred to her because he was motor-delayed. He couldn't roll over or sit up. He started to see her when he was about nine months old, and that relationship lasted a long time. It was through his physical therapist that we figured out many of his other issues, and that his motor delay wasn't an isolated thing. Fortunately, he loved going to see her, and it definitely helped him. He continued it for a long time, and now he attends a special education school where there are physical therapists on the staff.

John was really uncoordinated as a small child. He had a lot of difficulty with the most basic things, like learning to go up and down the stairs. His physical therapist explained the combination of strength, coordination, and "motor planning" that is required to do something that seems so simple. He worked on strength and balance with her, walking on the balance beam, practicing going up and down the stairs, and worked with other kids with similar issues. He enjoyed it, though he was exhausted when it was over. As he got older, he worked more on ball skills and eye-hand coordination and developed confidence in those skills.

As kids grow, the options for physical therapy broaden in some communities. Many quirky kids develop basic motor skills but still have difficulty with the coordination and communication necessary for team sports or playground games. Continued individual or group work with a physical therapist is necessary for some of these kids, but there are a number of other activities that can foster improved coordination, confidence, and strength. Families whose children take martial arts classes like karate or tae kwon do swear by them as something that has helped in all three of these areas. There are growing numbers of gymnasium-based programs, staffed by special educators, for kids who can benefit from some good old-fashioned physical activity with co-operative gross motor games and small-group processing sessions with a counselor afterward. These kinds of programs address both motor and social skills in each session.

Some schools offer *adaptive physical education programs* for kids with physical handicaps or more severe coordination problems, which can be complicated by perceptual difficulties. Adaptive physical education is not available in all schools but is worth knowing about, because the gym teacher may be willing to team up with an occupational or physical therapist to create such a program. Chances are good that a number of kids in any given school could benefit from an adaptive physical education program.

OCCUPATIONAL THERAPY

Occupational therapy (OT) is the therapy most likely to be recommended for a quirky child. It is a huge and growing field with many areas of specialization within it. There are occupational therapists who specialize in the small muscles of the hand or in feeding and swallowing disorders or in visual and perceptual differences, and there is a growing number who are obtaining certification in sensory integration treatment. As with physical therapists, occupational therapists can have a bachelor's degree, a master's degree, or a Ph.D. There are also a number of OTAs, or occupational therapy assistants, working in this field. OTs can be found working in virtually all early intervention programs and most schools and hospitals, and an increasing number are working in large private organizations with all the equipment in one place.

Younger kids may be seen by occupational therapists as part of their early intervention evaluation or may be referred specifically to OT because of feeding difficulties or generally low tone or inability to use both hands together in a coordinated fashion. Toddlers or preschoolers with developmental delays in fine motor skills, unusual reactions to textures (like Play-Doh or certain foods), extreme irritability or whininess, or difficulty following directions or quirky kids with preoccupations with unusual objects that prevent interactions with toys or other people are all good candidates for occupational therapy intervention. School-age kids with attentional, organizational, or fine motor deficits may benefit from working with an OT.

Charlie started occupational therapy in his early intervention program when he was about eighteen months old, and now he receives it at our local public school. At first, he was working on basic things like play skills, following directions, and staying with a task. As he has gotten older, his OT has helped him with fine motor skills like holding a marker or crayon properly, and now they are working more on sensory integration. He is learning to maintain his balance and keep his trunk erect. His OT has many different kinds of swings, and this is supposed to help him with his balance and coordination. His occupational therapist visits his preschool class periodically to observe and educate the staff about his stuff. When his preschool teacher was worried about his silly behavior and not paying attention at story time, his OT noticed that he was flopping all over the place because it is hard for him to maintain his posture if he has nothing to lean back on. As soon as he was moved to a place where he could lean against the wall, his attention improved and he was less disruptive. Sometimes he would refuse to participate in activities that the other kids loved, like art or dance. His OT helped us to see that he was overwhelmed by the happy chaos all around him and that his difficulty with things like cutting and drawing made it easier for him to ob-serve rather than participate. Occupational therapists seem to have an eye for this sort of thing. It worries me that, without her perspective, Charlie would have been seen as a behavior problem, when the solution was so simple. Ultimately, it was the insight of his OT that helped us realize that Charlie was in the wrong preschool setting. We moved him to another school where there was more struc-ture and many more adults to help kids with transitions and play skills, and he has absolutely thrived.

Occupational therapists are terrific at helping kids, families, and schools make (sometimes quite simple) modifications that can help with day-to-day functioning. A particular kind of chair may help a child maintain his posture in class. Simple tools can attach to a pencil or pen and make it easier for the child to write. For some kids, the mechanics of writing are just too much, and occupational therapists can set them up with technology and software pro-grams and teach keyboarding skills. For kids who need strategies for following directions, OTs teach them how to break things down into small, discrete pieces to make it easier.

DOES IT WORK?

Once again, there is not a tremendous amount of scientific data to support occupational therapy—particularly sensory integration treatment. Still, many quirky kids will be referred for evaluation. In our experience, most parents whose kids receive OT believe it is helping. Part of the picture is a warm and supportive relationship with an adult who understands the child's difficulties interacting with the world around him. It helps him to develop a vocabulary to describe those difficulties and strategies to cope. This can be an enormous com-fort to kids struggling with these issues, and many keep coming back for more!

SENSORY INTEGRATION TREATMENT

Although the term *sensory integration disorder* is relatively new, the concept of sensory integration itself is not. *Sensory integration* refers to the ability of the nervous system to integrate incoming information to the senses and act on it. Most of us can appreciate a child's struggle with the senses of vision, hearing, taste, and smell, but it may be harder to see the subtleties of touch in its vari-ous components, balance and movement, body position. Each of these more subtle senses is addressed in SI evaluation and treatment. For a detailed and excellent description of these concepts, we refer you to Carol Stock Kranowitz's *The Out-of-Sync Child*.

Sensory integration dysfunction is a diagnosis of sorts that applies to many quirky kids. For some, it is the *main* diagnosis or the one that best explains a child's unusual behaviors, and some parents are quite relieved to have an explanation and a strategy for helping.

Jack was about six years old when we first heard the term sensory integration dysfunction, *and it made so much sense to us. He had been such a difficult baby, screaming and arching and barely sleeping, and he developed horrendous tantrums as he got older. We knew we were good parents, and this had to be something about the way he was wired. Finding a professional who understood him was a great relief, and now he is receiving SI therapy, and he loves it. We have new strategies to help him at home, and we just understand it better.*

Sensory integration evaluations and treatments should be conducted by occupational or physical therapists with certification in sensory integration. With a certified therapist, there will be at least some consistency in approach, which will enable you to make a more meaningful assessment of whether or not it is helpful. A typical sensory integration program lasts from six months to a couple of years, with frequent assessments throughout the treatment, though some families have used an on-again, off-again approach over the years with reasonable results.

When Gabriel started his EI program, the occupational therapist suggested that we try a "brushing program" to improve his sense of his body in space and to help him overcome some of his hypersensitivity to sensation. He was one of those kids who had to have the tags cut out of all his clothes and couldn't stand the seam on his socks. So we used to "brush" him vigorously with a surgical brush. He seemed to like it, and it would actually calm him down for a while afterward. Our problem was that we could never really keep it up.

As he got older, he saw another occupational therapist certified in sensory integration, and she worked with him on things like "gravitational insecurity"—the fact that he didn't like to have his feet off the ground. They worked with various types of swings, and he developed more strength and coordination and less anxiety about these things. I can't really put my finger on it, but it did seem to help him, and he is pretty coordinated now.

DOES IT WORK?

There are few scientific data regarding this form of treatment. Some people recoil at the sight of the stiff surgical brushes being rubbed on a toddler's skin, but many occupational therapists and parents swear by it. It's worth looking into while we're waiting for research results. Most kids find it quite fun and engaging!

PSYCHOTHERAPY

Growing up quirky can be pretty rough, and it is our belief that most kids will need some mental health intervention at one point or another. Anxiety, depression, obsessive-compulsive disorder, and tics are common and, if untreated, are additional obstacles to growth and development. As we have said before, a relationship with a caring psychologist, social worker, or psychiatrist (especially if you think medication might be necessary) over the years can be immensely comforting for quirky kids and their families. Different families need different kinds of help. What is available ranges from individual talk therapy to family therapy to groups. Some child psychologists run social-skills groups much like the pragmatic therapy groups described above under speech and language therapy.

INDIVIDUAL "TALK THERAPY"

Many people question whether a child on this spectrum can successfully engage in one-on-one talk therapy with a counselor or therapist. Because of these children's typically poor interpersonal skills and lack of insight, this is a reasonable question. Supporters of this type of therapy argue that there is much to be gained for the socially awkward child and that, in a good therapeutic relationship, a child should experience a positive social interaction with a caring adult. Challenging for the therapist as well as the child, it has the potential to help the child learn to identify feelings and the facial expressions and tone of voice that may accompany them. An "empathic attachment" (to borrow a phrase from the psycholingo!) with a therapist will foster improved communication and the development of empathy itself. A therapist may in fact start out by acting as a translator for the child, giving her clues to understand the actions of people in her world that she may not understand. Parents whose children have developed good relationships with therapists invariably tell us that it takes a long time for them to get the hang of it but that it can be a great help for the kids and for their exhausted parents.

David has a therapist at school whom he sees weekly. It took a while for him to understand the point of it, but he looks forward to it, and it helps us as a family that he has another trusting adult to talk to. He is developing a vocabulary for describing his feelings and experiences that will help him make it through adolescence.

Individual therapy with a child psychiatrist is actually a rare event these days; most therapists are social workers, psychologists, or guidance counselors. You will probably have to see a child psychiatrist if your child needs medications to manage his symptoms. Although some child psychiatrists are knowledgeable about quirky kids and may even have a particular interest in what makes them tick, few have the time to engage in real ongoing therapy with their patients. Many child psychiatrists function as consultants to other mental health professionals because there are too few psychiatrists, and at least for now, they are the ones who are licensed to prescribe medication to children. Pediatricians can perform this function, but we generally consult with our psychiatric colleagues as well. They understand the subtleties of psychiatric medicines the way we understand antibiotics!

What I have found is that child psychiatrists tend to know lots about garden-variety problems—depression, anxiety in kids without complex learning/behavior problems—and they know and are experts in dealing with major mental illness in kids. Unless they have gotten additional training or done a lot of reading about these kinds of kids, they know very little about them. They are not the most open about considering the work of allied health professionals like occupational therapists, for example, who have contributed to the understanding of these kids and, as such, limit themselves in their understanding. I would tell parents to be sure a psychiatrist has experience with these kids before signing on with him.

GROUP THERAPY

Highly structured psychotherapy groups are sometimes recommended for quirky kids to help them address individual and interpersonal goals and to teach them about forming and negotiating relationships with others and about how to follow rules and directions. These groups usually take the form of social-skills groups or friendship groups aimed at kids who are learning about body language and social cues, about understanding the perspectives of others, and about communicating their confusion or lack of understanding in an acceptable way. Some psychology practices offer relaxation groups, growing-up groups, groups in which kids work on "social stories" together. Sessions can even take the form of going out for a meal together or some other social activity.

Whether or not a group experience works for a particular child depends on a number of factors:

- Is she motivated and interested, or young enough to go along with you if *you* are interested and believe it's indicated?
- Does the therapist have experience with this population of kids and agree that your child is a good candidate?
- Has the therapist thoughtfully chosen a group of kids who can work together?

The group itself is also critical. Kids referred for these kinds of groups are, by definition, having difficulty getting by socially. They might be excessively shy and uncommunicative or, alternatively, boisterous and loud. For some, their attention issues or nervous habits get in the way or are distracting or disturbing to the other kids. Kids with psychotic features may have behaviors frightening to other kids. Check it out for a few weeks. If you're lucky, some of these group therapy rooms have facilities for parents to sit and watch through a one-way mirror. Ask your son or daughter if the group is enjoyable, and ask the therapist how it's going. Again, this is a significant time commitment. It's good to cut your losses if you conclude that it isn't going to help.

BEHAVIORAL THERAPY

Many psychologists advocate behavioral approaches for quirky kids and their sometimes disturbing habits or behaviors. One well-known type of behavioral therapy is *cognitive behavioral therapy*, or CBT—sometimes recommended for the subset of kids characterized by anxiety or anxiety-like symptoms, strong special interests or hobbies, and a tendency to like structure and negotiating or making deals. CBT is goal-directed. There are specific goals such as reducing (or replacing) an undesirable behavior—an obsession or a habit, like picking one's nose or pulling out hair. It tends to work best with kids who can be taught to negotiate and parents who are willing partners in helping a child work toward a given goal. Once a behavior is targeted and its frequency measured, the child and her parents work together with the therapist to decide how the behavior should change. *Not* a lot of time or energy is spent determining why the behavior exists. Rather, the goal is to eliminate it, reduce it to a more reasonable level, or replace it with something else altogether. The next step is choosing a reinforcer for the desired change. Of course, the child herself gets first dibs on this one! What can work well are treats like baseball cards or a time to play an electronic game—some reasonably small guaranteed pleasure that means something to the child. This is the basic framework of the CBT approach. It can be a terrific plan for the right quirky kid, but not all have the capacity to negotiate or have such control over their undesirable behaviors that they can actually suppress them or replace them with alternative behaviors, whatever the incentive.

Behavioral psychologists are also known for teaching kids to manage their anxiety, using techniques like relaxation, guided imagery, teaching a "competing behavior" that prevents the anxiety-driven one (for example, you can't pull out your hair if you're squeezing a ball in your pocket), role-playing, and humor. Lots of kids respond to these strategies, and most parents prefer to start with these rather than moving right to medications—often the next step.

The therapies already discussed are most familiar, but they are by no means the only interventions out there, and parents may be referred to many others. The list is growing, and the data supporting the emerging therapies are even more scant than the data for the more traditional ones.

EMERGING THERAPIES FOR QUIRKY KIDS

There are a number of newer therapies designed to address the more subtle neurological differences that parents and teachers of quirky kids often describe. Difficulties in communicating and learning are sometimes attributed to *visual dysfunction* (in children with perfectly normal vision) or problems in *auditory processing* (in children with perfectly normal hearing). Therapies aimed at improving these skills have gained popularity in recent years. As yet, there are few data to support vision training or auditory-integration therapy, but these therapies have clearly helped some children. Parents who recognize one of these disorders in their own children may find them worth a try.

Activities in the Community and at Home

Many activities for kids have the potential to be therapeutic. A caring and sensitive Little League coach can make a world of difference to a quirky child. At times, it is necessary to talk with an adult who is supervising an activity about your child's particular quirks. Sometimes it doesn't make the least bit of difference. Many adults who work with children on a regular basis are going to figure things out on their own. Over time, many parents develop a kind of sixth sense about these issues—whom to tell, what to tell, and how to get the child the kind of support he needs.

Sam has been taking piano lesson for a couple of years with a couple of different teachers. He is intensely musical, but his techniques for learning and playing music are not at all standard-issue. His first teacher was pretty rigid and simply did not get him, and could only see his odd behaviors as defiance or hostility. Unfortunately, it was a negative experience for Sam. This year, we are working with someone new, who is less rigid and more accepting of Sam's stuff, but I can see that she, too, is confused and bewildered that this clearly very talented boy is such a struggle to work with. I have started talking to her more openly about what a struggle life in general is for him, and it seems to have helped the two of them relax and enjoy each other.

All families involved in any of the therapies or activities described above learn to incorporate some of these interventions in their day-to-day family life. Using organizational charts or dry-erase boards to keep your child on track, keeping simple pictures on the refrigerator to help a preverbal child with communication, using pragmatic language techniques at the dinner table, engaging in rough-and-tumble play that your child enjoys at physical therapy, using SI techniques like brushing to decrease tactile sensitivity—these are all familiar to many quirky-kid families and come naturally over time. Most therapists actively encourage parents to augment these programs at home.

There are a couple of programs that specifically lend themselves to the home environment.

Carol Gray, an educator, developed social stories and comic strip conversations to address the particular areas of difficulty for most quirky kids: understanding the rules of social behavior and understanding the perspectives of others. Although originally designed for use in the school and used heavily by speech and language pathologists, they are easily learned by parents and kids alike. Kits are available to help you get started. A social story is a simple story written by an adult who knows the child well. Stories are written according to a formula in which certain rules are followed and are then reviewed with the child. Social stories have the capacity to help parents and other adults understand a child's perspective and special areas of difficulty and to increase the child's awareness of the social world.

Comic strip conversations are joint projects in which an adult and a child create a simple comic strip in which the characters have bubbles (for thoughts or words) coming out of their heads. These can help a child process an event that she may have found disturbing or plan for an event in the future at which certain behaviors are expected (such as a birthday party or wedding). They are used to help the child understand the perspective of others; for example, that what someone says is not the same as what that person may be thinking, especially when sarcasm is used. Sarcasm is one of the hardest things for quirky kids to understand. Drawing a comic strip and working with your child to fill in the blanks provides a good opportunity to explain what comes naturally to you but not so naturally to him.

Stanley Greenspan's floor time technique, discussed earlier, lends itself to the home environment. Many families swear by it for helping to bring a child out of his shell. Once again, you've got little to lose and a lot to gain by making these activities part of your family life.

How to Decide What to Do for Your Child

Here are some questions to consider as you look at possible therapies, therapists, and therapeutic regimens:

- Does therapy target the problems that are really getting in my child's way? Keep in mind what *you* are targeting. What skills do you want him to gain, or which behaviors would you like to decrease? Does this therapy seem like the place to start?

- How will we know if it's working? This is a good question to ask of the therapist during an initial evaluation. How does the therapist herself decide? What kinds of assessments are done at the beginning, and how often is the child reassessed?
- What if it isn't helping? Can you trust the therapist to let you know if she believes that the program isn't working or that she and your child aren't a good match?
- What kind of commitment are we making if we start this course of therapy? Is there any danger in stopping the program cold turkey if it isn't effective? If it's a group, how important is it for your child to stick it out for an entire semester or year? How would it affect the other kids in the group if she didn't?
- How long will it take? How much time a therapeutic intervention will take—and how intense it is—is quite variable. None of the therapies we discuss here are intended as quick fixes.
- Is my child at the right age for this kind of therapy? There is good evidence to suggest that you can make better progress if you start addressing some of the more troublesome behaviors, or the most significant delays, at an early age. Younger children who don't get help may become relatively more delayed, or their behaviors more troublesome, as time passes. For parents, it's a lot easier to cart around a toddler, or work with her at home, than it may be with an older child who has more demands on her time and energy. At a certain point, an older child may balk at all this so-called help. It becomes harder to continue with a therapy—no matter how much good it's doing—if the child won't go!

For many parents, it may be easy to read down the list of problems and indications and think: yes, indeed, she needs help with her fine motor coordination; oh, and her social skills; and of course, the sensory integration stuff; and certainly, she needs to see a counselor . . . You won't possibly be able to do all the different things that are out there, and you won't be able to spend all your home time following therapeutic regimens either. You're going to have to pick and choose. Follow your instincts and pay close attention to how your child is doing.

Be sure your child doesn't have so many appointments that there is no time for playing with siblings or kids in the neighborhood or going to visit cousins or grandparents. Learning the basics of hanging out at home can be challenging for quirky kids, especially those with excess physical energy and those who engage in their special interests to an extreme degree. Create quiet hanging-out time for your family—whether it's reading or crossword puzzles on Sundays, playing word games or board games or doing projects together, or watching movies on Friday nights. This is good for all families and can easily get lost in the hectic pace of life for families with working parents and quirky kids. Make it a priority. You will see improvement in your child's ability to relax and enjoy the company of others, although this may take a long time!

What we all want for our children is that they be happy with themselves and live the best lives they possibly can. If your daughter never learns to ride a bike or hates the sand at the beach, so be it. If your son types all his assignments because he never mastered legible handwriting, fine. (He'll make a great doctor!) The world is much more tolerant of these idiosyncrasies in adults. There is no expectation that all adults will like soccer or science fiction movies, no requirement that they all have neat handwriting or perfect table manners.

The program you develop to help your child along the way will depend on what is available within a reasonable distance, on which individual therapists you respond to most positively, on your resources in terms of money and time, and once again, on the notorious schlepp factor.

References and Resources

Cohen, Donald J., and Fred R. Volkmar, eds. *Handbook of Autism and Pervasive Developmental Disorders.* 2d ed. Hoboken, N.J.: Wiley, 1997. The term *handbook* is a bit of a misnomer for this comprehensive text by highly respected clinicians and researchers from the Yale Child Study Center in New Haven, Connecticut. Section 5 of this volume, "Interventions," is a good place to read about the data on the various therapies.

Frost, Lori A., and Andrew S. Bondy. *PECS: The Picture Exchange Communication System.* Newark, Del.: Pyramid Educational Consultants, 1996. Details a system for communicating with a less verbal child that involves picture cues.

Greenspan, Stanley I., and Serena Weider, with Robin Simons. *The Child with Special Needs: Encouraging Intellectual and Emotional Growth.* Cambridge, Mass.: Perseus, 1998. The child psychiatrist who developed the "floor time" technique addresses a range of developmental issues and gives strategies for helping children.

Kranowitz, Carol Stock. *The Out-of-Sync Child: Recognizing and Coping with Sensory Integration Dysfunction.* New York: Perigee, 1998. Once again, we recommend this book written for parents by an educator with expertise in sensory integration. It's full of stories that resonate for many parents of quirky kids and explains the basis of this seemingly mysterious treatment in straightforward language.

Quill, Kathleen Ann. *Do-Watch-Listen-Say: Social and Communication Intervention for Children with Autism.* Baltimore: Paul H. Brookes, 2000. One of the few books available that describes the helpful speech and language interventions.

TEACCH (Treatment and Education of Autistic and Related Communication-Handicapped Children) curriculum. To learn more about the TEACCH curriculum, check out the Web site at www.teacch.com.

10

○ ○ ● ○

Mind-Altering Substances:
MEDICATIONS AND THE QUIRKY CHILD

It has been our experience that a trial of medications is suggested at some point for more than half of the children about whom we are talking. The small amount of data in the medical literature, and our personal correspondence with prescribing physicians who care for this group of kids, suggest a similar proportion of children on medications in other practices. In part, this reflects the general increase in the use of these medications in children, but it also reflects the special issues of this group of kids. Most schoolteachers are aware of at least a few children on medication in regular education classrooms. A higher number of children in special education or integrated classrooms will be taking drugs to alleviate behaviors or symptoms that interfere with learning.

This chapter is an attempt to make sense of the questions that usually come up, to explain the current wisdom of the professionals who usually prescribe psychotropic medications, and to review what scanty data are available regarding the use of these medications in quirky kids. There is justifiably a certain amount of anxiety and discomfort about side effects. Those worries must be weighed against the benefits of their use.

The well-documented increase in the use of psychiatric medications for children shows no signs of leveling off. Occasionally, the suggestion to consider medication comes early in the child's life or early in the diagnostic workup. More commonly, it occurs as the child enters the school-age years, when the academic and social demands are greater, when conformity to some ideal of normal is expected, and when the child and his family are feeling the stresses more acutely. The early childhood years, when parents can keep their child close to home, even if that means carting her around to different appointments and evaluations, are a bit of a honeymoon period for most families— though it may seem so only in retrospect!

Different kids show stress in different ways, but the most notable feature of a child's distress—anxiety, obsessiveness, moodiness, irritability, attentional difficulties—will be the target of the suggested drug. In other words, you medicate a symptom, not a diagnosis. Medications are offered in the spirit of helping children and families through these times and often of helping children function and succeed in the school setting, which becomes such an important part of their world.

Parents go through stages in the process of accepting (or not accepting) the reality that a medication may help, not unlike the Kübler-Ross stages of the process of grief. In fact, there is an element of grief in this process as well. Each time a new therapy is recommended, it serves as a reminder that this is a life-long process that most would not have chosen. For many parents, giving a drug—in particular, a psychiatric drug—is crossing a line; it means something is really wrong; it puts the child into a different category. Many parents initially feel a strong reaction of shock, denial, or anger. We all have mixed emotions about medications—especially psychotropic medications, the mood-changing, behavior-changing drugs. They seem mysterious, frightening, potentially harmful. Or they seem like a crutch, a sedative, a way of avoiding the real problem.

He is on no meds and never has been. His father and I both feel that all other avenues should be exhausted first. Medications should only be used as a last resort. I worry that medication would make him into a zombie, and he has a very nice disposition. He's very affectionate and loving, and despite everything, he's a happy kid.

Trevor has never been on any medications, and meds have never been suggested for him by any of the doctors he has seen. We're both happy about this, but we suspect that medications may be in his future for his anxiety, which is his biggest area of difficulty and will probably get worse.

I am looking for strategies to help with Aidan's tantrums. For now, I'm opposed to medications. I don't like to take medicines myself, and I'd rather not give them to him.

Some parents prefer other approaches—perhaps nontraditional therapies, perhaps a change in schools or school programs. Depending on where on the spectrum a particular child falls, that decision may be the best one at a given point in time. Sometimes you find the right school, and the stress lessens notably. Sometimes your child takes a developmental step or makes a friend, and things get easier. Families often revisit the question later on—a different age, a different developmental stage, new and different challenges. No decision needs to be set in stone. Similarly, a decision to start medication is not a lifetime commitment. You need to look at what is most helpful for your own child at this particular time.

When Caitlin was about six, we tried a course of Zoloft [an antidepressant also used to treat anxiety in kids] on the recommendation of her psychologist. We had already changed her school environment, hired a full-time aide, and involved her in a lot of different therapies, and she still needed something to help with her rigidity and her phobias. It helped her tremendously. It freed her up verbally and with communication. She stayed on it for a year and a half and then gradually tapered off.

That drugs are being recommended suggests that the child is having significant stress, that the activities of normal everyday life are just too much for her. Almost all parents initially resist the idea of using a medication to alter their children's behavior and would prefer to try any number of nonmedical therapies first. However, some reach a place at which they feel that the child's problem is just too great—causing the child and his family too much suffering—and they find themselves willing to try anything that might help. If the medication does indeed help, these same parents may start to feel that it's essential and that withholding medications is actually cruel.

In the fifth grade, George became very anxious and depressed. By the third week of school, he had pulled out all his eyelashes and had a giant bald spot on the top of his head. He said things like, "I think my school would be better off without me," and "I think I should go away and live in a box with the homeless people." I knew this was very serious and couldn't stand to see him suffering. I quickly got him to a psychiatrist, who prescribed medications (Zoloft and Seroquel), with tremendous relief.

There are a few rules of thumb that we have learned from working with families as they go through this process:

- Be sure that you trust the professional making the recommendation. Since medications need to be prescribed by a physician (in almost all states), this means finding a doctor you like and trust. General pediatricians should have a trusted child psychiatrist or behavioral and developmental pediatrician to whom families can be referred for detailed discussions about the use of medications. This physician must be someone who understands the potential benefits of the possible drugs, has experience in prescribing them and in following children on these medicines, and is committed to communicating with you around these issues.

- Some communities have a few experts who practice in the world of quirky kids—kids in the pervasive developmental disorder (PDD), Asperger's, and nonverbal learning disability (NLD) categories—doctors who see hundreds of families and have tremendous experience in prescribing medications. Usually, there is a long waiting list to see such people, but it's often well worth the wait. It's a terrific asset to have a long-term partner in the professional world who knows the child in question over time. As the child progresses through different developmental and educational stages, the experience of the disabilities will change. It may be appropriate to reconsider the pharmaceutical choices. These decisions are more easily made with the assistance of a consultant who knows the child well. In addition, she should be able to answer questions about the downside of treating with a particular medicine and the ramifications of not treating with a medicine at all.

- Be wary of specific suggestions for medication made by people who don't have the responsibility of prescribing these drugs and tracking their effects. Be wary as well of those who condemn the use of medication in all children.

- You need to stay flexible, and you need a doctor who's flexible. The prescribing physician must be open-minded and attentive to the experience of the child and family, ready to try different doses or juggle medications around a little until a good result is achieved. All children do not react alike to a given medicine or a given dosage. This is even more true for quirky kids, with their different neural wiring. You need a prescribing physician with the ability to listen with care and compassion, to accept that a particular carefully chosen medication may not have been exactly right for a particular child, that the side effects are overwhelming, or that the target symptoms are not being touched. These skills distinguish the truly seasoned and objective practitioner from one who is familiar with only a limited repertoire of therapies or is limited somehow by his own agenda. No one should ever make you feel that it's your child's fault if the medicine wasn't right—or your fault because you won't admit to an improvement that isn't there!

• It takes time to get it right or at least to get it better. That can be hard on children and maybe especially on parents. You need to be able to get help and answers from your doctor. Many parents find it frightening to watch as a doctor juggles around a child's medicines. We are far more tolerant of a change in an antibiotic when the first one didn't work for an ear infection. The psychotropic medications are newer and scarier, and the average family has little experience with them. This makes the process of finding just the right drug or the right combination much more stressful. The prescribing physician has to work as a partner with the child and family. That means not just listening at appointments but also being available for short consultations and questions when they are needed, which may happen at unexpected times. Many of these physicians are overscheduled and excessively busy. They can be hard to reach for a quick question. Be sure you ask the doctor about how you can get in touch if you have a sudden question or problem.

It took us a while to get it right. With the kids on medicines, questions come up all the time, and one of us wants a quick conversation with their doctor. We were shy at first about bothering him by paging him on his beeper when he might be busy with someone else, but eventually, we got more comfortable doing it when we feel we have to.

• A course of medications has helped many kids through particularly rough patches at school or at home. This doesn't mean signing up for a chemical solution forever. It is clear that children can benefit from other therapies (their occupational therapy, their speech and language therapy, their social-skills training) somewhat more when their disabling symptoms—whether anxiety, inattention, moodiness, or obsessiveness—are reduced or eliminated by the use of medications.

This chapter on medication is not intended to take the place of consultation with an appropriate prescribing physician. The use of psychiatric medications in children is a relatively new frontier, and there is often new information. What is up-to-date at the time of writing may well have changed before you read it. Do not, under any circumstances, change your child's medication, dosage, or schedule because of what you read here. Do not ever, under any circumstances, give your child a medication that has been prescribed for someone else. Every child is different, every case is different, and information and recommendations are constantly changing. Use this book for background information, to inform yourself about what you want to discuss with your doctor. Be aware that there is no substitute for proper evaluation by an experienced physician who understands the issues particular to *your* child.

- *A good diagnostic assessment means better treatment.* Maybe you didn't want a diagnosis at first, maybe you resisted the idea of a label—but generally, if it's time to think about medications, it's important to know which overall diagnostic category best fits the child. The team involved in the care of the child needs to be aware of previous evaluations that have been done, and you and they need to agree on the best diagnostic category for the child. In addition, it is helpful to agree on which symptom or symptoms, and for which settings, you're targeting with the medication. We do children a great service when we perform thorough evaluations and come to appropriate classifications of their overall combinations of symptoms or behaviors. It should also be said, however, that many different symptoms do get treated with the same drugs. In particular, the SRIs, or serotonin reuptake inhibitors (such as Prozac), get used a great deal in kids, and it may sometimes seem, as you read through this chapter, that all roads lead in that one particular direction.

  No medication will correct the underlying neurology of quirky kids, but there is a lot of experience with psychiatric medicines that have been used to treat some of the symptoms that these children are likely to manifest. The target symptom should be kept in mind at all times. That is your most valuable index for assessing whether a medication is helping or not. Many families can tolerate a given behavior or mood up to a point. When it emerges to a degree that interferes with the child's or the family's daily functioning, it is no longer a nuisance but a symptom worth directed treatment.

When Sam's moods and reactivity started causing chaos in the whole family and his tantrums were affecting his two brothers, we felt at a loss. We had tried so hard to help him with therapy and various groups as well as lots of support and compassion for his stuff. His child psychiatrist started him on medications, and things became much smoother at home. It's not perfect, but it's a lot better.

- *What are we treating?* Parents and professionals with experience with quirky kids describe their rigidity, their social difficulties, their obsessive tendencies, their attention issues, their anxiety, irritability, reactivity, and moodiness tending toward depression, especially as they approach adolescence and become more aware of their differences. Some children may engage in what is referred to as "self-mutilating" or "self-injurious" behavior—such as picking at their skin or head-banging—symptoms that have a big impact on parents and teachers and can lead to medical complications. Many of these behaviors have been successfully addressed by medications when other approaches have failed.

When John's picking at himself reached the point that he was making himself bleed every day, we knew we needed more help than he was getting in his therapies and asked our pediatrician to recommend a specialist for a medication evaluation. We have not regretted it.

- *Can medications help with learning problems?* Learning disabilities and learning differences cannot be directly affected by medications, but children may be able to focus better and use effective learning strategies when their overwhelming anxiety or their obsessive tendencies are under better control or when their attention deficits are at least modified. This may be a reason that school personnel sometimes seem eager to have their students on medications!

- *It seems wrong to medicate a child for not fitting in!* Many people are troubled by the idea that children who somehow fail to fit into their surroundings end up medicated so that they won't stick out. Bear in mind, though, that we are not just talking about the mildly eccentric child in an intolerant world. We're talking about kids who truly can't function in school because they're so anxious or rigid, so unable to concentrate, or so troubled by physical restlessness or tics. If you've made reasonable attempts to tailor a child's environment to his strengths and weaknesses and something is still getting in the way of his learning and his development and his joie de vivre, it's not immoral or cowardly to consider medication. As pediatricians, we know that there's no guarantee that medications will work. We have certainly heard the stories in which kids don't do well on particular medications, but we feel they get an awful lot of publicity, considering how many children are helped by medication and grateful for the help. Still, we have included comments by parents whose children have had mixed or negative reactions to specific medications. These are strong medications, and no one should ever treat them lightly.

  Other parents are deeply disturbed by the idea that with medications, the child's personality is somehow coming from the medicine bottle. Our experience, however, is that when children who have been severely affected by one of these symptoms have a successful medication trial, what parents report is not in any way a personality change. Rather, parents describe finally being able to see—and enjoy—the child's true personality, the personality that they have always known was there but that has been obscured or pushed aside, at least for a while, by the obsessions or the depression or the anxiety or the hyperactivity.

Despite our reservations, we started Sam on meds when his behavior was making him and everyone around him miserable. Within a few weeks, he was much calmer and enjoying himself again. We all breathed a sigh of relief. We tried to wean him off his medicine after about a year, but he just wasn't ready, and neither were we.

- *How do the medicines work?* Psychotropic medications act in a wide variety of ways, which we are only beginning to understand. Many messages in the brain are sent via chemicals, called neurotransmitters, which carry impulses from one neuron (nerve cell) to the next. These chemicals are usually released by the first neuron, cross the space where the two adjoin (called a synapse), and bind to specific binding sites on the next neuron, carrying a message. Many psychotropic medications act by increasing or decreasing the amount of a certain neurotransmitter—by competing for those binding sites, for example, or by reducing the ability of the first neuron to vacuum up the transmitter again, thus increasing the amount of time it spends passing the message. There are a few neurotransmitters that will come up again and again in this discussion: serotonin, dopamine, gamma-aminobutyric acid (GABA), and norepinephrine.

- *Can we anticipate what medications the doctor is likely to recommend?* A useful way to think about the psychotropic medications is to consider which medications might be used for a given symptom or for a comorbid condition affecting a child. (*Comorbidity* is the medical term used to describe conditions that may affect many quirky kids but are not the primary diagnosis. Thus, attention deficit disorder or anxiety may be a comorbid condition in a child with pervasive developmental disorder.) In this way, you can approach the recommendation with some prior knowledge and assess the likelihood that a particular medication may help. A thoughtful professional will be knowledgeable about the pros and cons of a variety of medications and will be able to answer questions regarding your individual situation. There are also a number of books and Web sites with information about these questions, and some select references are listed at the end of this chapter.

- *What does it mean for a medication to be "approved"?* When we say that a certain medication is approved for use in someone with a particular diagnosis or that it is approved for use in children above a certain age, we mean that the Food and Drug Administration has examined evidence from a considerable body of research and given an official stamp of approval. The FDA looks at risks and side effects and also at whether there is real evidence that the drug treats the particular symptom or disease. The approval process is long and intense, so official FDA approval is a sign that these medications have a good safety profile for use in kids. On the other hand, if a drug is not approved for use in children, that probably means it simply has not been fully studied in this age group—not that it has been tested and found to be dangerous. In fact, physicians frequently prescribe medications for symptoms other than the approved indications. We are also allowed to prescribe outside the approved age ranges. There are many situations in which that becomes necessary when you take care of children, just because many important drugs are tested first in adults. This is called "off-label" prescribing. You will note, as we go along, that many of the psychotropic medications we discuss have not yet been approved for use with children, though they are frequently prescribed. The FDA also monitors safety and side effects and may change guidelines; in June 2003 the FDA recommended that doctors stop prescribing Paxil, one of the commonly used antidepressants, to children under eighteen, because of concerns about a link between Paxil and suicidal behavior.

How to Use This Chapter

No list of psychiatric medications for quirky kids is completely up-to-date or all-inclusive. New medications, new formulations of older ones, and off-label prescribing basically make that nearly impossible. The recommendation against Paxil came out as we were editing this book; by the time you are reading this, there may be new recommendations about other medicines.

This chapter is organized by symptoms. Look up the symptoms that concern you, and you will see what your medication options are. Similarly, if a particular drug has been mentioned, you can look up that drug—which may be used to treat several different symptoms. There's a great deal of information here, and some of it may seem scary. Almost every psychiatric drug has at least rare serious side effects. A list of medications is not where any parent starts with a quirky child—but if this is where you've arrived, then knowledge is power.

Target Symptoms and Comorbidities: What Can We Treat with Medications?

ANXIETY
The single symptom most likely in any child with one of the quirky-kid diagnoses is anxiety, which can take many forms. In younger children, it is some-

times interpreted as an attentional problem. Many quirky children are described as worriers, but one may also see more specific syndromes like social phobia or obsessive or perseverative disorders. Some kids will manifest true panic re-actions. Younger children with anxiety are generally able to get along in the safety of their families without medications. Parents often unwittingly accom-modate their child's fears by gradually changing their routines in order to avoid situations that might bring on anxiety or make it worse. Eventually, they realize how restricted their lives have become:

We learned to avoid any animals, especially unpredictable puppies, windy days, loud noises or crowds, water, or sand. We couldn't attend any movies or concerts, go outside if it was breezy, or go to the beach. No dinners in restaurants, especially kid-friendly ones! We disconnected the doorbell and stopped grinding our coffee. We felt like we were in prison!

Antianxiety medications have been used a long time in adults and children with primary anxiety disorders and also when anxiety is a feature of another overall problem, like depression or attention deficit disorder. When they work, people describe being able to go about the business of living again, going through their days without intrusive worries interfering with their pleasure, their sleep, their ability to concentrate. In treating anxiety, you need to work with your prescribing physician to consider what other aspects of your child's behavior or experience you may want to address.

Antianxiety drugs, sometimes called anxiolytics, fall into several classes. Most commonly used are the antihistamines, antidepressants, and benzodi-azepines. There is a relatively new "atypical anxiolytic" that we will discuss as well. Each class of drugs has a spectrum of strengths and side effects, and the prescribing practitioner will be able to discuss these with you.

ANTIHISTAMINES
Atarax (hydroxyzine)
Benadryl (diphenhydramine)

> Use: Most familiar as allergy medicines, not officially approved for use as anxiety medications but of limited utility for mild intermittent anxi-ety. Also used for sleeplessness due to short-term anxiety.

Side effects: Rare but well-described "hyper" reaction. This is a short-lived and not dangerous effect. Not recommended for long-term use because of sedating effects.

If your child has intermittent short-term episodes of anxiety that are predictable—say, he can't sleep for the first week of school or camp—an antihistamine may just do the trick. Bear in mind, however, that even though Benadryl is a common over-the-counter allergy medication, you should consult a physician before you use it for anxiety. If your child is one of the few unfortunates to have a paradoxical reaction and becomes "wild" after a dose of Benadryl, no long-term harm has been done. It simply means that the antihistamines are off the list of potentially helpful medicines—even for allergies.

SEROTONIN REUPTAKE INHIBITORS (SRIs)

These newer antidepressants are frequently recommended for children with anxiety as an accompanying feature of depression or obsessive disorders and are often prescribed for quirky kids. They work by making more of the neurotransmitter serotonin available to the central nervous system. These drugs are useful in treating anxiety in adults, and their use in childhood anxiety has increased dramatically in recent years. Because they are short-acting, several doses may be needed over the course of the day.

Celexa (citalopram)

Luvox (fluvoxamine): Has sedative properties; sometimes recommended for the child with marked nighttime anxiety, as well as obsessive or repetitive behavioral symptoms, and for depression.

Paxil (paroxetine): As we said earlier, the FDA has recommended that Paxil not be prescribed to children under eighteen.

Prozac (fluoxetine): While Prozac was the first SRI and remains the best known, its long half-life (length of time it remains in the bloodstream) and length of time it takes to work make it a less likely first choice for kids.

Zoloft (sertraline)

Prescribed use: Depression and obsessive-compulsive disorder. Some SRIs are approved for anxiety disorder, social phobia, and post–traumatic stress disorder.

Off-label use: Anxiety, repetitive behavior.

Side effects: Generally safer than the older generation of antidepressants. Most of the side effects are transient and include gastrointestinal upset, headaches, sleep disturbance, and agitation, though again, there have been concerns about suicidal behavior. If a child is deriving significant benefit in treatment of the target symptom, it's usually worth waiting a while to see if the side effects diminish.

Other warnings: When a child stops taking one of these drugs, it should be tapered gradually under physician supervision. Some of the SRIs interact with other medications. The prescribing physician should be aware of all medicines the child is taking.

A prescribing physician needs to take a thorough history about the child, the symptoms, and the family history. For example, does she have great difficulty falling asleep at night? Are her mood swings dramatic? If there is a component of depression, how would you describe its onset—gradual or sudden? The answers to these questions and others may help guide the choice. An agitated child or one with a family history of bipolar disease or one who becomes depressed suddenly is at an increased risk of becoming manic (more agitated, poor sleep, erratic behavior, irritable or silly, disorganized) while taking an SRI. If such a child is going to try one of these medications, it's safer to start with a shorter-acting drug, which will be quickly excreted when discontinued and should leave no long-term effects.

Drug interactions can be a concern with the SRIs. Prozac, for example, can increase blood levels of drugs used to treat seizure disorders. The prescribing physician needs to know about other medications taken.

We have worked with families for whom the SRIs were not especially helpful or who needed to discontinue the drugs due to side effects. Other families found the drugs immensely beneficial. Effective medical treatment for the sometimes-disabling anxiety that afflicts quirky kids can make a great difference in their lives. Once again, many children improve over time and are able to stop taking medications. Others can learn to reduce their anxiety with

296 ° Quirky Kids

techniques like relaxation and biofeedback, though they may be able to learn how only when their anxiety is temporarily alleviated by means of a medical intervention.

I was able to see Sam's "stuff" in a new light. Even though many well-meaning friends and doctors had told me to see it as a medical or biological problem, I couldn't understand that until I saw how much better he was on Zoloft. Then I felt I could begin to accept this as biologically based, just the way he was born rather than something my wife and I had done to him.

OTHER CLASSES OF ANTIDEPRESSANTS

Tricyclic antidepressants, atypical antidepressants, and *monoamine oxidase inhibitors* have been used to treat anxiety in childhood for many years. They are no longer considered first-line treatments for children because the side effects of almost all the medicines in these classes can be so concerning. We discuss them in greater detail when addressing depression.

BENZODIAZEPINES

The oldest and best-known class of antianxiety drugs, dating back to Valium.

More Potent Benzodiazepines
Sometimes recommended for kids who have panic attacks.
Ativan (lorazepam)
Klonopin (clonazepam)
Xanax (alprazolam)

Less Potent Benzodiazepines
Librium (chlordiazepoxide)
Serax (oxazepam)
Tranxene (clorazepate)

> **Use:** While often a first choice for straightforward or "uncomplicated" anxiety in children, benzodiazepines are used *less* frequently in quirky kids, who are by definition "complicated."
> **Side effects:** Short-term side effects (which generally resolve quickly) include behavior changes, sleepiness, mental "dullness," and rarely, in-

creased anxiety. Longer-term use is associated with *tolerance* (increased doses are required over time) and *dependence* (a slow taper is required to discontinue the drug in order to prevent physical symptoms of withdrawal).

ATYPICAL ANXIOLYTIC DRUG
BuSpar (buspirone)

Use: Has been used to treat aggression in children with pervasive developmental disorder and children with anxiety associated with attention deficit hyperactivity disorder. Sometimes used in conjunction with an SRI to enhance the antidepressant effect of the SRI.
Side effects: Few but serious, including confusion, sedation, and disinhibition.

DEPRESSION
Quirky kids suffer from depression at higher rates than children in the general population. As a well-known developmental pediatrician said to one of us, "Parents can only be as happy as their saddest child." Depression in a child can bring a whole family down, and most families look eagerly for help and advice. There has been much discussion about whether depression in these kids is primary or secondary—that is, are they innately more prone to it, or is it a reaction to the many other difficulties they face? What child wouldn't become depressed if he is constantly subjected to teasing at school, if he feels that he has no friends, and if he is constantly reminded that he is different?

When George became depressed, I longed for the days when he was oblivious to his differences. When he became more tuned in to what was going on around him, it hit him really hard. I am hoping that a short trial of medication will be enough to help him through, but I have no way of knowing if that will turn out to be true.

Antidepressants have proved so effective in treating depression that there has been a lot of discussion about whether it works better than old-fashioned talk therapy for this condition. For the children we are addressing, a supportive relationship with a professional in the mental health field can go a long way toward helping the child understand the condition, learn to cope with it, and develop strategies for the future. Combining therapy with medication, if indicated, is probably the most effective strategy.

The medications that are indicated for the treatment of depression fall into four classes: serotonin reuptake inhibitors, atypical antidepressants, tricyclic antidepressants, and monoamine oxidase inhibitors.

SEROTONIN REUPTAKE INHIBITORS (SRIs)

The SRIs, discussed above in terms of their antianxiety properties, are likely to be recommended as first-line therapy for depressive symptoms in a child. They are preferred over the older classes of antidepressants because blood levels do not need to be monitored, and there is no need for electrocardiograms (ECGs) because they have no cardiac side effects. They are not as dangerous when taken in overdose as some of the older antidepressants, and the side effects are fewer. Because SRIs are indicated for treatment of anxiety and obsessive symptoms as well, they are a reasonable first choice for the quirky child who suffers from this combination of symptoms. Paxil is no longer recommended for children under eighteen.

ATYPICAL ANTIDEPRESSANTS

These medications are *atypical* in their mechanism of action. That is, they affect other neurotransmitter systems in addition to the serotonin system.

> **Desyrel** (trazadone), **Serzone** (nefazodone): These two medicines are more effective in the treatment of depression with anxiety, sleep disturbance, and oppositional behavior. Desyrel is used primarily for its sedative rather than its antidepressant effect.
>
> **Effexor** or **Effexor XR** (for extended release) (venlafaxine): Approved for use in adults with depression, anxiety, and social anxiety.
>
> **Remeron** (mirtazapine): Most sedating, so is especially helpful for children with major difficulty falling asleep at night.
>
> **Wellbutrin** (bupropion): Also approved for smoking cessation in adults and can be helpful in treating attention deficit hyperactivity disorder as well as depression in children prone to mood swings.

Use: All are approved for use in adult depression; used with increasing frequency in childhood depression and associated symptoms.

Side effects: Irritability, increased or decreased appetite, insomnia (Wellbutrin), excess sedation (Serzone, Desyrel, Remeron), dry mouth, constipation, upset stomach.

Other warnings: Wellbutrin is not used in children with a history of seizures. Like the stimulants, Wellbutrin may cause an increase in tics or sleep disturbance.

TRICYCLIC ANTIDEPRESSANTS

Known as an effective treatment in adults, this class of antidepressants has proved less effective in childhood depression.

Anafranil (clomipramine)
Elavil (amitriptyline)
Norpramin (desipramine)
Pamelor (nortriptyline)
Tofranil (imipramine)
Vivactil (protriptyline)

Use: Occasionally used for the treatment of tic disorders, anxiety disorders such as obsessive-compulsive disorder, depression, and attention deficit disorder.

Side effects: Numerous, including constipation; dry mouth; headaches; abdominal discomfort; red, itchy rash. All are reversible with tapering and discontinuing the medication.

Other warnings: These drugs have the potential to cause changes in the electrical activity of the heart. Therefore, an electrocardiogram (ECG) is recommended prior to starting any of them and periodically during the course of treatment. Safe storage is critical because tricyclics can be fatal in overdose.

MONOAMINE OXIDASE INHIBITORS

Mentioned here largely for completeness; MAO inhibitors have been used for decades in adults.

Nardil (phenelzine)
Parnate (tranylcypromine)

> **Use:** Approved for use in adult depression; rarely used in children.
>
> **Side effects:** High blood pressure can result from their use if a tyramine-containing food is ingested. Most forms of cheese contain at least some tyramine. Since it is nearly impossible to expect strict dietary compliance from children or teenagers (for whom pizza is a requirement), this class of drugs is very rarely prescribed for children.
>
> **Other warnings:** Many over-the-counter cold preparations can interact with these medicines to induce dangerously high blood pressure.

No drugs that treat depression come without side effects. Many offer slightly different profiles in terms of the symptoms they treat best. As always, it is absolutely essential to be working with a doctor whom you trust and who is available to answer questions when they arise.

OBSESSIVE AND PERSEVERATIVE QUALITIES

Many of the children we are discussing have a tendency to perseverate—to think about something over and over to the exclusion of other things—or to become obsessive in their interest in a topic. Others may have a compulsive behavior such as chewing on their clothes or picking at themselves. When quirky kids have a "special interest," the interests themselves may have a peculiar quality. There are stories about kids who become incredibly knowledgeable about deep-fat fryers or about the Civil War and can talk about nothing else. Although this may be charming or endearing in kids, it becomes less so as they grow up and is positively annoying in adults. Still, parents have told us that when their child is engaged in his particular interest, he is at his happiest. It is only when the interest has so absorbed the child that he cannot engage in the world around him or his experience with others is completely dependent on the obsession that a child's intense special interest needs attention. And if behavioral approaches have failed to help, it may be necessary to consider medication or to try the two approaches together.

He couldn't talk to anyone about anything except the weather. All conversations revolved around the temperature, the reading on the hygrometer, the fore-

cast, the wind speed, the barometric pressure, the likelihood of a hurricane or tornado, precipitation. At first, it was kind of cute—here was this small boy engaging everyone about the weather. Over time, we realized that he really couldn't talk about anything else and needed the conversation to be about his topic. When we stopped indulging him every single time he wanted to talk about weather, he became very anxious.

It is worth reiterating that although children on this spectrum often have obsessive or perseverative qualities as a manifestation of their anxiety, they usually do not have classic obsessive-compulsive disorder (OCD), in which the obsessions cannot be avoided at any cost and create even more anxiety for the affected individual.

SEROTONIN REUPTAKE INHIBITORS (SRIs)
The most commonly recommended class of medicines for children with these features.

Luvox (fluvoxamine)
Zoloft (sertraline): Approved for children ages six and up and has been the most often prescribed in recent years for this use.

Use: Used to treat obsessive and perseverative behaviors and thoughts.
Side effects: Discussed above in the subsection on anxiety.
Other warnings: While not exactly a warning, it is important to remember that the benefits of therapy with this class of drugs aren't always immediate. It generally requires a few weeks at the specified dose for the therapeutic effect to take hold.

Chrissie's trichotillomania [twirling her hair until it came out of her scalp] was really hard to deal with, and that's when we turned to medications. We tried a variety of medicines to help with this and with her anxiety. First Zoloft, which caused vomiting, then Risperdal, which kept her awake all the time and made her weepy. Adderall was of no benefit. Now she's on BuSpar for her anxiety and Luvox for her OCD symptoms. She still wears a scarf on her head to keep her fingers away, but it was the Luvox that helped the most. We had tried so many strategies before that, and none of them really helped.

ATTENTION DEFICIT DISORDER

The features of attention deficit disorder (ADD) and attention deficit hyperactivity disorder (ADHD) often overlap with those of quirky kids. For this reason, many are first diagnosed with attentional problems or carry that diagnosis along with another. For years, pediatricians believed that a combination of behavioral and medical approaches had the greatest benefit. More recently, there is evidence to suggest that medication alone may have the best record, as most pharmacological treatments of ADD have about a 70 percent response rate. Although behavioral therapies will help certain children develop strategies to cope with this disorder over time, they are not as effective if used alone.

Untreated, kids with ADHD almost invariably develop self-esteem issues and have greater rates of school failure and substance abuse, particularly marijuana use. About half of children diagnosed with attentional problems continue to have symptoms of ADD in adulthood, so treatment is extremely important and involves a real commitment to finding the right therapy for any given stage of life.

STIMULANTS

Stimulants have a long history of use for inattention, impulsive behavior, and distractibility. In general, they are more helpful when the inattention is accompanied by hyperactivity or "fidgetyness." They work through effects on the neurotransmitters dopamine and norepinephrine. The reaction is paradoxical: in a revved-up child, a stimulant calms the nervous system down by increasing focus and attention.

Shorter-Acting Stimulants
Dexedrine (dextroamphetamine)
Ritalin (methylphenidate)

Longer-Acting Stimulants
Adderall (dextroamphetamine and amphetamine)
Dexedrine Spansule (dextroamphetamine)

Extended-Release Stimulants
Adderall XR: Longer-acting form of Adderall; requires only a single morning dose.
Concerta: Longer-acting form of methylphenidate.

Newer Formulations

Focalin (dexmethylphenidate), **Metadate** (methylphenidate): The newer stimulants contain only the active part of the drug, thus requiring lower doses and having fewer side effects.

> **Use:** All are approved for use in children with a diagnosis of ADD.
>
> **Side effects:** Appetite suppression and sleep disturbance are common; other side effects include headaches, dizziness, stomachaches, sadness or sedation, irritability, and tics.
>
> **Other warnings:** It is important to monitor the child's reaction to the drug over the course of the day. Changes in dose, timing, or medication itself are frequent, based on a child's reaction. Some become irritable when the dose wears off; some rebound or become even more moody or disorganized. Occasionally, an additional medication is added to help with these effects, if the child seems to be deriving real benefit from the stimulant.

Certainly, there has been controversy around the use—or overuse—of Ritalin and the other stimulants. We have seen occasional kids whose parents felt they became zombies on stimulants. In this situation, a quick discontinuation is in order. Fortunately, with the exception of the potential for slightly slower growth due to appetite suppression when used long-term, the side effects of the stimulants are generally short-lived and reversible.

There are a couple of caveats regarding stimulant use that are worth mentioning. Stimulant use in a child with a tendency toward tics can be the catalyst that gets the tics started. About 15 percent of children with a diagnosis of ADD will also have tics. Quirky kids are believed to have higher rates of tics and tic disorders like Tourette's syndrome. The actual percentage is not known. Still, it is worth bearing this in mind when deciding about stimulant use and when monitoring the effects of such use. Second, there is a potential for abuse. Although the doses at which they are used to treat ADD symptoms are not abuse doses, we have both experienced adolescents selling their stimulants or offering them to friends. One advantage of Concerta is that it is difficult to abuse. If crushed, the tablet turns to a gel.

NEW NONSTIMULANT MEDICATION

Norepinephrine Reuptake Inhibitor

Strattera (atomoxetine): This is the new kid on the block in the treatment of attention deficit disorder and is the first medication to be approved for use in affected adults. There are many advantages to the fact that it is not a stimulant: it has no addiction potential and thus is not a controlled substance. Further, it does not induce tics or euphoria.

> **Use:** At this point, atomoxetine is used as a second-line treatment for attention deficit disorder, largely in children who cannot tolerate stimulants. Since it is not a controlled substance, refills are more convenient for prescribers and families. Like the stimulants, it has about a 75 percent response rate. Children with developmental disabilities tend to respond at somewhat lower rates.
>
> **Side effects:** Include headache, sleepiness, appetite suppression (which is generally transient), and stomach upset. It is recommended that atomoxetine be taken with a meal that is high in protein. For children who become sleepy, an evening dose provides the benefits while minimizing fatigue during the day.
>
> **Other warnings:** Use along with an SRI (serotonin reuptake inhibitor) must be carefully monitored. Atomoxetine is not recommended for individuals who have taken a monoamine oxidase inhibitor in the previous two weeks.

ANTIDEPRESSANT AND ANTIANXIETY MEDICATIONS

For those children for whom the stimulants are not helpful or for those with a more complex picture—including many quirky kids—other classes of medications may be indicated for inattentiveness.

Tricyclic Antidepressants
Norpramin (desipramine)
Pamelor (nortriptyline)
Tofranil (imipramine)

Atypical Antidepressants
Effexor (venlafaxine)

Serzone (nefazadone)
Wellbutrin (bupropion)

> **Use:** These classes of medications are often recommended for children with anxiety or depression combined with ADD.
>
> **Side effects and other warnings:** Discussed in the subsection on depression.

Occasionally, a medication targeting the anxiety may be added to one that seems to be working well for attentional issues. The antianxiety medicines have been discussed in detail in the subsection on anxiety above. For children with depression *and* attentional issues, the same classes of antidepressant medications are recommended or may be added, at a low dose, to a stimulant.

ANTIHYPERTENSIVES

Originally used to treat high blood pressure in adults, the antihypertensives are used in children to treat ADHD, tic disorders, and sleep disturbances. Sometimes used in the preschool age group for hyperactivity because they are quite safe and are much less likely to cause sleep problems or a decrease in appetite. Used as a first line of therapy for kids with preexisting tics, who cannot take a stimulant.

Catapres (clonidine)
Tenex (guanfacine)

> **Use:** Used in children for whom aggression or hyperactivity is the target symptom, clonidine is also indicated for treatment of tic disorders. Because it is quite short-acting, multiple doses throughout the day are sometimes required. A skin patch that slowly releases the medication throughout the day is also available. Guanfacine is more likely to improve inattention than clonidine but has similar effects on tics.
>
> **Side effects:** Clonidine is most likely to cause sedation as a side effect and for this reason is given in tiny doses. Over time, this effect lessens. Some children become irritable or depressed, and at the highest doses, there can be confusion. These side effects are less likely with guanfacine.
>
> **Other warnings:** Although these medicines have little or no impact on

the blood pressure of children taking them, abrupt discontinuation is not recommended. A slow taper under supervision is best.

OFF-LABEL DRUG TREATMENTS

Recently, medications originally used for other purposes—such as **Provigil** (modafinil; approved for use in narcolepsy, a sleep disorder) and **Aricept** (donepezil; used in Alzheimer's disease)—have been used with good results for young adults with ADHD who did not respond to the more traditional treatments described here.

TIC DISORDERS

Tic disorders, of which Tourette's syndrome is the best described, occur with increased frequency in quirky kids. A proper diagnosis is especially important in this population because tics can be mistaken for nervousness in these children (and vice versa), and the treatment options will be dictated by the correct diagnosis. Children with Tourette's syndrome have greater rates of obsessive-compulsive symptoms and attention deficit hyperactivity disorder (ADHD), and it is important to take all these factors into consideration when evaluating a child and considering treatment.

ANTIHYPERTENSIVES

Catapres (clonidine): Used for tics, ADHD, and sleep disturbance; sometimes added to a stimulant to help with sleeplessness; also effective in treating aggression. Potent and short-acting, it is taken in tiny doses over the course of the day for tics. Also comes as a skin patch, which releases small amounts of the drug over the course of the day.

Tenex (guanfacine): Prescribed for tics, Tourette's syndrome, ADHD, and aggression.

Use: Originally approved for use in treating high blood pressure, these medications are effective in about two-thirds of children with tics.

Side effects: Fatigue, irritability, sedation, decreased blood pressure, dry mouth.

Other warnings: Both of these medicines should be tapered gradually rather than stopped abruptly, to avoid the potential for a rebound increase in blood pressure.

TRICYCLIC ANTIDEPRESSANTS

The tricyclic antidepressants are used to treat attention deficit hyperactivity disorder (ADHD) and tics more frequently than to treat depression in children. They are prescribed both for primary tic disorders and for tics that arise during use of a stimulant to treat ADHD. This is just the kind of complication feared by many parents, in which you give one medication and then have to give a second to control the symptoms caused or exacerbated by the first. Even so, if the initial problem is debilitating enough, some children have to live with multiple medications.

ANTIPSYCHOTICS

Also called *neuroleptics*, the antipsychotics are major tranquilizers sometimes used to address tics when the other classes of medications have failed. Originally developed for truly psychotic individuals, they are currently used for a number of other indications as a second- or third-line option.

Typical Neuroleptics
Haldol (haloperidol)
Orap (pimozide)
Thorazine (chlorpromazine)

> **Use:** Quite effective for controlling tics but do not address any coexisting conditions like attentional issues or obsessiveness.
> **Side effects:** They are potentially serious, and for this reason, typical neuroleptics are rarely prescribed for children. Side effects are discussed below.

Atypical Neuroleptics
Abilify (aripiprazole)
Geodon (ziprasidone)
Risperdal (risperidone)
Seroquel (quetiapine)
Zyprexa (olanzapine)

> **Use:** These newer antipsychotic medications are used with great frequency in quirky kids with tics because they also address a number of

additional aspects of the quirky-kid personality—compulsive or obsessive behaviors, mood swings, reactivity, self-mutilating or picking at oneself, and explosive or aggressive behavior. In fact, the atypical neuroleptics are used to address these issues in quirky kids *without* tics as well.

Side effects: Similar to those of the more traditional antipsychotics, but the risk appears to be much, much lower. Weight gain is by far the greatest concern for children on these medicines.

Other warnings: Several of these medicines have specific warnings worth noting. Risperdal can produce an increased pulse rate. Seroquel has been associated with cataracts in animals. An electrocardiogram (ECG) is recommended prior to starting Geodon, due to a potential change in heart rhythm.

More on the Side Effects of Antipsychotics

Families who are considering antipsychotic meds for their children are generally suffering a great deal, and finding an effective treatment can be a lifesaver. The difference between this class of drugs and most of the other ones we have discussed is that the side effects here can be *irreversible* with long-term use. Therefore, the length of treatment and overall cumulative dose must be monitored carefully.

The short-term side effects of the older generation of antipsychotics are generally manageable and reversible: increased appetite with subsequent weight gain, and some degree of drowsiness, dry mouth, nasal stuffiness, and blurry vision. The higher-potency drugs—Haldol and Orap among them—are more likely to cause side effects involving the muscles, including spasm, eye-rolling, and restlessness.

The two most important serious side effects of the antipsychotics are *tardive dyskinesia* and *neuroleptic malignant syndrome.* Tardive dyskinesia describes involuntary muscular movements, usually starting in the facial muscles around the mouth or eye, that look like lip-smacking, eye-rolling, or facial grimacing. This side effect is potentially irreversible. Neuroleptic malignant syndrome, an exceedingly rare but serious reaction, involves the sudden onset of fever associated with severe muscle pain and tightness, profuse sweating, and mental confusion.

OFF-LABEL DRUG TREATMENTS

Other classes of medicines are sometimes used off-label to treat tic disorders and Tourette's syndrome. The antiseizure medicine **Tegretol** (carbamazepine), approved for children over the age of six with seizures, is the most likely to be used for tic disorder.

BIPOLAR (MANIC-DEPRESSIVE) DISORDER

Quirky kids are diagnosed with bipolar disorder at higher rates than the general population. However, bipolar disease in children—and in quirky kids in particular—is not always the classic cycling from deep depression to euphoria or mania that is described in adults. Children and adolescents with this disorder describe feeling agitated or restless and depressed *at the same time*. Episodes of extreme irritability or explosiveness may represent the mania component in these kids, when they simply cannot control their inner energy.

Depending on the features of the disorder in a particular child, a number of classes of drugs may be recommended, some of which have been described in detail previously. As with the other comorbidities or target symptoms we have described, bipolar disorder in quirky kids is not classic, and the other aspects of the child's situation must be addressed as well.

MOOD STABILIZER
Lithium

> **Use:** The mainstay of treatment for bipolar disease for decades, lithium will stabilize mood over time and smooth out the wide swings that can occur over the course of the day or even over an hour or two.
> **Side effects:** Short-term problems like upset stomach, tremor, acne, sleepiness, and excessive fluid intake and urination.
> **Other warnings:** Lithium is a salt—like sodium and potassium—and it is metabolized and excreted by the kidneys. Maintaining hydration is important to prevent any damage to the kidneys over the long term. Blood levels are monitored for this reason and because toxic levels are associated with other undesirable effects such as slurred speech, excess fatigue, or visual changes.

ANTICONVULSANTS
Depakote (valproic acid or valproate)
Tegretol (carbamazepine)

> **Use:** The anticonvulsants have been widely used to treat seizures in children and are used off-label for their mood-stabilizing effects, with very good effectiveness.
>
> **Side effects:** Short-term effects include dizziness and blurry vision with Tegretol and appetite suppression with Depakote. Both can cause stomach upset. Longer-term use can be associated with effects on blood cells and inflammation of the liver, which reverses upon discontinuation of the medicine. Pancreatitis has been associated with Depakote use.
>
> **Other warnings:** Blood levels are required to keep a therapeutic level and to avoid a toxic level.

NEWER ANTICONVULSANTS
Gabitril (tiagabine)
Lamictal (lamotrigine): May prevent recurrence of depression in individuals with bipolar disorder.
Neurontin (gabapentin)
Topamax (topiramate)
Trileptal (oxcarbazepine): No data are available for use in childhood.

> **Use:** All the newer anticonvulsants are approved for children with seizure disorders and are being used as mood stabilizers as well.
>
> **Side effects:** Fatigue, difficulty walking, and dizziness have all been described. The use of the newer anticonvulsants is quite recent, and no long-term effects have been reported.

Symptoms That Are "around the Edges"

Many features of quirky kids do not fit neatly into the above categories but may be amenable to medical therapy: their rigid natures, difficulties with transitions, anger, stereotypic motor behaviors that are not exactly tics, and sometimes bizarre social behaviors. Talk with your physician about what these features may represent. Your physician should be able to help tease out the meanings of these qualities and recommend a helpful approach—with or without the use of medications.

How Long Will I Have to Medicate My Child?

Many children take a single medication, successfully targeting a specific symptom—a tic, a high level of anxiety around starting school, a compulsive habit—and find that that medication is all they need to help them along, either for a brief period or over many years. However, it's important to note that for some children, life involves multiple medications, often needing adjustment or correction. This can be hard, but it offers some a chance to learn and live, to function in the world, on a level that would otherwise be impossible for them. Often the children themselves grow to understand this. We offer these stories not as cautionary tales about the evils of medication but as realistic accounts of the heavy burdens some quirky children carry and the risks and benefits of psychopharmacology.

After Ben was diagnosed with attention deficit hyperactivity disorder with obsessional features, and with a question of pervasive developmental disorder, he saw a psychopharmacologist, who started him on Serzone for his anxiety and "emotionality." At first, the Serzone helped; he was calmer, happier. After about a year—he was in first grade at the time—it didn't help anymore, and he switched over to an SRI. Then, in second grade, he was started on Remeron, and he threatened suicide. He was at camp and he couldn't swim, and he told the counselor that he wanted to jump off the end of the dock and let the snapping turtles eat him up. He came off Remeron. He remained very reactive and impulsive. Then a psychiatrist recommended lithium, but I really wasn't comfortable with that, since I don't think he's bipolar, and he ended up on Depakote. So his current regimen is Depakote and an SRI, and yes, he's still wound-up and reactive, but it's better. He has also been on Tenex, which didn't help, and clonidine, which made him too sleepy in class.

It took us two years to find the right combination of medicines to help Megan, but we felt we had to keep trying because she was so miserable and hard to live with. It had a big impact on the entire family. Megan fought the meds. She'd say things like, "You don't like me for who I am. When I'm eighteen, I'm not going to take them anymore. I know my rights." But when she was leaving for college a few years later, she said, "Where's my prescription? I think I need an evening dose of Dexedrine to get my homework done." She has accepted that these meds have really helped her and knows she is more successful with them than without them. Her current regimen is Dexedrine and Zoloft.

Probably the best news we can give you is to remind you of three comforting truths: First, the decision to move forward with a trial of medications, or even to have a child take multiple medications for a period of time, does not mean the child will need pharmaceutical support forever. Second, if you do need to try medications, the serious side effects, while worrisome, are rare. And third, many children are freed by these medications and find themselves able to thrive and experience pleasure from life when their bothersome symptoms are alleviated. When thinking about the medication option, a trusted partner in the medical profession is an important and meaningful part of your decision.

References and Resources

Bashe, Patricia Romanowski, and Barbara L. Kirby. *The Oasis Guide to Asperger Syndrome: Advice, Support, Insight, and Inspiration.* New York: Crown, 2001. This book has an excellent chapter on medication use, with many anecdotes from families regarding their own experiences.

Diller, Dr. Lawrence H. *Should I Medicate My Child?: Sane Solutions for Troubled Kids with—and without—Psychiatric Drugs.* New York: Basic Books, 2003. This useful book, by a behavioral and developmental pediatrician in California, is a well-balanced look at the complex decision process most of us experience when confronted with the issue of medication use in children.

Internet. Increasing numbers of parents are seeking information on the Internet. Although this has been tremendously helpful to many of us at times, the information on the Internet is usually anecdotal—that is, based on the experience of an individual or a family—and not scientifically based. So, again, by all means inform yourself, but don't let other people's stories have too great an impact on your decisions about your child. Seek out professionals in the field to guide you, to answer your questions, and to offer information.

Physician's Desk Reference. Montvale, N.J.: Thomson Medical Economics, 2003. The PDR is the most detailed and comprehensive resource around, and the average physician refers to it almost daily. The problem with the PDR is that it usually has more information than you want or need while the information you seek is buried somewhere. Also, because virtually every side effect ever reported—no matter how rare—finds its way into the PDR, it can be frightening reading for parents. So if you read the PDR for information, do so with a grain of salt and ask your prescribing physician about the things that concern you.

Wilens, Dr. Timothy. *Straight Talk about Psychiatric Medications for Kids.* New York: Guilford Press, 2002. Dr. Wilens is a child psychiatrist on the staff of Massachusetts General Hospital. The MGH child psychiatry department has done a tremendous amount of research on the use of psychiatric medications in children. This book has many more details about dosing and drug interactions than this chapter, and we recommend reading it.

11

○ ○ ● ○

Medical Perspectives
on the Quirky Child

In this chapter, we review quirkiness from the medical perspective and give you the most up-to-date science and opinions we can. We admit two things right off the bat: First, these issues include areas of intense current research. Anything we write may be out-of-date before you read it. Second, when it comes to the important questions of etiologies (causes), effectiveness of therapies, and long-term prognosis, there are not yet a lot of data to support definitive answers. So when we discuss the most controversial theories about etiology—for example, the ideas about vaccines being responsible for brain damage or the environmental toxins theory—we'll tell you what is known and what is thought, and then we'll join you in waiting for more data and a better understanding.

The risk in talking about quirkiness as a syndrome, of course, is that quirky kids are such a heterogeneous group. Some are mildly eccentric, some deeply challenged in many different ways. Their diagnostic labels are varied, and an individual child can move out of one diagnostic category and into another.

The problem with research on kids in this category is that most of the fundamental scientific research is actually based on the autistic end of the spectrum and extrapolated from there. Does our understanding of severely autistic children actually help us understand the mildly quirky? It's not always clear, but it does provide some new and fascinating hard science that will enhance our understanding of normal and abnormal development and perhaps some clues as we try to puzzle out the quirky children for whom we are responsible.

Epidemiology: Are There More Quirky Kids Than Before, and If So, Why?

Whereas forty and fifty years ago, it was a bit of an embarrassment to have a special-needs child in the family, it is openly discussed now, and there are many instances of such special children; I believe more so today than previously. Sometimes we hear of geographic clusters the way we hear of clusters of cancer cases, but I personally have not seen this, except that my son tells us there are five in our grandson Max's class, including Max, from his own area. Among my family, friends, and in the school where I taught, I had no previous acquaintance with autism in any form.

Our combined experience as pediatricians in practice and all we've seen as mothers of school-age kids have certainly suggested to us that the numbers of children that fall into these categories are increasing. Discussions with teachers and educators in all kinds of settings reflect this same awareness. The number of children receiving special education services outside those dedicated classrooms has risen sharply—and some of these kids are definitely quirky. Schools specifically designed to meet the needs of quirky kids, with their learning profiles or differences, are popping up in communities all over the United States as well as in other parts of the world. As we've been working on this book, we've found that mentioning the topic in any social situation whatsoever always yields someone in the group who knows a child who fits within this spectrum.

We were on vacation at the beach, and I saw another child who reminded me of my son Max. He was flapping his hands and avoiding the water. I approached his parents, and sure enough, he was "one of us"! The kids enjoyed each other in their own peculiar way, and I was relieved to feel that I wasn't alone.

This is all well and good, but it's hardly science. What do we know about the incidence and epidemiology of quirky kids? The Centers for Disease Control and Prevention have funded four states to do surveillance studies in order to assess the current prevalence of the autistic spectrum disorders. The best estimate at this time is that 1 child in 200 to 250 children is so affected. In our home state of Massachusetts, the Department of Public Health is tracking "service demand" among children in the first three years of life whose parents are seeking intensive home-based services in addition to early intervention services. The number of children for whom these services are provided doubled between the state fiscal years 1999 and 2002, which suggests that children with a variety of developmental needs were turning up at a rate of about 1 child in 200, based on the number of births in the state during that time period. These children would include quirky kids as well as a wide range of others.

The Department of Education in the state of Massachusetts offered grants to school districts in the state to improve the quality of their services to children with developmental delays who were thought likely to end up with autistic spectrum diagnoses. There were ninety applicants for twenty-five grants—another indication that educators are feeling the challenge of trying to meet the needs of these kids.

The media have devoted a lot of attention to the question of whether there is an epidemic of autistic disorders in the United States and around the world. There are certainly increasing numbers of kids who carry the *diagnoses* of these disorders. Does that mean there are actually more kids being born and growing up with the problems, or does it suggest that we've got better at assigning the diagnoses? No one really knows for sure how much the numbers are truly up and how much is an artifact of how and whom we diagnose. Asperger's syndrome, for example, was introduced into the *Diagnostic and Statistical Manual* of the American Psychiatric Association in 1994. Before 1994, the diagnosis didn't officially exist, and children with these traits were called by other names or went without diagnoses—peculiar in their ways but not fitting into any recognized category. One definite effect of this new nomenclature is that kids around the edges are now more likely to have a diagnosis than they were in the past. Think about what happens when a new diagnostic term is coined. The term *sensory integration dysfunction* is relatively new, and yet many people recognize themselves—or their kids—in its criteria. Before there was such a term as *sensory integration dysfunction*, many of those people had no name for their preferences, their peculiarities, or their unusual behaviors.

At the same time as the numbers of kids with autistic spectrum disorders have been climbing, the numbers of children diagnosed with mental retardation have been decreasing. Could this represent a shift in the terminology used to diagnose kids with developmental delays, with language and learning problems? Some of the change may reflect a better understanding of what's really going on with these children, and some may have to do with how the label is perceived. It may be easier on both parents and professionals if the diagnosis is pervasive developmental disorder rather than mental retardation. Even if a child's IQ might place him squarely in the mental retardation range, another diagnosis might also fit the facts or account for the delays, and those other words may be easier for parents to accept.

There's controversy among researchers about what is behind the rise in diagnoses. Most people would certainly agree that some of the increases we see are directly related to these terminology shifts, but that doesn't mean that there are not also more quirky kids being born. From an epidemiological point of view, there is a lot of work to be done investigating these questions. Given that the diagnostic criteria are somewhat soft—that is to say, no one diagnostic test will make the diagnosis—studies concerning prevalence are fraught with difficulties.

Another difficult epidemiological question is geographic variation. Are there really some quirky-kid hot spots where the problems are much more common? In California, high rates are quoted in particular areas. A study published in November 2001 in the journal *Pediatrics* quotes an even higher rate for the autistic spectrum disorders, 6.7 children per 1,000 (or 3.3 per 500) children in the community of Brick Township, New Jersey. Some of these effects may be magnified when an area with a high preponderance of quirky children develops good educational services to meet their needs and word gets out, so that other families, knowing their diagnoses, start moving in.

As with other medical issues—towns that seem to be hot spots for particular cancers or other medical syndromes—these findings provoke all kinds of theories and suspicions. It's in the water, it's the toxic waste buried too close to town, it's all those supernerds in Silicon Valley having kids with one another. Not to say that any of these theories are necessarily wrong or nonsensical, but it remains very difficult to determine cause and effect.

However, we do think that children who would once have carried no diagnosis at all, or would have carried another diagnosis altogether, are now being diagnosed as having developmental disorders. But we also think that the phenomenon we're describing—the combination of developmental variations and interpersonal eccentricities we're calling quirkiness—is becoming more common. We think it's more than just increasing skill at recognizing certain diagnoses. We think there are more children around with these traits than there used to be.

Etiology: What Do We Actually Understand about the Causes of Quirkiness?

All parents of quirky kids find themselves asking, "Where did this come from?" Unfortunately, most of the time, there simply isn't any easy answer. Yes, in the setting of our office, we will ask questions about family history, and sometimes there is a relative with a similar picture, which does at least suggest a genetic component to what is going on, though it doesn't offer any definite explanations. Often there isn't even that much of a clue, and we are as mystified as the parents about why *their* child is so affected.

We often wonder where this came from in our kids. Yes, we have some funny relatives on both sides, but is that really it? We don't think about it as much as we used to, but whenever there is a new crisis, we wonder, "What did we do to deserve this?"

My pregnancy with Chrissie was very stressful because of my career. I was working very hard, and the company was in financial trouble. I wonder about increased stress hormones in my pregnancy being a factor in Chrissie's diagnosis.

I read on a Web site of the Autism Research Institute about their belief that there is a link between mercury and autism, particularly thimerosal, a form of mercury used in some vaccines. Jacob had a hair analysis done that revealed an increased level of mercury. I have stopped giving him any vaccines.

Whole books have been written in support of individual theories, often by people who have devoted their lives to crusading against something they see as dangerous to children. Keep in mind, as you think about etiology and causation, that quirkiness is a heterogeneous phenomenon. There is no reason to expect one definitive answer, one single all-embracing, all-explaining root cause. There's a lot of work to be done teasing out the possible contributors and understanding the kids we see around us.

Here are some of the hypotheses that have been put forward:

- It's purely genetic. These differences in development and behavior reflect differences in brain structure and hardwiring. Maybe we're seeing more quirky kids because people who were once less likely to have children are now reproducing—all those computer nerds, perhaps, or maybe the increasing numbers of older parents.
- It's something that happens during fetal development—maybe because of some infection or exposure that affects the mother.
- There is a toxin in the environment that is affecting babies' brains. It is well established that certain toxins, specifically mercury and lead, can cause damage to the developing brain. Perhaps increased levels in our environment explain the increased numbers of neurodevelopmental disorders.
- Overuse of antibiotics in young children has caused many of them to be colonized with yeast, and the excessive growth of yeast can cause damage to the brain.
- An allergy or intolerance to certain foods is responsible in some children, and if you change a child's diet, you could change the behavior and development of that child.
- Developmental differences can be traced to vitamin deficiencies and treated with megadoses of a variety of vitamins.
- One or another of the increased number of childhood immunizations is responsible.
- Assisted reproductive technologies may be playing a role—either because the new high-tech processes somehow affect the brain of the embryo or because they enable people who would once not have successfully reproduced to have genetic offspring.
- We know there have always been quirky kids among us, but now we notice them more because we notice *everything* more. Are we simply less tolerant of these quirky kids than we used to be, now that everyone wants their child to go to an Ivy League college?

From our perspective *at this moment in time*, there seems to be more science to back up the genetic roots of many kinds of quirkiness than there is to support any of the other causes. To say "genetics" is not to suggest that we know exactly which gene or genes are responsible for any given pattern or how patterns of inheritance really work. However, there is clearly a high degree of genetic susceptibility to at least some of these disorders, based on data from family studies and twin studies.

Among identical twins, there is a 60 percent concordance rate for full classic autism—that is, a twin is also affected 60 percent of the time. For the milder forms, such as pervasive developmental disorder, there is a 92 percent concordance. Among siblings who are not twins, there is a generally accepted recurrence risk of 4 to 7 percent in subsequent children, and this risk increases with more severe forms.

This, of course, raises the question: if it's genetic, why does it appear to be on the rise? Many experts in the field agree that the degree to which quirky individuals are procreating may account for some of the increase in numbers. One intriguing, and rather entertaining, theory was proposed by Steve Silberman in the December 2001 edition of *Wired* magazine. Mr. Silberman points to the recent surge in the number of Silicon Valley children with ASD diagnoses and wonders whether the math-and-tech genes are to blame.

> As more women enter the IT workplace, guys who might never have had a prayer of finding a kindred spirit suddenly discover that she's hacking Perl scripts in the next cubicle.
>
> One provocative hypothesis that might account for the rise of spectrum disorders in technologically adept communities like Silicon Valley, some geneticists speculate, is an increase in *assortative mating.* . . . There are additional pressures and incentives for autistic people to find companionship—if they wish to do so—with someone who is also on the spectrum.[1]

So although there is definitely a genetic component to at least some of the quirkiness we see, and although certain families are clearly more affected than others, genetics is not going to be the whole story. Genes and environment interact. It's possible, for example, that genetic heritage makes some developing brains more vulnerable than others, so that when there's an insult—an infection, a toxin, a particular problem in either the fetal or the early childhood environment—those vulnerable brains are more likely to be affected, more likely to be damaged.

Many parents—and some experts—do not accept the idea that quirkiness is genetically determined. They feel there must be some other force at work. Something is damaging children, hurting their brains, changing their lives forever. Along with the increased numbers of affected families, there has been a huge increase in attention to questions about etiology that are largely outside the scope of traditional medical science. People look to dietary intolerance or allergies, to vitamin deficiencies, to exposure to environmental toxins, to overgrowth of yeast as a result of antibiotic therapy, and perhaps most prominently to childhood immunizations as possible culprits. There has been a real explosion of literature in the popular press and on the Internet, followed more slowly to some degree by discussion in the scientific and medical literature. These theories have passionate adherents, and many parents have shaped their children's daily lives around them.

I am interested in nonconventional approaches. I have investigated many organizations interested in studying this issue. Jacob was evaluated by an allergist who suggested yeast as a possible culprit and prescribed an antiyeast medicine. Jacob started to talk and had fewer tantrums. He has seen a nutritionist. The Defeat Autism Now (DAN) group recommends a B-vitamin complex. Jacob took it and went crazy at school and bit two kids. Jacob now takes cod liver oil, vitamin B, TMG [trimethylglycine], friendly flora, vitamin C, and folic acid.

As pediatricians, we are not big believers in any of these theories. We think they are, at best, unsupported by real evidence and, at worst, dangerous. We try hard not to send the parents of our patients down paths that will lead them to complex and labor-intensive regimens with no research backing them. We know that a certain number of the parents we see will pursue these paths and will perhaps end by writing us off as hopelessly mainstream. However, we have no intention of telling parents to abandon anything that seems to be working. We freely acknowledge that there is a great deal more research to be done.

Are there dietary triggers that set off the unusual development of the quirky child? For a given child, are there particular foods that affect day-to-day behavior? Many parents are deeply concerned about this question, though there are few pediatric gastroenterologists (physicians who specialize in the care of children with difficulties around eating, digestion, growth, and elimination) with a special interest in this area. Little well-done research is available. Among the experts, however, there is accumulated anecdotal evidence that quirky kids suffer from problems related to the gastrointestinal (GI) tract at a higher rate than more typical kids. Many parents we've interviewed have discussed their children's unusual food preferences, their growth disturbances, their problems with constipation, and their allergic reactions to food.

What's the difference between *allergy* and *intolerance* to a particular food or substance? This terminology can be confusing. A true *allergy* is a diagnosis made on the basis of blood tests that can document a response by the immune system to a given food. An *intolerance* refers to a particular reaction when a food is ingested—such as a rash, vomiting or diarrhea, or a change in behavior—that is *not* associated with an abnormal blood test result. We have seen many examples of food intolerance in practice—the child who vomits every time he eats seafood, for example, but shows no abnormalities on allergy testing. The absence of an immune marker can provide a certain reassurance that the child is unlikely to have a dangerous allergic reaction to that food—but of course, he may still have the vomiting or the rash or the behavior change. Most kids will avoid foods that cause physical discomfort, once they're old enough to make the connection. They are less likely to monitor their own behavior. Parents, however, may notice, if a behavior change happens every time the child eats a certain food.

Dr. Timothy Buie is a pediatric gastroenterologist who takes care of roughly four hundred children with autistic spectrum disorders in the pediatric GI clinic at Massachusetts General Hospital. His impression, based on his personal experience, is that about a third of the kids on the autistic spectrum will have positive tests for food allergies, compared to about 5 percent of typical kids. More than half, when their parents are questioned, have a history of some suggestion of food allergy or intolerance as infants—in that their formula was changed or a breast-feeding mother was herself put on a special diet. In addition, high rates of lactose intolerance, or difficulty digesting cow's milk, have been observed in his group of patients.

Among people who believe that changing a child's diet can improve or even cure quirky-child behavior problems, the foods that have received the most attention are dairy products, along with wheat products containing gluten. There are stories in which parents have altered their child's diet and seen dramatic improvements in behavior and development. Some parents swear by their experience of their children's remarkably improved development after switching to a diet free of casein (a dairy protein) and gluten (a wheat protein). Other parents whose children have similar problems have moved heaven and earth to make these dietary adjustments and seen no effect whatever.

What's our take on this? As physicians, we are always skeptical. Our thought process goes something like this: "With so few data to support this theory, how can we recommend it? How can we know that it was the actual diet and not the extra attention and care the child received from parents intent on providing such a labor-intensive diet? Has it been replicated in other settings? What other variables should we consider?" The casein-free, gluten-free diet has not been studied in any scientific manner, so there is no evidence to support its use. As pediatricians, we are concerned about the overall health of the children, not to mention the well-being of the parent responsible for providing this fairly extreme diet. So we certainly wouldn't go around telling people to adopt this diet. If they want to try it, we would worry about the child's growth and monitor it closely. And the truth is, we recommend all kinds of interventions for quirky kids for which there are no data! Many of our patients, quirky and not, are on different diets because of food allergies or other conditions that make certain foods dangerous. We take care of kids who are on dairy-free diets because of milk-protein allergy or lactose intolerance, and those kids are doing just fine. We also follow a number of kids on gluten-free diets because of celiac disease—a not so terribly rare condition of the bowel associated with gluten intolerance. Children can survive perfectly well on these diets. If you're monitoring the child's nutrition carefully, and if calcium and protein are delivered in other ways, we're not going to tell you that trying these diets is a bad idea. We would never try to discourage someone from feeding her child a nutritionally balanced diet that she thought was helping him out. But without scientific data to support these diets, no parent should feel obligated to follow them or feel less than thorough because she can't make them work.

We have more difficulty with some other theories. There are "experts" and diagnosticians out there offering all kinds of testing—for example, hair analysis for trace metals like mercury or lead, or stool analysis looking for yeast, or blood testing for vitamin levels. Not surprisingly, people who test for these problems usually find them and offer explanations and regimens to parents. Quite frankly, there's no evidence to support this hair analysis—or to suggest that there's any relationship at all between the level of a trace metal in the hair and the child's developmental path. Yeast infections have been offered as alternative explanations for every mysterious condition from chronic fatigue syndrome to chemical sensitivity—without a shred of real medical evidence emerging. Treating with antifungal agents or loading up on high doses of vitamins may have adverse effects for the health of the child in question. We think there are people out there making money off families with quirky children and essentially peddling snake oil.

WHAT'S THE STORY ABOUT CHILDHOOD IMMUNIZATIONS?

There has been a significant amount of publicity and concern around the issue of childhood immunizations, most particularly the MMR (measles-mumps-rubella) vaccine and the hepatitis B vaccine. You can find terrifying first-person accounts on the Internet by parents who feel their children were absolutely well until a certain shot was given and then deteriorated dramatically. There are whole organizations, with publications and conferences and publicity campaigns, dedicated to spreading the word that vaccines cause autism.

We're pediatricians; we give vaccines, and we don't think they cause autism. But the question has been raised by serious people. It deserves intense attention and proper research. Some of that has already happened, which is why we're comfortable saying we don't think that vaccines are causing these problems. If you believe that they do, we probably won't convince you otherwise, but we do mean to give a fair account of these theories and of the evidence that has accumulated around this question.

The MMR is generally administered for the first time between twelve and fifteen months and then again as a booster shot between the ages of four and six years. A link to autism was first proposed by Dr. Andrew Wakefield, a researcher who suggested that the MMR vaccine triggers an inflammatory condition of the intestines, causing the gut to become leaky, or more permeable to toxins, which can then get access to the brain and cause damage. His original paper, published in 1998, ignited a fiery debate that is still very much alive.

One problem is that the age when a child gets a first MMR—twelve to fifteen months—is right around the time that many parents start noticing developmental concerns. This is the age, between one and two years, when children are making huge strides in their development, particularly with emerging speech, and differences become more apparent. Many developmental problems do become evident around the time of the MMR vaccine. Cause and effect is a trickier question.

Over the past four or five years, a number of large epidemiological studies in several countries have looked for a link between the MMR and developmental disorders and have failed to find one. The Institute of Medicine, the Centers for Disease Control and Prevention, and the American Academy of Pediatrics have all issued policy statements regarding the absence of data proving an association between the two.

Most recently, and most impressively, a study in Denmark looked at every child born from 1991 to 1998—more than 537,000 children—questioning whether autism was diagnosed more often in children who received the MMR. The results of this study? That there was no difference between the two groups. When you looked at the whole population, the autism diagnoses were not clustered in the months immediately after the MMR shots were given. And there was no difference in the rates of other related developmental disorders between vaccinated and unvaccinated children.

So, yes, we go on giving the MMR vaccine, and yes, all of our own children are fully immunized. There is no evidence to show this link, however devoutly some people believe that it exists. It's also worth pointing out that measles, which many people in this country have never seen, is wildly contagious and can be a serious disease. A major cause of infant and child death in developing countries, measles itself can have devastating neurological aftereffects, including mental retardation, blindness, and seizures. Mumps, the viral infection most familiar for the swelling of the parotid glands of the face, also causes orchitis (infection of the testicles), which can result in sterility. Rubella is best known for the syndrome in which the offspring of a mother who contracted the illness in pregnancy has congential cataracts, heart defects, and mental retardation.

The other vaccine that has attracted a great deal of concern is the hepatitis B vaccine, which in this country is administered to babies three times in the first year of life, with the first dose often given at birth. The issue raised about the hepatitis B vaccine is that these vaccines used to contain thimerosal, a preservative that includes mercury. Mercury is a potent toxin, particularly dangerous to the nervous system. In cases of mercury poisoning in the medical literature, doses were hundreds or thousands of times higher than any baby ever got in vaccines. Nevertheless, some doctors became concerned about the possibility that even minute doses of mercury might harm some infants.

Thimerosal had been used in vaccines as a preservative since the 1930s, but in the 1980s and 1990s, as the number of vaccines recommended in childhood increased, so did the potential dose to which a child was exposed. In 1999, the American Academy of Pediatrics and the United States Public Health Service asked vaccine manufacturers to remove thimerosal from vaccines and delayed the newborn dose of hepatitis B vaccine until mercury-free vaccine was available. Hepatitis B vaccine, along with all the other vaccines we give, now contains no mercury. A great deal of research is now under way to look at whether thimerosal may have caused neurological damage in some children.

Even if the research ends up by showing that some children may have been harmed, the hepatitis B vaccine is not going to explain the autism epidemic. Thimerosal has been gone from vaccines for four years, and yet the numbers of young children diagnosed with developmental delays and autistic spectrum disorders continue to increase.

For those who hate vaccines, this will not be convincing. They will find another vaccine to blame, because they start from the assumption that vaccines are dangerous. As we said at the outset, we start from the other side. During our training, we watched children suffer from *Haemophilus influenzae* type B (Hib) infections, from sepsis and meningitis and life-threatening infections of the epiglottis. We saw them die or live with complete devastation of their brains and bodies. We know why we give babies those Hib vaccines, and we never want to see a case of Hib meningitis again. We don't want to see our patients suffer the high fever and irritability and encephalitis that can come with measles or to take care of any babies born with the mental retardation of congenital rubella or to see a child paralyzed by polio or to watch an adolescent's liver destroyed by chronic hepatitis B. We worry about what the thimerosal studies will show, and we worry that other vaccine problems may emerge, but we go on giving vaccines and feeling grateful for them, as we watch our patients grow up free of all these terrible diseases.

Yes, we have nightmares about the possibility of doing damage. But we have faith in the systems and safeguards—faith that has been strengthened by the removal of thimerosal and again recently by the recall of a new vaccine against rotavirus, a widespread cause of diarrhea. That vaccine was taken off the market—and off the vaccine schedule—very soon after being released because of some very preliminary reports that it might cause intestinal problems. Some vaccines have probably harmed some children, but they've saved millions from death and debilitation. There is no evidence at all that these enormous populations of autistic, autistic spectrum, and just plain quirky children can be explained by immunizations.

We admit that there's no one overarching theory of etiology—just as there is probably no one satisfying explanation of why this happened to your individual child in the way that it did. There are theories and speculations and interesting ideas. There are tantalizing pieces of genetic information. There is certainly reassuring evidence about the MMR vaccine. But there are not yet the answers that parents want.

Pathophysiology: What Can Basic Science Tell Us about the Neurobiological Underpinnings of Quirkiness?

BRAIN DIFFERENCES

There is clear evidence from basic research that the brain development of quirky kids is different in a number of ways. Keep in mind that most of the research is based on the *more affected* individuals within the group and that most of these individuals studied have been adults. The ideas about children's brains, and the differences we would be likely to see, have been extrapolated from these data. This is by no means perfect, but it's the best we can offer at this time.

Much of this work, though it's been carried out on adult brains, has been done by people who are first and foremost pediatric researchers with an intense interest in quirky kids. Dr. Margaret Bauman at Massachusetts General Hospital, along with Dr. Pauline Filipek at the University of California, Irvine, have devoted highly successful careers to deciphering the basic neural differences in the brains of the quirky.

First, a brief biology lesson. The key concepts of early brain development are actually quite straightforward. It's the terminology that all scientists love to use that serves to confuse us. We'll define some terms in the process of explaining the ideas about what goes haywire in early brain development for quirky kids.

In the first couple of years of life, the brain is most *plastic*, most able to be shaped by life experiences. *Dendrites*, the long, spindlelike fingers that attach brain cells to one another and enable them to communicate with one another, are more numerous at this point in development than at any other point throughout life. The neural circuits of the brain become more efficient over time, as a child's life experience fosters the *pruning down* of the number of these dendritic connections in the brain. Once this pruning has taken place, children are more able to focus on the matter at hand, to tune out extraneous information or sensations. Furthermore, the brain activity centers for language shift at this moment, from the cerebellum, in the back of the head, to the cerebral cortex, in the front of the brain. The stage is set for learning and communication.

For children on the autistic spectrum, this process seems to go awry, which may account for the sense of many parents that "everything was fine until he was about eighteen months old." Without the normal pruning down, there remain a huge number of connections in the brain that serve to keep the gates open for sensory experience that can be overwhelming and lead to an apparent arrest or regression of normal development. Between eighteen and nineteen months of age, a typical child becomes more mature in *associative memory*—that is, in memory that involves associations among all the senses—and applies emotional meaning to experience. This is a critical period for the developing child in terms of emotional connections to the world around her and to the development of language. Without an emotional context, skills like language that have been gained before this period may actually be lost.

This information is useful because it lends credence to the neurological underpinnings of the delays and behaviors we see in these kids. On the other hand, a typical CAT scan or magnetic resonance image of the brain will not reveal any of these differences, as they are too subtle and require more sophisticated technology to uncover. Furthermore, the fact that there *are* brain differences doesn't help that much in terms of interventions.

CHEMICAL DIFFERENCES

Many families are told at one time or another that the chemistry of their child's brain is different or that something is missing. Although this isn't the whole story, it isn't completely off the mark. The study of neurotransmitters, the chemicals that enable brain cells to talk to one another, is valuable. There are good data suggesting that the concentrations of various neurotransmitters in the brains of these children are different than the concentrations in typically developing children. In a fascinating study published by Dr. Karin B. Nelson in 2000, the newborn screening filter papers (remember those papers onto which a sample of your new baby's blood was put?) from the state of California over the past twenty years were reviewed. A class of transmitters called the neuropeptides (which include morphinelike substances such as the opioids) were quantified and evaluated with attention to any known diagnoses of those infants throughout childhood and adolescence. *Ninety-seven percent* of children later diagnosed with ASDs had elevated levels of these chemicals in the first few days of life! Although it raises more questions than it answers, this kind of information can be built upon to help us understand the children in question. The information we have about neurotransmitter concentrations does provide some of the basic science upon which much of the work with medications is based.

What do we know about the other neurotransmitters? There are a number of major neurotransmitter systems that appear to vary in the brains of affected individuals: *serotonin, GABA (gamma-aminobutyric acid), acetylcholine, dopamine, norepinephrine,* and *glutamate.* Each of these has been studied extensively and found to be different than in a "neurotypical" brain.

- *Serotonin:* This transmitter is well known as the neurotransmitter targeted by some of the new drugs to treat depression. Drugs like Prozac and Zoloft act by increasing serotonin levels. Baseline serotonin levels are believed to be altered in the brains of ASD children. Typically developing children in the first five years of life have a serotonin surge, in which the levels of serotonin reach two hundred times that of a normal adult brain.

There is some evidence to suggest that this process bypasses at least some quirky kids.

- *GABA:* Gamma-aminobutyric acid, an inhibitory neurotransmitter, appears to be deficient in the hippocampus of ASD adults in which it has been studied. The hippocampus is a brain structure that involves all sensory modalities as well as certain aspects of cognition or thinking, and associations.

- *Acetylcholine, dopamine, norepinephrine, and glutamate:* There are data to support differences in the metabolism of each of these neurotransmitters as well.

WHAT DO WE DO WITH THIS INFORMATION?

Has this type of research changed our practice or that of our colleagues in the field? It has certainly changed our understanding and acceptance of these diagnoses as *biologically based.* At this point, however, whether an individual child has these differences in her brain is not generally something we can look at or something that a parent is likely to discover. Sometimes, by working backward, we can wager a guess about what neurotransmitter system is most likely to be involved when a behavior or symptom presents itself. Psychiatrists and psychopharmacologists are the most likely to think this way. They work to understand the biological basis for these disorders, and their pharmacological treatments are often based on their understanding of neurotransmitter systems. But even though they may be treating their best guesses at neurotransmitter problems, they and all the rest of us have a long way to go before we understand the part that neurotransmitters play and how to use the information to treat children more effectively.

Diagnosis and Differential Diagnosis: What Else Could This Be? What Should a Pediatrician Ask You, Look for, Check on Examination?

When our son was in his infancy, with his failure to thrive and his developmental delay, his pediatrician was thinking much more about medical syndromes. He had an MRI—we wondered if he could have a brain tumor. We wondered if he might have celiac disease or cystic fibrosis because he didn't gain weight. Ruling these things out was a relief on the one hand, but it also increased my anxiety. It was almost as if, if it was a medical thing, it wasn't my responsibility—there was a piece of me that just wanted him to have a little medical thing. Developmental things are so much more complicated, and there's no quick fix.

As pediatricians, we are usually the first professionals to whom parents turn when there are developmental concerns. We are responsible for checking things out thoroughly—for making sure that whatever is going on is a developmental variation and not some other problem or disease. Although we rarely make a diagnosis of an underlying organic or metabolic disorder, parents need and deserve this kind of attention and information.

There is a general consensus that an organic etiology is more likely for those disorders associated with lower cognitive function. In other words, the more severely affected the child, the more important it is to look for an underlying disease. The likelihood that a more mildly affected child suffers from any of these conditions is slim unless there is a family history or physical features that suggest one of them.

Our starting point as physicians, going back to our original medical-school training, is the medical history and the physical examination.

MEDICAL HISTORY

When it comes to developmental problems, we ask a lot of questions about the medical history of the families of both parents and about the circumstances surrounding conception, gestation, and birth of the child.

- *Family history:* Is there a family history of developmental delays, retardation, or autism? Sometimes parents don't know the answers to these questions but go on a fact-finding mission with their families of origin. Keep in mind that the diagnostic labels we use now have been around for less than a decade. It is therefore unlikely that such a relative will ever have been tagged with one of them. With careful questioning, we often do find that there is *someone* on one side or the other who may offer a mirror or an echo of a developmental difference.

When the doctor asked us about family history, our initial reaction was no, there has never been anything like this in either family. We soon realized that we had some adult relatives who were real oddballs, including one who has never lived independently and has never worked. We wonder what he was like as a child, how his family took care of him and prepared him for adulthood. Would he have one of these diagnoses if he were born today?

- *Prenatal problems:* Were there problems before birth? There is increasing interest among researchers in the question of whether prenatal factors might play a role. Does the mother have a number of miscarriages in her history? Is there a history of assisted conception such as in vitro fertilization (known to be associated with increased numbers of anatomic anomalies and now being studied with regard to developmental variations)? Were there complications or infections (especially rubella) during pregnancy?

I had a terrible case of the flu very early in my pregnancy. I hadn't gotten a flu shot because I thought it might be dangerous. Instead, I had a raging case of the flu with high fevers and shaking chills. Of course, I will always wonder if that has something to do with my son's issues, but nobody can really answer that for me, so I need to move on.

- *Perinatal events:* What events occurred around birth? Was the delivery difficult? Was the baby deprived of oxygen for any length of time? Did the baby spend any time in the neonatal intensive care unit? Did she require oxygen? For how long? Were there any serious illnesses such as meningitis or encephalitis in the early months of life?

- *Developmental history:* How has the child developed so far? Has her physical growth been normal? Were there motor or speech delays? Did she seem fine until a certain age when her development arrested or regressed? Are her eating habits peculiar or different in some way? If age-appropriate, is she toilet-trained? What developmental concerns are most apparent now? What kind of temperament does the child have, and how does it fit with the temperaments of her parents? How does she express affection? Does she crave or avoid physical contact?

- *Current functioning:* How is the child functioning in his present setting? Are there difficulties with learning or attention? Does he engage with you in "shared attention"—that is, pointing at something to interest you in it or looking at something to which you are drawing his attention? Does he make sustained eye contact? Does he respond when his name is called? How are his play skills? How does he handle frustration? Is he explosive or otherwise difficult to manage at home? How do other children respond to him? Does he have friends in his community? What do his teachers say about him? Does he have any unusual skills—reading at a high level, telling time, a photographic memory, or perfect pitch? Does he have a hyperfocused interest?

- *Parental concerns:* Are the *parents* concerned about a possible medical problem? Parents often have specific worries related to an aspect of their child's behavior or development or perhaps to something in the family history. On more than one occasion, we have had parents tell us they are specifically concerned about bipolar disease, obsessive-compulsive disorder, or a seizure disorder because of an affected relative.

We have had many conversations of this type with families, and our antennae are up for possible developmental issues. What is of concern to one parent may be of no concern whatsoever to the other. In addition, parents have different expectations of their child's development. The same child may be viewed entirely differently depending on his parents. We need to be mindful of this and read between the lines to some extent. In retrospect, many parents tell us, they were concerned long before we realized it. Is this a combined denial on all parts? Or is it that the parents realize only in retrospect that there were really signs that something was amiss or at least not quite right?

PHYSICAL EXAMINATION

After the medical history, the next step is a careful look at the child. With small children, this can be done quickly, although a terrified child or one who is sensitive to touch will not appreciate it! Before even touching the child, careful observation of his behavior in the exam room can provide a fair amount of information in a short time. What is the pediatrician looking for?

- Does the child make eye contact? Is it sustained or brief and fleeting?
- Does he express interest or curiosity about equipment or toys in the office?
- Does he point or try to get your attention onto something in another way?
- Will she follow your gaze when *you* point at something?
- Is she carrying a transitional object like a blanket or stuffed animal?
- Is he spinning an object on the floor?
- Does he look at things from a funny angle?
- Does she use language? Is it functional? Does she echo what others in the room are saying?
- Can she carry on a conversation with her parent or sibling?
- Does he use "scripted speech"—that is, recite lines from books or movies that, albeit somewhat relevant, aren't his own words?
- What is his prosody (the character of the voice and the fluency) like?
- What about the level of physical energy: is she still or constantly moving or sitting all curled up in her mother's lap?
- Does she have any stereotyped movements, tics, or nervous habits that may be more likely to present themselves in the stressful environment of a doctor's office?
- Does he seem overly anxious?

A pediatrician with an interest in these issues and the time for proper observation will take notice of unusual behaviors or development. A second look may be necessary, or perhaps one visit will be spent entirely in observation and you'll make a new appointment for the physical exam. In any case, if you have concerns, don't wait for six months before going back to see your pediatrician again!

What are the specific aspects of a physical exam to which we pay particular attention?

- *Dysmorphic features:* Does the child have an unusual appearance? Are his eyes or ears different in any way? How large is his head (one-quarter of the children diagnosed with autistic spectrum disorders have large heads—that is, their head circumference is greater than that of 95 percent of children their age). Children with dysmorphic features are more likely to have an underlying genetic syndrome. Fragile X syndrome is an example:

this is an abnormality of the X chromosome, affecting mostly boys. It is a cause of mental retardation, and affected boys can have autistic behaviors. These children sometimes have large heads and large ears.

- *Skin lesions:* Some of the "neurocutaneous syndromes"—specifically, tuberous sclerosis or neurofibromatosis—can first show up as developmental differences due to small lesions or tumors in the brain. The associated skin lesions have a characteristic appearance ("café au lait spots" or "ash-leaf spots"), though sometimes a special lamp, called a wood's lamp, is required to see them clearly. These syndromes are serious but rare. A small number of kids will turn out to have one of the neurocutaneous syndromes.

- *Abdominal exam:* Does the child have an enlarged liver or spleen? Enlargements in these abdominal organs are associated with certain rare metabolic disorders in which a missing enzyme can lead to buildup of a metabolite in the abdominal organs as well as the brain, sometimes affecting behavior and development.

- *Careful neurological examination:* Not the easiest thing to do on an uncooperative toddler, a neurological examination can uncover subtle weakness or low muscle tone, poor coordination, and poor fine motor control. In addition to checking the reflexes, we usually ask a child to draw something with a marker or pencil to observe the manner in which he holds and uses the writing instrument. Depending on the child's age, we may ask her to stand on one foot to assess balance or to close her eyes to see whether she can maintain her posture without the visual input. These sorts of maneuvers will sometimes expose the subtle neurological weakness or poor coordination that's frequently seen in these children.

What's the Optimal Pediatric Management for These Kids as They Grow?

There is no single test that will make a diagnosis. These diagnoses are made on the basis of history and observation of behaviors. Additional evaluations from neuropsychologists, occupational therapists, speech and language pathologists, and the like provide further information, but there is no gold standard for a diagnosis. Where, then, does this leave the family? Which tests are generally recommended for most quirky kids, and which tests are targeted for those with specific findings on the medical history or physical exam? There is no consensus on this question, but there are general rules of thumb.

Any child with a speech delay should have a hearing test. It should be repeated in a few months if the child's speech doesn't improve. All children, and most especially children with developmental delays, should be tested for lead poisoning. These simple tests should be part of the evaluation of any child with a suspected delay. A speech and language evaluation is indicated for any child with a clear delay in the development of speech, particularly if there are other concerning aspects of development. Because there are certain chromosomal abnormalities identified with the autistic spectrum disorders, a chromosomal analysis may be useful, especially if there is unexplained mental retardation in the family history. Some experts in the field recommend a chromosomal analysis, including an analysis for the fragile X chromosome, for all affected kids.

If an underlying disorder is suspected on the basis of the child's history, the family history, or the physical exam, however, certain targeted laboratory tests are indicated. If there is a concern about a prenatal infection, tests on both mother and child may be done to evaluate that. For children who regress most severely when they have a minor viral illness, a search for a metabolic disease is indicated. Kids whose parents describe cyclic periods of abnormal behavior may have an electroencephalogram (EEG) looking for a seizure disorder; seizures are more common in children with the various quirky-kid diagnoses, though usually they happen at later ages. Many pediatricians and child neurologists will order an imaging study of the brain such as an MRI. These are almost always normal and not usually necessary unless there is an abnormality on physical exam. More sophisticated *functional* imaging studies, such as a functional MRI or PET (positron-emission tomography) scan are generally only available as part of a research study.

Although there is an increased incidence of seizures—particularly a rare kind called complex partial seizures—in older children with autistic spectrum disorders, there is one neurological disorder associated with seizures that is worth special mention: Landau-Kleffner syndrome. This rare syndrome can show up as developmental delays or developmental regression in a slightly older child. The diagnosis is made according to a specific pattern on the EEG, and about 25 percent of affected children will respond dramatically to treatment with seizure medications or steroids.

Other developmental disorders can be associated with eccentric behaviors or mannerisms as well, which is often a challenge for the diagnostic team. Children with visual disturbances, developmental language disorders, auditory-processing disorders, or attentional issues or learning disabilities can all present a puzzle to their parents as well as their pediatricians. Only through careful evaluation with a team of specialists will these diagnoses come to light.

Although we support the targeted medical evaluation, the majority of the quirky kids we see are highly unlikely to have a clear medical etiology for their developmental differences. Still, a medical evaluation may help set a parent's mind at rest, may rule out some scary possibilities, and may be important for genetic counseling and planning for future children.

Genetic Implications: What about Future Children?

Caitlin's diagnosis has family-planning implications for us. We will not have a third child because of it.

The search for an individual etiology usually ends without an answer, just as the deep basic questions about epidemiology have no single clear answer. *Most* quirky kids do not have an underlying syndrome or a congenital infection or a chromosomal abnormality. The first question many parents ask after "Why?" is "Will it happen again?" No one can tell you exactly. There is no prenatal diagnosis that can be made on an amniocentesis for any of the quirky-kid diagnoses we've discussed. But we do know that there is a genetic component. We know families with more than one affected child and many who have decided to call it quits after the first. The frequently quoted recurrence rate is 4 to 7 percent.

These are intensely personal decisions. There is no question that raising a quirky child involves heartache, but the prospects may look worse when the child is very young and all you have are unanswered questions about what the future holds. If you have time, wait it out a bit before making such a lifelong decision. By all means, consult with a geneticist. These consultations can be helpful. Because the exact gene or combination of genes responsible for transmitting these disorders is not known, most geneticists will offer advice based on a family's genetic history in addition to chromosomal analyses. When a careful analysis of both families is complete, a geneticist or genetic counselor is in a better position to offer more specific risks for recurrence based on each family's history.

Associated Conditions: Are There Medical Problems We Should Expect as Our Child Grows Up?

As you go about helping your child, dealing with the implications of the diagnosis for his life and for your future decisions, as you invoke the help of specialists and therapists, be sure to keep the lines of communication open with your pediatrician. Our job in primary care does not end just because a medical etiology for the quirks has been considered and ruled out. Many questions remain to be answered, and a number of associated medical and psychiatric conditions may need attention in the years ahead—though it is impossible to predict which ones might affect a given quirky child. Once again, look to the family history. If there is a cousin or an uncle or a brother or sister with a seizure disorder, that will increase the likelihood of seizures in your child. If there are family members with depression or obsessive-compulsive disorder or Tourette's syndrome, these, too, may be more likely to become a part of your child's picture.

Seizures are probably the single most common medical condition associated with these disorders—specifically with the autistic spectrum diagnoses—yet less than a quarter of kids on the spectrum will have seizures, and they do not usually appear until adolescence. *Partial complex seizures* are the most common type and are not always immediately obvious as seizures to observers. Partial complex seizures usually present with facial grimacing and twisting, sometimes with staring or drooling or lip-smacking, and are sometimes confused with strokes because they can make the face look strange. These seizures are treatable with medications.

Some quirky kids don't grow well—because of their peculiar dietary habits or just because, once again, they seem to be wired differently. Many suffer from constipation; many are slow to become toilet-trained. They may have more trouble handling their allergies or following any other medical regimen that's prescribed. You and your child will benefit from a close relationship with a doctor who understands the whole package.

And of course, quirky kids will suffer the usual ear infections and strep throats, stomach viruses and drippy noses. You want those problems treated by someone familiar with your child's patterns and preferences—someone who understands, for example, that it's hard for her to swallow medicine or that she just can't cope with wiping a runny nose and needs the strongest anti-histamines possible.

Be on the lookout as the years pass. Talk with your pediatrician or with whatever doctor knows your child best. Most quirky kids are pretty healthy, but it will help to have an ally who knows your child over time. As pediatricians and other primary-care providers become more familiar with the quirky-kid world, this will become easier. For the time being, however, we have to say that parents are the leaders and educators more often than not. Quirky kids deserve pediatric providers who understand their experience of the world.

We have a wonderful pediatrician whom we cannot praise enough. In the early years of our son's life, he was a learner along with us. He bought books and attended conferences to educate himself. Now he really gets it. His staff knows that we simply cannot wait for the usual time in the waiting room when Ben is sick. He is just too restless and becomes agitated. He asks us to call in advance so his staff can set up a room for us, and then he sees us as promptly as possible. This is so kind and understanding, so generous, and it makes a huge difference. He actually likes going to the doctor and thinks of Dr. John as his friend.

Rebecca's doctor is exceptionally understanding of our family—one child with autism, one child with pervasive developmental disorder–not otherwise specified. The doctor has told his staff that if I come in, I need to be brought right to an exam room. These kids cannot be expected to wait a long time to see the doctor. He is lovely with the kids and always asks me, "How are you?" I can't always answer that, or sometimes I don't want to, but I really appreciate that he seems to understand the trials of my life with my kids.

References and Resources

The most up-to-date medical and research information available is going to be in articles published in the professional literature; many of these are cited in the full bibliography at the end of this book.

Bauman, Margaret, and Thomas Kemper, eds. *Neurobiology of Autism.* Baltimore: Johns Hopkins University Press, 1997. This book, by prominent researchers, covers topics like genetics, neurophysiology, imaging studies, and neurotransmitters.

Gillberg, Christopher, and Mary Coleman. *The Biology of the Autistic Syndromes.* 3d ed. London: MacKeith Press, 2000. This is a revision of a classic text (be warned that it's expensive!); it reviews epidemiology, genetics, and biochemistry.

Lewis, Lisa. *Special Diets for Special Kids: Understanding and Implementing Special Diets to Aid in the Treatment of Autism and Related Developmental Disorders.* Arlington, Tex.: Future Horizons, 1998. A book of recipes for parents who want to make major modifications in their children's diets. Again, we suggest it as a resource without endorsing either the science or the program.

PART IV

Looking Ahead

Quirky Characters

Among the many people, fictional and real, about whom it has been suggested that they have Asperger's syndrome or that they have a few autistic traits:

Dilbert
Professor Henry Higgins
Sherlock Holmes
Mr. Spock

Jane Austen
Emily Dickinson
Thomas Edison
Albert Einstein
Glenn Gould
Alfred Hitchcock
Wolfgang Amadeus Mozart
Isaac Newton
Henry David Thoreau
Andy Warhol

Introduction

○ ○ ● ○

I worry about my daughter's future. Will she ever find someone to be with, of either gender? How would that person live with her? What if he or she also has a disorder on the spectrum? Should she ever have a baby? With the increased risk that she would have a special-needs child, I really don't think she could manage. I am not sure she could manage with a typical child. But of course, these aren't my decisions; they're hers. I think there is a place for her in the science world, and she will probably be able to live independently, but other aspects of life, I just don't know. She will need more support than a typical young adult, that's for sure.

I have managed to live a whole lifetime—I'm seventy-one—and somehow, I could never learn things. I didn't learn to drive until I was forty-five years old. But I am an artist, the greatest artist in the world. I had to teach myself how to draw and how to paint. I can teach anyone to draw like an old master. I give talks a lot about art. And I didn't really know that something was truly wrong until one day I heard my wife on the phone with my daughter, saying, "Look at your father and how far he has come!" I thought, what the hell is that? There are only two people in my life I can listen to—my wife and my singing teacher, who is a gospel singer. She says, "It's a good thing I believe in Jesus, because you are very challenging!"

Once your quirky child has graduated from high school, he is in certain respects no longer a child. Eighteen-year-olds—with driver's licenses and draft cards and the right to vote—have to be allowed a certain adult status, however nervous it makes us as their parents. Your child always remains in a certain sense your child, though, and you go on watching closely and hoping for the best and vicariously experiencing both triumphs and tragedies. For the parents of a quirky child—bound a little closer together by having come a more difficult, more unusual, and often more roundabout road together—the tendency is often to hover a little more closely and keep on smoothing the way.

That is by no means necessarily a bad thing. Yes, you have to learn to hold back a little, as your child grows into an adult. All parents do. Most likely, the high school years have already started teaching you that lesson. You will now probably have even less say over many details of how your child chooses to live her life. There's still no getting around it: quirky kids can have different issues or different timetables. Some of them aren't adults yet, despite their chronological ages, and some are deeply troubled or not completely functional adults. Keep in mind that because many of these diagnoses are relatively new, we are all going to learn a lot about high school, college, and adulthood as this cohort of children grows up. We know you're in this for the long haul, and in Part IV, we want to talk a little bit about perspectives on quirky adulthood. We can't hope to cover all the many situations that may arise or tell you how best to handle even the most common problems, but we can offer a little bit of thought about how quirkiness fits (or doesn't fit) into various corners of adult life, some realistic looks at the accommodations that sometimes have to be made, and some hopeful stories and happy endings.

We don't want in any way to patronize or offend those parents who are beginning to suspect that their children's whole futures will be circumscribed and even blighted by the adult versions of their quirks. Neither would it be fair to paint too bleak a picture, since many quirky children either will outgrow some of their problems, will look less odd against the wider range of choices available to adults, or will actually find more or less triumphant ways of making their special traits work to their advantage as their lives unfold. It would be wrong to promise you that your eccentric child may well turn out to be Einstein and equally wrong to warn you that he's likely to grow up to be the Unabomber. These children represent a wide spectrum. It can be difficult, looking at them when they're young, to predict how things will develop and change.

Brian's outlook is so much brighter than we ever imagined during his elementary school years. There were a lot of bleak times, when we thought he needed a residential program, when we worried that his options were severely limited. He's had a lot of help, but he has surprised all of us, even his psychiatrist. This summer he has a job ghostwriting proposals and doing spreadsheets. This is the same boy who couldn't get a sentence on a page until he was in fifth grade. It's just amazing what kids can outgrow.

12

o o • o

Adolescence and Adulthood

Our main message about adult life, to which we will return again and again in this chapter, is this: On the one hand, adult life poses certain specific challenges—which, for some quirky kids, are especially difficult and, for some few, frankly impossible:

- To live independently and care for yourself
- To hold a job and support yourself
- To maintain the human relationships you need to make you happy

These are tall orders, and not just for the quirky; they are the stuff of lifetime goals and internal struggles and a great deal of help-seeking for many people. However, adult life offers considerably more scope for quirkiness than the rigid everybody-needs-to-be-good-at-everything sociology of childhood. Quirky adults can shape their own worlds to fit themselves, choosing niches and platforms and hiding places and stages from an almost infinitely vast array of possibilities. Your job with your quirky child was at times to bend and rearrange his school so that his life fit better on his back. His job as an adult is to choose the work and the home and the social lives that fit him best and in which he functions most happily and most fully.

What Happens after High School?

College is not for everybody. Kids, quirky or not, for whom academics are either uninteresting or incredibly difficult and who have interests or talents leading them in some other direction should wave their friends and classmates off to college without a second thought. There are vocational-training opportunities or entry-level jobs. If you're lucky, you've started thinking about this before that last year of high school, and your child has had a chance to find out whether she really does love working in a garden-supply store as much as she thought she would. It's often true that in a more academically oriented family, the parents have difficulty with a child's decision not to go to college or not to go right away.

Help your child look into vocational-training possibilities. A kid who is good with his hands, who has a knack for working with machines or computers or dough or puppies, may be able to find a job that will actually pay him while he learns. Or there may be a particular certification toward which to work, a course to take at a community college or a specialized academy.

College isn't for everybody right away, either. Quirky kids do tend to lag a little bit behind their chronological ages. They may not be ready for a full-time college experience, let alone living away from home. Your child can stay home and attend a local school as a commuter or day student or enroll in school part-time at a community college or an extension school, an opportunity to try out college-level academics while still living in a familiar situation, with all familiar supports. Anyone who starts out this way—or who starts out assuming that she isn't going to college at all—has the option of changing directions later on and going to college when she feels she's ready and eager for it.

I don't know if George will make it to college. If the music thing takes off, maybe he will go to a conservatory. I worry about a career, and I think I will need to stay very involved in his life and planning. I have talked to his older sister about the fact that we are paying forty thousand dollars a year for her to go to college and that George will get some similar amount of money, but it may be in the form of a condo rather than a fancy private college.

Many parents send their quirky kids off to a college not too far away, choosing a school within an hour's drive, so they can visit regularly and welcome the child back home on weekends. That leaves those parents more clued in to what's going on in a college student's life than an occasional E-mail asking for money and those unsatisfactory phone calls parents make late at night.

In many high schools, and among many social groups both of parents and of adolescents, the college-admissions process is the one true arbiter of success and failure. For some quirky kids, going off to the best possible college may loom as the great and single goal. Parents get caught up in this as well, and the whole senior year of high school, in many places, is about your board scores and your college visits and your essays and your applications.

College is a rich intellectual and social opportunity and also a high-pressure environment. Parents need to recognize that high pressure and to think realistically about their child's history, his vulnerabilities, and the supports that will most help him thrive.

Let's bring up the whole question of a therapist or a psychiatrist or a counselor one more time. Should you think about getting your child hooked up with someone in the new setting? You want to find out what the student health services offer. If they don't seem to have too much going on from the mental health point of view, you probably want to ask about outside referrals. If your child has already been seeing a therapist for some time, that person may be able to find you a college-years replacement, the right person in the right place at the right time. The other advantage of doing a certain amount of self-exploration in high school is that, with any luck at all, your child will have a much greater degree of self-awareness, a stronger sense of his own emotional balance, and of danger signals that something may be going wrong: more anxiety, obsessive thoughts, depressive moods.

Any child planning to go away to college right after high school ought to have been away from home before that for at least a couple of weeks. Parents of quirky kids sometimes tend to hold them close, but if he can't go to math camp for fourteen days the summer after his junior year of high school, he probably isn't ready to move to another city and live in a dormitory.

I was pretty sure Megan would be able to handle college because she had gone to overnight camp. Now I am really glad she did that, though at the time, it never occurred to me how important it would be. I read a book about good colleges where a different kid might be OK and get a good education. I looked for places that said they liked individuals and that were not very sports-oriented. I went

with her on her college trips, and we helped her a lot with her applications, espe-
cially editing the essay. I knew that she had to see the places herself so she could
know if she could do it. We decided not to say that she has Asperger's on her appli-
cation. We did disclose her learning disability and the attention deficit disorder,
assuming that there would be other kids with those, but not the Asperger's, be-
cause it is so new and so few kids her age carry the diagnosis. She was admitted
everywhere she applied, except for one place where she was wait-listed, and she
decided to go to one that appealed to her because it was all-girl and small, about
fourteen hundred girls who are bright and working hard.

College is a challenging time for everyone. A certain number of kids just go off the deep end in college, in one direction or another: nonstop partying, academic crash-and-burning, eating disorders, destructive relationships, or withdrawal and depression. Also, colleges vary enormously in the level of support and supervision they provide. Consider the size of the school and its level of intensity. More fragile students do better in a smaller school where adults know them and watch them and can help them if they're in trouble. Despite their best efforts, most big universities and state schools are pretty anonymous places to be a freshman. That includes the Ivy League schools and many other very prestigious seats of higher learning. At these places, supervision and support are likely to mean a dorm proctor or adviser, often a graduate student with no particular training in counseling or psychology, and an academic adviser, often a required signature on a study plan or a drop/add petition and nothing more. And although there is usually more available if you ask for it— trained counselors and clergy and doctors—the truth remains, at many big schools, a student can get pretty deeply into trouble of one kind or another before anyone in authority notices.

A kid who gets into a big and prestigious university but is not quite up to dealing with this level of anonymity and fend-for-yourself spirit may be better off turning it down to go someplace smaller and more personalized—even if this means breaking a sacred family tradition and wasting all that money the parents have been donating to the alumni fund. Or it may mean that for the child to function successfully at that big school, her parents have to take responsibility for seeing that she is well supported with all the help—both inside and outside the school—that they think she needs. Whether the school is big or small, parents need to try to keep track of what is going on—and to remember that if things start going awry, no one's grade point average or dream of graduate school in engineering is worth a breakdown.

College may also mean living on close terms with others. Some adolescents who may be academically ready are definitely not able to cope with dormitory life. When it comes to college living arrangements, think hard about what will work and what will be a problem. Many schools are willing to arrange a single room for a student who has special issues.

The first year, Megan had a roommate. I had written to the school about her issues and her peculiarities and what she would need in order to have any chance at a successful roommate experience. On parents' weekend in October, Megan and her roommate came to meet us, arm in arm, and I teared up, because this had never happened before. But it didn't last. By March, the roommate had moved out. We never got the whole story, but it had to do with the fact that the roommate had a boyfriend and he was spending time in their room, and this led to a lot of conflict. Other girls in the dorm sided with the roommate, and Megan lost friends and ended up living on her own. We didn't even know this had happened until she came home for the summer. She told us that it was none of our business but said, "Could you tell when you met her that she was evil?" That was her black-and-white way of explaining it to us.

Certainly, all colleges are making more and more arrangements for students with learning disabilities. Special programs or special adjustments in the program or special arrangements for taking tests or for handing in assignments are increasingly available, and the student who needs to write all his essay exams on a computer is likely to be easily accommodated. You should make sure that the relevant office at your child's college (the bureau of study counsel or the office of learning disabilities or the dean of student academic affairs) is fully provided with information about your child and his learning needs.

Megan's college has a special education coordinator, like virtually all colleges now. She is there to help kids with accommodations they may need, but the kids have to go to her to get any help. She doesn't go looking for them. When we took Megan down for the first time, we went to meet her. I did tell her about the Asperger's, and she knew what we were talking about. When Megan did poorly on a physics test, she did go to see her and took the next test untimed and did much better.

Now that we've covered college in terms of breakdowns and disasters, let's come back to the good news. The most important thing about college, from the quirky person's point of view, is that it is the most glorious golden opportunity to sort yourself out according to your interests and preferences. High school may sometimes be a bigger and more varied world than middle school, but college is a much bigger, more interesting, even more tolerant universe. Do you want to hang out with the Trekkies who congregate every evening before dinner to watch *Star Trek* reruns? Do you belong in the science center library that stays open until two in the morning? College is a time for trying on new intellectual and personal interests and identities, and it can be a very forgiving place in which to experiment. Many quirky kids come into their own in college, with the social peculiarities and rigid hierarchies of high school long ago and far away.

Megan is doing well academically and likes the college a lot.

Identity

The tasks of adulthood, in college and after, are large but also elastic. It can be hard for parents to accept this, in the sense that parameters vary—that's what we mean by elastic. Your child may feel she is successfully living independently, and your only response may be, "You call that living?" You have to try to hold back on this, of course, along with its sequels ("You call that a job?" "You call that a boyfriend?"), and to cling tightly to the notion that growing up is about finding your place in the world. One person's paradise is another's punishment. For almost all of us, while growing up, there are some slips and errors and false starts along the way.

One important theme in your child's engagement with these daunting adult responsibilities will be his sense of himself, of who he is and where he is on the spectrum of humanity, including his understanding of all that we have been lumping together as quirkiness. Does your child see herself as belonging in a particular diagnostic category: a person living with Asperger's syndrome or with attention deficit disorder or with obsessive-compulsive disorder—or with all three? That can make for a different sense of identity than might evolve in a kid whose understanding of himself was that he was a math genius who gets anxious sometimes and has to take some medicine for it. We're not saying that those are two different ways of describing the same person but rather that each person formulates a sense of who he is and what can be expected of him based in part on how he interprets his quirks and his challenges.

One tempting syndrome, from which many medical students suffer, is the tendency to diagnose yourself with any syndrome you read about. In writing and researching this book, we have both realized that we have, at various times, sensory integration dysfunction, attentional difficulties, autistic features, and obsessional thought patterns. A young adult who has actually already carried several diagnoses in his life may be particularly susceptible to this syndrome and may be constantly constructing and reconstructing himself according to different combinations of mental and developmental disorders. However, the ever-expanding use of psychotropic medications in the general adult population means that there are now enormous numbers of functional adults taking antidepressants or antianxiety medications. The child who felt different because she had to go to the nurse once a day to take her meds may grow into the adult who complains that every single guy she meets seems to be on Zoloft.

How quirky young adults formulate their ideas of self—identity, level of success, happiness in the world—will depend on many things. There will always be a family context, a cultural context, a social context. We all know people who consider themselves failures despite multiple successes in life and people who consider themselves successes on the basis of making it from day to day. Some will define themselves to one extent or another by their quirks— whether that means identifying with one particular diagnosis and forming a social circle from its support group and its Web page or just limiting their lives strictly to some other category of people with whom they have a great deal in common. Others will resolutely refuse to define themselves in this way, insisting absolutely and completely, perhaps, that it's the rest of the world that's weird.

Some young adults will choose to identify themselves with specific syndromes and support groups. Others may decide to reject the diagnosis completely in adulthood—call it denial or call it free choice—and construct their identities in other ways. As a parent, be sensitive to the kind of experimentation that goes on in these years of self-discovery and self-definition and, as far as possible (with safety always in mind), let your child set the terms of how you talk to him, talk about him, and attempt to forge together a new and somewhat different bond, one adult to another.

Living Independently

The parents of children who just don't seem quite able to function in the standard child world often worry tremendously about whether those children will ever, as adults, live independently and take care of themselves. And it is certainly true that at the more troubled—or disabled—end of the spectrum, there may be children who take much longer to achieve any kind of independent life or whose independence, when it comes, may need regular support and propping up by nearby family members or who need special arrangements: a halfway house, a supervised situation, a group home. If this is what your child needs when the time comes, you will be out there looking for the best options, protecting and assisting the adult as you have protected and assisted the child. It's also true that many people choose to live at home for all or part of their adult lives and that this choice does not necessarily reflect an inability to manage out in the world. How many of us have adult siblings still living with the folks or a brother who moved back in after his divorce?

For the great majority of quirky young adults, however, there will indeed be that challenge of learning how to take care of themselves. Every detail of adult life, from paying the rent to cooking your favorite kind of macaroni and cheese, can pose a different challenge to someone who looks at the world from a different angle.

Some quirky kids, as they achieve adulthood and independence, take the opportunity to cast off certain conventions or behaviors that have just never made sense to them. These can be anything from hanging curtains in the window to shaving every day. They may live in chaos and squalor—or else in rigidly neat and ordered environments, where nothing is ever allowed to be the tiniest bit out of place. Without family members or college roommates dictating a slightly more normal setup (remember that normal for a dorm room full of college boys can mean pyramids of empty beer cans and a sofa with the stuffing coming out), some quirky young adults take the opportunity to indulge, finally, their preferences to the absolute extreme.

Many of these young adults thrive on routine of one kind or another and will shop for a few items in large multiples and ritually prepare the same meals day after day. Others seem to have been waiting for the chance to let all routine slip and, in extreme cases, abandon even those basic personal hygiene lessons you worked so hard to imprint upon them.

You can help your child get ready to take care of herself, and you probably have to do it much the same way you once helped her get ready to go to a birthday party. Break down the tasks of independent adult living and make sure she's got them figured out.

- ✓ *Food:* Every quirky adult (well, every adult, if you ask us) should know how to prepare a few basic items and, most important, know how to buy, store, and prepare the things that he really likes to eat and drink regularly. If you know how to scramble an egg, construct your favorite kind of sandwich, make the kind of coffee you most like to drink, and prepare two or three of your favorite easy dinners, you're ready for your diploma.

- ✓ *Money:* Make sure your child knows how money is transferred and stored (checks, cash cards, debit cards, credit cards) and make sure she has some sense of relative sums. In other words, she should understand that spending ten dollars on a whim, or lending it to someone you know only slightly, is different from doing that with a thousand dollars. Explain how different bills are paid—the rent with a check left in the landlord's mailbox, the phone bill on-line, and so on. If she is going to have access to a credit line—either through credit cards or through a bank account cash reserve—make sure she understands that these debts accumulate interest at high rates.

- ✓ *Medical care:* Figure out how your child will get his health insurance. There's no one easy answer to this (although anyone with a severe disability of any kind ought to be eligible for any of several programs), but it's not something that can safely be left up to most young adults, since the medical insurance world is a maze of confusing options, and most young adults believe they're immortal.

- ✓ *Special medical care:* Does your child know whom to call if her problems act up? If her medication stops working or starts to produce funny side effects? Be sure she's connected in all the ways she needs to be but shift some of the responsibility for making and keeping appointments to her, if she's ready.

✓ *Maintenance:* Whom do you call when the toilet won't flush or the stove burner won't light or the wall starts to crumble? Well, many of us can remember calling our parents! Be available for consultations, but also make sure your child has a little basic grounding in changing a lightbulb or tightening a loose screw.

✓ *Logistics of daily life:* Opening a bank account, registering to vote, renewing a driver's license—all of these are hard to figure out the first time around. Once again, quirky kids and the young adults they become often have a harder time figuring out even the things that come naturally to other people. The more you can help them break life down into manageable tasks and then get through those tasks, the easier it will be for them to keep safe, functional, and well connected.

It's generally a parent's job to provide a place of refuge if all this independence just gets to be too much. Most parents who have reared decidedly quirky kids accept this as a special responsibility: *if you need to, you can come home and start again.* There are certainly lots of quirky people who spend some part of their adult lives living at home with their parents, and if you find yourself in that situation, you will quickly realize that it raises some hard questions, maybe questions you've been thinking about and wrestling with for a long time. If you have a child who is not completely able to live independently and take care of himself, who is going to be responsible for whatever care and support are necessary when you are no longer able to do it? Is this going to devolve on your child's sibling or siblings? Are you going to make special financial arrangements, set up a trust fund or a special annuity account? Are you going to write a will that leaves house and money to one child, the one you think needs it most? If so, have you discussed it with the others? We just felt the need to raise this issue—certainly not any parent's favorite long-term fantasy for a child—in the context of the quirky young adult's experiments in independent living.

You may not like the way your adult offspring lives. You may be troubled or sad or mildly disgusted at the arrangements he makes for himself, at the state of his kitchen or bathroom, or his junk-food dependence, or the rag he calls a bathrobe. For the most part, keep quiet about these things. Yes, you need to be there as backup and resource and refuge, and you're certainly entitled to your opinion. But when your child starts to live independently as an adult, give her some space. Stand back a little—harder for parents who know their children often have a more difficult time. But independence is independence. As long as there doesn't seem to be anything unsafe about the situation, you need to let your child make these adult attempts and explorations.

Holding a Job

Chrissie has said—and I agree with her—that she'd like to do design work or something where she doesn't have to be around people too much. I don't think she'd be happy in the back office of a bank feeding data into a computer, but she also isn't going to be a public relations maven. Anything that requires a lot of quick changes during the day, like journalism, won't be her strong suit.

There are an awful lot of eccentric adults out there, some in particular jobs that they have chosen to fit their kinks or to allow them full-time access to their obsessions—anything from feeding the animals at the zoo to scheduling trains to splitting subatomic particles. Others are working at more generic jobs—office jobs, civil service jobs—but are unmistakably different from most of their colleagues in one way or another. Some choose jobs that require no social skills, thus finally escaping for most of the day the repeated ordeal of trying to figure out what other people are all about. Others pursue an all-consuming interest to the very top of academia—or of Silicon Valley. Still others are creating art or playing music.

What this means is important: most quirky kids grow up to be quirky adults who find ways to function and to contribute to society. Most of them find places in the world. You need to help your child find that place and, above all, not fix your own and your child's ambitions too firmly on any one particular professional destiny. She has to choose, and you have to be proud of her, not disappointed, once she's chosen.

Some quirky children grow up to go as far as anyone can go—start the company, make the discovery, write the symphony, win the Nobel Prize. Most of them, however, just like most of the rest of us, will live reasonably decent lives and do their best. The parents who make such a child feel like a failure are the parents who are having so much trouble giving up some dearly loved fantasy that they are willing to wreck their child's reality on the rocks of that illusion. So make suggestions, but let your child take the lead and show you where she wants to go.

The world is easier on quirky adults than it is on quirky kids. No one minds if an adult doesn't want to have anything to do with animals or likes to keep things lined up precisely or hates the water. By the nature of the schools and summer camps and activities that we set up for them, we often make children suffer if they have trouble with any one thing on the long list of what we feel normal children should do and enjoy and accomplish, but we allow adults much more latitude in charting their own paths.

Relationships

I think George will marry a nurse, some sweet and nurturing type. And he'll be a good husband.

Marriage and children are Chrissie's dream, but I don't know if she'll be able to handle it. What I really worry about is her loving spirit being taken advantage of.

We all want our children, as adults, to find the interpersonal connections and the important relationships that will lead to happiness and even love. We want them not to be alone but to be surrounded by people who appreciate them, understand them, value them, take care of them, and love them. We don't have the ability to make that happen just because we want it to. It's up to those adults themselves and to chance and fate and circumstance.

Some quirky children always got along better with adults than with children their own ages. Once they are adults themselves and no longer have to deal with children at all, social life can get easier. Their colleagues and social contacts are much less likely to tease or bully them, although they may certainly perceive them as odd, eccentric, or downright weird. However, adult life is full of alternative places to meet and greet. By choosing their venues carefully, most adults can find at least sporadic situations in which to assort themselves with like-minded folks.

Probably the most hopeful and most useful advice you can give quirky adults is to do exactly that: find your own special peer group, the club or clubs of which you are a member. The existence of the Internet, as has often been remarked, has made it much, much easier for small groups of people with rarefied interests to find one another and connect. Certainly, there are quirky adults who live their realest, truest lives in the times they spend at particular kinds of conventions—from historical reenactments to fantasy game sessions. Some of these people have complete alter egos, characters they assume— down to the attitudes, the accent, and the costume—when they are outside their own often humdrum daily lives and able to associate with their true friends and comrades.

Is any of this particular comfort to a parent who fears that, in a basic sense, this quirky child—now quirky adult—will always be alone, will never establish a long-term relationship or find a mate or build a truly secure base of home and family? We have no way to answer this question. Thus, taking our place in a rich tradition of people with no firm answers, we can offer only a little philosophy.

There are some really quirky adults who find long-term relationships, astonishingly good fits. There are also, of course, lots and lots of not-at-all-quirky adults who never find the long-term relationships for which they earnestly and endlessly seek. And there are many adults, quirky and not, who are in no way seeking a single permanent long-term relationship but have other ways of living their lives and establishing their places in the world. It's probably more important to think in terms of the many relationships that keep most people connected in the world and look at strategies for finding them if you happen to be a little bit eccentric. Quirky adults, as we said above, often need to search out a peer group, not necessarily as a way of finding that one special someone but as a way of finding a setting in which they are not seen as even faintly odd.

Many adults find connections and contacts through church groups or through community groups or through volunteering. The more different ways you can help your quirky young adult link himself up with those around him, the more likely it becomes that he will find friends, companions, and even perhaps something more.

Some of the quirky children we love will grow up to be relatively solitary and definitely quirky adults. Others will find ways to make their quirks work for them and will draw friends, admirers, and even disciples. You can't predict an adult's social future from watching a child on the playground or even on the high school dance floor. Though there are sad and disappointing adult lives, there are also remarkably happy endings out there, many of them downright quirky.

A Final Word

The world would be a poorer, plainer place without the quirky. Without the quirky children, who extend the range of normal in the schoolroom, in the pediatrician's office, or on the playground. Without the quirky adults, who remind us that not all lives are alike or predictable or easily explained in our simplest terms. The world would be a duller and more monochrome place without the artists and musicians and writers who have seen and heard and felt a little differently from the rest. And the world would be a less-well-understood place without the scientists and visionaries who have seen around corners with their unusual eyes and thought through walls with their strangely wired brains. We honor the different drummer among adults when we hear the beats as creativity or even as conviction and principle.

Children, on the other hand, live in a more conformist and regulated world. Despite a great deal of romantic twaddle about the freedom and innocence of childhood, the truth is that many children's lives are strictly regulated, and no major deviations from the norm are tolerated. A child can't wake up one morning and decide, *That's it. I'm through forever with math . . . with riding those damn buses . . . with pretending I like the great outdoors.* But adults can easily make such arrangements for themselves.

Quirky children, as you know, can be frustrating, inspiring, puzzling, delightful, devastating, and highly entertaining. Our goal in writing this book has been to offer some practical help and some general philosophy about doing the always hard and always different parental job with these children, and to do that at least in part from this standpoint: the world needs its quirky children, its quirky adults, its quirky minds, and its quirky sensibilities; for all the challenges they face, quirky people enlarge and enhance life for us all.

References and Resources

Grandin, Temple. *Thinking in Pictures: And Other Reports from My Life with Autism.* New York: Vintage Books, 1996. Temple Grandin is the ambassador for adults with autistic spectrum disorders, and her books are an inspiration. She has a very successful and unusual career in animal husbandry and writes about her experiences with candor and remarkable insight.

Hallowell, Edward M., and John J. Ratey. *Driven to Distraction: Recognizing and Coping with Attention Deficit Disorder from Childhood through Adulthood.* New York: Simon & Schuster, 1995. This excellent book on ADD includes much material about adults and young adults who suffer with the condition.

Ratey, John, and Catherine Johnson. *Shadow Syndromes: The Mild Forms of Major Mental Disorders That Sabotage Us.* New York: Bantam Books, 1998. This is a wonderful book for those of us who think, "Don't we all have some of these qualities?" The chapter entitled "Autistic Echoes" will resonate when a child's diagnosis has raised questions about other family members.

Weeks, David, and Jamie James. *Eccentrics: A Study of Sanity and Strangeness.* New York: Kodansha, 1996. Fascinating stories of eccentric adults managing to function brilliantly in the worlds of science and the arts.

NOTES

CHAPTER 2: SPECIALISTS, LABELS, AND ALPHABET SOUP

1. Janice Ware, "Autism, PDD, and Asperger's Syndrome: A Spectrum of Disorders," *Pediatric Views*, December 2001, 2–3, Children's Hospital Boston, Departments of Public Affairs and Marketing.

PART II: GROWING UP QUIRKY: INTRODUCTION

1. Kenneth Hall, *Asperger Syndrome, the Universe and Everything* (London: Jessica Kingsley Publishers, 2001), 114.

2. Bob Stuart, in *Disclosure and Asperger's Syndrome: Our Own Stories* (Newton, Mass.: Asperger's Association of New England, 2000), 7.

CHAPTER 11: MEDICAL PERSPECTIVES ON THE QUIRKY CHILD

1. Steve Silberman, "The Geek Syndrome," *Wired*, issue 9.12 (December 2001), 182.

BIBLIOGRAPHY

Allen, A. "The Not-So-Crackpot Autism Theory." *New York Times Magazine*, November 10, 2002.

Allen, D. A., and L. Mendelson. "Parent, Child, and Professional: Meeting the Needs of Young Autistic Children and Their Families in a Multidisciplinary Therapeutic Nursery Model." *Psychoanalytic Inquiry* 20 (2000): 704–731.

American Academy of Pediatrics, Committee on Children with Disabilities. "The Pediatrician's Role in the Diagnosis and Management of Autistic Spectrum Disorder in Children." *Pediatrics* 107, no. 5 (2001): 1221–1226.

American Psychiatric Association. *Diagnostic and Statistical Manual of Mental Disorders: DSM-IV.* 4th ed. Arlington, Va.: American Psychiatric Publishing, 1994.

Anderson, Elizabeth, and Pauline Emmons. *Unlocking the Mysteries of Sensory Dysfunction: A Resource for Anyone Who Works with, or Lives with, a Child with Sensory Issues.* Arlington, Tex.: Future Horizons, 1996.

Attwood, Tony. *Asperger's Syndrome: A Guide for Parents and Professionals.* London: Jessica Kingsley Publishers, 1998.

Ayres, J. *Sensory Integration and the Child.* Los Angeles: Western Psychological Services, 1979.

Bailey, A., W. Phillips, and M. Rutter. "Autism: Towards an Integration of Clinical, Genetic, Neuropsychological, and Neurobiological Perspectives." *Journal of Child Psychology and Psychiatry* 37, no. 1 (1996): 89–126.

Barkley, R. A., M. Fischer, L. Smallish, and K. Fletcher. "Does the Treatment of

Attention-Deficit/Hyperactivity Disorder with Stimulants Contribute to Drug Use/Abuse? A 13-Year Prospective Study." *Pediatrics* 111, no. 1 (2003): 97–109.

Baron-Cohen, S., J. Allen, and C. Gillberg. "Can Autism Be Detected at 18 Months? The Needle, the Haystack, and the CHAT." *British Journal of Psychiatry* 161 (1992): 839–843.

Baron-Cohen, Simon. *Mindblindness: An Essay on Autism and Theory of Mind.* Cambridge, Mass.: MIT Press, 1997.

Barton, M., and F. Volkmar. "How Commonly Are Known Medical Conditions Associated with Autism?" *Journal of Autism and Developmental Disorders* 28, no. 4 (1998): 273–278.

Bashe, P. R., and B. L. Kirby. *The Oasis Guide to Asperger Syndrome: Advice, Support, Insight, and Inspiration.* New York: Crown, 2001.

Bauman, M. L. "Brief Report: Neuroanatomic Observations of the Brain in Pervasive Developmental Disorders." *Journal of Autism and Developmental Disorders* 26, no. 2 (1996): 199–203.

Bauman, M. L., and T. Kemper, eds. *The Neurobiology of Autism.* Baltimore: Johns Hopkins University Press, 1997.

Bellis, T. J. *When the Brain Can't Hear: Unraveling the Mystery of Auditory Processing Disorder.* New York: Pocket Books, 2002.

Blumenthal, R. "An Artist's Success at 14, Despite Autism." *New York Times,* January 16, 2002.

Brazelton, T. Berry. *Touchpoints: Your Child's Emotional and Behavioral Development.* Cambridge, Mass.: Da Capo Press, 1994.

Brumback, R. A., C. R. Harper, and W. A. Weinberg. "Nonverbal Learning Disabilities, Asperger's Syndrome, Pervasive Developmental Disorder—Should We Care?" *Journal of Child Neurology* 11 (1996): 427–429.

Burd, L., W. Fisher, D. Knowlton, and J. Kerbeshian. "Hyperlexia: A Marker for Improvement in Children with Pervasive Developmental Disorder?" *Journal of the American Academy of Child and Adolescent Psychiatry* 26 (1987): 407–412.

Caronna, E. B., and N. Halfon. "Dipping Deeper into the Reservoir of Autistic Spectrum Disorder." (editorial) *Archives of Pediatrics and Adolescent Medicine* 157, no. 7 (2003): 619–621.

Casey, J. E., B. P. Rourke, and E. M. Picard. "Syndrome of Nonverbal Learning Disabilities: Age Differences in Neuropsychological, Academic, and Socioemotional Functioning." *Development and Psychopathology* 3 (1991): 329–345.

Chakrabarti, S., and E. Fombonne. "Pervasive Developmental Disorders in Preschool Children." *Journal of the American Medical Association* 285 (2001): 3093–3099.

Chudley, A. E., E. Gutierrez, L. J. Jocelyn, and B. N. Chodirker. "Outcomes of Genetic Evaluation in Children with Pervasive Developmental Disorder." *Journal of Developmental and Behavioral Pediatrics* 19, no. 5 (1998): 321–325.

Citro, T. A., ed. *The Experts Speak: Parenting the Child with Learning Disabilities.* Weston, Mass.: Learning Disabilities Association of Massachusetts, 2001.

Cohen, C. *Raise Your Child's Social IQ: Stepping Stones to People Skills for Kids.* Silver Springs, Md.: Advantage, 2000.

Cohen, D. J., J. Jankovic, and C. Goetz, eds. *Tourette Syndrome.* Philadelphia: Lippincott Williams and Wilkins, 2001.

Cohen, D. J., and F. R. Volkmar, eds. *Handbook of Autism and Pervasive Developmental Disorders.* Hoboken, N.J.: Wiley, 1997.

Cohen, S. *Targeting Autism: What We Know, Don't Know, and Can Do to Help Young Children with Autism and Related Disorders.* Updated ed. Berkeley: University of California Press, 2002.

Davis, R. L., Piotr Kramarz, Kari Bohlke, Patti Benson, Robert S. Thompson, John Mullooly, Steve Black, Henry Shinefield, Edwin Lewis, Joel Ward, S. Michael Marcy, Eileen Eriksen, Frank DeStefano, and Robert Chen. "Measles-Mumps-Rubella and Other Measles Containing Vaccines Do Not Increase Risk for Inflammatory Bowel Disease: A Case Control Study from the Vaccine Safety Datalink Project." *Archives of Pediatrics and Adolescent Medicine* 155, no. 3 (2001): 354–359.

Denckla, M. B. "The Neuropsychology of Social-Emotional Learning Disabilities." *Archives of Neurology* 40 (1983): 461–462.

DeStefano, F., and R. T. Chen. "Autism and Measles, Mumps and Rubella Vaccine: No Epidemiological Evidence for a Causal Association." *Journal of Pediatrics* 136 (2000): 125–126.

Diller, L. H. *Should I Medicate My Child?: Sane Solutions for Troubled Kids with—and without—Psychiatric Drugs.* New York: Basic Books, 2003.

Ehlers, S., and C. Gillberg. "The Epidemiology of Asperger Syndrome: A Total Population Study." *Journal of Child Psychology and Psychiatry* 34, no. 8 (1993): 1327–1350.

Eisenberg, A., H. E. Murkoff, and S. E. Hathaway. *What to Expect the First Year.* New York: Workman, 1996.

Eliot, L. *What's Going on in There?: How the Brain and Mind Develop in the First Five Years of Life.* New York: Bantam, 2000.

Faherty, C. *Asperger's: What Does It Mean to Me?: A Workbook Explaining Self-Awareness and Life Lessons to the Child or Youth with High Functioning Autism or Asperger's.* Arlington, Tex.: Future Horizons, 2000.

Filipek, P. A., P. J. Accardo, S. Ashwal, G. T. Baranek, E. H. Cook Jr., G. Dawson, B. Gordon, J. S. Gravel, C. P. Johnson, R. J. Kallen, S. E. Levy, N. J. Minshew, S. Ozonoff, B. M. Prizant, I. Rapin, S. J. Rogers, W. L. Stone, S. W. Teplin, R. F. Tuchman, and F. R. Volkmar. "Practice Parameter: Screening and Diagnosis of Autism: Report of the Quality Standards Subcommittee of the American Academy of Neurology and the Child Neurology Society." *Neurology* 55 (2000): 468–479.

Filipek, P. A., P. J. Accardo, G. T. Baranek, E. H. Cook Jr., G. Dawson, B. Gordon, J. S. Gravel, C. P. Johnson, R. J. Kallen, S. E. Levy, N. J. Minshew, S. Ozonoff, B. M. Prizant, I. Rapin, S. J. Rogers, W. L. Stone, S. Teplin, R. F. Tuchman, and F. R. Volkmar. "The Screening and Diagnosis of Autistic Spectrum Disorders." *Journal of Autism and Developmental Disorders* 29 (1999): 439–484.

Fletcher, P. C., F. Happe, U. Frith, S. C. Baker, R. J. Dolan, R. S. Frackowiak, and C. D. Frith. "Other Minds in the Brain: A Functional Imaging Study of 'Theory of Mind' in Story Comprehension." *Cognition* 57, no. 2 (1995): 109–128.

Fombonne, E. "Is the Prevalence of Autism Increasing?" *Journal of Autism and Developmental Disorders* 26 (1996): 673–676.

Frankel, F. *Good Friends Are Hard to Find: Help Your Child Find, Make and Keep Friends.* Glendale, Calif.: Perspective, 1996.

Frost, Lori A., and Andrew S. Bondy. *PECS: The Picture Exchange Communication System.* Newark, Del.: Pyramid Educational Consultants, 1996.

Gardner, H. *Frames of Mind: The Theory of Multiple Intelligences.* New York: Basic Books, 1993.

Gerland, G. *Finding Out about Asperger's Syndrome, High-Functioning Autism, and PDD.* London: Jessica Kingsley Publishers, 2000.

Ghaziuddin, M., and L. Gerstein. "Pedantic Speaking Style Differentiates Asperger Syndrome from High-Functioning Autism." *Journal of Autism and Developmental Disorders* 26, no. 6 (1996): 585–595.

Gillberg, C. "Autistic Children Growing Up: Problems during Puberty and Adolescence." *Developmental Medicine and Child Neurology* 26 (1984): 125–129.

Gillberg, C., and M. Coleman. *The Biology of the Autistic Syndromes.* 3d ed. London: MacKeith Press, 2000.

Gillberg, C., H. Melanders, A. von Knorring, L. Janols, G. Thernlund, B. Hagglof, L. Eidevall-Wallin, P. Gustafsson, and S. Kopp. "Long-Term Stimulant Treatment of Children with Attention-Deficit Hyperactivity Disorder Symptoms: A Randomized, Double-Blind, Placebo-Controlled Trial." *Archives of General Psychiatry* 54 (1997): 857–864.

Goleman, D. *Emotional Intelligence.* New York: Bantam, 1995.

Gorman, C. "Do Vaccines Cause Autism?" *Time,* November 18, 2002.

Grandin, T. "Needs of High-Functioning Teenagers and Adults with Autism: Tips from a Recovered Autistic." *Focus on Autistic Behavior* 5 (1990): 1–16.

————. *Thinking in Pictures: And Other Reports from My Life with Autism.* New York: Vintage Books, 1996.

Grandin, T., and Margaret M. Scariano. *Emergence: Labeled Autistic.* New York: Warner Books, 1996.

Gravel, J. S. "Auditory Integration Training: Placing the Burden of Proof." *American Journal of Speech and Language Pathology* 5 (May 1994): 25–29.

Gray, Carol. "Gray's Guide to Bullying." The Gray Center for Social Learning and Understanding (mailing address: The Gray Center, 2020 Raybrook SE, Suite 101, Grand Rapids, MI 49546; phone: [616] 954-9747; fax: [616] 954-9749; Web site: www.thegraycenter.org).

————. *The New Social Story Book.* Arlington, Tex.: Future Horizons, 2000.

Green, W. H. *Child and Adolescent Clinical Psychopharmacology.* 3d ed. Baltimore: Lippincott Williams and Wilkins, 2001.

Greene, R. W. *The Explosive Child: A New Approach for Understanding and Parenting Easily Frustrated, Chronically Inflexible Children.* 2d ed. New York: Harper-Collins, 2001.

Greenspan, S. I., and N. T. Greenspan. *First Feelings: Milestones in the Emotional Development of Your Baby and Child.* Reprint. New York: Penguin USA, 1994.

Greenspan, S. I., with Jacqueline Salmon. *The Challenging Child: Understanding, Raising, and Enjoying the Five "Difficult" Types of Children.* Cambridge, Mass.: Perseus Publishing, 1996.

Greenspan, S. I., and S. Wieder, with R. Simons. *The Child with Special Needs: Encouraging Intellectual and Emotional Growth.* Cambridge, Mass.: Perseus, 1998.

Gurney, J. G., M. S. Fritz, K. K. Ness, P. Sievers, C. J. Newschaffer, and E. G. Shapiro. "Analysis of Prevalence Trends of Autism Spectrum Disorder in Minnesota." *Archives of Pediatrics and Adolescent Medicine* 157, no. 7 (2003): 622–627.

Haddon, Mark. *The Curious Incident of the Dog in the Night-Time.* New York: Doubleday, 2003.

Hall, Kenneth. *Asperger Syndrome, the Universe and Everything.* London: Jessica Kingsley Publishers, 2001.

Hallowell, E. M., and J. J. Ratey. *Driven to Distraction: Recognizing and Coping with Attention Deficit Disorder from Childhood through Adulthood.* New York: Simon & Schuster, 1995.

Handen, B. L., H. M. Feldman, A. Lurier, and P. J. Murray. "Efficacy of Methylphenidate among Preschool Children with Developmental Disabilities and ADHD." *Journal of Child and Adolescent Psychiatry* 38, no. 7 (1999): 805–812.

Happe, F., S. Ehlers, P. Fletcher, U. Frith, M. Johansson, C. Gillberg, R. Dolan, R. Frackowiak, and C. Frith. " 'Theory of Mind' in the Brain: Evidence from a PET Scan Study of Asperger Syndrome." *Neuroreport* 8, no. 1 (1996): 197–201.

Happe, F., and U. Frith. "The Neuropsychology of Autism." *Brain* 119 (1996): 1377–1400.

Harris, R. H. *It's Perfectly Normal: Changing Bodies, Growing Up, Sex, and Sexual Health.* Illustrated by M. Emberley. Cambridge, Mass.: Candlewick, 1996.

———. *It's So Amazing! A Book about Eggs, Sperm, Birth, Babies and Families.* Illustrated by M. Emberley. Cambridge, Mass.: Candlewick, 2002.

Hoopmann, K. *Blue Bottle Mystery: An Asperger's Adventure.* London: Jessica Kingsley Publishers, 2001.

Horvath, K., J. C. Papadimitriou, A. Rabsztyn, C. Drachenberg, and J. T. Tildon. "Gastrointestinal Abnormalities in Children with Austic Disorder." *Journal of Pediatrics* 135, no. 5 (1999): 559–563.

Houston, Rab, and Uta Frith. *Autism in History: The Case of Hugh Blair of Borgue.* Oxford, U.K.: Blackwell, 2000.

Hyman, S. L., P. M. Rodier, and P. Davidson. "Pervasive Developmental Disorders in Young Children." *Journal of the American Medical Association* 285 (2001): 3141–3142.

The Interdisciplinary Council on Developmental and Learning Disorders. *Clinical Practice Guidelines: Redefining the Standards of Care for Infants, Children, and Families with Special Needs.* Bethesda, Md.: ICDL Press, 2000.

Ives, Martine, and Nell Munro. *Caring for a Child with Autism: A Practical Guide for Parents.* London: Jessica Kingsley Publishers, 2002.

Jensen, V. K., J. A. Larrieu, and K. K. Mack. "Differential Diagnosis between Attention-Deficit/Hyperactivity Disorder and Pervasive Developmental Disorder–Not Otherwise Specified." *Clinical Pediatrics* 36 (1997): 555–561.

Kaye, J. A., M. del Mar Melero-Montes, and H. Jick. "Mumps, Measles, and Rubella Vaccine and the Incidence of Autism Recorded by General Practitioners: A Time Trend Analysis." *British Medical Journal* 322 (2001): 460–463.

Kelly, D. L., R. R. Conley, R. C. Love, D. S. Horn, and C. M. Ushchak. "Weight Gain in Adolescents Treated with Risperidone and Conventional Antipsychotics over Six Months." *Journal of Child and Adolescent Psychopharmacology* 8, no. 3 (1998): 151–159.

Kliman, G. W. "Child Psychoanalysis Applied in Public Special Education Classes: The Cornerstone Project." *The American Psychoanalyst,* April 1997.

Klin, A., W. Jones, R. T. Schultz, F. R. Volkmar, and D. J. Cohen. "Defining and Quantifying the Social Phenotype in Autism." *American Journal of Psychiatry* 159 (2002): 895–908.

Klin, A., F. R. Volkmar, and S. S. Sparrow, eds. *Asperger Syndrome.* New York: Guilford Press, 2000.

Kranowitz, C. S. *The Out-of-Sync Child: Recognizing and Coping with Sensory Integration Dysfunction.* New York: Perigee, 1998.

Kurcinka, M. S. *Raising Your Spirited Child: A Guide for Parents Whose Child Is More Intense, Sensitive, Perceptive, Persistent, Energetic.* Reprint. New York: Harper Perennial, 1992.

Landrigan, P. J., and J. J. Witte. "Neurologic Disorders Following Live Measles-Virus Vaccination." *Journal of the American Medical Association* 223 (1973): 1459–1462.

Leach, P. *Your Baby and Child: From Birth to Age Five.* New York: Knopf, 1997.

Leicester City Council and Leicestershire County Council. *Asperger Syndrome— Practical Strategies for the Classroom: A Teacher's Guide.* Shawnee Mission, Kans.: Autism Asperger Publishing Co., 2002.

Levine, M. *A Mind at a Time: America's Top Learning Expert Shows How Every Child Can Succeed.* New York: Touchstone Books, 2003.

Levine, Mel. *All Kinds of Minds: A Young Student's Book about Learning Abilities and Learning Disorders.* Cambridge, Mass.: Educators Publishing Service, 1992.

Lewis, L. *Special Diets for Special Kids: Understanding and Implementing Special Diets to Aid in the Treatment of Autism and Related Developmental Disorders.* Arlington, Tex.: Future Horizons, 1998.

Lord, C. "Follow-up of Two-Year-Olds Referred for Possible Autism." *Journal of Child Psychology and Psychiatry* 36, no. 8 (1995): 1365–1382.

Lord, C., M. Rutter, and A. Le Couteur. "Autism Diagnostic Interview—Revised: A Revised Version of a Diagnostic Interview for Caregivers of Individuals with Possible Pervasive Developmental Disorders." *Journal of Autism and Developmental Disorders* 24, no. 5 (1994): 659–685.

Lovaas, O. I. "Behavioral Treatment and Normal Educational and Intellectual Functioning in Young Autistic Children." *Journal of Consulting and Clinical Psychology* 55 (1987): 3–9.

Lyon, G. R., and N. A. Krasnegor, eds. *Attention, Memory, and Executive Function.* Baltimore: Paul H. Brookes, 1996.

Makela, A., J. P. Nuorti, and H. Peltola. "Neurologic Disorders after Measles-Mumps-Rubella Vaccination." *Pediatrics* 110 (2002): 957–963.

Martin, A., L. Scahill, A. Klin, and F. R. Volkmar. "Higher-Functioning Pervasive Developmental Disorders: Rates and Patterns of Psychotropic Drug Use." *Journal of the American Academy of Child and Adolescent Psychiatry* 38, no. 7 (1999): 923–931.

Maurice, C. *Let Me Hear Your Voice: A Family's Triumph over Autism.* Reprint. New York: Fawcett Columbine, 1994.

Maurice, C., ed.; coedited by G. Green and S. C. Luce. *Behavioral Intervention for Young Children with Autism: A Manual for Parents and Professionals.* Austin, Tex.: PRO-ED, 1996.

McEachin, J. J., T. Smith, and O. I. Lovaas. "Long-Term Outcome for Children with Autism Who Received Early Intensive Behavioral Treatment." *American Journal of Mental Retardation* 97 (1993): 359–372.

Michelson, D., D. Faries, J. Wernicke, D. Kelsey, K. Kendrick, F. R. Sallee, and T. Spencer. "Atomoxetine in the Treatment of Children and Adolescents with Attention-Deficit Hyperactivity Disorder: A Randomized, Placebo-Controlled, Dose-Response Study." *Pediatrics* 108, no. 5 (2001): E83.

The Morning News. Jenison High School, 2140 Bauer Road, Jenison, MI 49428; phone (616) 457-8955; fax (616) 457-4070.

Moyes, Rebecca A. *Incorporating Social Goals in the Classroom: A Guide for Teachers and Parents of Children with High-Functioning Autism and Asperger Syndrome.* London: Jessica Kingsley Publishers, 2001.

Nash, J. M. "The Secrets of Autism." *Time,* May 6, 2002, 46–56.

Nelson, K. B., J. K. Grether, L. A. Croen, J. M. Dambrosia, B. F. Dickens, L. L. Jelliffe, R. L. Hansen, and T. M. Phillips. "Neuropeptides and Neurotrophins in Neonatal Blood of Children with Autism or Mental Retardation." *Annals of Neurology* 49, no. 5 (2001): 597–606.

Nelson, K. B., and M. L. Bauman. "Thimerosal and Autism?" *Pediatrics* 111, no. 3 (2003): 674–679.

Newman, B. *When Everybody Cares: Case Studies of ABA with People with Autism.* New York: Dove and Orca, 1999.

Nicolson, R., G. Awad, and L. Sloman. "An Open Trial of Risperidone in Young Autistic Children." *Journal of the American Academy of Child and Adolescent Psychiatry* 37 (1998): 372–376.

Nowicki, S., Jr., and M. P. Duke. *Helping the Child Who Doesn't Fit In.* Atlanta: Peachtree, 1992.

Osterling, J., and G. Dawson. "Early Recognition of Children with Autism: A Study of First Birthday Home Videotapes." *Journal of Autism and Developmental Disorders* 24 (1994): 247–257.

Ozonoff, S., and R. E. McEvoy. "A Longitudinal Study of Executive Function and

Theory of Mind Development in Autism." *Development and Psychopathology* 6 (1994): 415–431.

Ozonoff, S., and J. N. Miller. "Teaching Theory of Mind: A New Approach to Social Skills Training for Individuals with Autism." *Journal of Autism and Developmental Disorders* 25 (1995): 411–434.

Ozonoff, Sally, Geraldine Dawson, and James McPartland. *A Parent's Guide to Asperger Syndrome and High-Functioning Autism: How to Meet the Challenges and Help Your Child Thrive.* New York: Guilford Press, 2002.

Paradiž, Valerie. *Elijah's Cup: A Family's Journey into the Community and Culture of High-Functioning Autism and Asperger's Syndrome.* New York: Free Press, 2002.

Physician's Desk Reference. Montvale, N.J.: Thomson Medical Economics, 2003.

Quill, K. A. *Do-Watch-Listen-Say: Social and Communication Intervention for Children with Autism.* Baltimore: Paul H. Brookes, 2000.

———. *Teaching Children with Autism: Strategies to Enhance Communication and Socialization.* New York: Delmar, 1995.

Rapee, R. M., S. H. Spence, V. Cobham, and A. Wignall. *Helping Your Anxious Child: A Step-by-Step Guide for Parents.* Oakland, Calif.: New Harbinger, 2000.

Rapin, I. "The Autistic-Spectrum Disorders." *New England Journal of Medicine* 347 (2002): 302–303.

———. "An 8-Year-Old-Boy with Autism." *Journal of the American Medical Association* 285 (2001): 1749–1757.

Rapin, I., ed. *Preschool Children with Inadequate Communication: Developmental Language Disorder, Autism, Low IQ.* London: MacKeith Press, 1996.

Rappaport, N., and P. Chubinsky. "The Meaning of Psychotropic Medications for Children, Adolescents, and Their Families." *Journal of the American Academy of Child and Adolescent Psychiatry* 39, no. 9 (2000): 1198–1200.

Ratey, J. J., and C. Johnson. *Shadow Syndromes: The Mild Forms of Major Mental Disorders That Sabotage Us.* New York: Bantam Books, 1998.

Robins, D. L., D. Fein, M. L. Barton, and J. A. Green. "Modified Checklist for Autism in Toddlers (M-CHAT)." *Journal of Autism and Developmental Disorders* 31, no. 2 (2001): 131–144.

Rourke, B. P. *Nonverbal Learning Disabilities: The Syndrome and the Model.* New York: Guilford Press, 1989.

———. "The Syndrome of Non-verbal Learning Disabled Children: Developmental Manifestations of Neurological Disease." *The Clinical Neuropsychologist* 2 (1988): 293–330.

Sacks, O. *Uncle Tungsten: Memories of a Chemical Boyhood.* New York: Knopf, 2001.

Schopler, E., G. Mesibov, and L. J. Kunce, eds. *Asperger Syndrome or High-Functioning Autism?* New York: Plenum, 1998.

Shaw, W. *Biological Treatments for Autism and PDD.* 2d ed. Lenexa, Kans.: Great Plains Laboratory, 2002.

Shore, Stephen M. *Beyond the Wall: Personal Experiences with Autism and Asperger Syndrome.* 2d ed. Shawnee Mission, Kans.: Autism Asperger Publishing Company, 2003.

Siegel, B. *The World of the Autistic Child: Understanding and Treating Autistic Spectrum Disorders.* Reprint. New York: Oxford University Press, 1998.

Siegel, L. M. *The Complete IEP Guide: How to Advocate for Your Special Ed Child.* 2d ed. Berkeley: Nolo Press, 2001.

Silberman, S. "The Geek Syndrome." *Wired,* issue 9.12 (December 2001), 174–183.

Silver, L. B. *Attention-Deficit/Hyperactivity Disorder: A Clinical Guide to Diagnosis and Treatment for Health and Mental Health Professionals.* 2d ed. Washington, D.C.: American Psychiatric Press, 1999.

———. *Dr. Larry Silver's Advice to Parents on ADHD.* 2d ed. New York: Times Books, 1999.

———. *The Misunderstood Child: Understanding and Coping with Your Child's Learning Disabilities.* New York: Three Rivers Press, 1998.

Snider, L. A., L. D. Seligman, B. R. Ketchen, S. J. Levitt, L. R. Bates, M.A. Garvey, and S. E. Swedo. "Tics and Problem Behaviors in Schoolchildren: Prevalence, Characterization, and Associations." *Pediatrics* 110, no.2 (2002): 331–336.

Stein, M. T., S. D. Dixon, and C. Cowan. "A Two-Year-Old Boy with Language Regression and Unusual Social Interactions." *Pediatrics* 107 suppl. (2001): 910–915.

Stewart, K. *Helping a Child with Nonverbal Learning Disorder or Asperger's Syndrome: A Parent's Guide.* Oakland, Calif.: New Harbinger Publications, 2002.

Stigler, Kimberly A., M.D.; David J. Posey, M.D.; and Christopher J. McDougle, M.D. "Two Drug Therapy Algorithms Target Autism's Problem Behaviors." *Current Psychiatry Online* 2, no. 4 (April 2003).

Stone, W. L., B. B. Lee, L. Ashford, J. Brissie, S. L. Hepburn, E. Coonrod, and B. H. Weiss. "Can Autism Be Diagnosed Accurately in Children under 3 Years?" *Journal of Child Psychology and Psychiatry* 40, no. 2 (1999): 219–226.

Tanguay, P. "Pervasive Developmental Disorders: A 10-Year Review." *Journal of the American Academy of Child and Adolescent Psychiatry* 39, no. 9 (2000): 1079–1095.

Tanguay, P. B. *Nonverbal Learning Disabilities at Home: A Parent's Guide.* London: Jessica Kingsley Publishers, 2001.

———. *Nonverbal Learning Disabilities at School: Educating Students with NLD, As-*

perger Syndrome and Related Conditions. London: Jessica Kingsley Publishers, 2002.

Tantam, D. "Asperger's Syndrome." *Journal of Child Psychology and Psychiatry* 29 (1988): 245–255.

Taylor, B., E. Miller, C. P. Farrington, M. C. Petropoulos, I. Favot-Mayaud, J. Li, and P. A. Waight. "Autism and Measles, Mumps, and Rubella Vaccine: No Epidemiological Evidence for a Causal Association." *Lancet* 353 (1999): 2026–2029.

Taylor, B., E. Miller, R. Lingam, N. Andrews, A. Simmons, and J. Stowe. "Measles, Mumps, and Rubella Vaccination and Bowel Problems or Developmental Regression in Children with Autism: A Population Study." *British Medical Journal* 324 (2002): 393–396.

Thompson, M. *Best Friends, Worst Enemies: Understanding the Social Lives of Children.* New York: Ballantine, 2002.

Thompson, S. *The Source for Nonverbal Learning Disorders.* East Moline, Ill.: LinguiSystems, 1997.

Turecki, S., with L. Tonner. *The Difficult Child.* 2d ed. New York: Bantam, 2000.

Twachtman-Cullen, D., and J. Twachtman-Reilly. *How Well Does Your IEP Measure Up?: Quality Indicators for Effective Service Delivery.* Higganum, Conn.: Starfish Specialty Press, 2002.

Twemlow, S. W., P. Fonagy, F. C. Sacco, M. E. O'Toole, and E. Vernberg. "Premeditated Mass Shootings in Schools: Threat Assessment." *Journal of the American Academy of Child and Adolescent Psychiatry* 41 (2002): 475–477.

Van Bourgondien, M. E., and A. V. Woods. "Vocational Possibilities for High-Functioning Adults with Autism." In *High-Functioning Individuals with Autism,* edited by E. Schopler and G. B. Mesibov, 227–239. New York: Plenum Press, 1992.

Van der Wal, M. F., C. A. M. de Wit, and R. A. Hirasing. "Psychosocial Health Among Young Victims and Offenders of Direct and Indirect Bullying." *Pediatrics* 111, no. 6 (2003): 1312–1317.

Volkmar, F., E. H. Cook Jr., J. Pomeroy, G. Realmuto, and P. Tanguay. "Practice Parameters for the Assessment and Treatment of Children, Adolescents, and Adults with Autism and Other Pervasive Developmental Disorders." *Journal of the American Academy of Child and Adolescent Psychiatry* 38 suppl. (1999): 32S–54S.

Volkmar, F. R., A. Klin, B. Siegel, P. Szatmari, C. Lord, M. Campbell, B. J. Freeman, D. V. Cicchetti, M. Rutter, W. Kline, J. Buitelaar, Y. Hattab, E. Fombonne, J. Fuentes, J. Werry, W. Stone, J. Kerbeshian, Y. Hoshino, J. Bregman, K. Loveland, L. Szymanski, and K. Towbin. "DSM-IV Autism/Pervasive Developmental Disorder Field Trial." *American Journal of Psychiatry* 151 (1994): 1361–1367.

Wakefield, A. J., and S. M. Montgomery. "Measles, Mumps, Rubella Vaccine:

Through a Glass, Darkly." *Adverse Drug Reactions and Toxicology Review* 19 (2000): 265–283.

Wakefield, A. J., S. H. Murch, A. Anthony, J. Linnell, D. M. Casson, M. Malik, M. Berelowitz, A. P. Dhillon, M. A. Thomson, P. Harvey, A. Valentine, S. E. Davies, and J. A. Walker-Smith. "Ileal-Lymphoid-Nodular Hyperplasia, Non-specific Colitis, and Pervasive Developmental Disorder in Children." *Lancet* 351 (1998): 637–641.

Weeks, D., and J. James. *Eccentrics: A Study of Sanity and Strangeness.* New York: Kodansha, 1996.

Whitney, R. V. *Bridging the Gap: Raising a Child with Nonverbal Learning Disorder.* New York: Perigee, 2002.

Wilens, T. E. *Straight Talk about Psychiatric Medications for Kids.* New York: Guilford Press, 2002.

Willey, L. H. *Asperger Syndrome in the Family: Redefining Normal.* London: Jessica Kingsley Publishers, 2001.

———. *Pretending to be Normal: Living with Asperger's Syndrome.* London: Jessica Kingsley Publishers, 1999.

Wilson, K., E. Mills, C. Ross, J. McGowan, and A. Jadad. "Association of Autistic Spectrum Disorder and the Measles, Mumps, and Rubella Vaccine." *Archives of Pediatrics and Adolescent Medicine* 157, no. 7 (2003): 628–634.

Wing, L. *The Autistic Spectrum: A Parents' Guide to Understanding and Helping Your Child.* Berkeley, Calif.: Ulysses Press, 2001.

Wright, P.W.D., and P. D. Wright. *Wrightslaw: Special Education Law.* Hartfield, Va.: Harbor House Law Press, 1999.

Wudarsky, M., R. Nicolson, S. D. Hamburger, L. Spechler, P. Gochman, J. Bedwell, M. C. Lenane, and J. L. Rapoport. "Elevated Prolactin in Pediatric Patients on Typical and Atypical Antipsychotics." *Journal of Child and Adolescent Psychopharmacology* 9 (1999): 239–245.

INDEX

ABOUT THE AUTHORS

Perri Klass, M.D., and Eileen Costello, M.D., are pediatricians on the staff of Boston University School of Medicine. Both Harvard graduates who trained in pediatrics at Boston Medical Center and Boston Children's Hospital, they have practiced pediatrics together at Dorchester House, a community health center in Boston, for ten years. Klass has written for *The New York Times*, and is a contributing editor at *Parenting*. She has written both fiction and non-fiction, including the novel *Other Women's Children* and the memoir *Baby Doctor: A Pediatrician's Training*. Each is the mother of three children, and they both live in the Boston area.